Breaking Free

The Transformative Power of Critical Pedagogy

Edited by

PEPI LEISTYNA
ARLIE WOODRUM
STEPHEN A. SHERBLOM

Reprint Series No. 27
Harvard Educational Review

Third Printing, 1999

Copyright © 1996 by President and Fellows of Harvard College.

All rights reserved. No part of this publication may be reproduced or transmitted in any form or by any means, electronic or mechanical, including photocopy, recording, or any information storage and retrieval systems, without permission in writing from the publisher.

Library of Congress Catalog Card Number 95-78432

ISBN 0-916690-29-6

Harvard Educational Review
Gutman Library Suite 349
6 Appian Way
Cambridge, MA 02138

Typesetting by Sheila Walsh
Editorial Production by Dody Riggs
Cover Design by Dody Riggs
Cover Artwork by Pepi Leistyna: "The idea was inspired by the work of a Native American artist whose name I do not know, but whose gift I carry with me with great appreciation."

Contents

	Introduction	v
1	Context and Culture: What Is Critical Pedagogy? *Pepi Leistyna and Arlie Woodrum*	1

Part One: Education in Its Social Context

	Introduction: A Call for Multiple Literacies	9
2	In Search of a Critical Pedagogy *Maxine Greene*	13
3	Literacy for Stupidification: The Pedagogy of Big Lies *Donaldo P. Macedo*	31
4	Transitional Bilingual Education and the Socialization of Immigrants *David Spener*	59
5	Doing Cultural Studies: Youth and the Challenge of Pedagogy *Henry A. Giroux*	83
6	A Dialogue with Noam Chomsky *With Pepi Leistyna and Stephen Sherblom*	109
7	Academic Freedom and the Parameters of Knowledge *William G. Tierney*	129
8	Rethinking Liberal and Radical Perspectives on Racial Inequality in Schooling: Making the Case for Nonsynchrony *Cameron McCarthy*	149
9	A Tentative Description of Post-Formal Thinking: The Critical Confrontation with Cognitive Theory *Joe L. Kincheloe and Shirley R. Steinberg*	167

Part Two: The Process of Learning and Teaching

	Introduction: A Call for Critical Educators	197
10	A Dialogue: Culture, Language, and Race *Paulo Freire and Donaldo P. Macedo*	199
11	Beyond the Methods Fetish: Toward a Humanizing Pedagogy *Lilia I. Bartolomé*	229
12	A Discourse Not Intended for Her: Learning and Teaching within Patriarchy *Magda Lewis and Roger I. Simon*	253
13	Teachers as Political Actors: From Reproductive Theory to the Crisis of Schooling *Dennis Carlson*	273
14	Teacher Education and the Politics of Engagement: The Case for Democratic Schooling *Henry A. Giroux and Peter McLaren*	301
	Glossary	333
	Recommended Reading	345
	About the Contributors	365
	About the Editors	369

Introduction

At its most basic, critical pedagogy provides a lens through which educators are better able to examine and interact with the politics of education. By "politics" we do not mean the "Republican/Democrat" type of politics, but, rather, the real, underlying power relationships that structure our world: for example, how we make meaning of commonplace events, the purpose and goals of public education, how schools are structured, the type of preparation teachers receive, the way students are perceived and treated, the curriculum we use, and so forth. *Breaking Free: The Transformative Power of Critical Pedagogy,* a collection of essays originally published in the *Harvard Educational Review,* was conceptualized with the central purpose of serving as an introduction to this field. It offers readers several editorial supports to facilitate their understanding of the complexity of such work. Chapter One, "Context and Culture: What Is Critical Pedagogy?" provides an explanation of the central concepts and theories that are generally grouped under the term "critical pedagogy." The remainder of the book is divided into two parts. The first part offers various perspectives on the larger social and political context within which educational policies and practices exist. Part Two focuses on the role of teachers and students in the process of learning and teaching.

The book is designed to help readers begin to explore critical pedagogy's wide range of styles and ideas. To ease the reader's entry into this complex field, we provide two editorial aids. First, each chapter begins with an editors' introduction (in bold) that locates the particular author in the broader conversation of the book. Second, the key terms and concepts in each chapter, if not defined within an author's text, are defined in an editors' footnote at the bottom of the page. Some definitions appear in more than one chapter in order to facilitate readers' understanding of these terms in various contexts. A glossary at the back of the book provides a more extensive description of many key concepts and theoretical positions, and both the glossary and the annotated bibliography offer suggestions for further study. Although each of the chapters can be read independently, this collection is designed as an integrated whole.

We wish to point out to the reader that the work of the authors included in this collection is ever-evolving as the cultural and political landscape and language usage continues to change. However, our efforts to link earlier work to more current thinking is an attempt to provide a historical perspective on some of the ways in which critical inquiry has responded to various and shifting social and political concerns.

It is our hope that the accessibility of this book and the diversity of articles chosen will inspire readers to explore further the implications of critical pedagogy, and that *Breaking Free* will serve as a stepping-stone for those who are willing to pursue participatory dialogue, self-empowerment, and educational transformation. We offer the following insights in the hope that they will serve us all in our diverse efforts to realize meaningful, democratic change.

                                Pepi Leistyna
                                Arlie Woodrum
                                Stephen A. Sherblom
                                Harvard Graduate School of Education

1

Context and Culture: What Is Critical Pedagogy?

PEPI LEISTYNA and ARLIE WOODRUM

In the classroom and on the streets, everyday experiences of racism, discrimination, and violence bespeak the reality of a great many Americans. Even though exclusionary practices and social unrest in the United States are being discussed within the discourse of social and educational reform, both the conservative and liberal efforts to restructure public schooling are severely limited by the paradigm from which they work, and are thus inadequate and ineffective in dealing with the plethora of today's societal dilemmas and tensions.

Conservative *technocratic*[a] models that dominate mainstream educational programs (which narrowly conceptualize teaching and learning as a discrete and scientific undertaking) embrace depersonalized methods for educating students, that often translate into the regulation and standardization of teacher practices and curricula. As such, the role of the teacher (who is "trained") is reduced to that of a passive, "objective," and "efficient" distributor of information.

Endorsing a mechanical approach to reading, writing, and math, this movement, referred to as "*back to basics*," focuses primarily on the transfer of basic skills from the instructor to the student through mindless drills and rote memorization of selected "facts" that can easily be measured through standardized testing. Such a pedagogical model, which focuses exclusively on preparing students for the work force, abstracts education from the challenges of developing a critically conscious, socially responsible, and politically active student body and citizenry. In fact, conservatives have argued that attempts to reveal the underlying power relationships that structure educational policies and practices have corrupted the academic environment. A

---

[a] Words in italics are defined within the text, as well as in the glossary located in the back of the book. These terms are frequently used in the literature on critical pedagogy.

consequence of these technocratic models is that the larger historical, ideological, economic, and cultural conditions out of which today's social and institutional crises have grown generally go unquestioned in schools.

Even the more progressive popular reform efforts — the mainstream multicultural movement, for example — fail to challenge effectively this prevailing paradigm. Under the rubric of "multicultural education," a great deal of research, literature, curricula, and classroom practices presently attempts to address the issues of cultural diversity, as well as racial and economic inequalities. However, the majority of this work, which endeavors simply to affirm diversity and identities through positive images of subordinated groups, does so in a limited fashion, focusing on color coordination, food festivals, cut-and-paste add-ons to the existing canon, and group-based methodologies. These efforts, by abstracting particular groups' similarities from an understanding of their various complexities (such as differences among them in terms of gender, class, sexual orientation, etc.), often fall into the trap of *essentializing* (e.g., perceiving all Blacks to be the same), *objectifying* (i.e., seeing people as objects of educational policies and practices, rather than as self-determining subjects with a say in their education), or even *romanticizing* the lives of those on the margins. Within such limited models that focus exclusively on the "Other," the concept of "difference" is often not taken up in terms of recognizing and critically engaging the *dominant referent group* — the invisible norm of the White, middle-class, heterosexual male by which all others are measured. Consequently, this all too common depoliticized, liberal "multiculturalism" fails to examine adequately the ideologies that inform unequal power relations and social stratification along such lines as race, ethnicity, class, gender, and sexual orientation. These mainstream endeavors can invite surface reforms, but merely recognizing our differences will not lead to a transformation of the exclusionary structural and ideological patterns of our unequal society.

Critical pedagogy, on the other hand, while widely misunderstood and misinterpreted, challenges us to recognize, engage, and critique (so as to transform) any existing undemocratic social practices and institutional structures that produce and sustain inequalities and oppressive social identities and relations. While this type of work has been influential across the social sciences, its vast literature and history have often been superficially dismissed within schools of education as being too ideological and too opaque, or as offering simplistic "big bang" solutions. As a result, teacher education programs and policies, as well as educational research and classroom practices, are largely bereft of the dialogue, insights, and contributions that such perspectives offer. In order to clarify some of these misconceptions and facile dismissals, this chapter sets for itself two tasks: to introduce readers to critical pedagogy, and to debunk some of the myths that have grown up around its theories and practices.

Contrary to common misperceptions of critical pedagogy as a monolithic *discourse*, that is, one particular way of seeing the world — the vast literature and positions (as represented in volumes such as *Breaking Free: The Transformative Power of Critical Pedagogy*) demonstrate that not only are there multiple versions, but there is also no generic definition that can be applied to the term. However, there are important theoretical insights and practices that are woven through these various approaches, which often grow out of a common set of issues and conditions, that provide the focus for critical pedagogy within the shifting spheres of political conflict. As new questions evolve out of these controversies, so does the call for new and more inclusive theoretical and practical responses.

Critical pedagogy is primarily concerned with the kinds of educational theories and practices that encourage both students and teachers to develop an understanding of the interconnecting relationship among ideology, power, and culture. *Culture* in this sense is shaped by the lived experiences and institutional forms organized around diverse elements of struggle and domination. In other words, culture also embodies the lived experiences and behaviors that are the result of the unequal distribution of power along such lines as race, gender, class, ethnicity, age, and sexual orientation. As people interact with existing institutions and social practices in which the values, beliefs, bodies of knowledge, styles of communication, and biases of the dominant culture are imposed, they are often stripped of their power to articulate and realize their own goals. For example, the efforts in the United States to enforce a *common culture* (an unnegotiated foundation of values, ethics, meaning, histories, and representations — "our cultural heritage") or a *common sense* (a selective view of social reality in which difference is viewed as deviant or a deficit), is in fact the imposition of a homogenizing social paradigm (known as ideological domination or *hegemony*) that severely limits the possibility for a critical multicultural democracy. As race and culture, and class and culture are inextricably related in the United States — middle-class realities are certainly different from those of the working-class, as Black and Latino are from White — the critical question is, whose perspectives and interests are defining what it means to be an American? Focusing on the imposition of particular values in society, as well as the antagonistic relations and the resistance (opposition) that surfaces as a response to such domination, critical pedagogues view the contemporary cultural landscape, not as a vista of common traditions and memories, but, rather, as a terrain of conflict of differences.

As microcosms of the larger society, schools also produce this social turmoil by maintaining dominant beliefs, values, and interests — cultural identities — through particular bodies of knowledge, pedagogical practices, and curricula. Examining schooling as a form of cultural politics, critical pedagogy contests *modernist* traditions (which, for the most part, direct mainstream educational theories, policies, and practices) that are based on the notion that emancipation is only realizable through objective inquiry, universal reason, and absolute truth. Rejecting any claim to a universal foundation for truth and culture, as well as any claim to objectivity, critical pedagogy reveals that educational practices and knowledge are always produced within particular social and historical conditions, and therefore any understanding of their production and dissemination must be accompanied by, not only an investigation of their relation to ideology and power, but also, an inquiry into the researchers' inherently subjective perspectives — that is, as a product of their own sociohistorical environment: With what lens do they look upon the world? Education, for example, as an integral part of the socialization process, is directed by particular beliefs, interests, and thus, ideologies. Knowledge, which in broad terms is understood as the way a person explains or interprets reality, is similarly constructed. The questions posed by critical pedagogues are, Whose values, interpretations, and goals constitute the foundation of public education — the "official" core curriculum — and how is this body of knowledge, which is often falsely presented as being objective and universal, imposed on the greater society?

Teachers who work within the traditional paradigm, with its model of teacher as knower/lecturer and student as passive recipient of information, inevitably reproduce and maintain particular forms of identity, meaning, authority, and interaction, whether they are aware of it or not. At the same time, teachers work and speak from within historically and socially determined relations of power and privilege that are based on their race, ethnicity, class, and gender. While the possession and wielding of the dominant values and beliefs serve to legitimate the voices of some teachers and students, they can also work to silence others. In the same way, curricula can either affirm or exclude certain voices and lifestyles. What is worse, it can demean, deny, or disfigure the lived experience of a great many people who are not part of the dominant group. As Cameron McCarthy contends in "Rethinking Liberal and Racial Perspectives on Racial Inequality in Schooling: Making the Case for Nonsynchrony," "American schools are principal sites for the production and naturalization of myths and ideologies that systematically disorganize and neutralize minority cultural identities" (p. 163). Pedagogy and curricula are thus not only composed of particular experiences and interests, but also represent a site of struggle over whose values and versions of authority and history will be central to the educational process.

Another important insight of critical pedagogy is that pedagogy — that is, how, and in what context, we learn what we learn — does not simply take place in schools. The electronic media — for example, television news, movies, and music — not only serve up information, but also shape our perceptions. As Henry Giroux argues in "Youth and the Challenge of Pedagogy," popular texts such as movies are not simply expressive, but also formative, in that they can influence how we see ourselves and others and thus affect the ways in which we interact with one another. Giroux contends that the pedagogy (the messages) implicit in most Hollywood films about youth culture reinforce dominant racist and cultural stereotypes. For example, he illustrates how violence is often portrayed as being endemic to the Black community. However, making no effort to identify and challenge the oppressive conditions within which crime is inevitable, such images confirm through the conditioned eyes of the White middle-class mainstream, that Blacks, as well as other groups, need to be both culturally and physically contained. This struggle over identity and representation (that is, over who has the power to articulate experience, fashion identities, define the nature of problems, and legitimate solutions) contributes to shaping the social relations of everyday life — how we look at, feel about, fear, and interact with one another.

Whether it be in or out of schools, students and teachers involved in critical learning and teaching are encouraged to examine the values, assumptions, ideologies, and interests reflected in bodies of knowledge and representations, link such information to their own experiences, and subsequently pose the kinds of questions that William Tierney asks in "Academic Freedom and the Parameters of Knowledge": "How is knowledge conceived? Whose interests have been advanced by these forms of knowledge? How has what we have defined as knowledge changed over time? How does the organization's culture promote or silence some individuals? How are some topics marginalized and others promoted?" (p. 145). In their efforts to understand the sociopolitical, economic, and historical realities that shape their lives, students and teachers struggle to make new meaning and develop cultural practices that are critical, transformative, and liberatory. This ongoing process of reflection and action is referred to in critical pedagogy as *praxis*.

In order to affirm and engage the complexity of diverse human histories and perceptions, and cross the socially and economically constructed borders of race, gender, ethnicity, class, sexual orientation, etc., a fundamental tenet of critical pedagogy is the need to include both teachers' and students' voices in the learning process. By including both of these voices, educators move away from traditional relational restraints (that is, the limits of the relation of knowledge imparter to passive recipients). This move makes the teachers' and students' *location* (the place that a person occupies within a set of social relationships — often determined by such categories as gender, class, race, etc.), experiences, and perceptions in their private and public lives the point of departure for dialogue and a text for debate. In examining the social construction of knowledge, values, and interaction across "difference," the idea is not for teachers to be abusive by silencing students or placing their identities on trial. Instead, the process is to be unsettling only to the degree that it forces all of those involved to recognize their role in accepting and perpetuating oppression of any kind. Critically examining our own perspectives enables everyone to avoid the debilitating ramifications of "relativism" in which any and all cultural practices are equally acceptable. The critical reflection, debate, and negotiation in such dialogue affords the necessary conditions for all classroom participants to act as knower, learner, and teacher, and to reach beyond our own cultural boundaries. This in turn creates space for a more critical and democratic exchange of ideas.

Critical pedagogy is thus rooted in a democratic project that emphasizes new theories and languages of critique, resistance, and possibility capable of *engaging* (critically examining and transforming) the standard academic boundaries and social and educational practices that maintain the de facto social code in the United States. These new theories and languages provide the necessary analytic stepping-stones for realizing a truly democratic process through which we can better identify the sociopolitical realities that shape our lives, begin to negotiate our differences, and, where necessary, transform our practices.

One of the major obstacles of transformative education in the United States is that theory is often devalued among educators. This ambivalence is not surprising considering the fact that most educational theory has been removed from everyday practice and left in the hands of academic "experts" who have little contact with the actual classroom dynamic. Further, as argued by Joe Kincheloe and Shirley Steinberg in "A Tentative Description of Post-Formal Thinking: The Critical Confrontation with Cognitive Theory," theory is commonly relegated to the realm of cognition, abstracted from the inherently sociohistorical and political nature of learning and teaching, and is often uncritically passed on to future teachers to inform more "efficient" ways that students can assimilate "basic skills." When asked about educators in the United States, Paulo Freire responded:

> There are always the mechanistic questions, how tos, how tos with no theory behind them. They want to know the facts. I like facts too, but I like to know where they came from.
> (Personal communication, 1994)

This divorce of theory and practice is reflected in a system of public primary and secondary schooling that continues to be inundated with the practical — prepackaged methods, teacher-proof materials, and standardized evaluation.

The theory in critical pedagogy, in contrast, creates the self-empowering pedagogical conditions within which both teachers and students can better make sense of the world and their interactions therein — to engage and thus interact as *participants* (shapers) of history, rather than simply *objects* (passive recipients) to be acted upon, manipulated, and controlled. Emphasizing the need for political awareness, critical work is enormously important for developing a theoretical framework that historically and socially situates the deeply embedded roots of racism, discrimination, violence, and disempowerment in this country. Instead of perpetuating the assumption that such realities are inevitable, the theories presented in critical pedagogy invite the reader to further explore the relationship between these larger historic, economic, and social constructs and their inextricable connection to ideology and power.

What is important to recognize is that critical pedagogy is not its own universal theory or methodology that transfers neatly from one situation to another. Nor is it meant to be the imposition of a particular ideology. It is an interdisciplinary process that changes with each unique social/classroom context and creates a space for teachers and students to engage in critical dialogue in which the objective is the production of their own ideas and values rather than the mere reproduction of those of the dominant groups. Theory and practice in this sense work actively through and not on students by helping both teachers and students to reflect on how domination works, and consequently to develop, as they interact with one another, their own transformative practices. In becoming aware of both the positions they inhabit and the locations from which they speak, students and teachers are better able to take responsibility for their beliefs and actions.

Through the various definitions, differences, and commonalties, critical pedagogy is not simply (as it is often accused of being) some macro, theoretical, abstract undertaking in which realistic applications are beyond reach. On the contrary, there is, in fact, an inextricable relationship between critical social theory and practice. Lilia Bartolomé, for example, in "Beyond the Methods Fetish: Toward a Humanizing Pedagogy," illustrates how such theory has direct implications for methodological considerations and curricular decisions. Critical social theories thus function as both political and pedagogical practice. They should inspire the reconceptualization of different ways of knowing that rupture entrenched epistemologies, and they can equally help to foster participatory spaces for the sharing and production of knowledge, and the mobilization of agency to effect changes in the world. The very act of engaging one another and theorizing around the issue of oppression is inherently a form, if not the first seeds, of transformative practice.

Critical pedagogy is not only interdisciplinary in content, but also draws upon the lived experience of scholars from a diversity of backgrounds who cross and engage the multiple and shifting interconnecting relationships that constitute a pedagogy and politics of identity and difference. The interdisciplinary framework illustrates why the struggle over language, meaning, and identity is fundamental to any discourse and pedagogy that is working towards a more critical multicultural democracy. Our desire is to inspire educators, researchers, and others to undertake the political and ethical roles they might assume as public intellectuals and to prepare students in the kind of broad, critical thinking necessary for responsible democratic citizenship. Creating and negotiating languages of inclusion and possibility that go beyond critique and demystification allows us to analyze ourselves and society from our multiple locations and to decide how we will define and live our lives. We trust that critical pedagogy, with its sharing of insights, strategies, and critical reflections, significantly moves such efforts forward.

Part One: Education in Its Social Context

INTRODUCTION: A CALL FOR MULTIPLE LITERACIES

If the United States is ever to achieve a critical, pluralistic democracy, it is essential that all society's members possess a clear understanding of difference. In order to develop such clarity, people need to be literate in multiple ways of perceiving and speaking about reality. Engaging a full range of perspectives is not an argument for a particular position or ideology, but, rather, it leads us to recognize that there are multiple audiences, and demands a willingness to strive to understand and make ourselves understood in speaking and acting across our differences. Unfortunately, instead of emphasizing the need to interact with a diversity of perspectives and modes of expression, many educators too often dismiss work that does not fall neatly into the category of "Standard English" as being "jargonistic" or "inaccessible." In doing so, these educators deter the readers/learners from struggling through diverse languages and theoretical and political positions, thus ignoring how multiple audiences read and comprehend the word and the world differently; discounting the insights, contributions, and legitimacy of experience of all those who do not speak or write in a particular fashion.

This call for "plain prose" ignores the inherent relationship among ideology, power, and language and, thus, between language and experience. That is, it ignores the way that systems of communication, which are all social and historical constructions informed by particular ideologies, play a significant role in shaping (rather than simply reflecting) human perceptions and world views, and can work either to confirm or deny the life histories and experiences of the people who use them. Recognizing the inherently political nature of language, Trinh Minh-ha contends that

> accessibility, which is a process, is often taken for a "natural," self-evident state of language. What is perpetuated in its name is a given form of intolerance and an unacknowledged practice of exclusion.[1]

Because language can never be situated outside of history, power, and struggle, *languages of resistance and possibility* (that is, resistance to various forms of oppression and the possibility of transformation of the status quo) must always be *productive* (critical and inclusive, producing new meaning) rather than simply reproductive. In practice, this translates into the development of new theories, bodies of knowledge, and transformed relationships, rather than the mere reification of existing paradigms. Therefore, the call for "plain prose" can be interpreted one of two ways: either people are sincerely seeking to understand, or they are consciously refusing to acknowledge the inherently ideological nature of all language. This attempt to mask the politics of language often plays out in a reactionary dismissal of new critical discourses as being too ideological and opaque, and thus unworthy of engaging. As Noam Chomsky states in the following dialogue,

> If you simply talk about the world in the accepted ways, that would not be called politics, that would be being reasonable. It becomes "ideological" or "extremist" when it deviates from the accepted patterns. . . . If you repeat the clichés of the propaganda system, that's not ideological. On the other hand, if you question them, that's considered ideological and very strident. (pp. 125–126)

The critical appropriation of different discourses have enormous implications for educational theory and practice. Without such an effort, we are certain to become what Donaldo Macedo, in "Literacy for Stupidification" (p. 42), terms "semiliterate"; that is, only able to deal with the simple language that masks the intricacies of the reality being examined, thus absolving the examiner from the need to engage the resultant multiple perspectives.

The central purpose of *Breaking Free: The Transformative Power of Critical Pedagogy* is to serve as an introductory scaffold for educators who are unfamiliar with critical pedagogy. We have employed several devices to facilitate the reader's understanding. In addition to chapter introductions that situate the particular author in the broader conversation of the book, each essay is supplemented with general definitions of complex terms.[a] A glossary at the end of the book provides a more extensive description of some of the key concepts and theoretical positions presented. Our objective in providing these heuristics should not be misinterpreted as an endorsement of fixed definitions and the mechanical process of rote memorization; we are simply attempting to provide the unfamiliar reader with the necessary signposts to enter the discussion. Reflective reading should always be a challenge to push us beyond our immediate ability and understanding. The ideas in this book, instead of being uncritically consumed, are to be understood, linked to one's

---

[a] Words in bold in each essay are defined by the editors at the bottom of the page on which they appear. Editors' footnotes are meant to be broad understandings of terms used and are not meant to provide fixed definitions. For the most part, the interpretation of concepts taken from the text is the work of the editors, not of the authors. More extensive definitions are found in the book's glossary, beginning on page 333.

own experience, and subsequently reinvented to fit one's particular needs. Discussing "The Act of Study" in *The Politics of Education* (1985), Paulo Freire states,

> Understanding a text isn't a gift from someone else. It requires patience and commitment from those who find it problematic. To study is not to consume ideas. Studying is a form of reinvention, re-creating, rewriting, and this is a subject's, not an object's, task.[2]

This first section of essays offers various perspectives on the broad social and political context that subsumes educational policies and practices. As they all need to be understood, engaged, and reinvented by the critical reader, these essays nevertheless embody the kind of critical research and theorizing that we all should do in order to inform our practices.

NOTES

1. Trinh Minh-ha, *When the Moon Waxes Red* (New York: Routledge, 1991), pp. 228–229.
2. Paulo Freire, *The Politics of Education: Culture, Power and Liberation* (New York: Bergin & Garvey, 1983), pp. 3–4.

2

In Search of a Critical Pedagogy

MAXINE GREENE

In this essay, Maxine Greene contextualizes the role (or lack) of critical thought in our society by examining some facets of the intellectual legacy of Western history. As with all of the authors in this collection, Greene grapples with ways of extracting and expanding the productive elements that emanated from the Age of Enlightenment (such as democracy and human rights) while eliminating the forms of domination that also accompanied this period, often referred to as the era of modernity or humanism. (See the glossary for a more in-depth discussion of "modernity" and "postmodernity.") For example, the author rejects the modernist notion of positivism, which makes claims to objectivity, truth, and certainty, in defense of a scientific basis for the study of culture. Such claims to objective universals — absolute truths — contradict the basis of democracy, in that multiple voices cannot be heard if, in fact, only one truth or reality is given legitimacy.

Greene asserts that because the problems of education are profound, and educators' notions of the possibilities for change are limited by this constrained discourse of modernity, it is often difficult even to envision more humane, more just, and more democratic alternatives. Yet, without that vision, one cannot develop a critical pedagogy in which students resist materialism, conformity, and oppressive practices, and begin to think for themselves.

Greene's attention to context reminds us that critical pedagogy is not a one-size-fits-all methodology, but, rather, a process that must take into consideration social, political, and historical conditions, as well as the perspectives and considerations of the participants of that moment. She suggests ways educators can begin to create a pedagogy that, working through and beyond the confines of modernist thought, is relevant and meaningful to the multiple experiences and realities that students face.

14   *Breaking Free*

In what Jean Baudrillard describes as "the shadow of silent majorities" in an administered and media-mystified world, we try to reconceive what a critical pedagogy relevant to this time and place ought to mean.¹ This is a moment when great numbers of Americans find their expectations and hopes for their children being fed by talk of "educational reform." Yet the reform reports speak of those very children as "human resources" for the expansion of productivity, as means to the end of maintaining our nation's economic competitiveness and military primacy in the world. Of course we want to empower the young for meaningful work, we want to nurture the achievement of diverse literacies. But the world we inhabit is palpably deficient: there are unwarranted inequities, shattered communities, unfulfilled lives. We cannot help but hunger for traces of utopian visions, of critical or **dialectical**[a] engagements with social and economic realities. And yet, when we reach out, we experience a kind of blankness. We sense people living under a weight, a nameless inertial mass. How are we to justify our concern for their awakening? Where are the sources of questioning, of restlessness? How are we to move the young to break with the given, the taken-for-granted — to move towards what might be, what is not yet?

Confronting all of this, I am moved to make some poets' voices audible at the start. Poets are exceptional, of course; they are not considered educators in the ordinary sense. But they remind us of absence, ambiguity, embodiments of existential possibility. More often than not they do so with passion; and passion has been called the power of possibility. This is because it is the source of our interests and our purposes. Passion signifies mood, emotion, desire: modes of grasping the appearances of things. It is one of the important ways of recognizing possibility, "the presence of the future as *that which is lacking* and that which, by its very absence, reveals reality."² Poets move us to give play to our imaginations, to enlarge the scope of lived experience and reach beyond from our own grounds. Poets do not give us answers; they do not solve the problems of critical pedagogy. They can, however, if we will them to do so, awaken us to reflectiveness, to a recovery of lost landscapes and lost spontaneities. Against such a background, educators might now and then be moved to go in search of a critical pedagogy of significance for themselves.

Let us hear Walt Whitman, for one:

---

[a] While there are a number of definitions and interpretations of **dialectics**, for the general purposes of critical pedagogy, this concept refers to the interconnecting and contradicting relationships that constitute a particular phenomenon, for example, among the economic, political, social, and cultural dimensions of society. A dialectical analysis is also often used to show how every idea or force has its opposite/contradiction. For example, the dialectic of "oppressor" is the reality of the "oppressed." Such an analysis holds both "opposing" concepts together at once to see how they interconnect and play off each other.

> I am the poet of the Body and I am the poet of the Soul,
> The pleasures of heaven are with me and the pains of
> hell are with me.
> The first I graft and increase upon myself, the latter I
> translate into a new tongue.
>
> I am the poet of the woman the same as the man,
> And I say it is as great to be a woman as to be a man,
> . . . .
> I chant the chant of dilation or pride.
> We have had ducking and deprecating about enough,
> I show that size is only development.
>
> Have you outstript the rest? are you the President?,
> It is a trifle, they will more than arrive there every one,
> and still pass on.[3]

Whitman calls himself the poet of the "barbaric yawp"; he is also the poet child going forth, of the grass, of comradeship and communion and the "en masse." And of noticing, naming, caring, feeling. In a systematized, technicized moment, a moment of violations and of shrinking "minimal" selves, we ought to be able to drink from the fountain of his work.

There is Wallace Stevens, explorer of multiple perspectives and imagination, challenger of objectified, quantified realties — what he calls the "ABC of being . . . the vital, arrogant, fatal, dominant X," questioner as well of the conventional "lights and definitions" presented as "the plain sense of things." We ought to think of states of things, he says, phases of movements, polarities:

> But in the centre of our lives, this time, this day,
> It is a state, this spring among the politicians
> Playing cards. In a village of the indigenes,
> One would still have to discover. Among the dogs
> and dung,
> One would continue to contend with one's ideas.[4]

One's ideas, yes, and blue guitars as well, and — always and always — "the never-resting mind," the "flawed words and stubborn sounds."

And there is Marianne Moore, reminding us that every poem represents what Robert Frost described as "the triumph of the spirit over the materialism by which we are being smothered," enunciating four precepts:

> Feed imagination food that invigorates.
> Whatever it is, do with all your might.
> Never do to another what you would not wish done to yourself.
> Say to yourself, "I will be responsible."
>
> Put these principles to the test, and you will be inconvenienced by being over-trusted, overbefriended, overconsulted, half adopted, and have no leisure. Face that when you come to it.[5]

Another woman's voice arises: Muriel Rukeyser's, in the poem "Käthe Kollwitz."

> What would happen if one woman told the truth about her life?
> The world would split open[6]

The idea of an officially defined "world" splitting open when a repressed truth is revealed holds all sorts of implications for those who see reality as opaque, bland and burnished, resistant both to protest and to change.

Last, and in a different mood, let us listen to these lines by Adrienne Rich:

> A clear night in which two planets
> seem to clasp each other   in which the earthly grasses
> shift like silk in starlight
>   If the mind were clear
> and if the mind were simple   you could take this mind
> this particular state   and say
> *This is how I would live if I could choose:*
> *this is what is possible*[7]

The poem is called "What Is Possible," but the speaker knows well that no mind can be "simple," or "abstract and pure." She realizes that the mind has "a different mission in the universe," that there are sounds and configurations still needing to be deciphered; she knows that the mind must be "wrapped in battle" in what can only be a resistant world. She voices her sense of the contrast between the mind as contemplative and the mind in a dialectical relation with what surrounds.

They create spaces, these poets, between themselves and what envelops and surrounds. Where there are spaces like that, desire arises, along with hope and expectation. We may sense that something is lacking that must be surpassed or repaired. Often, therefore, poems address our freedom; they call on us to move beyond where we are, to break with submergence, to transform. To transform what — and how? To move beyond ourselves — and where? Reading such works within the contexts of schools and education, those of us still preoccupied with human freedom and human growth may well find our questions more perplexing. We may become more passionate about the possibility of a critical pedagogy in these uncritical times. How can we (decently, morally, intelligently) address ourselves both to desire and to purpose and obligation? How can we awaken others to possibility and the need for action in the name of possibility? How can we communicate the importance of opening spaces in the imagination where persons can reach beyond where they are?

Poets, of course, are not alone in the effort to make us see and to defamiliarize our commonsense worlds. The critical impulse is an ancient one in the Western tradition: we have only to recall the prisoners released from the cave in *The Republic,* Socrates trying to arouse the "sleeping ox" that was the

Athenian public, Francis Bacon goading his readers to break with the "idols" that obscured their vision and distorted their rational capacities, David Hume calling for the exposure of the "sophistries and illusions" by which so many have habitually lived. In philosophy, in the arts, in the sciences, men and women repeatedly have come forward to urge their audiences to break with what William Blake called "mind-forg'd manacles." Not only did such manacles shackle consciousness; their effectiveness assured the continuing existence of systems of domination — monarchies, churches, land-holding arrangements, and armed forces of whatever kind.

The American tradition originated in such an insight and in the critical atmosphere specific to the European Enlightenment. It was an atmosphere created in large measure by rational, autonomous voices engaging in dialogue for the sake of bringing into being a **public sphere.**[b] These were, most often, the voices of an emerging middle class concerned for their own independence from anachronistic and unjust restraints. Their "rights" were being trampled, they asserted, rights sanctioned by natural and moral laws. Among these rights were "life, liberty, and the pursuit of happiness," which (especially when joined to justice or equity) remain normative for this nation: they are goods *to be* secured. Liberty, at the time of the founding of our nation, meant liberation from interference by the state, church, or army in the lives of individuals. For some, sharing such beliefs as those articulated by the British philosopher John Stuart Mill, liberty also meant each person's right to think for himself or herself, "to follow his intellect to whatever conclusions it may lead" in an atmosphere that forbade "mental slavery."[8]

The founders were calling, through a distinctive critical challenge, for opportunities to give their energies free play. That meant the unhindered exercise of their particular talents: inventing, exploring, building, pursuing material and social success. To be able to do so, they had to secure power, which they confirmed through the establishment of a constitutional republic. For Hannah Arendt, this sort of power is kept in existence through an ongoing process of "binding and promising, combining and covenanting." As she saw it, power springs up between human beings when they act to constitute "a worldly structure to house, as it were, their combined power of action."[9] When we consider the numbers of people excluded from this process over the generations, we have to regard this view of power as normative as well. It is usual to affirm that power belongs to "the people" at large; but, knowing that this has not been the case, we are obligated to expand the "worldly structure" until it contains the "combined power" of increasing

---

[b] **Public spheres** in the critical sense are public arenas for citizens in which political participation, outside of direct government and economic influence and intervention, is enacted through dialogue and debate. Schools are envisioned by critical pedagogues as "public spheres," wherein classrooms are active sites of public intervention and social struggle, rather than mere adjuncts of corporate and partisan interests. Because mainstream society is constituted by particular oppressive ideologies, these critical spheres are also referred to as "counterpublics."

numbers of articulate persons. A critical pedagogy for Americans, it would seem, must take this into account.

For the school reformers of the early nineteenth century, the apparent mass power accompanying the expansion of manhood suffrage created a need for "self-control" and a "voluntary compliance" with the laws of righteousness.[10] Without a common school to promote such control and compliance, the social order might be threatened. Moreover, the other obligations of the school — to prepare the young to "create wealth" — could not be adequately met. Even while recognizing the importance of providing public education for the masses of children, we have to acknowledge that great numbers of them were being socialized into factory life and wage labor in an expanding capitalist society. Like working classes everywhere, they could not but find themselves alienated from their own productive energies. The persisting dream of opportunity, however, kept most of them from confronting their literal powerlessness. The consciousness of objectively real "open" spaces (whether on the frontier, "downtown," or out at sea) prevented them from thinking seriously about changing the order of things; theoretically, there was always an alternative, a "territory ahead."[11] It followed that few were likely to conceive of themselves in a dialectical relation with what surrounded them, no matter how exploitative or cruel. As the laggard and uneven development of trade unions indicates, few were given to viewing themselves as members of a "class" with a project to pull them forward, a role to play in history.

The appearance of utopian communities and socialist societies throughout the early nineteenth century did call repeatedly into question some of the assumptions of the American ideology, especially those having to do with individualism. The founders of the experimental colonies (Robert Owen, Frances Wright, Albert Brisbane, and others) spoke of communalism, mental freedom, the integration of physical and intellectual work, and the discovery of a common good. Socialists called for a more humane and rational social arrangement and for critical insight into what Orestes Brownson described as the "crisis as to the relation of wealth and labor." He said, "It is useless to shut our eyes to the fact and, like the ostrich, fancy ourselves secure because we have so concealed our heads that we see not the danger."[12] Important as their insights were, such people were addressing themselves to educated humanitarians whose good offices might be enlisted in improving and perfecting mankind. Critical though they were of exploitation, greed, and the division of labor, they did not speak of engaging the exploited ones in their own quests for emancipation. No particular pedagogy seemed required, and none was proposed, except within the specific contexts of utopian communities. Once a decent community or society was created, it was believed, the members would be educated in accord with its ideals.

There were, it is true, efforts to invent liberating ways of teaching for children in the larger society, although most were undertaken outside the confines of the common schools. Elizabeth Peabody and Bronson Alcott, among others, through "conversations" with actual persons in classrooms, toiled to inspire self-knowledge, creativity, and communion. Like Ralph Waldo Emerson, they were all hostile to the "joint-stock company" that society seemed to have become, a company "in which the members agree, for the better securing of his bread to each shareholder, to surrender the liberty and culture of the eater."[13] Like Emerson as well, they were all hostile to blind conformity, to the ethos of "Trade" that created false relations among human beings, to the chilling routines of institutional life. It is the case that they were largely apolitical; but their restiveness in the face of an imperfect society led them to find various modes of defiance. Those at Brook Farm tried to find a communal way of challenging the social order: Fuller found feminism; Emerson, ways of speaking intended to rouse his listeners to create their own meanings, to think for themselves.

The most potent exemplar of all this was Henry David Thoreau, deliberately addressing readers "in the first person," provoking them to use their intellects to "burrow" through the taken-for-granted, the conventional, the genteel. He wanted them to reject their own self-exploitation, to refuse what we would now call **false consciousness**[c] and artificial needs. He connected the "wide-awakeness" to actual work in the world, to projects. He knew that people needed to be released from internal and external constraints if they were to shape and make and articulate, to leave their own thumbprints on the world. He understood about economic tyranny on the railroads and in the factories, and he knew that it could make political freedom meaningless. His writing and his abolitionism constituted his protests; both *Walden* and *On Civil Disobedience* function as pedagogies in the sense that they seemed aimed at raising the consciousness of those willing to pay heed. His concern, unquestionably, was with his "private state" rather than with a public space; but he helped create the alternative tradition in the United States at a moment of expansion and materialism. And there are strands of his thinking, even today, that can be woven into a critical pedagogy. Whether building his house, hoeing his beans, hunting woodchucks, or finding patterns in the ice melting on the wall, he was intent on *naming* his lived world.

There were more overtly rebellious figures among escaped slaves, abolitionists, and campaigners for women's rights; but the language of people like Frederick Douglass, Harriet Tubman, Sarah Grimke, Susan B. Anthony, and Elizabeth Cady Stanton was very much the language of those who carried on the original demand for independence. The power they sought, however,

---

[c] Linked to the notion that social institutions like schools are agents of ideological control that work to maintain dominant beliefs, values, and forms of oppression, **false consciousness** is the point at which members of society buy into their own exploitation and subordination, and become uncritical tools of production and consumption. More contemporary concepts referring to similar phenomena are: *domestication, mystification of reality, dysconsciousness, anesthetized, the social construction of not seeing, manufactured consent,* and *colonization of the mind.*

was not the power to expand and control. For them — slaves, oppressed women, freedmen and freedwomen — the idea of freedom as endowment solved little; they had to take action to *achieve* their freedom, which they saw as the power to act and to choose. Thomas Jefferson, years before, had provided the metaphor of *polis* for Americans, signifying a space where persons could come together to bring into being the "worldly structure" spoken of above. Great romantics like Emerson and Thoreau gave voice to the passion for autonomy and authenticity. Black leaders, including Douglass, W. E. B. Du Bois, the Reverend Martin Luther King, Jr., and Malcolm X, not only engaged dialectically with the resistant environment in their pursuit of freedom; they invented languages and pedagogies to enable people to overcome **internalized oppression.**[d] Struggling for their rights in widening public spheres, they struggled also against what the Reverend King called "nobodiness" as they marched and engaged in a civil disobedience grounded in experiences of the past. Du Bois was in many ways exemplary when he spoke of the "vocation" of twentieth-century youth. Attacking the industrial system "which creates poverty and the children of poverty . . . ignorance and disease and crime," he called for "young women and young men of devotion to lift again the banner of humanity and to walk toward a civilization which will be free and intelligent, which will be healthy and unafraid."[14] The words hold intimations of what Paulo Freire was to say years later when he, too, spoke of the "vocation" of oppressed people, one he identified with "humanization."[15] And the very notion of walking "toward a civilization" suggests the sense of future possibility without which a pedagogy must fail.

Public school teachers, subordinated as they were in the solidifying educational bureaucracies, seldom spoke the language of resistance or transcendence. It is well to remember, however, the courageous ones who dared to go south after the Civil War in the freedmen's schools. Not only did they suffer persecution in their efforts to invent their own "pedagogy of the oppressed" — or of the newly liberated; they often fought for their own human rights against male missionary administrators and even against the missionary concept itself.[16] It is well to remember, too, the transformation of the missionary impulse into settlement house and social work by women like Jane Addams and Lillian Wald. Committing themselves to support systems and adult education for newcomers to the country and for the neighborhood poor, they supported union organizations with an explicitly political awareness of what they were about in a class-ridden society. They were able, more often than not, to avoid what Freire calls "malefic generosity" and develop the critical empathy needed for enabling the "other" to find his or her own way.

---

[d] **Internalized oppression** occurs when a member(s) of an oppressed group, after a period of abuse and criticism, comes to believe the dominant group's description of them as "inferior."

For all the preoccupations with control, for all the schooling "to order," as David Nasaw puts it,[17] there were always people hostile to regimentation and manipulation, critical of constraints of consciousness. Viewed from a contemporary perspective, for example, Colonel Francis Parker's work with teachers at the Cook County Normal School at the end of the nineteenth century placed a dramatic emphasis on freeing children from competitive environments and compulsions. He encouraged the arts and spontaneous activities; he encouraged shared work. He believed that, if democratized, the school could become "the one central means by which the great problem of human liberty is to be worked out."[18] Trying to help teachers understand the natural learning processes of the young, he was specifically concerned with resisting the corruptions and distortions of an increasingly corporate America. In the Emersonian tradition, he envisioned a sound community life emerging from the liberation and regeneration of individuals. And indeed, there were many libertarians and romantic progressives following him in the presumption that a society of truly free individuals would be a humane and sustaining one.

This confidence may account for the contradictions in the American critical heritage, especially as it informed education within and outside the schools. Structural changes, if mentioned at all, were expected to follow the emancipation of persons (or the appropriate molding of persons); and the schools, apparently depoliticized, were relied upon to effect the required reform and bring about a better world. If individual children were properly equipped for the work they had to do, it was believed, and trained to resist the excesses of competition, there would be no necessity for political action to transform economic relations. The street children, the tenement children, those afflicted and crippled by poverty and social neglect, were often thrust into invisibility because their very existence denied that claim.

John Dewey was aware of such young people, certainly in Chicago, where he saw them against his own memories of face-to-face community life in Burlington, Vermont. Convinced of the necessity for cooperation and community support if individual powers were to be released, he tried in some sense to recreate the Burlington of his youth in the "miniature community" he hoped to see in each classroom.[19] In those classrooms as well, there would be continuing and open communication, the kind of learning that would feed into practice, and inquiries arising out of questioning in the midst of life. Critical thinking modeled on the scientific method, active and probing intelligence: these, for Dewey, were the stuff of a pedagogy that would equip the young to resist fixities and stock responses, repressive and deceiving authorities. Unlike the libertarians and romantics, he directed attention to the "social medium" in which the individual growth occurred and to the mutuality of significant concerns.

Even as we question the small-town paradigm in Dewey's treatment of community, even as we wonder about his use of the scientific model for social inquiry, we still ought to be aware of Dewey's sensitivity to what would later be called the **"hegemony,"**[e] or the ideological control, implicit in the dominant point of view of a given society. He understood, for instance, the "religious aureole" protecting institutions like the Supreme Court, the Constitution, and private property. He was aware that the principles and assumptions that gave rise even to public school curricula were so taken for granted that they were considered wholly natural, fundamentally unquestionable. In *The Public and Its Problems,* he called what we think of as ideological control a "social pathology," which "works powerfully against effective inquiry into social institutions and conditions." He went on, "It manifests itself in a thousand ways: in querulousness, in impotent drifting, in uneasy snatching at distractions, in idealization of the long established, in a facile optimism assumed as a cloak, in riotous glorification of things 'as they are,' in intimidation of all dissenters — ways which depress and dissipate thought all the more effectually because they operate with subtle and unconscious pervasiveness."[20] A method of social inquiry had to be developed, he said, to reduce the "pathology" that led to denial and to acquiescence in the status quo. For all his commitment to scientific method, however, he stressed the "human function" of the physical sciences and the importance of seeing them in human terms. Inquiry, communication, "contemporary and quotidian" knowledge of consequence for shared social life: these fed into his conceptions of pedagogy.

His core concern for individual fulfillment was rooted in a recognition that fulfillment could only be attained in the midst of "associated" or intersubjective life. Troubled as we must be fifty years later by the "eclipse of the public," he saw as one of the prime pedagogical tasks the education of an "articulate public." For him, the public sphere came into being when the consequences of certain private transactions created a common interest among people, one that demanded deliberate and cooperative action. Using somewhat different language, we might say that a public emerges when people come freely together in speech and action to take *care* of something that needs caring for, to repair some evident deficiency in their common world. We might think of homelessness as a consequence of the private dealings of landlords, an arms build-up as a consequence of corporate decisions, racial exclusion as a consequence of a private property-holder's choice. And then we might think of what it would mean to educate to the end of caring for something and taking action to repair. That would be *public* education informed by a critical pedagogy; and it would weave together a number of American themes.

---

[e] **Hegemony**, as derived from the work of Italian theorist Antonio Gramsci, is used to express how certain groups manage to dominate others. An analysis of hegemony is especially concerned with how the imposition of particular ideologies and forms of authority results in the reproduction of social and institutional practices through which dominant groups maintain not only their positions of privilege and control, but also the consensual support of other members of society.

Certain of these themes found a new articulation in the 1930s, during the publication of *The Social Frontier* at Teachers College. An educational journal, it was addressed "to the task of considering the broad role of education in advancing the welfare and interests of the great masses of the people who do the work of society . . . those who labor on farms and ships and in the mines, shops, and factories of the world."[21] Dewey was among the contributors; and, although it had little impact on New Deal policy or even on specific educational practices, the magazine did open out to a future when more and more "liberals" would take a critical view of monopoly capitalism and industrial culture with all their implications for a supposedly "common" school.

In some respect, this represented a resurgence of the Enlightenment faith. Rational insight and dialogue, linked to scientific intelligence, were expected to reduce inequities and exploitation. A reconceived educational effort would advance the welfare and interests of the masses. Ironically, it was mainly in the private schools that educational progressivism had an influence. Critical discussions took place there; attention was paid to the posing of worthwhile problems arising out of the tensions and uncertainties of everyday life; social intelligence was nurtured; social commitments affirmed. In the larger domains of public education, where school people were struggling to meet the challenges of mass education, the emphasis tended to be on "life-adjustment," preparation for future life and work, and "physical, mental, and emotional health."

There is irony in the fact that the progressive social vision, with its integrating of moral with epistemic concerns, its hopes for a social order transformed by the schools, was shattered by the Second World War. The terrible revelations at Auschwitz and Hiroshima demonstrated what could happen when the old dream of knowledge as power was finally fulfilled. Science was viewed as losing its innocence in its wedding to advanced technology. Bureaucracy, with all its impersonality and literal irresponsibility, brought with it almost unrecognizable political and social realities. It took time, as is well known, for anything resembling a progressive vision to reconstitute itself; there was almost no recognition of the role now being played by "instrumental rationality,"[22] or what it would come to signify. On the educational side, after the war, there were efforts to remake curriculum in the light of new inquiries into knowledge structures in the disciplinary fields. On the side of the general public, there were tax revolts and rejections of the critical and the controversial, even as the McCarthyite subversion was occurring in the larger world. Only a few years after the Sputnik panic, with the talent searches it occasioned, and the frantic encouragement of scientific training, the long-invisible poor of America suddenly took center stage. The Civil Rights Movement, taking form since the Supreme Court decision on integration in 1954, relit flames of critical pedagogy, as it set people marching to achieve their freedom and their human rights.

Viewed from the perspective of a critical tradition in this country, the 1960s appear to have brought all the latent tendencies to the surface. The civil rights movement, alive with its particular traditions of liberation, provided the spark; the war in Vietnam gave a lurid illumination to the system's deficiencies: its incipient violence; its injustices; its racism; its indifference to public opinion and demand. The short-lived effort to reform education and provide compensation for damages done by poverty and discrimination could not halt the radical critique of America's schools. And that many-faceted critique — libertarian, Marxist, romantic, democratic — variously realized the critical potentialities of American pedagogies. Without an Emerson or a Thoreau or a Parker, there would not have been a Free School movement or a "deschooling" movement. Without a Du Bois, there would not have been liberation or storefront schools. Without a social reformist tradition, there would have been no Marxist voices asking (as, for instance, Samuel Bowles and Herbert Gintis did) for a "mass-based organization of working people powerfully articulating a clear alternative to corporate capitalism as the basis for a progressive educational system."[23] Without a Dewey, there would have been little concern for "participatory democracy," for "consensus," for the reconstitution of a public sphere.

Yes, the silence fell at the end of the following decade; privatization increased, along with consumerism and cynicism and the attrition of the public space. We became aware of living in what Europeans called an "administered society";[24] we became conscious of technicism and **positivism**[f] and of the one-dimensionality Herbert Marcuse described.[25] Popular culture, most particularly as embodied in the media, was recognized (with the help of the critical theorist Theodor Adorno) as a major source of mystification.[26] The schools were recognized as agents of **"cultural reproduction,"**[g] oriented to a differential distribution of knowledge.[27] Numerous restive educational thinkers, seeking new modes of articulating the impacts of ideological control and manipulation, turned towards European neo-Marxist scholarship for clues to a critical pedagogy. In an American tradition, they were concerned for

---

[f] Associated with the Enlightenment and modernism, **positivism** refers to a belief system or paradigm that makes claims to objectivity, truth, and certainty in defense of a scientific basis for the study of culture. As such, knowledge and reason are seen as neutral and universal, rather than as social constructions that reflect particular interests and ideologies. This uncritical call to science has resulted in an obsession with finding and using the "right" technique to understand a phenomenon or solve a problem. For example, "technocratic" models, which conceptualize teaching as a discrete and scientific undertaking, embrace depersonalized methods for educating students that often translate into the regulation and standardization of teacher practices and curricula, and rote memorization of selected "facts" that can easily be measured through standardized testing. As such, the role of the teacher is reduced to that of an uncritical, "objective," and "efficient" distributor of information.

[g] Critical social theorists argue that dominant ideologies and knowledge are built into social institutions that both privilege and exclude particular perspectives, voices, authorities, and representations. Within theories of **cultural reproduction**, schools, educators, and curricula are generally viewed as mechanisms of ideological control that work to reproduce and maintain dominant beliefs, values, norms, and oppressive practices. This reproductive process is mediated, in part, through the "hidden curriculum" — the hidden agenda of maintaining the status quo through specific schooling practices.

the individual, for the subject, which late Marxism appeared to have ignored; and the humanist dimension of **Frankfurt School**[h] philosophies held an unexpected appeal. Moreover, what with its concern for critical consciousness and communicative competence, Frankfurt School thinking held echoes of the Enlightenment faith; and, in some profound way, it was recognized.

There is, of course, an important sense in which the Frankfurt School has reappropriated philosophical traditions (Kantian, Hegelian, phenomenological, psychological, psychoanalytical) which are ours as well or which, at least, have fed our intellectual past. But it also seems necessary to hold in mind the fact that European memories are not our memories. The sources of European critical theory are to be found in responses to the destruction of the Workers' Councils after the First World War, the decline of the Weimar Republic, the rise of Stalinism, the spread of fascism, the Holocaust, the corruptions of social democracy. As climactic as any contemporary insight was the realization that reason (viewed as universal in an Enlightenment sense) could be used to justify the application of technical expertise in torture and extermination. Europeans saw a connection between this and the rationalization of society by means of bureaucracy, and in the separating off of moral considerations long viewed as intrinsic to civilized life. The intimations of all this could be seen in European literature for many years: in Dostoevsky's and Kafka's renderings of human beings as insects; in Musil's anticipations of the collapse of European orders; in Camus's pestilence, in Sartre's nausea, in the Dionysian and bestial shapes haunting the structures of the arts. We have had a tragic literature, a critical literature, in the United States. We need only recall Twain, Melville, Crane, Wharton, Hemingway, Fitzgerald. But it has been a literature rendered tragic by a consciousness of a dream betrayed, of a New World corrupted by exploitation and materialism and greed. In background memory, there are images of Jeffersonian agrarianism, of public spheres, of democratic and free-swinging communities. We do not find these in European literature, *nor* in the writings of the critical theorists.

One of the few explicit attempts to articulate aspects of the Western tradition for educators has been the courageous work of Freire, who stands astride both hemispheres. He has been the pioneer of a pedagogy informed by both Marxist and existential-phenomenological thought; his conception of critical reflectiveness has reawakened the themes of a tradition dating back to Plato and forward to the theologies of liberation that have taken hold in oppressed areas of the Western world. His background awareness, however, and that of the largely Catholic peasants with whom he has worked, are not that of most North Americans. It must be granted that his own

---

[h] This German institute of social research, frequented by the likes of Marcuse, Fromm, Horkheimer, Adorno, Habermas, Arendt, Brecht, Lukacs, and a great many others, had an enormous impact on the sociological, political, and cultural thought of this century. It was in this institute that the term "critical theory" and its ideas evolved.

culture and education transcend his Brazilian origins and make him something of a world citizen when it comes to the life of ideas. Like his European colleagues, however, he reaches back to predecessors other than Jefferson and Emerson and Thoreau and William James and Dewey; his social vision is not that of our particular democracy. This is not intended as criticism, but as a reminder that a critical pedagogy relevant to the United States today must go beyond — calling on different memories, repossessing another history.

We live, after all, in dark times, times with little historical memory of any kind. There are vast dislocations in industrial towns, erosions of trade unions; there is little sign of class consciousness today. Our great cities are burnished on the surfaces, building high technologies, displaying astonishing consumer goods. And on the side streets, in the crevices, in the burnt-out neighborhoods, there are the rootless, the dependent, the sick, the permanently unemployed. There is little sense of agency, even among the brightly successful; there is little capacity to look at things as if they could be otherwise.

Where education is concerned, the discourse widens, and the promises multiply. The official reform reports, ranging from *A Nation at Risk* to the Carnegie Forum's *A Nation Prepared,* call for a restructuring of schools and of teacher education to the end of raising the levels of literacy in accord with the requirements of an economy based on high technology.[28] The mass of students in the schools, including the one-third who will be "minorities," are to be enabled to develop "higher order skills" in preparation for "the unexpected, the nonroutine world they will face in the future."[29] The implicit promise is that, if the quality of teachers is improved (and "excellent" teachers rewarded and recognized), the majority of young people will be equipped for meaningful participation in an advanced knowledge-based economy wholly different from the mass-production economy familiar in the past.

On the other hand, there are predictions that we will never enjoy full employment in this country, that few people stand any real chance of securing meaningful work. If the military juggernaut keeps rolling on, draining funds and support from social utilities, daycare centers, arts institutions, schools and universities, we will find ourselves devoid of all those things that might make life healthier, gentler, more inviting, and more challenging. At once we are reminded (although not by the authors of the educational reports) of the dread of nuclear destruction (or of Chernobyls, or of Bhopal) that lies below the surface of apparent hope for the future. This dread, whether repressed or confronted, leads numbers of people to a sense of fatalism and futility with respect to interventions in the social world. For others, it leads to a sad and often narcissistic focus on the "now." For still others, it evokes denial and accompanying extravagances: consumerism increases; a desire for heightened sensation, for vicarious violence, grows. And for many millions, it makes peculiarly appealing the talk of salvation broadcast by evangelists and television preachers; it makes seductive the promise of Armageddon.

As young people find it increasingly difficult to project a long-range future, intergenerational continuity becomes problematic. So does the confidence in education as a way of keeping the culture alive, or of initiating newcomers into learning communities, or of providing the means for pursuing a satisfying life. Uncertain whether we can share or constitute a common world, except in its most fabricated and trivialized form, we wonder what the great conversation can now include and whether it is worth keeping alive. Michael Oakeshott spoke eloquently of that conversation, "begun in the primeval forests and extended and made more articulate in the course of centuries." He said it involves passages of argument and inquiry, going on in public and in private, that it is an "unrehearsed intellectual adventure. . . ." Education, for him, "is an initiation into the skill and partnership of this conversation," which gives character in the end "to every human activity and utterance."[30] We know now how many thousands of voices have been excluded from that conversation over the years. We know how, with its oppositions and hierarchies, it demeaned. As we listen to the prescriptions raining down for "common learnings" (which may or may not include the traditions of people of color, feminist criticism and literature, Eastern philosophies) and "cultural literacy," we cannot but wonder how those of us in education can renew and expand the conversation, reconstitute what we can call a common world.

Yes, there are insights into humane teaching in the latest reports; but, taking the wide view, we find mystification increasing, along with the speechlessness. We have learned about the diverse ways we Americans interpret our traditions: about those who identify with the old individualism, those who yearn for old communities, those who seek new modes of justice, those who want to lose themselves in a cause.[31] We know something about the persistence of a commitment to freedom, variously defined, and to the idea of equity. At once, we are bound to confront such extremes as a moral majority usurping talk of intimacy and family values, while neoliberals seek out technocratic, depersonalized solutions to quantified problems and speak a cost-benefit language beyond the reach of those still striving for public dialogue.

People have never, despite all that, had such vast amounts of information transmitted to them — not merely about murders and accidents and scandals, but about crucial matters on which public decisions may some day have to be made: nuclear energy, space vehicles, racism, homelessness, life-support systems, chemotherapies, joblessness, terrorism, abused children, fanatics, saints. There are whole domains of information that arouse frustration or pointless outrage. All we need to do is think of the persecution of the sanctuary-movement leaders, of children living in shelters, of the *contras* in Honduras, of adolescent suicides, of overcrowded jails. At the same time, no population has ever been so deliberately entertained, amused, and soothed into avoidance, denial, and neglect. We hear the cacophonous voices of special interest groups; we hear of discrete acts of sacrifice and martyrdom; we seldom hear of intentionally organized collaborative action to repair what is felt to be missing, or known to be wrong.

Complacency and malaise; upward mobility and despair. Sometimes we detect feelings of shame and helplessness perceived as personal failure. To be dependent, to be on welfare, is to be certified as in some manner deviant or irresponsible since good Americans are expected to fend for themselves. Even as oppressed peasants internalize their oppressors' images of them as helpless creatures, so unsuccessful Americans (young or old) internalize the system's description of them as ineffectual. They are unable to live up to the culture's mandate to control their own lives and contribute to the productivity of the whole. Our institutional responses are ordinarily technical (and we are drawn to technical solutions out of benevolence, as well as out of helplessness). Yet we know that to think mainly in terms of techniques or cures or remedies is often to render others and the earth itself as objects to be acted upon, treated, controlled, or used. It is to distance what we believe has to be done (efficiently, effectively) from our own existential projects, from our own becoming among other incomplete and questing human beings. It is to repress or deny the prereflective, tacit understandings that bind us together in a culture and connect us to our history.

Having said all this, I must ask again what a critical pedagogy might mean for those of us who teach the young at this peculiar and menacing time. Perhaps we might begin by releasing our imaginations and summoning up the traditions of freedom in which most of us were reared. We might try to make audible again the recurrent calls for justice and equality. We might reactivate the resistance to materialism and conformity. We might even try to inform with meaning the desire to educate "all the children" in a legitimately "common" school. Considering the technicism and the illusions of the time, we need to recognize that what we single out as most deficient and oppressive is in part a function of perspectives created by our past. It is a past in which our subjectivities are embedded, whether we are conscious of it or not. We have reached a point when that past must be reinterpreted and reincarnated in the light of what we have learned.

We understand that a mere removal of constraints or a mere relaxation of controls will not ensure the emergence of free and creative human beings. We understand that the freedom we cherish is not an endowment, that it must be achieved through dialectical engagements with the social and economic obstacles we find standing in our way, those we have to learn to name. We understand that a plurality of American voices must be attended to, that a plurality of life-stories must be heeded if a meaningful power is to spring up through a new "binding and promising, combining and covenanting." We understand that the Enlightenment heritage must be repossessed and reinterpreted, so that we can overcome the positivism that awaits on one side, the empty universalism on the other. But we cannot and ought not escape our own history and memories, not if we are to keep alive the awarenesses that ground our identities and connect us to the persons turning for fulfillment to our schools.

We cannot negate the fact of power. But we can undertake a resistance, a reaching out towards becoming *persons* among other persons, for all the talk of human resources, for all the orienting of education to the economy. To engage with our students as persons is to affirm our own incompleteness, our consciousness of spaces still to be explored, desires still to be tapped, possibilities still to be opened and pursued. At once, it is to rediscover the value of care, to reach back to experiences of caring and being cared for (as Nel Noddings writes) as sources of an ethical ideal. It is, Noddings says, an ideal to be nurtured through "dialogue, practice, and confirmation," processes much akin to those involved in opening a public sphere.[32] We have to find out how to open such spheres, such spaces, where a better state of things can be imagined; because it is only through the projection of a better social order that we can perceive the gaps in what exists and try to transform and repair. I would like to think that this can happen in classrooms, in corridors, in schoolyards, in the streets around.

I would like to think of teachers moving the young into their own interpretations of their lives and their lived worlds, opening wider and wider perspectives as they do so. I would like to see teachers ardent in their efforts to make the range of symbol systems available to the young for the ordering of experience, even as they maintain regard for their vernaculars. I would like to see teachers tapping the spectrum of intelligences, encouraging multiple readings of written texts and readings of the world.

In "the shadow of silent majorities," then, as teachers learning along with those we try to provoke to learn, we may be able to inspire hitherto unheard voices. We may be able to empower people to rediscover their own memories and articulate them in the presence of others, whose space they can share. Such a project demands the capacity to unveil and disclose. It demands the exercise of imagination, enlivened by works of art, by situations of speaking and making. Perhaps we can at last devise reflective communities in the interstices of colleges and schools. Perhaps we can invent ways of freeing people to feel and express indignation, to break through the opaqueness, to refuse the silences. We need to teach in such a way as to arouse passion now and then; we need a new camaraderie, a new en masse. These are dark and shadowed times, and we need to live them, standing before one another, open to the world.

NOTES

1. Jean Baudrillard, *In the Shadow of Silent Majorities* (New York: Semiotexte, 1983).
2. Jean-Paul Sartre, *Search for a Method* (New York: Knopf, 1968), p. 94.
3. Walt Whitman, *Leaves of Grass* (New York: Aventine Press, 1931), pp. 49–50.
4. Wallace Stevens, *Collected Poems* (New York: Knopf, 1963), p. 198.

5. Marianne Moore, *Tell Me, Tell Me* (New York: Viking Press, 1966), p. 24.
6. Muriel Rukeyser, "Käthe Kollwitz," in *By a Woman Writt,* ed. Joan Goulianos (New York: Bobbs Merrill, 1973), p. 374.
7. Adrienne Rich, *A Wild Patience Has Taken Me This Far* (New York: Norton, 1981), p. 23.
8. John Stuart Mill, "On Liberty," in *The Six Great Humanistic Essays* (New York: Washington Square Press, 1963), p. 158.
9. Hannah Arendt, *On Revolution* (New York: Viking Press, 1963), pp. 174–175.
10. Horace Mann, "Ninth Annual Report," in *The Republic and the School: Horace Mann on the Education of Free Men,* ed. Lawrence A. Cremin (New York: Teachers College Press, 1957), p. 57.
11. Mark Twain, *The adventures of Huckleberry Finn* (New York: New American Library, 1959), p. 283.
12. Orestes Brownson, "The Laboring Classes," in *Ideology and Power in the Age of Jackson,* ed. Edwin C. Rozwenc (Garden City, NY: Anchor Books, 1964), p. 321.
13. Ralph Waldo Emerson, "Self-Reliance," in *Emerson on Education,* ed. Howard Mumford Jones (New York: Teachers College Press, 1966), p. 105.
14. W. E. B. Du Bois, *W. E. B. Du Bois: A Reader,* ed. Meyer Weinberg (New York: Harper Torchbooks, 1970), pp. 153–154.
15. Paulo Freire, *Pedagogy of the Oppressed* (New York: Continuum, 1970), pp. 27 ff.
16. Jacqueline Jones, "Women Who Were More Than Men: Sex and Status in Freedmen's Teaching," *History of Education Quarterly, 19* (1979), 47–59.
17. David Nasaw, *Schooled to Order* (New York: Oxford University Press, 1981).
18. Colonel Francis Parker, *Talks on Pedagogics* (New York: Harper, 1894).
19. John Dewey, "The School and Society," in *Dewey on Education,* ed. Martin Dworkin (New York: Teachers College Press, 1959), p. 41.
20. John Dewey, *The Public and Its Problems* (Athens, OH: Swallow Press, 1954).
21. Lawrence A. Cremin, *The Transformation of the School* (New York: Knopf, 1961), pp. 231–232.
22. Jürgen Habermas, *Knowledge and Human Interests* (Boston: Beacon Press, 1972).
23. Samuel Bowles and Herbert Gintis, *Schooling in Capitalist America* (New York: Basic Books, 1976), p. 266.
24. Herbert Marcuse, "Some Social Implications of Modern Technology," in *The Essential Frankfurt School Reader,* ed. Andrew Arato and Eike Gebhardt (New York: Urizen Books, 1978), pp. 138–162.
25. Herbert Marcuse, *One-Dimensional Man* (Boston: Beacon Press, 1966).
26. Theodor Adorno, "Cultural Criticism and Society," in *Prisms* (London: Neville Spearman, 1961), pp. 31–32 ff.
27. See Pierre Boudieu and Jean-Claude Passeron, *Reproduction* (Beverly Hills: Sage, 1977).
28. The National Commission on Excellence in Education, *A Nation at Risk: The Imperative for Educational Reform* (Washington: U.S. Department of Education, 1983); and Carnegie Forum on Education and the Economy, *A Nation Prepared: Teachers for the 21st Century* (New York: Carnegie Forum, 1986).
29. Carnegie Forum, *A Nation Prepared,* p. 25.
30. Michael Oakeshott, *Rationalism in Politics and Other Essays* (London: Methuen, 1962), pp. 198–199.
31. Robert N. Bellah, Richard Madsen, William M. Sullivan, Ann Swidler, and Steve M. Tipton, *Habits of the Heart: Individualism and Commitment in American Life* (Berkeley: University of California Press, 1985).
32. Nel Noddings, *Caring: A Feminine Approach to Ethics and Moral Education* (Berkeley: University of California Press, 1984).

3

Literacy for Stupidification: The Pedagogy of Big Lies

DONALDO P. MACEDO

Elaborating on what Maxine Greene refers to as "these uncritical times," Donaldo Macedo confronts in this essay the ideological forces that shape public institutions of learning and, in turn, the ways in which those institutions work pedagogically to construct forms of conformity, discrimination, and socioeconomic inequality. Macedo argues that ignoring the politics of literacy practices and learning helps to maintain dominant ideological mechanisms that produce uncritical thinkers (what he refers to as "semiliterates"). Within this constricting paradigm, schools function as sites for indoctrination and enforcing compliance — systems of control characterized by mindless drills and exercises. Macedo presents events like the Gulf War and the first Rodney King verdict as evidence that, without the ability to understand and engage the world critically (that is, to be able to understand and transform the ideological, economic, and sociopolitical realities that shape our lives) Americans are subject to political manipulation, exploitation, and complicity with an oppressive system of privilege based on gender, skin color, class, sexual orientation, etc.

Begging the question of why a supposedly highly literate society frequently demonstrates the inability to think critically, Macedo contends that the educational system in the U.S. is not failing, and that the majority of people were never meant to be educated and have access to the dominant political and economic spheres. At most, the overwhelming majority are to be prepared to meet the demands of global economic competition in an ever-expanding technological society. Those who do receive an "education," Macedo argues, specialize in very specific areas/disciplines, so as to be fragmented/disconnected and unable to link their work to the world. For example, science and engineering students are not encouraged to be critical in terms of the political and social implications of their research.

Macedo challenges educators to examine potentially dangerous educational practices that ignore the need to make linkages between pedagogy (that is, how and in what context we learn what we learn) and ideology and power. Otherwise, from his perspective, democratic processes will continue to be undermined by the positions of privilege that constitute and sustain existing and unjust institutions.

> The great masses of people . . . will more easily fall victims to a big lie than to a small one.
> — Adolf Hitler

Most Americans would cringe at the thought that they have repeatedly fallen victim to big lies by their government. In fact, they would probably instinctively point out that the manipulation of people through big lies would only occur in totalitarian, fascist governments such as Hitler's. Within the same breath, they might remind us that their ancestors gave their lives in the great wars so we could enjoy the freedom and democracy we now have. They might also hasten to recite our national slogans such as "live free or die," "freedom of speech," and "freedom of information," among others.

While busily calling out slogans from their patriotic vocabulary memory warehouse, these same Americans dutifully vote, for example, for Ronald Reagan, giving him a landslide victory under a platform that promised to balance the budget, cut taxes, and increase military spending. This "unreason of reason" led George Bush to characterize Reagan's economic plan as voodoo economics — even though he himself later became entranced by the big lie of this same voodooism. What U.S. voters failed to do was to demand that Reagan tell the whole truth and nothing but the truth. In other words, they failed to require that Reagan acknowledge that, in order for his proposition to be true (and not a lie), the voters would have to give him and Bush a blank credit card with $4.3 trillion in deficit credit to create the false sense of economic prosperity enjoyed under their leadership. I say a false sense not only because of the present economic malaise, but also because the Reagan economic boom was a bust. According to Samuel Bowles, David M. Gordon, and E. Thomas Weisskopf,

> output growth did not revive during the 1980's cycle. Far from stimulating investment through massive tax cuts and concessions to the wealthy, Reagan-Bush economic policy has dealt investment a blow; compared with the previous business cycle, the pace of real net productive investment . . . declined by a quarter during the most recent business cycle.[1]

Despite concrete evidence indicating that the Reagan-Bush economic plan was a failure, U.S. voters swept Bush into office in 1988 with the same voodoo trickledown economics, now ornamented with a thousand points of short-circuited lights. These same voters ascended to Bush's morally high-minded call to apply international laws against Saddam Hussein's tyranny and his invasion of Kuwait. The great mass of voters who rallied behind Bush, pushing his popular approval rating beyond 90 percent during the Gulf War, failed to realize that these same international laws had been broken by Bush a year or so before in Panama, and by his predecessor in Grenada, Libya, and Nicaragua. This begs us to question why we supposedly highly literate and principled citizens of a great democracy frequently demonstrate the inability to separate myth from reality. This inability pushes us to perpetual flirtation with historical hypocrisy.

However, not all Americans suffer from the inability to separate myths from reality, to read the world critically. For example, David Spritzler, a 12-year-old student at Boston Latin School, faced disciplinary action for his refusal to recite the Pledge of Allegiance, which he considers "a hypocritical exhortation to patriotism" in that there is not "liberty and justice for all." According to Spritzler, the Pledge is an attempt to unite the

> oppressed and the oppressors. You have people who drive nice cars, live in nice houses and don't have to worry about money. Then you have the poor people, living in bad neighborhoods and going to bad schools. Somehow the Pledge makes it seem that everybody's equal when that's not happening. There's no justice for everybody.[2]

Spritzler was spared disciplinary action only after the American Civil Liberties Union wrote a letter on his behalf, citing a 1943 case, *West Virginia State Board of Education v. Barnett*, in which the U.S. Supreme Court upheld a student's right not to say the Pledge of Allegiance and to remain seated.

What remains incomprehensible is why a 12-year-old boy could readily see through the obvious hypocrisy contained in the Pledge of Allegiance, while his teachers and administrators, who have received much higher levels of education, cannot. As Noam Chomsky pointed out in reference to a similar situation, these teachers' and administrators' inability to see through the obvious represents "a real sign of deep indoctrination [in] that you can't understand elementary thoughts that any 10-year-old can understand. That's real indoctrination. So for him [the indoctrinated individual] it's kind of like a theological truth, a truth of received religion."[3] These teachers and administrators should know that history shows us convincingly and factually that the United States has systematically violated the Pledge of Allegiance, from the legalization of slavery, the denial of women's rights, and the near genocide of Native Americans, to the contemporary discriminatory practices against people who, by virtue of their race, ethnicity, class, or gender, are not treated with the dignity and respect called for in the Pledge. If we did not suffer from historical amnesia, we would easily recall that, once upon a time, the Massachusetts legislature promulgated a law that provided monetary rewards for dead Indians: "For every scalp of a male Indian brought in . . . forty pounds. For every scalp of such female Indian or male Indian under the age of twelve years that shall be killed . . . twenty pounds."[4] Even the abolitionist President Abraham Lincoln did not truly uphold the U.S. Declaration of Independence propositions of equality, life, liberty, and the pursuit of happiness, when he declared: "I will say, then, that I am not, nor ever have been in favor of bringing about in any way the social and political equality of the white and black races . . . I as much as any other man am in favor of having the superior position assigned to the white race."[5]

One could argue that the above-cited incidents belong to the dusty archives of our early history, but I do not believe that we have learned a great deal from historically dangerous memories, in so far as our leaders continue to incite racial tensions, as evidenced in the Willie Horton presidential campaign issue, or in Bush's opposition to job quotas on the pretext that it was a renewed invitation to racial divisiveness. This racial divisiveness actually has served the Republican Party's interest of splitting voters along class, racial, and ethnic lines. Our perpetual flirtation (if not marriage) with historical hypocrisy becomes abundantly clear if we imagine the juxtaposition of students reciting the Pledge of Allegiance in Charlestown High School in 1976, in classrooms ornamented with copies of the Declaration of Independence hanging alongside racial epithets scrawled on the walls: "Welcome Niggers," "Niggers Suck," "White Power," "KKK," "Bus is for Zulu," and "Be illiterate, fight busing."[6]

Our inability to see the obvious was never more evident than when a predominantly White jury found the four White policemen who brutally beat Rodney King "not guilty." Even though the world was shocked beyond belief by the raw brutality and barbarism of the Los Angeles law enforcers, the jurors who saw concrete video shots of King struggling on his hands and knees while being hit repeatedly by the policemen's batons concluded that "Mr. King was controlling the whole show with his action."[7] The racist ideology of Simi Valley, California, blinded these jurors such that they could readily accept that the savage beatings they had seen on the video were, as the defense attorneys claimed, nothing more than a mere "controlled application of fifty-six batons" in order to contain King, who had been portrayed as a dangerous "animal," like "gorillas in the mist."[8] However, one of the jurors did not fully accept the view of reality suggested by the defense attorneys: "I fought so hard to hang on, and hang on to what I saw on the video. . . . There was no way I could change the others. They couldn't see what I saw. . . . [But] they could not take away from what my eyes saw."[9]

The real educational question and challenge for us is to understand why most of the jurors either could not see, or refused to see, what their eyes and the eyes of the entire world saw on television. Unfortunately, in the present conjuncture of our educational system, particularly in our schools of education, it is very difficult to acquire the necessary critical tools that would unveil the ideology responsible for these jurors' blinders. A critical understanding of the savage beating of Rodney King and the subsequent acquittal of the four White police officers necessitates the **deconstruction**[a] of the intricate interplay of race, ethics, and ideology — issues that schools of education, by and large, neglect to take on rigorously. Courses such as race relations, ethics, and ideology are almost absent from the teacher preparation curriculum. This serious omission is, by its very nature, ideological, and constitutes the foundation for what I call the pedagogy of big lies.

At this juncture, I can easily frame my argument to demonstrate that many, if not all, of David Spritzler's teachers and administrators are either naive victims of a big lie, or are cognizant of the deceptive ideological mechanisms inherent in the Pledge and consciously reproduce them, even if it means violating the very rights the oath proclaims. I argue that the latter is true. Even if we want to give such educators the benefit of the doubt, their naivete is never innocent, but ideological. It is ideological to the degree that they have invested in a system that rewards them for reproducing and not questioning dominant mechanisms designed to produce power asymmetries along the lines of race, gender, class, culture, and ethnicity. This will become clearer in my analysis of the role of literacy in **cultural reproduction**,[b] in which I will show how collective experiences function in the interest of the dominant ruling elites, rather than in the interest of the oppressed groups that are the object of its policies.

Literacy for cultural reproduction uses institutional mechanisms to undermine independent thought, a prerequisite for the Orwellian "manufacture of consent" or "engineering of consent." In this light, schools are seen as ideological institutions designed to prevent the so-called crisis of democracy, another Orwellian concept, meaning the beginnings of democracy.[10]

In fact, this very perspective on schools was proposed by the Trilateral Commission, a group of international and essentially liberal elites, which included Jimmy Carter in its membership. This commission was created in response to the general democratic participation of masses of people in the Western world in questioning their governments' ethical behavior. Its major purpose as many understand it, was to seek ways to maintain the Western capitalist cultural **hegemony**.[c] The Trilateral Commission referred to schools

---

[a] Generally associated with the work of French theorist Jacques Derrida, **deconstruction** is an analytic process through which the deep, unconscious meaning of texts is examined. Within a critical pedagogical framework, deconstruction often refers to the analytic process of taking apart (i.e., dissecting, critically inquiring, problematizing) a phenomenon in order to understand its construction.

[b] Critical social theorists argue that dominant ideologies and knowledge are built into social institutions that both privilege and exclude particular perspectives, voices, authorities, and representations. Within theories of **cultural reproduction**, schools, educators, and curricula are generally viewed as mechanisms of ideological control that work to reproduce and maintain dominant beliefs, values, norms, and oppressive practices. This reproductive process is mediated, in part, through the "hidden curriculum" — the hidden agenda of maintaining the status quo through specific schooling practices.

[c] **Hegemony**, as derived from the work of Italian theorist Antonio Gramsci, is used to express how certain groups manage to dominate others. An analysis of hegemony is especially concerned

as "institutions responsible for the indoctrination of the young."[11] Noam Chomsky states it simply: the Trilateral Commission argues that schools should be institutions for indoctrination, "for imposing obedience, for blocking the possibility of independent thought, and they play an institutional role in a system of control and coercion."[12] This becomes clear in the conservative call for the control of the so-called "excess of democracy." For example, according to Henry Giroux, Boston University president John Silber, who prides himself on being an education "expert," "has urged fellow conservatives to abandon any civility toward scholars whose work is considered political."[13] What Silber fails to realize is that the very act of viewing education as neutral and devoid of politics is, in fact, a political act. In order to maintain schools as sites for cultural reproduction and indoctrination, Silber prefers an educational system that brooks no debate or dissent. This is apparent in his urging of "his fellow conservatives to name names, to discredit educators who have chosen to engage in forms of social criticism (work that the New Right considers political) at odds with the agenda of the New Right's mythic conception of the university as a warehouse built on the pillars of an unproblematic and revered tradition."[14]

Although it is important to analyze how ideologies inform various literacy traditions, in this article I limit my discussion to a brief analysis of the instrumentalist approach to literacy and its linkage to cultural reproduction. I also argue that the instrumentalist approach to literacy does not refer only to the goal of producing readers who meet the basic requirements of contemporary society, but also includes the highest level of literacy found in disciplinary specialism and hyper-specialism.

Finally, I analyze how the instrumentalist approach to literacy, even at the highest level of specialism, functions to **domesticate**[d] the consciousness via a constant disarticulation between the narrow **reductionistic**[e] reading of one's field of specialization and the reading of the universe within which one's specialism is situated. This inability to link the reading of the word with the world, if not combatted, will further exacerbate already feeble democratic institutions and the unjust, asymmetrical power relations that characterize the hypocritical nature of contemporary democracies. The inherent hypocrisy in the actual use of the term "democracy" is eloquently captured by Noam Chomsky in his analysis of the United States. Chomsky writes:

---

with how the imposition of particular ideologies and forms of authority results in the reproduction of social and institutional practices through which dominant groups maintain not only their positions of privilege and control, but also the consensual support of other members of society.

[d] The term **domesticate** refers to the process by which people learn to internalize the dominant values and behaviors that render individuals and groups unable, or unwilling, to recognize oppressive practices. Similar concepts: *manufacture consent, anesthetize, colonize the mind.*

[e] To be **reductionistic** is to simplify a particular phenomenon so as to mask its complexity. For example, arguing that social reality is shaped solely by socioeconomic status and class conflict obscures the multiple and interconnecting relationships of other significant human experiences (such as race, gender, and sexual orientation) and their effects on perception and struggle.

"Democracy" in the United States rhetoric refers to a system of governance in which elite elements based in the business community control the state by virtue of their dominance of the private society, while the population observes quietly. So understood, democracy is a system of elite decision and public ratification, as in the United States itself. Correspondingly, popular involvement in the formation of public policy is considered a serious threat. It is not a step towards democracy; rather, it constitutes a "crisis of democracy" that must be overcome.[15]

INSTRUMENTALIST APPROACH TO LITERACY

Both the instrumental literacy for the poor, in the form of a competency-based skills banking approach, and the highest form of instrumental literacy for the rich, acquired through the university in the form of professional specialization, share one common feature: they both prevent the development of the critical thinking that enables one to "read the world" critically and to understand the reasons and linkages behind the facts.

Literacy for the poor is, by and large, characterized by mindless, meaningless drills and exercises given "in preparation for multiple choice exams and writing gobbledygook in imitation of the psycho-babble that surrounds them."[16] This instrumental approach to literacy sets the stage for the anesthetization of the mind, as poet John Ashbery eloquently captures in "What is Poetry":

> In School
> All the thoughts got combed out:
> What was left was like a field.[17]

The educational "comb," for those teachers who have blindly accepted the status quo, is embodied in the ditto-sheets and workbooks that mark and control the pace of routinization in the drill-and-practice assembly line. Patrick Courts correctly describes the function of these workbooks and ditto-sheets:

Either you must fill in the blank (or does the blank fill you in? — they have lots of blanks) or you must identify the correct or incorrect answer by circling it, underlining it, or drawing an X through it. In addition to all this, students will find that learning to spell involves copying the same word five times and copying the definition; and learning the meaning of the word involves looking it up in the dictionary and copying the definition; and learning to write involves writing a sentence or two using the word they copied five times and looked up in the dictionary. Much of what they read in the first four or five grades, they will read-to-read: That is, they will be practicing reading in order to show that they can read, which much of the time means that they will be involved in "word-perfect" oral-reading activities, grouped as Cardinals (if they are good at it), or Bluebirds (if they are not). They will learn that reading has one of two functions: Either you read orally to show that you can "bark at print" well (delighting your teachers and boring your peers), or you read silently in order to fill in those blanks in the workbook.[18]

One would hope the students grouped as Cardinals, who survived reading-and-writing drill bootcamp to become fully literate, were empowered with some sort of ability for independent critical analysis and thought. Unfortunately, these Cardinals continue in their literacy practices to experience the same fragmentation of knowledge, albeit with more sophistication. The fragmentation of knowledge via specialization produces an intellectual mechanization that, in the end, serves the same function as the fragmentation of skills in the literacy for the poor. It is not a coincidence that the defense lawyers for the White policemen in the Rodney King trial insisted on showing the jurors the video frame by frame over and over again, instead of running the video at the normal speed. The fragmentation of the Rodney King beating served two important functions: 1) by showing each frame separately, the jurors were not allowed to see and experience the total impact of the violence incurred in the beatings, and 2) by repeating the frames over and over again, the defense lawyers were able to anesthetize the sensibilities of the jurors and routinize the action captured in each frame. Although the fragmentation of skills and bodies of knowledge is not the same as the fragmentation of the video into separate frames, the underlying principle serves the same function: it creates, on the one hand, the inability to make linkages, and on the other hand, it deadens the senses. This process leads to a de facto social construction of not seeing. My colleague Robert Greene (personal communication, Fall 1992) noted that this once again proves the old proverb that the eyes do not see; they only record while the mind sees. To the extent that the mind can be ideologically controlled, it filters in order to transform what the eyes record, as was the case in the transformation of Rodney King's brutal beating to a "systematic application of fifty-six batons." However, an African American colleague, Pancho Savery, correctly pointed out to me (personal communication, Fall 1992) that the defense attorney's manipulative mechanisms to prevent linkages and to deaden the jurors' senses could only work if jurors were already invested in the doctrinal system that imposed a willful blindness to realities that contradicted or questioned the system. In other words, the success of the ideological manipulation depends on the degree to which one invests in the doctrinal system and expects rewards from it. Savery argues that the fragmentization of the video frames and the playing of them over and over again would not deaden the senses of most African Americans. On the contrary, the more they see the video of King's beating, even in fragmented frames, the more enraged they would become, as they are not invested in the racist doctrinal system of which they are the victims.

For some, the instrumentalist approach to literacy may have the appeal of producing readers who are capable of meeting the demands of our ever more complex technological society. However, such an approach emphasizes the mechanical learning of reading skills while sacrificing the critical analysis of the social and political order that generates the need for reading in the first place. Seldom do teachers require students to analyze the social and political structures that inform their realities. Rarely do students read about the racist and discriminatory practices that they face in school and the community at large. The instrumentalist approach has led to the development of "functional literates," groomed primarily to meet the requirements of our contemporary society. The instrumentalist view also champions literacy as a vehicle for economic betterment, access to jobs, and increase in the productivity level. As it is clearly stated by UNESCO, "Literacy programs should preferably be linked with economic priorities. [They] must impart not only reading and writing, but also professional and technical knowledge, thereby leading to a fuller participation of adults in economic life."[19]

This notion of literacy has been enthusiastically incorporated as a major goal by the back-to-basics proponents of reading. It has also contributed to the development of neatly packaged reading programs that are presented as the solution to difficulties students experience in reading job application forms, tax forms, advertisement literature, sales catalogs, product labels, and the like. In general, the instrumentalist approach views literacy as meeting the basic reading demand of an industrialized society. As Henry Giroux points out:

> Literacy within this perspective is geared to make adults more productive workers and citizens within a given society. In spite of its appeal to economic mobility, functional literacy reduces the concept of literacy and the pedagogy in which it is suited to the pragmatic requirements of capital; consequently, the notions of critical thinking, culture and power disappear under the imperatives of the labor process and the need of capital accumulation.[20]

A society that reduces the priorities of reading to the pragmatic requirements of capital necessarily has to create educational structures that anesthetize students' critical abilities, so as to "domesticate social order for its self-preservation."[21] Accordingly, it must create educational structures that involve "practices by which one strives to domesticate consciousness, transforming it into an empty receptacle. Education in cultural action for domination is reduced to a situation in which the educator as 'the one who knows' transfers existing knowledge to the learner as 'the one who does not know.'"[22]

Paulo Freire's concept of banking refers to this treatment of students as empty vessels to be filled with predetermined bodies of knowledge, which are often disconnected from students' social realities. This type of education for domestication, which borders on stupidification, provides no pedagogical space for critical students like David Spritzler, who question the received knowledge and want to know the reasons behind the facts. His defiance of the rigid bureaucracy, his refusal to surrender his civil rights, are rewarded by a threat of disciplinary action. In other words, according to Freire, the real rewards go to the "so-called good student who repeats, who renounces critical thinking, who adjusts to models, . . . [who] should do nothing other than receive contents that are impregnated with the ideological character vital to the interests of the sacred order."[23] A good student is the one who piously recites the fossilized slogans contained in the Pledge of Allegiance. A good student is the one who willfully and unreflectively accepts big lies, as described in Tom Paxton's song:

> What did you learn in school today, dear little boy of mine?
> What did you learn in school today, dear little boy of mine?
>
> I learned that Washington never told a lie,
> I learned that soldiers seldom die,
> I learned that everybody's free,
> And that's what the teacher said to me.
>
> That's what I learned in school today,
> That's what I learned in school.
>
> I learned that policemen are my friends,
> I learned that justice never ends,
> I learned that murderers die for their crimes
> Even if we make a mistake sometimes.
>
> I learned our government must be strong,
> It's always right and never wrong
> Our leaders are the finest men
> And we elect them again and again.
>
> I learned that war is not so bad.
> I learned about the great ones we have had.
> We've fought in Germany and in France,
> And someday I may get my chance.
>
> That's what I learned in school today,
> That's what I learned in school.[24]

THE BARBARISM OF SPECIALIZATION OR THE SPECIALIZATION OF BARBARISM

Long before the explosion of hyper-specialization and the tragedies of the Holocaust and Hiroshima, Spanish philosopher José Ortega y Gasset cautioned us against the demand for specialization so that science could progress. According to Ortega y Gasset, "The specialist 'knows' very well his own tiny corner of the universe; he is radically ignorant of all the rest."[25] I am reminded of a former classmate of mine, whom I met while doing research work at MIT. When she learned that I was working with pidgin and creole languages, she curiously asked me, "What's a pidgin language?" At first I thought she was joking, but soon I realized that her question was in fact genuine. Here we had a perfect case of a **technician**[f] of linguistics doing the highest level theory available in the field without any clue about historical linguistics. It is not difficult to find other examples of such limited specialization in that, more and more, specialists dominate institutions of learning and other institutional structures of our society. The social organization of knowledge via rigidly defined disciplinary boundaries further contributes to the formation of the specialist class, i.e., engineers, doctors, professors, and so on. This sort of specialist is

> only acquainted with one science, and even of that one only knows the small corner in which he is an active investigator. He even proclaims it as a virtue that he takes no cognizance of what lies outside the narrow territory specially cultivated by himself, and gives the name 'dilettantism' to any curiosity for the general scheme of knowledge.[26]

This so-called "dilettantism" is discouraged through the mythical need to discover absolute objective truth. I remember vividly when I gave my linguist friend at MIT articles on pidgins and creoles to read. I later questioned her as to whether she had found the readings interesting and informative. Half apologizing but with a certain pride in her voice, she told me: "If I want to be a great theoretical linguist, I just can't be reading too much outside theoretical linguistics. I can't even keep up with all the reading in syntax alone." Obviously there are exceptions to this attitude, Noam Chomsky, bell hooks, Howard Zinn, Gayatri Spivak, and Henry Giroux being prime examples. However, it is quite frequent in specialization to divorce science from the general culture within which it exists.

Not only does specialization represent a rupture with philosophies of social and cultural relations, it also hides behind an ideology that creates and sustains false dichotomies rigidly delineated by disciplinary boundaries. This ideology also informs the view that "hard science," "objectivity," and "scientific rigor" must be divorced from the messy data of "soft science," and from the social and political practices that generate these categories in the first place. For example, those linguists and psycholinguists who "believe that what they study has little to do with social values or politics in any sense"[27] fail to realize that their research results are "the product of a particular

---

[f] Emanating from the positivist tradition, technocratic models, which conceptualize teaching and learning as a discrete and scientific undertaking, embrace depersonalized methods for educating students that often translate into the regulation and standardization of teacher practices and curricula, and rote memorization of selected "facts" that can easily be measured through standardized testing. As such, the role of the teacher is reduced to that of a **technician** — an uncritical, "objective," and "efficient" distributor of information.

model of social structures that gear the theoretical concepts to the pragmatics of the society that devised . . . the model to begin with."[28] That is, if the results are presented as facts determined by a particular ideological framework, "these facts cannot in themselves get us beyond that framework."[29] Too often, the **positivistic**[g] overemphasis on "hard science" and "absolute objectivity" has given rise to a form of "scientism" rather than science. By "scientism" I refer to the mechanization of the intellectual work cultivated by specialists, which often leads to the fragmentation of knowledge, as accurately understood by Ortega y Gasset: "A fair amount of things that have to be done in physics or in biology is mechanical work of the mind which can be done by anyone, or almost anyone . . . to divide science into small sections, to enclose oneself in one of these, and leave out all consideration of the rest."[30] Specialists of this sort have often contributed to a further fragmentation of knowledge due to their reductionistic view of the act of knowing. They have repeatedly ignored that their very claim of objectivity is, in fact, an ideological act. Objectivity always contains within it a dimension of subjectivity; thus, it is **dialectical.**[h]

Almost without exception, traditional approaches to literacy do not escape the fragmentation of knowledge and are deeply ingrained in a positivistic method of inquiry. In effect, this has resulted in an epistemological stance in which scientific rigor and methodological refinement are celebrated, while "theory and knowledge are subordinated to the imperatives of efficiency and technical mastery, and history is reduced to a minor footnote in the priorities of 'empirical' scientific inquiry."[31] In general, this approach abstracts methodological issues from their ideological contexts, and consequently ignores the interrelationship between the sociopolitical structures of a society and the act of reading and learning. In part, the exclusion of social, cultural, and political dimensions from literacy practices gives rise to an ideology of cultural reproduction that produces semiliterates. My linguist

---

[g] Associated with the Enlightenment and modernism, **positivism** refers to a belief system or paradigm that makes claims to objectivity, truth, and certainty in defense of a scientific basis for the study of culture. As such, knowledge and reason are seen as neutral and universal, rather than as social constructions that reflect particular interests and ideologies. This uncritical call to science has resulted in an obsession with finding and using the "right" technique to understand a phenomenon or solve a problem. For example, "technocratic" models, which conceptualize teaching as a discrete and scientific undertaking, embrace depersonalized methods for educating students that often translate into the regulation and standardization of teacher practices and curricula, and rote memorization of selected "facts" that can easily be measured through standardized testing. As such, the role of the teacher is reduced to that of an uncritical, "objective," and "efficient" distributor of information.

[h] While there are a number of definitions and interpretations of **dialectics**, for the general purposes of critical pedagogy, this concept refers to the interconnecting and contradicting relationships that constitute a particular phenomenon, for example, among the economic, political, social, and cultural dimensions of society. A dialectical analysis is also often used to show how every idea or force has its opposite/contradiction. For example, the dialectic of "oppressor" is the reality of the "oppressed." Such an analysis holds both "opposing" concepts together at once to see how they interconnect and play off each other.

friend at MIT, who reads only the theoretical work in syntax and dismisses relevant literature that links linguistics to the social and historical context, serves as a prime example of the highest level of instrumental literacy. In other words, at the lowest level of instrumental literacy, a semiliterate reads the word but is unable to read the world. At the highest level of instrumental literacy achieved via specialization, the semiliterate is able to read the text of his or her specialization but is ignorant of all other bodies of knowledge that constitute the world of knowledge. This semiliterate specialist was characterized by Ortega y Gasset as a "learned ignoramus." That is to say, "he is not learned, for he is formally ignorant of all that does not enter into his speciality; but neither is he ignorant, because he is a 'scientist' and 'knows' very well his own tiny portion of the universe."[32]

Because the "learned ignoramus" is mainly concerned with his or her tiny portion of the world disconnected from other bodies of knowledge, he or she is never able to relate the flux of information so as to gain a critical reading of the world. A critical reading of the world implies, according to Freire, "a dynamic comprehension between the least coherent sensibility of the world and a more coherent understanding of the world."[33] This implies, for example, that medical specialists in the United States, who have contributed to a great technological advancement in medicine, should have the ability to understand and appreciate why over thirty million Americans do not have access to this medical technology and why we still have the highest infant mortality rate of the developed nations. (The United States in 1989 ranked 24th in child mortality rate as compared to other nations.)[34]

The inability to make linkages between bodies of knowledge and the social and political realities that generate them is predominant even among those who recognize that a coherent comprehension of the world cannot be achieved through fragmentation of knowledge. For example, at a recent professional meeting, a concerned environmental scientist decried the absence of critical perspectives in his field of study. He eloquently called for an interdisciplinary approach to world environmental problems, particularly within the developing countries. His present research is linked with environmental concerns in Mexico. With a certain amount of pride he emphasized that his research breakthrough could be used as a commodity in Mexico, since that country is becoming more and more rigorous with respect to environmental laws. He failed, however, to ask a fundamental question: How can the U.S. package environmental technology for Mexico while we are establishing factories there that pollute the country because they can operate with less government regulation? This environmentalist was baffled that such a question should even be raised.

Although specialization may lead to a high level of literacy acquisition in a particular subfield of knowledge, it often produces a disarticulation of this same knowledge by dislodging it from a critical and coherent comprehension of the world that informs and sustains it. This disarticulation of knowledge anesthetizes consciousness, without which one can never develop clarity of reality. As suggested by Frei Betto, clarity of reality requires that a person transcend "the perception of life as a pure biological process to arrive at a perception of life as a biographical, and collective process."[35] Betto views his concept as "a clothesline of information." In other words, "on the clothesline we may have a flux of information and yet remain unable to link one piece of information with another. A politicized person is one who can sort out the different and often fragmented pieces contained in the flux."[36] The apprehension of clarity of reality requires a high level of **political clarity,**[i] which can be achieved by sifting through the flux of information and relating each piece so as to gain a global comprehension of the facts and their raison d'être.

We can now see the reasons why David Spritzler's teachers and administrators, who had attained a higher level of literacy through a banking model of transference of knowledge, could not relate each piece of this knowledge to separate the mythical dimension of the Pledge of Allegiance from factual reality. Part of the reason lies in the fact that the teachers, who, like most specialists, have accepted the dominant ideology, are technicians who, by virtue of the specialized training they receive in an assembly line of ideas, and aided by the mystification of this transferred knowledge, seldom reach the critical capacity of analysis to develop a coherent comprehension of the world. In reality, there is little difference between the pedagogy for school children described in Tom Paxton's song and the prevalent pedagogy in universities as described by Freire:

> Today at the university we learned that objectivity in science requires neutrality on the part of the scientist; we learned today that knowledge is pure, universal, and unconditional and that the university is the site of this knowledge. We learned today, although only tacitly, that the world is divided between those who know and those who don't (that is, those who do manual work) and the university is the home of the former. We learned today that the university is a temple of pure knowledge and that it has to soar above earthly preoccupations, such as mankind's liberation.
>
> We learned today that reality is a given, that it is our scientific impartiality that allows us to describe it somewhat as it is. Since we have described it as it is, we don't have to investigate the principal reasons that would explain it as it is. But if we should try to denounce the real world as it is by proclaiming a new way of living, we learned at the university today that we would no longer be scientists, but ideologues.

---

[i] Not to be confused with "political correctness," **political clarity** (which Paulo Freire refers to as "conscientization") is the awareness of the historical, sociopolitical, economic, cultural, and subjective reality that shapes our lives and our ability to transform that reality. Lilia Bartolomé further explains that "political awareness/clarity" is "the process by which individuals come to better understand possible linkages between macro-level political, economic, and social variables and subordinated groups' academic performance at the micro-level classroom" (p. 235).

We learned today that economic development is a purely technical problem, that the underdeveloped peoples are incapable (sometimes because of their mixed blood, their nature, or climatic reasons).

We were informed that blacks learn less than whites because they are genetically inferior.[37]

In short, this type of educational training makes it possible for us to rally behind our political leaders who ritualistically call for the protection of human rights all over the world without recognizing these same leaders' complicity in the denial of rights of human beings who live under dictatorships that we support either overtly or covertly. The selective selection of our strong support for human rights becomes glaringly clear in the case of Haitians. In fact, the *Boston Globe*, confident of readers' inability to link historical events, published a front page article on the U.S. Supreme Court decision that allowed the administration to repatriate thousands of Haitian refugees. On page two of the same issue, the *Globe* also ran a story about groups organized in Miami to search for and assist Cuban boat people to reach their final destination in Florida.[38] It is this lack of connectedness that helped Bush to prevail in erasing our historical memory file of foreign policy in order to garner support for his fabricated high-tech war in the Gulf. In what follows, I use the Gulf War as an example of how questions of literacy and ideology can be used to separate events from their historical contexts. This fragmentation serves to create a self-serving history that feeds the recontextualization of a distorted and often false reality, leading (sometimes) to a specialization of barbarism ipso facto. In other words, the high-tech management of the Gulf War celebrated technical wizardry while it dehumanized the tens of thousands of people who were victims of specialized technical prowess.

THE ILLITERACY OF LITERACY OF THE GULF WAR

It is not a coincidence that during the Gulf War we were saturated with information around the clock in the comfort of our homes, and yet we remained poorly informed. It is also not a coincidence that George Bush categorically and arrogantly stated there will be "no linkage" in any possible diplomatic settlements in the Gulf crisis. Bush's insistence on "no linkage" served to eclipse historicity so as to further add to a total social amnesia. How else could we explain that a highly developed society that prides itself on its freedom of information and high democratic values could ignore the clarity of the obvious? I say the "clarity of the obvious" because it is a well-known fact that the Reagan-Bush decade was characterized by a total disdain for the United Nations. The Reagan-Bush administration stopped paying the U.S. membership contribution to the United Nations and threatened to withdraw from the world body because the rest of the world was not, in their view, subservient enough to U.S. interests. And yet, during the Gulf crisis, the same George Bush found it convenient to hail the United Nations as the theater where "civilized" nations uphold international laws and high principles. If it had not been for the denial of linkage and the social amnesia, we could have easily referred to Daniel Patrick Moynihan's role as the ambassador to the United Nations. In his memoir, *A Dangerous Place*, Moynihan discusses the invasion of East Timor by Indonesia and sheds light on his role as the U.S. ambassador to the United Nations: "The U.S. government wanted the United Nations to be rendered ineffective in any measures that it undertook. I was given this responsibility and I filled it with no inconsiderable success."[39] Moynihan later recounts his success when he states that "within two months, reports indicated that Indonesia had killed about 60,000 people. That is roughly the proportion of the population that the Nazis had killed in Eastern Europe through World War II."[40] By not linking these historical events, the Bush administration was able to claim a moral high ground in the defense of international laws and the sanctity of national borders during the Gulf crisis.

The United States' defense of high principles and international laws that led to the Gulf War could only have moral currency if we were to obliterate our memory of recent history. Before proceeding, let me make it clear that Saddam Hussein's invasion of Kuwait was brutal, cruel, and unforgivable. The violation of international laws and borders by other nations, including the United States, is no small matter. According to Noam Chomsky, the irony of the United States' opposition to such violation and defense of high principles can be summed up as follows:

- The U.S. invasion of Grenada
- The U.S. invasion of Panama, where the United States installed a puppet regime of its choice with U.S. military advisors running it at every level.
- The U.S. mining of the Nicaraguan harbor. The World Court found the United States guilty, and the U.S. reaction was to arrogantly dismiss the World Court.
- The Turkish invasion and virtual annexation of northern Cyprus that killed several hundred people and drove out thousands more. The United States was in favor of the action.
- The Moroccan invasion of the western Sahara, also supported by the United States.
- The Israeli invasion of Lebanon, where the United States vetoed a whole series of resolutions in the Security Council, which was trying to terminate the aggression. In human terms, at least 20,000 were killed, mostly civilians.
- The Indonesian invasion of East Timor in which 60,000 people were massacred. The Carter administration provided 90 percent of the armaments to the invaders.[41]

Against this landscape of violation of international laws and aggression perpetrated by the United States, or by other countries with U.S. support, how can we explain the ease with which Bush convinced a supposedly highly literate and civilized citizenry that Saddam Hussein's invasion of Kuwait was an isolated case of aggression against a weaker nation and had nothing to do with the historical record? The inability to link and treat the "clothesline" of the Gulf War had to do with ideological obstacles that too often obfuscate political clarity. We need to develop a more critical literacy along Freirian lines where, "as knowing subjects (sometimes of existing knowledge, sometimes of objects to be produced), our relation to knowable objects cannot be reduced to the objects themselves. We need to reach a level of comprehension of the complex whole of relations among objects."[42] In his book *The Social Mind*, Jim Gee elegantly demonstrates that "to explicate the 'internal working' of the 'machine', and not the uses to which the machine is put in the world of value conflicts and political action," is to treat each piece of the "clothesline" separately so as to never allow us to reach a level of comprehension of the complex whole of relations among objects.[43] This functions as a form of illiteracy of literacy, in which we develop a high level of literacy in a given discourse while remaining semiliterate or illiterate in a whole range of other discourses that constitute the ideological world in which we travel as thinking beings.

In an era in which we are more and more controlled by ever increasing technological wizardry — ephemeral sound bites, metaphorical manipulations of language, and prepackaged ideas void of substance — it becomes that much more urgent to adhere to Gee's posture that we acquire literacies rather than literacy. Given our tendency as humans to construct "satisfying and often self-deceptive 'stories,' stories that often advantage themselves and their groups," the development of a critical comprehension between the meaning of words and a more coherent understanding of the meaning of the world is a prerequisite to achieving clarity of reality. As Freire has suggested, it is only "through political practice [that] the less coherent sensibility of the world begins to be surpassed and more rigorous intellectual pursuits give rise to a more coherent comprehension of the world."[44] Thus, in order to go beyond a mere word-level reading of reality, we must develop a critical comprehension of psychological entities such as "memories, beliefs, values, meanings, and so forth . . . which are actually out in the social world of action and interaction."[45] We must first read the world — the cultural, social, and political practices that constitute it — before we can make sense of the word-level description of reality.

The reading of the world must precede the reading of the word. That is to say, to access the true and total meaning of an entity, we must resort to the cultural practices that mediate our access to the world's semantic field and its interaction with the word's semantic features. Since meaning is, at best, very leaky, we have to depend on the cultural models that contain the necessary cultural features responsible for "our stories," and "often self-deceptive stories."[46] Let's look at the Gulf War again to exemplify how the role of cultural practices not only shapes, but also determines, metaphorical manipulations of language, which are facilitated by the electronically controlled images and messages through "the strategic use of doublespeak to disguise from television viewers the extent of the real terror and carnage of the military campaign against Iraq."[47] According to William Lutz, doublespeak "is a language that avoids or shifts responsibility, language that is at variance with its real or purported meaning. It is a language that conceals or prevents thought; rather than extending thought, doublespeak limits it."[48]

The Gulf War coverage represented the production of doublespeak par excellence. The success to which the media and the government used euphemisms to misinform and deceive can be seen in the transformation of the horrible carnage of the battlefield into a "theater of operation," where the U.S. citizenry became willfully mesmerized by the near-precision zapping of "smart bombs" during the aseptic "surgical strikes." The "theater of operation" positioned viewers to see "human beings become insentient things while weapons become the living actors of war. 'Smart' weapons that have eyes and computer 'brains' make decisions when and where to drop seven and a half tons of bombs, taking away the moral responsibility of the combatants themselves."[49]

The effective outcome of the doublespeak during the Gulf War was not only to give primacy to sophisticated weaponry with its newly acquired human attributes; it also functioned as a means to dehumanize human beings by removing them from center stage. The preoccupation of reporters and so-called "experts" was to narrate zealously the "accuracy" of the "smart bombs" while showing over and over again Star-Wars-like images of "surgical strikes." What these reporters did not show was that 92.6 percent of the bombs dropped were not "precision-guided ordinances," which amounted to roughly 82,000 tons. Even the 7.4 percent of "smart bombs" dropped during the war had a widely varied reliability rate of between 20 percent and 90 percent.[50] However, it would be considered unpatriotic and un-American to question the Pentagon-controlled deceit of the U.S. public. Even after the Gulf War was all but faded in our national consciousness, the Pentagon ordered Theodore Postal, an MIT professor and leading critic of the Patriot missile, "to cease all public discussion of his critique or face disciplinary action."[51] The Pentagon's gag order was summarized by Postal himself: "The Army and Raytheon are now using DIS [Defense Investigation Service] which appears to be more than an unwitting partner to suppress my speech on the subject of Patriot performance in the Gulf."[52] So much for independent thought, critical thinking, and freedom of speech. What the U.S. citizenry was less concerned with was the terror of war and the horrible carnage caused by the 82,000 tons of "delivered packages" that ended up as de facto carpet bombings. But then, the U.S. television viewers and newspaper readers had already been positioned in a "theater of operation" context as passive observers seduced and fascinated by the wizardry of exciting precision-guided missiles. The "theater" "overfloweth with computer graphics, night-vision lenses, cruise missiles and, best ever, the replay of the impact of laser guided bombs."[53] Missing from the "theater" center stage were the horrified human faces of tens of thousands of Iraqis, including women and children, who were decimated by the unparalleled bombing "sorties." The U.S. public's feelings were steered away from the reality of over 100,000 Iraqi casualties to the degree that the electronic management of the Gulf War vulgarly reduced human suffering and casualties to mere "collateral damage."

In "Media Knowledges, Warrior Citizenry, and the Postmodern Literacies," Peter McLaren and Rhonda Hammer accurately characterize the Gulf War as "a gaudy sideshow of flags, emblems, and military hardware — a counterfeit democracy produced through media knowledge able to effectively harness the affective currency of popular culture such that the average American's investment in being 'American' reached an unparalleled high which has not been approximated since the years surrounding the post World War II McCarthy hearings."[54] This unparalleled patriotism was cemented by the signifier yellow ribbon that functioned effectively to suffocate any truly democratic dialogue. The yellow ribbon ideologically structured the Gulf War debate so as to brook no dissent or dialogue. Criticizing the Bush administration's policies was viewed as not supporting the troops. In fact, the yellow ribbon did more to ideologically cage the American mind than all the speeches given by politicians. One could easily argue that the yellow ribbon patriotically tied American minds by making them sufficiently complacent so as to comply with the manufacture of consent for a fabricated war.

The complexity of networks of relations in our present **telecratic**[j] society is making our sensibilities of the world increasingly less coherent — leading to a real crisis of democracy, to the extent that the present "propaganda approach to media coverage suggests a systematic and highly political dichotomization in news coverage based on serviceability to important domestic interests. This should be observable in dichotomized choices of story and in the volume and quality of coverage."[55] This political dichotomization became flagrantly obvious when, on the one hand, George Bush, in a John Waynean style, rallied "civilized" nations to uphold high moral principles against aggression when Saddam Hussein invaded Kuwait. On the other hand, Bush sheepishly watched and allowed thousands of Kurds, whom he had incited to revolt, to be exterminated by the same forces of aggression. So much for high moral principles. What is at stake here is our ability as democratic citizens and thinking beings to see through the obvious contradictions and discern myth from reality. However, our level of critical con-

---

[j] A **telecratic** society is one, such as U.S. society, in which the electronic media have an enormous influence on the construction of meaning, identity, and social relations (that is, a media-oriented society).

sciousness is being rapidly eroded to the degree that "today's cultural and historical events bombard our sensibilities with such exponential speed and frequency, and through a variety of media forms, that our critical comprehension skills have fallen into rapid deterioration."[56] The deterioration of Americans' critical comprehension of the world became self-evident when they readily rallied behind the "Pentagon's vacuous military briefings, lists of aircraft types, missions, and losses [that] have become the sterilized equivalent of body counts recited in Saigon. Far more important elements — human and political — are being lost."[57] It is indeed a sad statement about the inability of the U.S. citizenry to make the necessary historical linkages so as to develop a rigorous comprehension of the world when, with the exception of a small minority, only Vice President Dan Quayle was able to read the Gulf War correctly by describing it as "a stirring victory for the forces of aggression."[58] President Bush became entrapped in a similar Freudian slip during an interview with Boston's Channel 5 TV news anchor, Natalie Jacobson. Referring to the Gulf War, Bush said, "We did fulfill our aggression," instead of the no doubt intended, "we did fulfill our mission."[59]

The seemingly misspoken words by both Bush and Quayle denude the pedagogy of big lies to the extent that their statements more accurately capture the essence of Ortega y Gasset's proposition that civilization, if "abandoned to its own devices" and put at the mercy of specialists, would bring about the rebirth of primitivism and barbarism.[60] In many instances, the attainment of a high level of technical sophistication has been used in the most barbaric ways, as evidenced in the gassing of the Jews and the bombing of Hiroshima. It is certainly not an illuminated civilization that prides itself in reducing Iraq to a preindustrial age — killing tens of thousands of innocent victims, including women and children, while leaving Saddam Hussein, our chief reason for war, in power and with unreduced capacity to perpetuate genocide against his own people. Ask the Africans who endured the chains of slavery, the Indians who were victims of a quasi-genocide, the Jews who perished in the Holocaust, or the Japanese who experienced first hand the destructive power of science to measure our so-called advanced Western civilization. If they apply the same rigorous objective standards of science, intellectual honesty, and academic truth in their inquiry, their response would have to be unequivocally primitive and barbaric. Ortega y Gasset could not have been more insightful on this issue:

> It may be regrettable that human nature tends on occasion to this form of violence, but it is undeniable that it implies the great tribute to reason and justice. For this form of violence is none other than reason exasperated. Force was, in fact, the "ultima ratio." Rather stupidly it has been the custom to take ironically this expression, to methods of reason. Civilization is nothing else than the attempt to reduce force to being the "ultima ratio." We are now beginning to realize this with startling clearness, because "direct action" consists in inventing the order and proclaiming violence as

"prima ratio," or strictly as "unica ratio." It is the norm which proposes the annulment of all norms, which suppresses all intermediate process between our purpose and it execution. It is the Magna Carta of barbarism.[61]

Ortega y Gasset's profound thoughts enable us to deconstruct Bush's policy of violence parading under the veil of reason and justice. In fact, Bush successfully made force not only the "ultima ratio," but also the "unica ratio." His total disregard for a multitude of proposals to negotiate a settlement in the gulf characterized the "norm which proposes the annulment of all norms, which suppresses all intermediate process between our purpose and its execution."[62] Flip-flopping from a defensive stance to the protection of our oil and the invocation of international laws and the sanctity of national borders, Bush simply refused to negotiate. When Saddam Hussein proposed to withdraw from Kuwait with the condition that an international conference be held to discuss the Middle East situation, Bush flatly refused the offer, which, incidentally, was very much in line with the U.N. General Assembly vote of 142 to 2 that called for an international peace conference in the Middle East. It was just such a conference that Bush and his administration aggressively promoted after the execution of the violence and terror that reduced Iraq to a preindustrial age. Had Bush accepted Saddam's condition for an international conference, a condition passionately promoted after the war, he would have avoided the carnage that cost over 100,000 lives and an ecological disaster of enormous proportions. Bush's insistence on force led his administration to a constant double standard, which our uncritical citizenry, including the media and the intelligentsia, fail to see and question. While Bush often referred to the United Nations resolution of November 29, 1990, which gave "the U.S. a green light to use military means to expel Iraqi troops from Kuwait," he totally rejected a "U.N. General Assembly resolution, passed a week later by a vote of 142 to 2, which called for an international peace conference on the Middle East."[63] Bush's convenient selective selection of the United Nations as a forum for international dispute resolution and justice points to a systematic gun-boat diplomacy that views force as the "unica ratio" in our foreign policy. We do not have to dig too far in our historical memory files to understand that, over and over again, the United States resorts to force to settle its so-called "national interest," which is, more appropriately, the interest of capital and the ruling elite. When we mined the Nicaraguan harbor and supported the Contras as our proxy army and were censured by the World Court, we arrogantly dismissed the much-hailed world body, the theater of justice, and the mecca of international disputes and settlements. It is this same arrogance of power and force that justified and rationalized Desert Storm. And closer to home, it is this same arrogance of power and force that continues to justify and rationalize our war on drugs.

In order for us to better understand how our rationalization process works to transform force and violence into methods of reason, I will create two hypothetical scenarios. The first finds its parallel in the Gulf War, the second in the war on drugs. To begin the first scenario, let's imagine that the African countries, where over twenty million people die of hunger every year, decide to call the U.N. General Assembly to session to ask for permission to send a defensive armed force led by Ethiopia to the Canadian and Mexican borders with the United States to protect and guarantee the flow of grain in order to prevent the death of over twenty million people. These African countries would argue that the United States, being a major producer of food, should stop burning grain and paying farmers not to produce so prices will remain stable and profitable. The Africans would also passionately point out that the burning of grain and the limitation on production constitute a crime against humanity, and that the twenty million Africans who are at risk of dying of hunger should be protected by international laws that view hunger as a human rights violation. If this hypothetical scenario were to occur in reality and a half million African troops were dispatched to the U.S. borders with Canada and Mexico, most of us would find the move so ridiculous as to be laughable. Well, Bush's initial rationale to send troops to Saudi Arabia was to protect the flow of oil that otherwise would disrupt the economies of the developed and industrialized nations. Even though Bush later recanted his earlier position by claiming that the fight was not about oil, but about naked aggression, all evidence points to oil as the reason for the Gulf War. If Bush were defending the world order from naked aggression, he would first have to bomb Washington, DC, since we had recently been engaged in a number of naked aggressions, mainly the invasion of Panama, the war against Nicaragua via a proxy army, the bombing of Libya, the invasion of Grenada — to mention only a few of the most recent violations of the same international laws that Bush so passionately wanted to protect during the Gulf War. In fact, the oil rationale made infinitely more sense, given the architecture of our foreign policy throughout history. The question that we should now ask of ourselves is: Would it be ridiculous for the African nations to send an army to protect the flow of grain that would save the lives of millions of people who may die of hunger, but not ridiculous for the United States to send a half-million troops to the Gulf to protect the flow of oil so industrialized nations may avoid economic chaos?

Let's turn to the second scenario, which finds its parallel rationale in the war on drugs. Let's imagine that the developing countries, composed mainly of Latin American nations but including some African nations as well, were to call for a regional summit where a decision is made to send troops to the United States to put a halt to the steady supply of armaments to support what they have characterized as the death industry in their countries. By death industry these nations are referring to the monies spent arming their military forces. Many developing countries, because of the never ending military rule often supported by the Western powers, spend between 25 percent and 50 percent of their GNP on armaments. This militarization of their societies is not only destroying their economies, but also leading to the killing of great numbers of people every year. Thus these developing countries would send their troops to strategically select locations in the United States where research and production of destructive armaments are contributing to economic chaos in their own countries and the killing of millions worldwide. Their troops would be trained to bomb and destroy all research laboratories and armament factories — such as Raytheon, General Dynamics, Boeing, and so forth — in the hope of stopping the flow of arms to their countries. All of this would have international approval, since this measure would constitute the national interests of these countries. If this hypothetical scenario were to be enacted, we can readily imagine the panic of all of those highly trained specialists who would be jobless once their factories and research laboratories had been destroyed. We can imagine as well the chaos that would ensue when these same specialists were left without a livelihood and abandoned to luck, or perhaps to some form of social welfare. A turn to the latter for support would entail a reliance on a social structure that they no doubt had fought most of their lives to destroy, or at least to curtail to a bare minimum.

I see little difference in what we are doing to fight the drug war. The United States has militarized many Latin American countries, including Colombia, Peru, Boliva, and Guatemala, to fight and destroy coca fields and drug laboratories, which constitute the only means of economic survival for millions of natives in these countries. By randomly destroying these people's only means of economic support in already poor countries with feeble economies, we are sentencing these native people to hunger and possibly death. However, we seldom think about the consequences and implications of the arrogance of power in the design of our drug war policy. That is to say, if we switch contexts and focus on our hypothetical scenario, we can clearly see through the infantile dimension and the lack of logic behind the imagined destruction of workplaces devoted to the production of armaments. I am arguing that it is the same infantile, illogical policy that we support when we ratify Bush's war on drugs. The only effective way to fight the war on drugs is to decrease demand. Even law enforcement officials and officials of these Latin countries have admitted that they are losing the drug war. In fact, by focusing only on the destruction of drug production while ignoring the social causes that breed a high demand for drugs, we are contradicting even our principle of capitalism. In other words, the best way to control production is to control demand. If we try to destroy production while leaving demand unchecked, production will resurface elsewhere — as is the case with drug production in Latin America that is finding its way to Europe and other safe ports.

These contradictions and instances of the unreason of reason are rarely understood and just as rarely questioned. If, by coincidence, we come to understand the blatant contradictions and question them, the ideological machine will tow us immediately into line. That is what happened to a reporter in San Antonio, Texas, who incessantly questioned Bush about the obvious failure of his drug war. He was immediately fired for being insistent and impolite to the president. Here politeness functioned as yet another mechanism to eliminate the possibility of knowing the truth. Since our society functions more and more on a pedagogy of lies, it depends on ideological institutions, such as schools and the media, to reproduce cultural values that work to distort and falsify realities so as to benefit the interest of the power elite. If schools were really involved in the development of critical thinking to arm students against the orchestrated distortion and falsification of reality, they would have both to teach the truth and teach to question. That includes, obviously, the deconstruction of the Pledge of Allegiance so as to make its hypocrisy bare, and the rewriting of history books to keep alive dangerous memories so that slavery, the Holocaust, genocide, and Hiroshima could not be repeated under the guise and protection of Western civilization.

I believe that we can now return, with greater understanding, to our original question: Why is it that David Spritzler, a 12-year-old boy, could readily see through the hypocrisy in the Pledge of Allegiance, while many of his teachers and administrators could not? According to Chomsky, in discussing other educational situations, these teachers and administrators, having been indoctrinated by schools, are unable to understand elementary thoughts that any 10-year-old can understand.[64] The indoctrination process imposes a willful blindness that views facts and contradictions as irrelevant. On the other hand, the more educated and specialized individuals become, the more vested interest they have in the system that provides them with special privileges. For this reason, we often see people whose consciousness has not been totally atrophied; yet they fail to read reality critically and they side with hypocrisy. In most cases, these individuals begin to believe the lies and, in their roles as functionaries of the state, they propagate the lies. That is why, for example, the majority of the educated population supported the war in Vietnam, while in 1982, according to a Gallup poll, over 70 percent of the general population were still saying that the Vietnam War was "fundamentally wrong and immoral, a mistake."[65] This is another example that supports the contention that more education does not necessarily entail a greater ability to read reality.

As I have tried to demonstrate, both the competency-based skill banking approach to literacy and the highest level literacy acquisition via specialization fail to provide readers with the necessary intellectual tools to denude reality that is often veiled through the ideological manipulation of language. It is safe to assume, given the way the educated class more often than not supports "theological truths" (or unquestioned truths), that the less educated one is, in the reproductive dominant model, the greater the chances to read the world more critically. Chomsky accurately captures this form of illiteracy of literacy when he states that the less educated . . . tend to be more sophisticated and perceptive about these matters, the reason being that education is a form of indoctrination, and the less educated are less indoctrinated. Furthermore, the educated tend to be privileged and they tend to have a stake in the doctrinal system, so they naturally tend to internalize and believe it. As a result, not uncommonly and not only in the United States, you find a good deal more sophistication among people who learn about the world from their experience rather than those who learn about the world from a doctrinal framework that they are exposed to and that they are expected as part of professional obligation to propagate.[66]

It is indeed ironic that in the United States, a country that prides itself on being the first and most advanced within the so-called "first world," over sixty million people are illiterate or functionally illiterate. If Jonathan Kozol is correct, the sixty million illiterates and functional illiterates whom he documents in his book *Illiterate America* do not constitute a minority class of illiterate.[67] To the sixty million illiterates we should add the sizable groups who learn how to read but are, by and large, incapable of developing independent and critical thought. In reality, the United States is in forty-ninth place among the 128 countries of the United Nations in terms of literacy rate. This ranking applies basically to the reading of the word and not the world. Our ranking, if applied to the reading of the world, would indeed be much lower.

Against this high illiteracy landscape, we can begin to wonder why a country that considers itself a model of democracy can tolerate an educational system that contributes to such a high level of illiteracy and failure. I am increasingly convinced that the U.S. educational system is not a failure. The failure that it generates represents its ultimate victory to the extent that large groups of people, including the so-called minorities, were never intended to be educated. They were never intended to be part of the dominant political and economic spheres. How else can we explain why we sit idly by and tolerate dropout rates that exceed 60 percent in many urban cities, with New York City at 70 percent?[68] I believe that, instead of the democratic education we claim to have, we really have in place a sophisticated colonial model of education designed primarily to train state functionaries and commissars while denying access to millions, which further exacerbates the equity gap already victimizing a great number of so-called "minority" students. Even the education provided to those with class rights and privileges is devoid of the intellectual dimension of teaching, since the major objective of a colonial education is to further deskill teachers and students so as to reduce them to mere technical agents who are destined to walk unreflectively through a labyrinth of procedures. What we have in the United States is not a system to encourage independent thought and critical thinking. Our colonial literacy model is designed to domesticate so as to enable the "manufacture of consent." The Trilateral Commission could not have been more accurate when they referred to schools as "institutions responsible for the indoctrination of the young." I see no real difference between the more or less liberal Trilateral Commission position on schooling and Adolf Hitler's fascist call against independent thought and critical thinking. As Hitler noted, "What good fortune for those in power that people do not think."

NOTES

1. Samuel Bowles, David M. Gordon, and E. Thomas Weisskopf, "An Economic Strategy for Progressives," *The Nation*, February 10, 1992, pp. 163–164.
2. Diego Ribademeina, "Taking a Stand, Seated," *Boston Globe*, November 14, 1991, p. 40.
3. Noam Chomsky, *Language and Politics* (New York: Black Rose Books, 1988), p. 681.
4. As cited in Howard Zinn, *Declarations of Independence: Cross-Examining American Ideology* (New York: Harper & Row, 1990), pp. 234–235.
5. As cited in Richard Hofstadter, *The American Political Tradition* (New York: Vintage Press, 1974), p. 148.
6. Alan Lukas, *Common Ground* (New York: Alfred A. Knopf, 1985), p. 281.
7. Herald Wire Services, *Boston Herald*, May 1, 1992, p. 2.
8. Herald Wire Services, *Boston Herald*, p. 2.
9. Herald Wire Services, *Boston Herald*, p. 2.
10. Chomsky, *Language and Politics*, p. 671.
11. As quoted in Chomsky, *Language and Politics*, p. 671.
12. Chomsky, *Language and Politics*, p. 671.
13. Henry A. Giroux, *Border Crossings: Cultural Workers and the Politics of Education* (New York: Routledge, 1992) p. 3.
14. Giroux, *Border Crossings*, p. 3.
15. Noam Chomsky, *On Power and Ideology* (Boston: South End Press, 1987), p. 6.
16. Patrick L. Courts, *Literacy and Empowerment: The Meaning Makers* (South Hadley, MA: Bergin & Garvey, 1991), p. 4.
17. As cited in Courts, *Literacy and Empowerment*, p. 46.
18. Courts, *Literacy and Empowerment*, p. 48.
19. UNESCO, *An Asian Model of Educational Development* (Paris: UNESCO, 1966), p. 97.
20. Henry A. Giroux, *Theory and Resistance in Education: A Pedagogy for the Opposition* (South Hadley, MA: Bergin & Garvey, 1983), p. 87.
21. Paulo Freire, *The Politics of Education* (South Hadley, MA: Bergin & Garvey, 1985), p. 116.
22. Freire, *Politics of Education*, p. 114.
23. Freire, *Politics of Education*, p. 117.
24. Freire, *Politics of Education*, p. 117.
25. José Ortega y Gasset, *The Revolt of the Masses* (New York: W. W. Norton, 1964; rpt. 1930), p. 111.
26. Ortega y Gasset, *Revolt of the Masses*, p. 110.
27. James Gee, *The Social Mind: Language, Ideology, and Social Practices* (South Hadley, MA: Bergin & Garvey, 1992), p. vii.
28. Richard Fowler, Bob Hodge, Gunter Kress, and Tony Trew, *Language and Control* (London: Routledge & Kegan Paul, 1979), p. 192.
29. Greg Myers, "Reality, Consensus, and Reform in the Rhetoric of Composition Teaching," *College English*, 48 (1986), 111.
30. Ortega y Gasset, *Revolt of the Masses*, p. 111.

31. Giroux, *Theory and Resistance*, 1983, p. 87.
32. Ortega y Gasset, *Revolt of the Masses*, p. 112.
33. Freire, *Politics of Education*, p. 131.
34. "U.S. Infant Mortality Hits Low," *Boston Globe*, February 7, 1992, p. 8.
35. As cited in Paulo Freire and Donaldo Macedo, *Literacy: Reading the Word and the World* (South Hadley, MA: Bergin & Garvey, 1987), p. 130.
36. Freire and Macedo, *Literacy*, p. 130.
37. Freire, *The Politics of Education*, p. 118.
38. Catherine Wilson, "U.S. Begins Returning Haitian Refugees," *Boston Globe*, February 2, 1992, pp. 2–3. Christopher Boyd, "Friends for Cubans Who Flee," *Boston Globe*, February 2, 1992, p. 2.
39. As cited in Noam Chomsky, "On the Gulf Policy," *Open Magazine*, Pamphlet Series, 1991, p. 8.
40. Chomsky, "On the Gulf Policy," p. 8.
41. Chomsky, "On the Gulf Policy," p. 8.
42. Freire and Macedo, *Literacy*, p. 131.
43. Gee, *Social Mind*, p. xv.
44. Freire and Macedo, *Literacy*, p. 132.
45. Freire and Macedo, *Literacy*, p. 132.
46. Gee, *Social Mind*, p. xi.
47. Peter McLaren and Rhonda Hammer, "Media Knowledges, Warrior Citizenry, and Postmodern Literacies," *Journal of Urban and Cultural Studies*, 1 (1992), p. 49.
48. William Lutz, *Doublespeak* (New York: Harper Collins, 1989), p. 1.
49. Peter McLaren and Rhonda Hammer, "Media Knowledges, Warrior Citizenry, and Postmodern Literacies," *Journal of Urban and Cultural Studies*, 1 (1992), p. 51.
50. Paul F. Walker and Eric Stambler, "The Surgical Myth of the Gulf War,"*Boston Globe*, April 16, 1991, p. 15.
51. "U.S. Ordered a Stop to Patriot Criticism MIT Professor Says," *Boston Globe*, March 18, 1992, p. 3.
52. "U.S. Ordered a Stop," *Boston Globe*, March 18, 1992, p. 3.
53. "Packaging the War," *Boston Globe*, January 20, 1991, p. 74.
54. McLaren and Hammer, "Media Knowledges," p. 50.
55. Edward S. Hermon and Noam Chomsky, *Manufacturing Consent: The Political Economy of Mass Media* (New York: Pantheon Books, 1988), p. 35.
56. McLaren and Hammer, "Media Knowledges," p. 44.
57. "Packaging the War," *Boston Globe*, January 20, 1991, p. 74.
58. As cited in "Quayle, in Boston, Tells of U.S. Relief Effort for Iraq Refugees," *Boston Globe*, April 12, 1991, p. 15.
59. Interview with Natalie Jacobson, "Nightly News at 6:00 pm," January 16, 1992.
60. Ortega y Gasset, *Revolt of the Masses*, p. 130.
61. Ortega y Gasset, *Revolt of the Masses*, p. 75.
62. Ortega y Gasset, *Revolt of the Masses*, p. 75.
63. Martin A. Lee and Norman Solomon, *Unreliable Sources: A Guide to Detecting Bias in News Media* (New York: Carol Publishing Group, 1991), p. xxii.
64. Chomsky, *Language and Politics*, 1988, p. 681.
65. Chomsky, *Language and Politics*, p. 673.
66. Chomsky, *Language and Politics*, p. 708.
67. For a complete discussion of this issue, see Jonathan Kozol, *Illiterate America* (New York: Anchor Press/Doubleday, 1985), pp. 3–40.
68. Giroux, *Border Crossings*, p. 111.

4

Transitional Bilingual Education and the Socialization of Immigrants

DAVID SPENER

Supporting Donaldo Macedo's contention that schools are in fact not failing, and that the majority of people were never meant to have access to dominant political and economic spheres, David Spener argues that U.S. educational policies and practices reflect an implicit economic need to socialize immigrants and members of oppressed groups to fill necessary, but undesirable, low-status jobs. Spener contends that transitional bilingual education programs, which provide only a limited period of native-language instruction and do not ensure English mastery, prevent most linguistic minority children from attaining academic fluency in either their native language or in English. The subsequent discrepancy between the learning capacities of these children and their monolingual peers reinforces stereotypes that serve to socially legitimize their limited access to better jobs.

Spener analyzes the politics of Americanization (an assimilation process in which U.S. society's dominant culture's values are imposed), the xenophobic views within the English Only Movement (which strives to make English the official, and only, language of the United States), and the conservative efforts to impose a "common culture." His conclusions not only debunk the myth of meritocracy, the "melting pot," and the "American dream," but also the deceit in the present system that continues to embrace the idea that education is the great equalizer. Under the assumption that institutions in this society are equally responsive to all groups, regardless of race, class, and sex, "meritocracy" refers to a system of education where the so-called "talented" are advanced by virtue of their achievements. Arguing that meritocracy is simply a mechanism of maintaining the status quo, David Spener contends that students who do not conform to dominant ideologies, language, and behaviors are punished through low grades and tracking, and eventually through job ceilings.

Controversy abounds in this country regarding the education of immigrant children in the public schools. Specifically, this controversy has centered upon the language, or languages, to be used in the instruction of language-minority students. Both advocates and opponents of bilingual education make many claims about the relative merits of English-only instruction versus the use of the students' mother tongue (Cummins, 1984; Gersten & Woodward, 1985; Hakuta, 1986; Ovando & Collier, 1985). Some light can be shed on this debate by looking beyond the immediate issue of language use in the classroom to the role of immigrants in the United States in general. This article will first examine the economic and social situation of immigrants and other minorities in the United States, and then, with this context established, will examine the role of transitional bilingual education in the socialization of immigrants and ethnolinguistic minorities.

Those concerned about how well public school students achieve their individual or familial goals in society cannot ignore the reverse side of educational policy: that is, how well the educational system prepares students to be able to perform tasks and occupy the social roles necessary to the social, political, and economic functioning of society. Educational policy at the macro level deserves scrutiny in conjunction with other aspects of governmental policy: By viewing the educational system as serving the needs of society instead of the individual student, we implicitly recognize that educational policy is not only related to, but is, in fact, largely determined by economic, social, and political factors.

Education is an integral part of the socialization process. It is future-oriented in that it prepares students to function productively in the niches of the social structures they will occupy as adults. As a part of the socialization process, education depends upon the features of the wider society — economic, technological, and political — for its direction. These features interact to form the *opportunity structure* of the society; that is, the array of social and economic positions open for a given individual to occupy on the basis of his or her particular socialization (Ogbu, 1978). How individuals confront society's opportunity structure may vary greatly, both in terms of starting position and degree of social mobility. How, then, immigrants to the United States confront its opportunity structure has important implications both for educational policy regarding immigrants and for their achievement levels in the educational system.

THE ROLE OF MINORITIES IN THE U.S. ECONOMY

The notion of the existence of an opportunity structure in U.S. society assumes that in order for available social and economic slots to be filled by appropriately "qualified" individuals, the nature of the structure itself must somehow be communicated to society members. It is the job of the family and the school to equip youth with skills, knowledge, attitudes, and personal attributes for both high- and low-status social roles as adults, so that all slots are filled and all necessary societal functions are served. Moreover, the skills, knowledge, attitudes, and personal attributes that determine a low-status position in this society must be differentiated from those suitable for a high-status position. Given this, and assuming that all the slots are in some sense "necessary," it follows that some individuals must be socialized to occupy high-status positions, while others must be socialized or adapted to fill low-status positions. Under these differential socialization processes, certain groups can be specially socialized to occupy certain positions in society. Indeed, historically, it has been the case that individuals from racial, ethical, and linguistic minority groups have tended to occupy low-status positions in our society.

The perceptions of both immigrant and majority groups concerning opportunities in U.S. society for immigrant groups who are also members of racial and ethnolinguistic minorities matter in two ways. First, how both parents and children perceive the opportunities open to them in society and the combination of knowledge, skills, and behaviors that must be acquired in order to take advantage of that has an effect on how children are trained. R. A. Levine (1967) has posited two hypotheses about how children acquire the attributes for upward social mobility within the opportunity structure. In one, he suggests that parents of socially mobile children train them to adopt the attributes of a "successful" person in the society, thus helping their children to gain access to high-status positions. In the other, he proposes that children develop accurate perceptions of the possibilities for social advancement in response to differing "messages" received from society and adapt their behavior accordingly. Both of these hypotheses assume that social mobility depends on an individual's ability to adapt to the norm for mobility (Levine, 1967, cited in Ogbu, 1978).

Secondly, the perceptions of the majority group in society regarding minority group members are important, because in a society such as the United States the members of the majority White group control the opportunity structure. In his book *Minority Education and Caste: The American System in Cross-Cultural Perspective,* John U. Ogbu (1978) discusses discrimination against minority groups in terms of their socialization through public education. He describes situations in which groups controlling the opportunity structure ascribe to members of different minority groups only those attributes specific to low-status social and economic situations. If such ascription is intense, it creates an invisible but effective job ceiling above which it may be extremely difficult to rise. Ogbu goes on to contrast the different kinds of minority groups that may be present in a society and the ways in which their relation to the opportunity structure may vary according to their relative ascribed status and their perception of that status. Additionally, he distinguishes between castelike minorities and immigrant minorities.

Castelike Minorities and Immigrant Minorities

According to Ogbu (1978), members of castelike minorities are perceived by the majority group to be inherently inferior in all aspects of intelligence and ability to carry out the tasks associated with high-status jobs. They "enjoy" a pariah status that sharply circumscribes their economic, political, and cultural participation in society. Members of castelike minorities do not compete freely with majority group members, but instead are summarily excluded from certain jobs solely because of their caste status. Thus, they occupy the least desirable positions in society and face job ceilings that only a few may surmount. Children of caste-minority parents may be socialized for inferiority based on their parents' and their own perceptions of the adult statuses open to them. In addition, public schools may play subtle roles in educating and socializing caste-minority children for low-status positions as adults. Such "inferiorating" education can result from the following causes: negative teacher attitudes and expectations toward these children; teachers recruited from the majority group who are isolated from the minority community, thus inhibiting parent/teacher collaboration in the children's education; biased testing, misclassification of students as learning disabled, and ability group "tracking"; biased textbooks and curricula; use of clinical definitions of caste-minority children's academic problems that place the blame on the minority family for producing "inferior" children; and classroom dynamics that favor the more active participation of majority-group children (Cummins, 1984; McDermott, 1976; Ogbu, 1978). In addition to these factors are the more commonly cited problems of overcrowding, decaying facilities, and drug abuse found in many schools with primarily minority children.

In Ogbu's classification scheme, immigrant minorities may be treated by the majority group in the host society much the same as castelike minorities. That is, their political, economic, and social roles are circumscribed, and they face job ceilings similar to those for caste-minority members. Members of immigrant minorities, however, may react to the same opportunity structure in ways very different from castelike minorities. Since a common reason members of immigrant minorities come to this country is to improve their condition relative to what they experienced in their homelands, they come into contact with the opportunity structure voluntarily. One of their personal measures of success, then, is not whether they have achieved parity in status with the majority group of the host society, but whether their situation has improved materially by immigrating — in which case, the member of an immigrant minority may actually accept discrimination as the price for personal advancement.

Furthermore, as strangers who may have established their own separate communities in the host country, immigrants are not as likely as native-born minorities to internalize the host society's caste ideology. Consequently, members of immigrant minorities may hold instrumental attitudes toward the host society, seeing it as a means to an end while holding on to either the hope of steady relative advance within it, or an improved economic position upon returning to the home country (Ogbu, 1978). Parents' instrumentalist attitudes toward the society in general may carry over to their children in school, who may see more immediate value in their education than caste-minority students whose families may not expect to advance.

There are several problems with Ogbu's castelike versus immigrant minority dichotomy in describing the current situation for immigrants in the United States. First is the issue of race, which is noted but not fully developed in Ogbu's analysis. For Ogbu, the major castelike minority in the United States is, of course, Black people, who constitute a pariah group whose main identifying characteristic is race. But Ogbu does not explicitly discuss the racial background of immigrant minorities in his classification scheme. This is an important omission, since historical experience in the United States has demonstrated that assignments of immigrant groups to low-status positions in the opportunity structure have often been made primarily upon the basis of race. During past waves of immigration to this country from Europe, the outward ethnolinguistic markers of immigrant minorities have disappeared after one or two generations. But for current immigrants from the Third World, race will not escape them even after linguistic and cultural barriers to their advancement have been overcome. The vast majority of those currently immigrating to the United States are non-White people from Latin America, the Caribbean, and Asia (Cockcroft, 1986; Dulles, 1966; Moyers, 1985; U.S. English, 1985).

Many current immigrants, especially Latin Americans, are racially and linguistically "lumped" by the White majority with Chicanos and Puerto Ricans, who, along with the Chinese in some areas, have become castelike minorities by establishing themselves permanently in the United States over the course of several generations. For example, the experiences of Chicanos and Puerto Ricans show that, over time, immigrant minorities may become castelike minorities who share a pariah status with Black people based principally on their race. The phenomenon of "lumping" new immigrants with ethnically similar caste minorities undermines Ogbu's contention that the children of immigrants may have a better chance at higher rates of success in school on the basis of their purported instrumentalist attitudes toward education. Failure to look at the racial background of immigrants also ignores the relatively ascribed statuses among different groups of recent immigrants. Numerous reports appear in the press comparing "successful" immigrant groups with those in the process of becoming castelike minorities. Thus, "Korean-ness" may come to carry a positive racial stereotype, whereas "Mexican-ness" may come to be stigmatized (Matthews, 1985).

It is also important to consider other changes in the nature of immigration to this country. One difference is that a large number of new immigrants to the United States are coming not so much to better their economic situation as to escape war and physical repression in their native countries in Central America, Indochina, and the Caribbean. Because of their experiences of violence and physical and emotional trauma, they may have different aspirations and adapt themselves to the opportunity structure here in ways that are quite different from both established caste minorities and traditional immigrant groups. How these new refugees are received also differs. Some are welcomed with open arms by the U.S. government, while others live under constant threat of deportation by the Immigration and Naturalization Service (INS). Indochinese refugees, for example, are clearly being sent a different message about the array of opportunities open to them in this society than are Central American or Haitian refugees. Indochinese (who are not policed by the INS, need not fear deportation, and are eligible for public assistance) are recognized as victims of Communist aggression and are welcome in this country, while Central Americans and Haitians (who are policed by the INS, have reason to fear deportation, and are not eligible for any kind of public assistance) are perceived as taking away jobs from U.S. citizens (MacEoin & Riley, 1982).

The nature of economically motivated immigration itself has also changed since the first part of this century. Earlier groups of immigrants, from Southern and Eastern Europe, came to the United States at a time of rapid industrial expansion and were actively recruited to work in nearly all segments of a burgeoning industry. They came at a time of very real labor shortage, and although exploited, had a relatively large array of opportunities for placement and advancement, at least *within* the working class. This relative mobility was possible not only because of the labor shortage, but also because quite a large percentage of the working class was drawn from the ranks of first- and second-generation immigrants (Dulles, 1966).

Current immigrants, from Asia and Latin America, are entering a post-industrial United States that faces economic stagnation, high levels of unemployment — especially among members of the industrial working class — and a shift in the economy away from the production of goods toward the provision of services. As such, the opportunities for these new non-White immigrants tend toward low-level employment in the expanding service sector, seasonal farm labor, or membership in the strata of the chronically unemployed or underemployed (Harrington & Levinson, 1985). If these, in fact, are the roles open to most new immigrants to the United States, then we might well expect that government policies, including educational policy, will work in favor of socializing immigrants for such roles.

THE ROLE OF "ILLEGAL ALIENS" IN THE U.S. ECONOMY

Tove Skutnabb-Kangas of Denmark's Roskilde University has examined how the immigration and educational policies of several European countries relate to the roles played by immigrants in those countries. In her article "Guest Worker or Immigrant: Different Ways of Reproducing an Underclass" (1981), she analyzes post-World War II immigration to several Western European countries. Immediately following the war, these countries initiated guest worker programs to meet a severe labor shortage. Rapid post-war reconstruction and economic growth led the governments of these countries to recruit and hire, for a finite amount of time, unskilled and uneducated workers from Southern Europe and the Balkans to fill low-paying industrial and service jobs undesired by domestic workers.

Forty-plus years have passed since the end of World War II, and Europe has been rebuilt, but many guest workers have yet to return home, even though industrial production has slowed or been exported to the Third World, and high levels of unemployment have become chronic in the host countries. The continued residence of alien workers and their families in Western Europe with the tacit or official approval of the host countries has led Skutnabb-Kangas (1981) and others (Cockcroft, 1986; Dixon, Martinez, & McCaughan, 1982) to propose that immigrants have taken on a new function in modern, post-industrial nations. In the past, a host country would encourage immigration in order to meet labor shortages in an expanding economy. A primary role for immigrants in modern, post-industrial countries is to serve as a buffer between the domestic population, specifically the native-born working class, and the effects of periodic downturns in the economy. In essence, Skutnabb-Kangas sees immigrants as coming to constitute the modern caste minorities of Europe — the last hired, the first fired, the lowest status members of society. Nowhere does this view of the situation seem more real than in Great Britain today, where non-White immigrants compose the vast majority of the British underclass. If one accepts that the economies of the United States and Western European countries are similar, immigrants to the United States can be seen as additions to the ranks of castelike minorities historically represented by Blacks, Chicanos, Chinese, Native Americans, and Puerto Ricans.

Although Skutnabb-Kangas's model for the new role of immigrants in post-industrial societies sheds some light on the situation in the United States, it does not directly address itself to one of the most provocative and controversial issues for U.S. immigration policy — the increasing presence of "illegal aliens" in the U.S. work force. Few public issues have generated as emotional a debate as the new wave of Hispanic immigration across our southern border. The alarm with which this migration has been treated in the press has fostered widespread misunderstanding of its nature and has fueled nativist and racist sentiments among large segments of the country's population. Even normally restrained and cautious public officials, such as former CIA Director William Colby, have expressed fears of the development of "a Spanish-speaking Quebec in the U.S. Southwest," and have viewed illegal immigration from Mexico as "a greater threat to national security than the Soviet Union" (Cockcroft, 1986, p. 39). Television specials present images of "an army of aliens waiting to move forth across the border when night falls," and reporters interview White workers who feel that the United States is "being invaded as surely as [if] we had an enemy dropping bombs on us" (Moyers, 1985).

Nonetheless, by using the tools of analysis developed by Skutnabb-Kangas and by Ogbu, illegal immigration can be viewed quite differently. Some leaders in this country are less alarmed and more rational about immigration, as illustrated by William French Smith, the Reagan administration's first attorney general. Smith commented that the administration's goal was not to stem the flow of foreign workers into this country, but rather to "reduce and regulate" the flow and to channel foreigners "into jobs where they are needed" (Cockcroft, 1986, p. 220).

As noted above, Skutnabb-Kangas has suggested that immigrant workers serve as a buffer between native-born workers and the effects of economic downturn in developed nations. The historian and political economist James Cockcroft, in his book *Outlaws in the Promised Land* (1986), develops this analysis more completely in examining the role of undocumented Mexican workers in the U.S. economy. Cockcroft argues that thousands of "bad" jobs in the U.S. economy need filling, and employers face an acute shortage of laborers willing to fill those jobs. For Cockcroft, a "bad" job is one that does not pay a worker an adequate living wage, does not provide health and life insurance benefits, and exposes a worker to unsafe working conditions and unhealthy hours. Furthermore, Cockcroft points out that often the difference between a "good" job and a "bad" job is not intrinsic to the nature of the work or the level of skill required to perform it. The large difference in wages and benefits between an auto worker and an assembler of calculator parts in Silicon Valley, for example, cannot be accounted for by differences in skills, since neither job requires an extended period of special education or training; essentially the work performed in both jobs is similar. The auto worker has a better job because the work force in the auto industry is organized and has benefited for decades from union contracts with the major auto firms. In other words, workers have the ability to organize collectively under certain free-labor conditions to transform low-paying, undesirable jobs into better paying positions that are relatively attractive and difficult to obtain. In reality, Cockcroft maintains, there is no shortage of unskilled workers in the U.S. economy. Instead, he argues, there is a shortage of employers willing to pay a living wage and provide decent working conditions for their employees.

If, for example, seasonal farm labor paid better, there would be no seasonal labor shortage to be filled by undocumented Mexican workers in California's Central Valley. Farm labor jobs pay poorly because the work force in the agricultural sector of the economy is unorganized. Native-born or naturalized citizens, who enjoy the protection of federal and state labor codes won by decades of union organizing and who are eligible for social services, have no interest in taking these "bad" jobs. It is the role of illegal immigrants — the "outlaws" whose lack of protection by U.S. laws renders them unable to organize to raise wages or improve working conditions — to fill the "bad" jobs in the U.S. economy (Cockcroft, 1986). Cockcroft argues that illegal immigrants are recruited on the basis of their special "illegal" status to fill low-status slots in the U.S. opportunity structure outlined by Ogbu.

By extrapolating from the work of Skutnabb-Kangas (1980), it can be said that undocumented workers in the United States are not significantly different from the guest workers of post-war Western Europe, although they may not be officially recognized as such. Guest workers serve at the pleasure of the host country and can be ordered to return to their country of origin at any time. Their legal status is that of a policed labor force tightly constrained by the host government. They are denied the right to make demands for higher wages or for the provision of social services from business or government. They are like the immigrant minorities of Ogbu's model in that, even under the most draconian conditions in the host country, they may "enjoy" a higher standard of living than in their home countries. Guest workers are brought into the host country to do its most menial work for lower wages than the native-born work force would accept. The presence of guest workers in a country can also serve to elevate the status and pay of native-born or naturalized workers. This is because guest workers contribute substantially to expanding the gross national product and pay taxes to the host country while drawing substandard wages and receiving only token government expenditures for social services (Skutnabb-Kangas, 1981). While there has not been an official government guest worker program in the United States for over twenty years, the continued participation of "illegal aliens" in the U.S. work force suggests a tacit government guest worker policy, although the benefits to the naturalized work force may not be as directly correlated as in Great Britain's guest worker program.

The immigrant reform legislation that was recently signed into law (Immigrant Reform and Control Act, 1986) by President Reagan has received much attention. On the surface, it appears to take strong measures to halt the influx of undocumented workers, who many citizens believe threaten the livelihoods of "legal" workers. The efficacy of the measures mandated by the bill must be questioned, however. Although sanctions against knowingly hiring undocumented workers may discourage some employers, enforcement of this provision may or may not be vigorous. Consider the Bracero Guest Worker Program, for example, in which the U.S. government imported Mexican workers to work in agriculture to meet labor shortages. The workers stayed well after the return to a peacetime economy. Many believe that the Bracero program survived because it preserved a docile, cheap labor force for U.S. agribusiness. The historical record shows that many regulations governing the import and employment of workers in this program generally went unenforced, allowing employers to violate them with impunity (Cockcroft, 1986).

In spite of the fact that vast new expenditures have authorized the INS to strengthen and expand law enforcement and investigative capabilities, most knowledgeable observers agree that the agency lacks the capability to close the border and prevent the employment of "illegals" in this country (Brinkley, 1986; Matthews, 1986). Finally, the inclusion of a guest worker program for seasonal farm labor gives an additional indication that many of those individuals presently working illegally in the United States are, in fact, needed economically. Cockcroft (1986) notes that in the past, mass importation of Mexicans as "guest workers" has occurred simultaneously with their mass deportation of "illegals." The new immigration law seems less likely to eliminate illegal aliens from the work force than to police their presence in order to keep the "bad" jobs filled.

The Effect of U.S. Economic Realities on Attitudes toward Minorities

If immigrants, guest workers, and "illegal aliens" are performing services that are important to the U.S. economy by filling undesirable jobs, contributing to the growth of the GNP, and paying taxes, and if the existence of an underclass artificially raises the status of the White working class, why should the United States be witnessing an outpouring of anti-immigrant sentiment from the White working class at this time? One explanation lies in the nature of the changes in the U.S. economy and its export of "good" jobs (as defined by Cockcroft) to other countries where wages and corporate taxes are lower than those in the United States. The greatest loss of jobs in the economy has been in those heavy-manufacturing industries which, because of unionization and high profits during the period between the end of World War II and the end of the U.S. involvement in the Vietnam War, had paid high hourly wages, provided good benefit packages for their workers, and had been regulated by the government for standards of worker health and safety (Harrington & Levinson, 1985). The greatest growth in jobs, on the other hand, has been in the so-called service sector, where jobs were traditionally filled by members of the underclass, and in the high-tech field, where most firms are non-union (Bluestone, 1987). Huge cuts in government expenditures on welfare, combined with the loss of "good" jobs in the economy, have forced many members of the White, native-English-speaking working class to seek lower status jobs in the growth sectors of the economy (Harrington & Levinson, 1985). For the first time, many majority group members are competing with members of castelike and immigrant minorities for suddenly scarce jobs (Bluestone, 1987). Traditionally, this competition has not existed, and it may be the perception of large numbers of White, native-born workers that such competition is unjust, especially when their chief competitors are not "Americans." Hostility toward foreigners from U.S. workers, however misplaced, should really come as no surprise under these conditions.

A second possible explanation concerns U.S. nationalism and its role in enhancing the self-perception of the domestic working class. The rise of the United States to the most powerful and economically successful nation in the world following World War II had the effect of raising the absolute status of all U.S. citizens in a world context, regardless of their relative status within the U.S. social hierarchy. Although mythical, this perceived status has had a powerful effect upon the psyche of U.S. workers. Another myth is that of the United States as a "melting pot," a nation of newcomers who have given up their old identities in order to assume the new, if somewhat vague, "American" identity. All newcomers then start at the bottom of the social ladder and climb in status as they progressively shed their foreign identities. As the economy is restructured, many assimilated Americans are experiencing a loss in relative status that forces them to work alongside and compete for jobs with foreign workers and other out-group members who, according to the myth, "belong" at the bottom of the social ladder because they are not Americanized. At this point, the fall in relative status is transformed into a fall in absolute status as the status of native-born within the United States falls to that of foreigners.

The perceived superior status of Americanized workers in the world might be preserved in several ways. One alternative, the deportation of foreigners so that the only workers remaining are culturally Americanized, is reflected in mounting pressures to stem the "tide" of illegal aliens entering the country and to deport those illegals already working. Another possibility is to drop the job ceiling for immigrant minorities even lower through intensified racial discrimination and violence. Consider the following recent events in Georgia, where the connection between anti-immigrant and non-English speakers has been used by lawmakers to prohibit the use of Spanish. In the small community of Cedartown, near the Alabama border, a meat-packing plant that was the town's largest source of jobs employed about one hundred Mexican workers alongside a large majority of White and Black employees. In 1985, many of the Anglo and Black workers walked off the job in a strike action organized by the Ku Klux Klan to protest the "discrimination" against U.S. workers by the company. The strike action followed the roadside slayings of two of the plant's Mexican employees in the previous three years by Klan members or associates ("Bill Pushes an Official State Prejudice," 1986). One of the Klan defendants was acquitted by an all-White jury ("Cedartown Strike," 1986). In 1986, the Georgia General Assembly passed a resolution declaring English to be the state's official language in order to reinforce "the cultural fabric of one language" within the state. The *Atlanta Constitution* stated in an editorial that it could not be seen as coincidence that the measure was introduced into the state legislature by the senator whose district includes Cedartown:

It is such an obvious slap at dozens of Mexicans who came to Cummings's northwest Georgia district to work in a local meat-packing plant, only to find themselves targets of intense hatred and violence by local yahoos, that one wonders at the short span of some of the lawmakers' memories ("Bill Pushes an Official State Prejudice," 1986, p. 22A)

The legislators' action in this light can be seen both as an effort to bestow official blessing upon state residents who speak English, and a repudiation of those residents who do not. The rapid growth in the number of Hispanic immigrants from diverse national and racial backgrounds to this country has contributed to the perception of the Spanish language as a racial characteristic, since Spanish is virtually the only feature common to all Hispanic immigrants (though not to all Hispanic residents), and because most new immigrants to the United States are coming from Latin America. If one accepts the notion that speaking Spanish functions as a racial characteristic of Hispanics in this country, can one ignore the racist implications of Georgia's English-language resolution?

In a related case in California, where there is a long history of violent crimes against Hispanic migrant workers and union organizers, and where it is traditional for the perpetrators of such crimes to go unpunished (Cockcroft, 1986), voters in 1986 overwhelmingly passed a ballot initiative declaring the primacy of the English language in public discourse ("An Official Language for California," 1986). The measure is intended to curtail the use of Spanish in the state government bureaucracy and in public schools.

A third alternative for preserving the status of Americanized workers, and the one that has the greatest implication for educational policy, is to insist that the immigrants who are allowed to remain in the United States become full-fledged, Anglicized Americans at the earliest possible date. Advocates of this path, among them the most strident critics of bilingual education, seem to fear that the price of cultural pluralism is the loss of a cultural basis for nationalism. All three of these remedies, however contradictory, were being applied simultaneously in the United States in the mid-1980s. At times, they were even cloaked in the rhetoric of the civil rights movement. An article written by a Black columnist in the *Washington Post,* for instance, questioned whether or not the United States could compete with a "homogeneous society like Japan" unless it, too, took steps towards homogenization by moving faster towards assimilating ethnic and racial minorities into the mainstream (Rowan, 1986).

THE ROLE OF U.S. EDUCATIONAL POLICY IN SOCIALIZING MINORITIES FOR A PART IN THE ECONOMY

Not surprisingly, current public demands to assimilate immigrant groups quickly, for their own good and for the good of the nation, have revolved around proficiency in the English language. English has become *the* public issue in the socialization of immigrant adults and children living in the

United States. Increasingly, attempts are being made to ensure that mastery of the "standard" or "core" dialect of American English is represented as emblematic of an "American" identity. The public debate on the English language issue raised two concerns. First, it has always been true that millions of native-born U.S. citizens have never mastered standard English as defined by school textbooks, and that, since its founding, the United States has been multilingual (Hakuta, 1986; Shor, 1986). Second, it is necessary to question the extent to which mastery of English is necessary to carry out the functions of the roles open to adult immigrants in the U.S. opportunity structure. If, as a consequence of the imposition of a job ceiling on the upward social mobility of their members, immigrant minorities are restricted to "immigrant" jobs which do not require high English proficiency, it may be unrealistic to expect that immigrants will ever master "standard" English. A number of eminent linguists, most notable among them John Schumann, have hypothesized that individuals become proficient in a second language not so much due to the effects of formal instruction, but rather to the degree that second language proficiency serves their social and economic needs (Schumann, 1976, 1980). In this sense, proficiency in standard English is not a causal variable in an individual's social status, but, rather, is reflective of the individual's opportunities to participate in social settings where standard English is the language of the participants (Schumann, 1980). The lack of proficiency in standard English on the part of many Black and White working-class Americans, in spite of years of public schooling, bears witness to the predictive value of Schumann's hypothesis.

Respect for the U.S. public education system has rested on the belief that public education is a great upward equalizer, giving children of low-status families the chance to surpass their parents' status through achievement in school (Shor, 1986). This belief parallels the melting pot myth that links social advancement to the process of "Americanization." Both notions presume that the opportunity structure of U.S. society will always have a surplus of higher status jobs to be filled by individuals who have adopted the language, values, and beliefs of the dominant White majority as they pass through the educational system. The presumption of a surplus of "good" jobs in the United States is dubious at best. Nonetheless, the "excellence in education" movement, spearheaded by the presidential commission's report on the nation's public schools (National Commission on Excellence in Education, 1983) rests on just such an assumption, and advocates the adoption of national curriculum standards aiming at the "Americanization" of students from groups outside the cultural mainstream. A focus on mastery of standard English is a major feature of the proposed new curriculum standards (Shor, 1986).

The "Excellence in Education" Movement
Educational curriculum theorists, including Ira Shor of the City University of New York, have extensively analyzed the proposals for restoration of "ex-

cellence" in the nation's schools. Shor has commented in particular on the curriculum standards heralded by excellence movement leader Albert Shanker, president of the American Federation of Teachers. Shanker was disturbed by tendencies towards "permissiveness" and "cultural relativism" in the schools in the 1960s and 1970s, and began to argue for the re-establishment of standards of academic excellence in public schools. The "core curriculum" formulated by Shanker is described by Shor as follows:

> This theme of a universal course of study embodying a singular dominant culture took shape as a "core curriculum." That core of knowledge emanated from the center of authority outward to the periphery. It is based in Standard English, a traditional reading list, and cleansed versions of history (the "American Heritage"). The "core curriculum" idea rejects the ideological diversity of the protest era. (Shor, 1986, p. 13)

Shor criticizes the concept of the "core curriculum" in general because, he says, it "transmits an official value system disguised as universal knowledge" (Shor, 1986, p. 23). He also criticizes the "core curriculum" for fostering a nationwide hysteria over an alleged "literacy" crisis in the United States based upon widespread lack of mastery of standard English, which has been a linguistic reality among Black people, immigrant groups, and lower class Whites in this country almost since its founding (Dulles, 1966; Hakuta, 1986; Johansen & Maestas, 1983; McDermott, 1976; Ovando & Collier, 1985; Rodriguez, 1981; Sennett & Cobb, 1972). Shor writes: "Curriculum and civilization were defined in the Literacy Crisis as resting on the authority of the elite language; that language was posed as a universal standard of culture rather than as a class-specific form of expression" (Shor, 1986, p. 65). Shor contrasts the English achievement standards of the core curriculum with more tolerant views regarding language usage:

> [In 1973] the largest organization of English teachers, the National Council of Teachers of English, had voted in its policy on "Students' Rights to Their Own Language." This egalitarian document described Standard English as a privileged dialect, and as one dialect among many in a diverse culture. It is no secret that most people speak a form of English different from the language of teachers, of literature, and of the elite. (Shor, 1986, p. 65)

The call for excellence in education, including the demand for assimilation of immigrant and castelike minorities in the United States, is justified as necessary to raise the skills and productivity of the U.S. work force as the U.S. economy moves into new technological and trade frontiers in the twenty-first century. In spite of the fact that most evidence points to a *decrease* in the need for skilled laborers as the complexity of goods produced in the economy increases (Bluestone, 1987; Braverman, 1974), proponents of the excellence movements insist that the shortage of skilled, literate personnel in the labor market restricts U.S. ability to compete with the rest of the world. As evidence, they point to the declining productivity of workers and the falling academic test scores of students. The workers and students responsible for these declines are then seen as dragging down the rest of the society as it strives to enter a new age of high-tech prosperity. Members of immigrant and castelike minorities, who often score lower on measures of academic achievement both because of cultural and dialectical differences and decades of discrimination, are easily targeted for this criticism. Minorities have, in fact, been scapegoated on numerous occasions, as shown in this excerpt from the conservative journal *Heritage Today:*

> The most damaging blows to science and mathematics education have come from Washington. For the past 20 years, federal mandates have favored "disadvantaged" pupils at the expense of those who have the highest potential to contribute positively to society. . . . By catering to the demands of special interest groups — racial minorities, the handicapped, women and non-English speaking students — America's public schools have successfully competed for government funds, but they have done so at the expense of education as a whole. (Gardner, 1983, pp. 6–7).

The question of how the call for excellence in education is compatible with the decline in the number of "good" jobs available and skilled laborers needed in the U.S. economy is important if one accepts Shor's proposition that the educational system is "functional or dysfunctional to society at any instance to the degree it prepares student attitudes appropriate to the needs of an unequal social order" (Shor, 1986, p. 168). On the surface, it would seem that accepting the excellence program in the schools would lead to just the sort of dysfunction to which Shor alludes. Returning to Ogbu's job ceiling notion helps to reveal a way in which the imposition of new standards of excellence in the schools is highly functional.

In a sense, the United States is not experiencing a literacy crisis, but a crisis of an "overeducated" work force. Well-compensated, higher status jobs in the economy are in short supply relative to the number of workers "qualified" by their education and socialization to fill them (Bluestone, 1987; Cockcroft, 1986; Harrington & Levinson, 1985; Shor, 1986). As competition among workers for "good" jobs intensifies, employers can arbitrarily raise the qualifications a worker must have. The excellence movement in education is also expanding the grounds for exclusion from high-status jobs without regard to the real needs of the economy. Because the excellence movement seeks through its meritocracy to reward the "excellent" student who "excels" in the language and behaviors of the dominant elite, and to punish (through low grades and tracking) the "inferior" student who does not master the language and behaviors of the elite, the outcome of the movement will be to maintain a job ceiling for minorities. This serves to preserve the perceived superior status of the native-born White worker who is increasingly being called upon to accept employment in occupations formerly reserved for the underclass.

The United States offers immigrants an ambiguous social contract. It reads, more or less, as follows: "In order to participate in a non-marginal way in the U.S. economy, you must become an American by giving up your loyalty to your home country and language, and you must learn the language of the American elite. In order to become an American, you must meet certain standards. This country is in the process of raising its standards because, unfortunately, there are already too many Americans. If you aren't allowed to become an American, there's still plenty of room for you in this country — at the bottom." Due to catastrophic economic conditions in much of the rest of the world, there are millions of people ready to sign on. A Mexican woman waiting to sneak across the U.S. border at Tijuana put it this way: "We're sad about it, but what can we do? There is no opportunity in Mexico. Mexico is very poor, and the government doesn't help the people. . . . We are born to die. We know where we were born, but we don't know where we will end up" (Kelly, 1986).

Assimilation as a Goal of Immigrant Educational Policies

In spite of all the limitations on the social mobility of immigrants within the United States, the goal of almost any educational policy directed toward them will be assimilationist in some measure. The pace of the assimilation will vary, as will the means of achieving it. The strategies that have been employed to implement immigrant educational policies in both the United States and Europe include so-called submersion, immersion, and transitional bilingual education programs. A question that must be raised at this point concerns the type of assimilation the United States aims to achieve through its educational policies. Is the goal to assimilate immigrant children into the dominant social group of the host society, or more to discourage their assimilation of the cultural and linguistic norms of their home country? In the United States, a long history of racism and the existence of a stratified opportunity structure combine to work against assimilation into the host society's higher status, dominant White group. What could be the rationale for assimilating immigrant children away from their own culture?

Ogbu's caste minority/immigrant minority model can provide some insight into this question. Ogbu (1978) noted that many immigrants hold instrumental attitudes toward the host society — by holding on to the hope of steady relative advancement within it or by an improved economic position upon returning to the home country. Viewing the host society instrumentally means concomitantly that immigrants view their stay as provisional, depending upon how they perceive their position in facing the opportunity structure. In Ogbu's view, it is the unassimilated status of immigrant minorities, best illustrated by the possibility of ultimately returning to the home country, that qualitatively distinguishes them from caste minorities. (A number of authors have studied the situation of immigrants standing at the crossroads between assimilation and return: See Ekstrand, Foster, Olkiewicz, & Stankovski, 1981.) That unassimilated status means that immigrants may hold onto attitudes, values, and behaviors that are incompatible with occupying a traditional caste-minority position within the U.S. opportunity structure.

The education of immigrant children enters the picture here in a most profound way. In order to prepare students for caste-minority status in the host society, whether in the United States or Europe, several things must be accomplished. First, children must let go their instrumentalist attitudes that view school and the host country as a means of personal advancement. Second, they must internalize the caste ideology of the host society. That is, they must not have a value system and a way of life independent of that of the society at large. Finally, they must be denied the possibility of returning to their home country should prospects for advancement in the host country dim. How can schooling accomplish these aims? Official indoctrination might be one way. Another more politically acceptable way is to take away the immigrant child's language and culture and replace them with some form more suited to the social roles he or she can be expected to occupy as an adult in the host society. All three strategies mentioned earlier — submersion, immersion, and transitional bilingual education — can be effective means of achieving both assimilation and a progressive disengagement from the home language and culture. They may also play a role in educating immigrant children for low-status roles as adults.

The aim of educational approaches that prohibit mother-tongue instruction for immigrants is unquestionably and strongly assimilationist. The so-called submersion approach, which places limited-English-proficient children in English-only classrooms in the hope that they will somehow learn the new language and adapt themselves to the new culture, has been shown to have devastating consequences on the average immigrant child's cognitive development and academic achievement (California State Department of Education, 1982; Hakuta, 1986; Ovando & Collier, 1985). The immersion approach is also English-only, though the academic outcomes of immersion programs in the United States have only recently begun to be studied (Gersten & Woodward, 1985). The few programs in the United States that do use some degree of mother-tongue instruction and that have been implemented on a large scale are transitional bilingual education (TBE) programs. Since bilingual education is currently embroiled in controversy, an examination of how it may function as an agent of socialization for immigrant children is worthwhile.

The goal of federally funded TBE programs in the United States has never been the "production" of bilingual, biliterate, bicultural adults capable of functioning competently in two languages and cultures. If this were the case, there would have to be numerous programs that promote the development of academic skills in immigrant students' native languages in all school subjects through the end of high school. Virtually no such programs exist in this country. Since the 1974 reauthorization of Title VII of the Elementary and Secondary Education Act, the primary aim of such programs has been to raise the English proficiency of non-English-speaking children such that they may be able to participate "effectively" in classrooms where English is the sole medium of instruction (Ovando & Collier, 1985). Transitional bilingual education programs typically last only two to three years. The mother tongues of children in such transitional programs are used as necessary to introduce content material and to begin to develop the literacy competencies that will presumably help children learn to read and write in English. English instruction focuses on the development of students' oral command of the language as well as communicative competencies in English. After three years, or when students are deemed sufficiently proficient in English (whichever comes first), they are "mainstreamed" into regular English-only classrooms (Ovando & Collier, 1985). With formal instruction in the mother tongue completely terminated both as the medium of instruction and as a content subject very early on in students' education, they may be put on the road to *limited bilingualism.*

Limited bilingualism, that is, less than native-like proficiency in either the mother tongue or the second language, has been associated with impeded cognitive development and lowered academic achievement in a number of studies (California State Department of Education, 1982; Cummins, 1981; Hakuta, 1986). Research into bilingualism as a cognitive phenomenon has shown that second-language acquisition is most successful when there is a strong foundation in the mother tongue, and that conversational skills in a second language are learned earlier than the ability to use the language for academic learning (Hakuta, 1985). Research has also indicated that in order for bilingual children to match their monolingual peers' levels of cognitive and academic achievement, they must first attain a minimum linguistic threshold of near native proficiency in at least one of their two languages (Cummins, 1981, 1984; Skutnabb-Kangas, 1979). Cummins (1981) has gone further to suggest that it takes at least three to four years of formal schooling to attain such a threshold.

It is now widely accepted among researchers studying language acquisition that there are two dimensions of language proficiency (California State Department of Education, 1982; Hakuta, 1986; Ovando & Collier, 1985). The first dimension has to do with those skills associated with casual conversational use of the language, what Cummins has called BICS — basic interpersonal communicative skills. The second dimension concerns more formal intellectual understanding of the language and the ability to use it for intellectual or academic purposes. Cummins has called this dimension CALP — cognitive academic learning proficiency. Proficiency in one dimension, however, does not necessarily correlate positively with proficiency in the other. Moreover, it is generally believed that the BICS dimension is acquired before the CALP dimension (California State Department of Education, 1982; Cummins, 1984; Hakuta, 1986). The minimum linguistic threshold includes the development of CALP-level skills in a formal academic setting (Cummins, 1981, 1984).

Transitional Bilingual Education Programs
Bilingualism research findings have important implications for transitional bilingual education programs. The overriding goal of TBE programs is to mainstream students into English-only classrooms. As a result, a major component of such programs is the development of English proficiency in the students. Unfortunately, most of the programs last only two to three years, not long enough for children to build up CALP level skills in either their mother tongue or English. Such children may be mainstreamed into English-only classes before they have attained the minimum linguistic threshold necessary to ensure their ability to carry out cognitively demanding academic tasks in English. Additionally, two to three years at the elementary level is regarded as insufficient time to allow for the development of CALP skills in the mother tongue. Students mainstreamed after only two to three years in bilingual classrooms will generally not be able to rely on a cross-language transfer of academic skills from their mother tongue to English to compensate for their CALP deficit in English. Consequently, language-minority students who are mainstreamed out of transitional bilingual programs may not be sufficiently prepared to participate and compete in English-only classrooms where English is the mother tongue of the majority of their peers.

The consequences of mainstreaming limited-English-proficient children into English-only classrooms extend beyond the cognitive and the personal. The social consequences include defining the terms of competition and social ranking in the public schools and influencing the perceptions that English mother-tongue students and teachers have of immigrant children in their classes. Immigrant children (as well as children of native-born linguistic minority parents) mainstreamed into regular classrooms from transitional bilingual programs may be presented before their teachers and classmates not as equal-but-different representatives of another language and culture, but rather as imperfect or inferior members of the domestic culture (Skutnabb-Kangas, 1981). The differences most noted may be the immigrants' imperfect use and understanding of English, their poorer academic performance, and the color of their skin.

The process of mainstreaming limited bilingual students may potentially reinforce the racist stereotypes in U.S. society that limit the advancement of caste or castelike minorities. The majority of recent immigrants to this country are non-White, and members of the White majority may consciously or subconsciously associate the cognitive deficits linked to poor educational policies with particular races and nationalities, particularly if transitional bilingual education programs are viewed in the same light as other forms of compensatory education. Intellectual inferiority would then be ascribed to immigrant groups on the basis of ascribed characteristics, since their school performance would still be perceived as deficient, even after they have received several years of special help in school. Blaming the victim, especially Black Americans, has been established as a given in the United States (Ogbu, 1978).

Research on bilingualism seems to indicate that early mainstreaming, the legal goal of short-term TBE programs, is flawed as a compensatory educational strategy for immigrant students (California State Department of Education, 1982; Cummins, 1981, 1984; Hakuta, 1985, 1986). It seems likely that many TBE programs are, in fact, turning out students whose CALP-dimension proficiency in both the mother tongue and English is inadequate for participation in English-only classrooms. On the surface, at least, it is on this issue that bilingual education is attacked. On another level, however, TBE may be an appropriate way for society to educate the children of immigrants.

If U.S. society needs to recruit and prepare new candidates for a growing number of low-status, poorly compensated slots in the opportunity structure, transitional bilingual education programs for non-English-speaking immigrants may be construed by the majority as part of a "reasonable" set of educational policies for the nation. If political and social considerations dictate that Black and other non-White and/or foreign-born people bear a greater share of the hardships, poverty, and unemployment in the U.S. economy, it is "reasonable" to expect the educational system to reflect such considerations. Black people and many new immigrants are already separated by means of race as they confront the opportunity structure. Educational policy can serve to reinforce caste distinctions in the society by providing, more or less intentionally, non-White people with an inferior education. In doing so, the educational system plays a role in creating a pool of adults who are "qualified" to be economically exploited, unemployed, or underemployed.

Reagan's Department of Education has vigorously attacked TBE programs because, it is claimed, they hinder non-English-speaking students' acquisition of English and keep them separated from mainstream students for too long. In fact, the criticism of TBE programs from within the government began under the Carter administration. Consider this statement by a former Secretary of Health, Education and Welfare, Joseph Califano: "[In bilingual programs] too little attention was paid to teaching English, and far too many children were kept in bilingual classes long after they acquired the necessary proficiency to be taught in English" (Califano, 1981). Further, Ronald Reagan did not wait long after entering the White House to begin to speak out against bilingual school programs:

> It is absolutely wrong and against American concept to have a bilingual education program that is now openly, admittedly dedicated to preserving their native language and never getting them adequate in English so they can go out into the job market. (quoted in Hakuta, 1985, p. 207)

The attacks on transitional bilingual education are not consistent with the available research evidence on bilingualism, but they can be seen as consistent with trends toward the further lowering of the job ceiling for immigrants in the United States. New regulations governing the expenditure of funds for bilingual education promulgated by William Bennett, the Secretary of Education, seek to discourage the use of languages other than English in instruction and to encourage the early "mainstreaming" of students out of bilingual programs. Furthermore, the aim of native-language instruction under the new regulations is not to provide for children's overall academic success, but rather, to foster the acquisition of English. To this end, the Department of Education hopes to renegotiate many districts' compliance with the civil rights provisions of Title VII legislation (Orum, 1985). The National Council of La Raza, a national Hispanic-American civil rights organization, has commented that the Secretary of Education seems to believe that instruction in English-as-a-Second-Language alone is a sufficient educational remedy to meet the department's civil rights obligations as set by the *Lau v. Nichols* Supreme Court case of 1974 (Orum, 1985).

The provisions of the Department of Education's proposed new rules governing bilingual education programs receiving Title VII monies are as follows:

- DOE will provide for "maximum flexibility" on the part of local districts in designing programs to meet the needs of limited-English-proficient students. (In practice, this means that the native component of such programs may be eliminated.)
- Bilingual education programs will use native language instruction only to the extent necessary to achieve competence in English and to meet grade promotions and graduation requirements.
- No minimum amount of time or instruction is to be established to meet the standards of achieving English competence and meeting grade promotion and graduation requirements. (In other words, early mainstreaming of students is permissible.)
- The Secretary will fund proposals only if they can demonstrate the ability, financial or otherwise, to continue the project after Title VII monies are exhausted. Increased local responsibility for funding programs will be a priority. (U.S. Department of Education, 1985)

The last provision is of particular interest because of its implications for the many bilingual education programs located in poor districts. It appears that the Department of Education will fund only those projects in districts that can afford bilingual programs after federal start-up monies are spent. It is conceivable, then, that many districts will be denied federal bilingual education funds not because there is no demonstrable need for a bilingual program, but because the economically marginal status of the populations served cannot manage to foot the bill for the programs (Crawford, 1986). In relation to this point, Navarro (1985) notes that the rollback of bilingual education programs in the state of California is largely attributable to the real powerlessness of Hispanics there. In addition, he says that it is increasingly true that those who have a direct interest in public education policy are the disenfranchised, impoverished ethnic and racial minorities, while members of the dominant majority group in society are less and less willing to pay for such educational programs.

It is interesting to look at how the new DOE-proposed regulations define a "program of transitional bilingual education." According to the department, TBE refers to programs designed to meet the educational needs of limited English-proficient students and provide "structured English language instruction, and, to the extent necessary to allow a child to achieve competence in the English language, instruction in the child's native language" (U.S. Department of Education, 1985). Clearly, the goal of such a program in this scheme — and the one criterion used to evaluate its success or failure (as well as the success or failure of the students participating in it) — is the acquisition of English as a badge of American identity. The insights gained from sociological and linguistic investigation seem to show that this goal serves the interest of society at the expense of the needs of language-minority students.

It remains to be seen whether or not TBE programs produce results in terms of student academic achievement. The research to date in bilingualism indicates, however, that in both the cognitive and affective domains, maintenance bilingual programs or two-way enrichment programs of longer duration (at least six years) would be far superior to transitional bilingual programs. Bilingual advocates need to consider whether or not they are preserving the essence of quality bilingual education when they seek to promote bilingual education through the defense of existing programs. If, in so doing, they defend compensatory programs whose graduates are consistently outperformed by their monolingual peers, they may inadvertently play a role in the negative stereotyping of the language and immigrant minorities whose cause they champion.

Finally, those who believe that compensatory educational programs for immigrants and language minorities play an important role in the advancement of minority civil rights need to be wary. The analysis presented in this article suggests that the existence of low-status social roles is necessary to U.S. society in some sense and that someone must fill those roles. Compensatory education assumes that low-status people suffer low status because of their lack of school success, and that if they were to become successful in school, their status would rise. In the United States, where race and ethnicity frequently form the basis of low status, such an assumption does not hold true. Educational advocates for immigrants and language minorities must look beyond strictly academic themes and examine the adult roles open to these students, in order to determine whether such programs do indeed facilitate both their advancement and mobility in our society.

REFERENCES

An official language for California. (1986, October 2). *New York Times*, p. A23.
Barreto, J., Jr. (1986, August 9). English isn't the only language we speak. *Washington Post*, p. A19.
Bill pushes an official state prejudice [Editorial]. (1986, February 18). *Atlanta Constitution*, p. 22A.
Bluestone, B. (1987). *The de-industrialization of America*. New York: Basic Books.
Braverman, H. (1974). *Labor and monopoly capital*. New York: Monthly Review Press.
Brinkley, J. (1986, June 26). U.S. set to act on border drug flow. *New York Times*, p. 1.
Califano, J. (1981). *Governing America: An insider's report from the White House and the Cabinet*. New York: Simon & Schuster.
California State Department of Education, Office of Bilingual and Bicultural Education. (1982). *Basic principles for the education of language-minority students: An overview*. Sacramento: Author.
Cedartown Strike. (1986, February 15). *Mundo Hispanico*, Atlanta, p. 10A.
Cockcroft, J. D. (1986). *Outlaws in the promised land: Mexican immigrant workers and America's future*. New York: Grove Press.
Crawford, J. (1986, February 12). Bennett's plan for bilingual overhaul heats up debate. *Education Week*, p. 1.
Cummins, J. (1981). The role of primary language development in promoting educational success for language minority students. *Schooling and language minority students: A theoretical framework*. Evaluation, Dissemination, and Assessment Center, California State University at Los Angeles.
Cummins, J. (1984). *Bilingualism and special education: Issues in assessment and pedagogy*. San Diego: College Hill Press.
Cummins, J. (1986). Empowering minority students: A framework for intervention. *Harvard Educational Review*, 56, 18–36.
Dixon, M., Martinez, E., & McCaughan, E. (1982, March). *Chicanas and Mexicanas within a transitional working class*. Paper presented at the Chicana History Project and Symposium, University of California at Los Angeles.
Dulles, F. R. (1966). *Labor in America: A history*. Arlington Heights, IL: AHM.
Ekstrand, L. H., Foster, S., Olkiewicz, E., & Stankovski, M. (1981). Interculture: Some concepts for describing the situation of immigrants. *Journal of Multilingual and Multicultural Development*, 2, 269–295.
Gardner, E. (1983). What's wrong with math and science teaching in our schools. *Heritage Today*, 3 (May–June), 6–7.
Georgia General Assembly. (1985). *Georgia State House of Representatives Bill Number 717*.
Gersten, R., & Woodward, J. (1985). A case for structured immersion. *Educational Leadership*, 43, 75–84.
Hakuta, K. (1985, September 27). Generalizations from research in second language acquisition and bilingualism. Testimony presented before the House Education and Labor Committee, Washington, DC.
Hakuta, K. (1986). *Mirror of language: The debate on bilingualism*. New York: Basic Books.
Harrington, M., & Levinson, M. (1985, September). The perils of a dual economy. *Dissent*, pp. 417–426.
Johansen, B., & Maestas, R. (1983). *El Pueblo: The Gallegos family's American journey, 1503 to 1980*. New York: Monthly Review Press.
Kelly, P. (1986, November 19). American bosses have jobs; Mexicans need work. *The Guardian*, New York, p. 11.
Levine, R. A. (1967). *Dreams and needs: Achievement and motivation in Nigeria*. Chicago: University of Chicago Press.

MacEoin, G., & Riley, N. (1982). *No promised land: American refugee policies and the rule of law.* Boston: Oxfam America.

Matthews, J. (1985, November 14). Asian-American students creating a new mainstream. *Washington Post,* p. A1.

Matthews, J. (1986, November 16). Few employers fear new immigration law: Threat of sanctions greeted with a shrug. *Washington Post,* p. A3.

McDermott, R. P. (1976). Achieving school failure: An anthropological approach to illiteracy and social stratification. In H. Singer & R. B. Russel (Eds.), *Theoretical models and processes of reading* (pp. 389–424). Newark, DE: International Reading Association.

Moyers, B. (1985, September). *Whose America is it?* Television documentary aired on CBS.

National Commission on Excellence in Education. (1983). *A nation at risk: The imperative for educational reform.* Washington, DC: U.S. Department of Education.

Navarro, R. (1985). The problems of language education and society: Who decides? In E. Garcia & R. V. Padilla (Eds.), *Advances in bilingual education research* (pp. 289–312). Tucson: University of Arizona Press.

Ogbu, J. U. (1978). *Minority education and caste: The American system in cross-cultural perspective.* New York: Academic Press.

Orum, L. S. (1985, October 31). Secretary Bennett's bilingual education initiative: Historical perspectives and implications. *Perspectivas Publicas,* a newsletter published by the National Council of La Raza, Washington, DC.

Ovando, C., & Collier, V. (1985). *Bilingual and ESL classrooms: Teaching in multicultural contexts.* New York: McGraw-Hill.

Rodríguez, R. (1981). *Hunger of memory: The education of Richard Rodríguez.* Boston: David R. Godine.

Rowan, C. T. (1986, October 7). The real issue Nakasone raised. *Washington Post,* p. A17.

Schumann, J. H. (1976). Second language acquisition: The Pidginization hypothesis. *Language Learning, 26,* 391–408.

Schumann, J. H. (1980). Affective factors and the problem of age in second language acquisition. In K. Croft (Ed.), *Readings on English as a second language* (2nd ed.). Cambridge, MA: Winthrop.

Sennett, R., & Cobb, J. (1972). *Hidden injuries of class.* New York: Random House.

Shor, I. (1986). *Culture wars: School and society in the conservative restoration, 1969–1984.* Boston: Routledge & Kegan Paul.

Skutnabb-Kangas, T. (1979). *Language in the process of cultural assimilation and structural incorporation of linguistic minorities.* Rosslyn, VA: National Clearinghouse for Bilingual Education.

Skutnabb-Kangas, T. (1981). Guest worker or immigrant: Different ways of reproducing an underclass. *Journal of Multilingual and Multicultural Development, 2,* 89–113.

U.S. Department of Education. (1985, November 22). Notice of proposed rule-making for bilingual program implementation and general provisions. *Federal Register, 50* (226), 48352–48370.

U.S. English. (1985). *A kind of discordant harmony: Issues in assimilation* (Pamphlet). Washington, DC: Author.

5

Doing Cultural Studies: Youth and the Challenge of Pedagogy

HENRY A. GIROUX

In this essay, Henry Giroux illustrates how pedagogy, as the production of knowledge, values, and social identities, takes place not only in schools, but in a variety of sites — especially the sphere of popular culture. Elaborating on Donaldo Macedo's critique of "domestication," and David Spener's paralleling analysis of the anti-immigrant sentiments explicit in television images and commentary, Giroux illustrates and analyzes how people are being portrayed and manipulated (what he refers to as "represented," "framed," or "positioned") through the popular media.

Perceiving pedagogy — how and in what contexts we learn — as a configuration of aural, verbal, visual, and written texts (that is, any aspect of reality that encodes meaning), Giroux reveals how the media are not simply expressive but formative in that they work to shape how we are seen, how we see others, and how we interact with one another. He describes how dominant modes of interpretation and expression actively control the ways in which identities are depicted or "represented" in the mainstream. For example, he illustrates how the pedagogy implicit in several Hollywood films about youth culture miseducates by reinforcing dominant racist and cultural stereotypes.

Giroux argues that educators need to fashion alternative analyses that address the representational politics (the struggle over how different groups are portrayed in the media and the public sphere) of popular culture in order to understand what is happening with and to today's youth. He demonstrates how cultural studies provides a new and transformative language for educators to work with youth, helping both teachers and students to identify, understand, and resist the hostile forces that are directed at them. The resulting critical pedagogical strategies work towards developing critical voices that are capable of challenging and transforming the social institutions that legitimate only particular bodies of knowledge and certain cultural portraits.

We recommend that readers not familiar with the debates over "modernity" and "postmodernity" check the glossary under "postmodernism" and "poststructuralism" before reading this chapter.

Note: The first seven pages of the original article are not reprinted here.

> In our society, youth is present only when its presence is a problem, or is regarded as a problem. More precisely, the category "youth" gets mobilized in official documentary discourse, in concerned or outraged editorials and features, or in the supposedly disinterested tracts emanating from the social sciences at those times when young people make their presence felt by going "out of bounds," by resisting through rituals, dressing strangely, striking bizarre attitudes, breaking rules, breaking bottles, windows, heads, issuing rhetorical challenges to the law.[1]

MASS CULTURE AND THE REPRESENTATION OF YOUTH(S)

Youth have once again become the object of public analysis. Headlines proliferate like dispatches from a combat zone, frequently coupling youth and violence in the interests of promoting a new kind of causal relationship. For example, "gangsta rap" artist Snoop Doggy Dogg was featured on the front cover of an issue of *Newsweek*.[2] This message is that young Black men are selling violence to the mainstream public through their music. But according to *Newsweek*, the violence is not just in the music — it is also embodied in the lifestyles of the rappers who produce it. The potential victims in this case are a besieged White majority of male and female youth. Citing a wave of arrests among prominent rappers, the story reinforces the notion that crime is a racially coded word for associating Black youth with violence.[3]

The statistics on youth violence point to social and economic causes that lie far beyond the reach of facile stereotypes. On a national level, U.S. society is witnessing the effects of a culture of violence in which

> close to 12 U.S. children aged 19 and under die from gun fire each day. According to the National Center for Health Statistics, "Firearm homicide is the leading cause of death of African-American teenage boys and the second-leading cause of death of high school age children in the United States."[4]

What is missing from these reports is any critical commentary on underlying causes that produce the representations of violence that saturate the mass media. In addition, there is little mention of the high numbers of infants and children killed every year through "poverty-related malnutrition and disease." Nor is the U.S. public informed in the popular press about "the gruesome toll of the drunk driver who is typically White."[5] But the bad news doesn't end with violence.

The representations of White youth produced by dominant media within recent years have increasingly portrayed them as lazy, sinking into a self-indulgent haze, and oblivious to the middle-class ethic of working hard and getting ahead. Of course, what the dominant media do not talk about are the social conditions that are producing a new generation of youth steeped in despair, violence, crime, poverty, and apathy. For instance, to talk about Black crime without mentioning that the unemployment rate for Black youth exceeds 40 percent in many urban cities serves primarily to conceal a major cause of youth unrest. Or to talk about apathy among White youth without analyzing the junk culture, poverty, social disenfranchisement, drugs, lack of educational opportunity, and **commodification**[a] that shape daily life removes responsibility from a social system that often sees youth as simply another market niche.

A failing economy that offers most youth the limited promise of service-sector jobs, dim prospects for the future, and a world of infinite messages and images designed to sell a product or to peddle senseless violence as another TV spectacle, constitutes, in part, the new conditions of youth. In light of radically altered social and economic conditions, educators need to fashion alternative analyses in order to understand what is happening to our nation's youth. Such a project seems vital in light of the rapidity in which market values and a commercial public culture have replaced the ethical referents for developing democratic **public spheres.**[b] For example, since the 1970s, millions of jobs have been lost to capital flight, and technological change has wiped out millions more. In the last twenty years alone, the U.S. economy lost more than five million jobs in the manufacturing sector.[6] In the face of extremely limited prospects for economic growth over the next decade, schools will be faced with an identity crisis regarding the traditional assumption that school credentials provide the best route to economic security and class mobility for a large proportion of our nation's youth. As Stanley Aronowitz and I have pointed out elsewhere:

---

[a] **Commodification** refers to the process by which culture is increasingly being held captive by the materialistic logic of capitalism in which everything and everybody are reduced to objects or commodities and thus to their market value. The consequence of this process is that people become uncritical tools of production and consumption — *commodified*. In this sense, schools function merely as adjuncts to corporations and the marketplace.

[b] **Public spheres** in the critical sense are public arenas for citizens in which political participation, outside of direct government and economic influence and intervention, is enacted through dialogue and debate. Schools are envisioned by critical pedagogues as "public spheres," wherein classrooms are active sites of public intervention and social struggle, rather than mere adjuncts of corporate and partisan interests. Because mainstream society is constituted by particular oppressive ideologies, these critical spheres are also referred to as "counterpublics."

The labor market is becoming increasingly bifurcated: organizational and technical changes are producing a limited number of jobs for highly educated and trained people-managers, scientific and technological experts, and researchers. On the other hand, we are witnessing the disappearance of many middle-level white collar subprofessions. . . . And in the face of sharpening competition, employers typically hire a growing number of low paid, part-time workers. . . . Even some professionals have become freelance workers with few, if any, fringe benefits. These developments call into question the efficacy of mass schooling for providing the "well-trained" labor force that employers still claim they require.[7]

In light of these shattering shifts in economic and cultural life, it makes more sense for educators to reexamine the mission of the school and the changing conditions of youth rather than blaming youth for the economic slump, the culture of racially coded violence, or the hopelessness that seems endemic to dominant versions of the future.

But rethinking the conditions of youth is also imperative in order to reverse the mean-spirited discourse of the 1980s, a discourse that has turned its back on the victims of U.S. society and has resorted to both blaming and punishing them for their social and economic problems. This is evident in states such as Michigan and Wisconsin, which subscribe to "Learnfare" programs designed to penalize a single mother with a lower food allowance if her kids are absent from school. In other states, welfare payments are reduced if single mothers do not marry. Micky Kaus, an editor at the *New Republic,* argues that welfare mothers should be forced to work at menial jobs, and if they refuse, Kaus suggests that the state remove their children from them. Illiterate women, Kaus argues, could work raking leaves.[8] There is an indifference and callousness in this kind of language that now spills over to discussions of youth. Instead of focusing on economic and social conditions that provide the nation's youth, especially those who are poor and live on the margins of hope, with food, shelter, access to decent education, and safe environments, conservatives such as former Secretary of Education William Bennett talk about imposing national standards on public schools, creating voucher systems that benefit middle-class parents, and doing away with the concept of "the public" altogether. There is more at work here than simply ignorance and neglect.

It is in the dominant **discourse**[c] on values that one gets a glimpse of the pedagogy at work in the culture of mean-spiritedness. Bennett, for instance,

---

[c] A **discourse** represents the ways in which reality is perceived through and shaped by historically and socially constructed ways of making sense; that is, language, complex signs, and practices that order and sustain particular forms of social existence. These systems of communication, which are constructions informed by particular ideologies, play a significant role in shaping human subjectivities and social reality, and can work to either confirm or deny the life histories and experiences of the people who use them. If the rules that govern what is acceptable in a particular society are exclusive, discourse can be a major site of contention in which different groups struggle over meaning and ideology.

in his new book, *The Book of Virtues: A Treasury of Great Moral Stories,* finds hope in "Old Mr. Rabbit's Thanksgiving Dinner" in which the rabbit instructs us that there is more joy in being helpful than being helped. This discourse of moral uplift may provide soothing and inspirational help for children whose parents send them to private schools, establish trust-fund annuities for their future, and connect them to the world of political patronage, but it says almost nothing about the culture of compressed and concentrated human suffering that many children have to deal with daily in this country. In part, this can be glimpsed in the fact that over seventy percent of all welfare recipients are children. In what follows, I want to draw from a number of insights provided by the field of cultural studies to chart out a different cartography that might be helpful for educators to address what might be called the changing conditions of youth.

FRAMING YOUTH

The instability and transitoriness characteristically widespread among a diverse generation of 18- to 25-year-old youth is inextricably rooted in a larger set of **postmodern cultural conditions**[d] informed by the following: a general loss of faith in the modernist narratives of work and emancipation; the recognition that the indeterminacy of the future warrants confronting and living in the immediacy of experience; an acknowledgment that homelessness as a condition of randomness has replaced the security, if not misrepresentation, of home as a source of comfort and security; an experience of time and space as compressed and fragmented within a world of images that increasingly undermine the **dialectic**[e] of authenticity and universalism. For many youth, plurality and contingency — whether mediated through media culture, or through the dislocations spurned by the economic system, the rise of new social movements, or the crisis of representation and authority — have resulted in a world with few secure psychological, economic, or intellectual markers. This is a world in which one is condemned to wander within and between multiple borders and spaces marked by excess, **other-**

---

[d] Theorists of postmodernity claim that new technologies and changes in the socioeconomic system are responsible, in part, for new social formations (**postmodern cultural conditions**). French theorist Jean Baudrillard, for example, has argued that we are facing "a new era of simulation in which computerization, information processing, media, cybernetic control systems, and the organization of society according to simulation codes and models replace production as the organizing principle of society. If modernity is the era of production controlled by the industrial bourgeoisie, the postmodern era of simulations by contrast is an era of information and signs governed by models, codes, and cybernetics." (Best & Kellner, 1991)

[e] While there are a number of definitions and interpretations of **dialectics**, for the general purposes of critical pedagogy, this concept refers to the interconnecting and contradicting relationships that constitute a particular phenomenon, for example, among the economic, political, social, and cultural dimensions of society. A dialectical analysis is also often used to show how every idea or force has its opposite/contradiction. For example, the dialectic of "oppressor" is the reality of the "oppressed." Such an analysis holds both "opposing" concepts together at once to see how they interconnect and play off each other.

ness,[f] and difference. This is a world in which old certainties are ruptured and meaning becomes more contingent, less indebted to the dictates of reverence and established truth. While the circumstances of youth vary across and within terrains marked by racial and class differences, the modernist world of certainty and order that has traditionally policed, contained, and insulated such difference has given way to a shared postmodern culture in which representational borders collapse into new hybridized forms of cultural performance, identity, and political agency. As the information highway and MTV condense time and space into what Paul Virilio calls "speed space," new desires, modes of association, and forms of resistance inscribe themselves into diverse spheres of popular culture.[9] Music, rap, fashion, style, talk, politics, and cultural resistance are no longer confined to their original class and racial locations. Middle-class White kids take up the language of gangsta rap spawned in neighborhood turfs far removed from their own lives. Black youth in urban centers produce a bricolage of style fashioned from a combination of sneakers, baseball caps, and oversized clothing that integrates forms of resistance and style later to be appropriated by suburban kids whose desires and identities resonate with the energy and vibrancy of the new urban funk. Music displaces older forms of textuality and references a terrain of cultural production that marks the body as a site of pleasure, resistance, domination, and danger.[10] Within this postmodern culture of youth, identities merge and shift rather than become more uniform and static. No longer belonging to any one place or location, youth increasingly inhabit shifting cultural and social spheres marked by a plurality of languages and cultures.

Communities have been refigured as space and time mutate into multiple and overlapping cyberspace networks. Bohemian and middle-class youth talk to each other over electronic bulletin boards in coffee houses in North Beach, California. Cafes and other public salons, once the refuge of beatniks, hippies, and other cultural radicals, have given way to members of the hacker culture. They reorder their imaginations through connections to virtual reality technologies and produce forms of exchange through texts and images that have the potential to wage a war on traditional meaning, but also run the risk of reducing critical understanding to the endless play of random access spectacles.

This is not meant to endorse a **Frankfurt School**[g] dismissal of popular culture in the postmodern age.[11] On the contrary, I believe that the new

---

[f] In a society in which the dominant referent for defining "difference" is based on White, middle-class, heterosexual male characteristics, **otherness** refers to anybody that is considered outside of or at odds with this prevailing paradigm. In the literature, one often finds the use of the term "decentering." This refers to an attempt to rupture the undemocratic hierarchy (or centrality) of the dominant beliefs, values, and practices.

[g] This German institute of social research, frequented by the likes of Marcuse, Fromm, Horkheimer, Adorno, Habermas, Arendt, Brecht, Lukacs, and a great many others, had an enormous impact on the sociological, political, and cultural thought of this century. It was in this institute that the term "critical theory" and its ideas evolved.

electronic technologies with their proliferation of multiple stories and open-ended forms of interaction have altered not only the pedagogical context for the production of subjectivities, but also how people "take in information and entertainment."[12] Produced from the centers of power, mass culture has spawned in the name of profit and entertainment a new level of instrumental and commodified culture. On the other hand, popular culture offers resistance to the notion that useful culture can only be produced within dominant regimes of power. This distinction between mass and popular culture is not meant to suggest that popular culture is strictly a terrain of resistance. Popular culture does not escape commodification, racism, sexism, and other forms of oppression, but it is marked by fault lines that reject the high/low culture divide while simultaneously attempting to affirm a multitude of histories, experiences, cultural forms, and pleasures. Within the conditions of postmodern culture, values no longer emerge unproblematically from the modernist pedagogy of foundationalism and universal truths, or from traditional narratives based on fixed identities with their requisite structure of closure. For many youths, meaning is in rout, media has become a substitute for experience, and what constitutes understanding is grounded in a decentered and diasporic world of difference, displacement, and exchanges.

The intersection among cultural studies and pedagogy can be made more clear through an analysis of how the pedagogy of Hollywood has attempted in some recent films to portray the plight of young people within the conditions of a postmodern culture. I will focus on four films: *River's Edge* (1986), *My Own Private Idaho* (1991), *Slacker* (1991), and *Juice* (1992). These films are important as arguments and framing devices that in diverse ways attempt to provide a pedagogical representation of youth. They point to some of the economic and social conditions at work in the formation of different racial and economic strata of youth, but they often do so within a narrative that combines a politics of despair with a fairly sophisticated depiction of the alleged sensibilities and moods of a generation of youth growing up amid the fracturing and menacing conditions of a postmodern culture. The challenge for progressive educators is to question how a critical pedagogy might be employed to appropriate the more radical and useful aspects of cultural studies in addressing the new and different social, political, and economic contexts that are producing the twenty-something generation. At the same time, there is the issue of how a politics and project of pedagogy might be constructed to create the conditions for social agency and institutionalized change among diverse sectors of youth.

WHITE YOUTH AND THE POLITICS OF DESPAIR

For many youth, showing up for adulthood at the fin de siècle means pulling back on hope and trying to put off the future rather than taking up the modernist challenge of trying to shape it.[13] Popular cultural criticism has captured much of the ennui among youth and has made clear that "what used to be the pessimism of a radical fringe is now the shared assumption of a generation."[14] Cultural studies has helped to temper this broad generalization about youth in order to investigate the more complex representations at work in the construction of a new generation of youth that cannot be simply abstracted from the specificities of race, class, or gender. And yet, cultural studies theorists have also pointed to the increasing resistance of a twenty-something generation of youth who seem neither motivated by nostalgia for some lost conservative vision of America nor at home in the New World Order paved with the promises of the expanding electronic information highway.[15] While "youth" as a social construction has always been mediated, in part, as a social problem, many cultural critics believe that postmodern youth are uniquely "alien," "strange," and disconnected from the real world. For instance, in Gus Van Sant's film *My Own Private Idaho,* the main character, Mike, who hustles his sexual wares for money, is a dreamer lost in fractured memories of a mother who deserted him as a child. Caught between flashbacks of Mom, shown in 8-mm color, and the video world of motley street hustlers and their clients, Mike moves through his existence by falling asleep in times of stress only to awaken in different geographic and spatial locations. What holds Mike's psychic and geographic travels together is the metaphor of sleep, the dream of escape, and the ultimate realization that even memories cannot fuel hope for the future. Mike becomes a metaphor for an entire generation of lower middle-class youth forced to sell themselves in a world with no hope, a generation that aspires to nothing, works at degrading McJobs, and lives in a world in which chance and randomness rather than struggle, community, and solidarity drive their fate.

A more disturbing picture of White, working-class youth can be found in *River's Edge.* Teenage anomie and drugged apathy are given painful expression in the depiction of a group of working-class youth who are casually told by John, one of their friends, that he has strangled his girlfriend, another member of the group, and left her nude body on the riverbank. The group at different times visits the site to view and probe the dead body of the girl. Seemingly unable to grasp the significance of the event, the youth initially hold off from informing anyone of the murder and with different degrees of concern initially try to protect John, the teenage sociopath, from being caught by the police. The youth in *River's Edge* drift through a world of broken families, blaring rock music, schooling marked by dead time, and a general indifference. Decentered and fragmented, they view death, like life itself, as merely a spectacle, a matter of style rather than substance. In one sense, these youth share the quality of being "asleep" that is depicted in *My Own Private Idaho.* But what is more disturbing in *River's Edge* is that lost innocence gives way not merely to teenage myopia, but also to a culture in which human life is experienced as a voyeuristic seduction, a video game, good for passing time and diverting oneself from the pain of the moment. Despair and indifference cancel out the language of ethical discriminations and social responsibility while elevating the immediacy of pleasure to the defining moment of agency. In *River's Edge,* history as social memory is reassembled through vignettes of 1960s types portrayed as either burned-out bikers or as the ex-radical turned teacher whose moralizing relegates politics to simply cheap opportunism. Exchanges among the young people in *River's Edge* appear like projections of a generation waiting either to fall asleep or to commit suicide. After talking about how he murdered his girlfriend, John blurts out, "You do shit, it's done, and then you die." Another character responds, "It might be easier being dead." To which her boyfriend replies, "Bullshit, you couldn't get stoned anymore." In this scenario, life imitates art when committing murder and getting stoned are given equal moral weight in the formula of the Hollywood spectacle, a spectacle that in the end flattens the complex representations of youth while constructing their identities through ample servings of pleasure, death, and violence.

River's Edge and *My Own Private Idaho* reveal the seamy and dark side of a youth culture while employing the Hollywood mixture of fascination and horror to titillate the audiences drawn to these films. Employing the postmodern aesthetic of revulsion, locality, randomness, and senselessness, the youth in these films appear to be constructed outside of a broader cultural and economic landscape. Instead, they become visible only through visceral expressions of psychotic behavior or the brooding experience of a self-imposed comatose alienation.

One of the more celebrated White youth films of the 1990s is Richard Linklater's *Slacker.* A decidedly low-budget film, *Slacker* attempts in both form and content to capture the sentiments of a twenty-something generation of middle-class White youth who reject most of the values of the Reagan/Bush era but have a difficult time imagining what an alternative might look like. Distinctly non-linear in format, *Slacker* takes place in a twenty-four-hour time frame in the college town of Austin, Texas. Building upon an anti-narrative structure, *Slacker* is loosely organized around brief episodes in the lives of a variety of characters, none of whom are connected to each other except to provide the pretext to lead the audience to the next character in the film. Sweeping through bookstores, coffee shops, auto-parts yards, bedrooms, and rock music clubs, *Slacker* focuses on a disparate group of young people who possess little hope in the future and drift from job to job speaking a hybrid argot of bohemian intensities and New Age pop-cult babble.

The film portrays a host of young people who randomly move from one place to the next, border crossers with little, if any, sense of where they have come from or where they are going. In this world of multiple realities, youth work in bands with the name "Ultimate Loser" and talk about being forcibly put in hospitals by their parents. One neo-punker even attempts to sell a Madonna pap smear to two acquaintances she meets in the street: "Check it out, I know it's kind of disgusting, but it's like sort of getting down to the real Madonna." This is a world in which language is wedded to an odd mix of nostalgia, popcorn philosophy, and MTV babble. Talk is organized around comments like: "I don't know . . . I've traveled . . . and when you get back you can't tell whether it really happened to you or if you just saw it on TV." Alienation is driven inward and emerges in comments like "I feel stuck." Irony slightly overshadows a refusal to imagine any kind of collective struggle. Reality seems too despairing to care about. This is humorously captured in one instance by a young man who suggests: "You know how the slogan goes, workers of the world, unite? We say workers of the world, relax?" People talk, but appear disconnected from themselves and each other; lives traverse each other with no sense of community or connection. There is a pronounced sense in *Slacker* of youth caught in the throes of new information technologies that both contain their aspirations and at the same time hold out the promise of some sense of agency.

At rare moments in the films, the political paralysis of narcissistic forms of refusal is offset by instances in which some characters recognize the importance of the image as a vehicle for cultural production, as a representational apparatus that can not only make certain experiences available but can also be used to produce alternative realities and social practices. The power of the image is present in the way the camera follows characters throughout the film, at once stalking them and confining them to a gaze that is both constraining and incidental. In one scene, a young man appears in a video apartment surrounded by televisions that he claims he has had on for years. He points out that he has invented a game called a "Video Virus" in which, through the use of a special technology, he can push a button and insert himself onto any screen and perform any one of a number of actions. When asked by another character what this is about, he answers: "Well, we all know the psychic powers of the televised image. But we need to capitalize on it and make it work for us instead of working for it." This theme is taken up in two other scenes. In one short clip, a graduate history student shoots the video camera he is using to film himself, indicating a self-consciousness about the power of the image and the ability to control it at the same time. In the concluding scene, a carload of people, each equipped with a Super 8 camera, drive up to a large hill and throw their cameras into a canyon. The film ends with the images being recorded by the cameras as they cascade to the bottom of the cliff in what suggests a moment of release and liberation.

In many respects, these movies largely focus on a culture of White male youth who are both terrified and fascinated by the media, who appear overwhelmed by "the danger and wonder of future technologies, the banality of consumption, the thrill of brand names, [and] the difficulty of sex in alienated relationships."[16] The significance of these films rests, in part, in their attempt to capture the sense of powerlessness that increasingly affects working-class and middle-class White youth. But what is missing from these films, along with the various books, articles, and reportage concerning what is often called the "Nowhere Generation," "Generation X," "13thGen," or "Slackers," is any sense of the larger political, racial, and social conditions in which youth are being framed, as well as the multiple forms of resistance and racial diversity that exist among many different youth formations. What in fact should be seen as a social commentary about "dead-end capitalism" emerges simply as a celebration of refusal dressed up in a rhetoric of aesthetics, style, fashion, and solipsistic protests. Within this type of commentary, postmodern criticism is useful but limited because of its often theoretical inability to take up the relationship between identity and power, biography and the commodification of everyday life, or the limits of agency in an increasingly globalized economy as part of a broader project of possibility linked to issues of history, struggle, and transformation.[17]

In spite of the totalizing image of domination that structures *River's Edge* and *My Own Private Idaho,* and the lethal hopelessness that permeates *Slacker,* all of these films provide opportunities for examining the social and cultural context to which they refer in order to enlarge the range of strategies and understandings that students might bring to them to create a sense of resistance and transformation. For instance, many of my students who viewed *Slacker* did not despair over the film, but interpreted it to mean that "going slack" was viewed as a moment in the lives of young people that, with the proper resources, offered them a period in which to think, move around the country, and chill out in order to make some important decisions about their lives. Going slack became increasingly more oppressive as the slack time became drawn out far beyond their ability to end or control it. The students also pointed out that this film was made by Linklater and his friends with a great deal of energy and gusto, which in itself offers a pedagogical model for young people to take up in developing their own narratives.

BLACK YOUTH AND THE VIOLENCE OF RACE

With the explosion of rap music into the sphere of popular culture and the intense debates that have emerged around the crisis of Black masculinity, the issue of Black nationalism, and the politics of Black urban culture, it is not surprising that the Black cinema has produced a series of films about the coming of age of Black youth in urban America. What is unique about these films is that, unlike the Black exploitation films of the 1970s, which were made by White producers for Black audiences, the new wave of Black cinema is being produced by Black directors and aimed at Black audiences.[18] With the advent of the 1990s, Hollywood has cashed in on a number of talented young Black directors such as Spike Lee, Allen and Albert Hughes, Julie Dash, Ernest Dickerson, and John Singleton. Films about Black youth have become big business — in 1991 *New Jack City* and *Boyz N the Hood* pulled in over 100 million dollars between them. Largely concerned with the inequalities, oppression, daily violence, and diminishing hopes that plague Black communities in the urban war zone, the new wave of Black films has attempted to accentuate the economic and social conditions that have contributed to the construction of "Black masculinity and its relationship to the ghetto culture in which ideals of masculinity are nurtured and shaped."[19]

Unlike many of the recent films about White youth whose coming-of-age narratives are developed within traditional sociological categories such as alienation, restlessness, and anomie, Black film productions such as Ernest Dickerson's *Juice* (1992) depict a culture of nihilism that is rooted directly in a violence whose defining principles are homicide, cultural suicide, internecine warfare, and social decay. It is interesting to note that just as the popular press has racialized crime, drugs, and violence as a Black problem, some of the most interesting films to appear recently about Black youth have been given the Hollywood imprimatur of excellence and have moved successfully as crossover films to a White audience. In what follows, I want briefly to probe the treatment of Black youth and the representations of masculinity and resistance in the exemplary Black film, *Juice*.

Juice (street slang for respect) is the story of four young Harlem African American youth who are first portrayed as kids who engage in the usual antics of skipping school, fighting with other kids in the neighborhood, clashing with their parents about doing homework, and arguing with their siblings over using the bathroom in the morning. If this portrayal of youthful innocence is used to get a general audience to comfortably identify with these four Black youth, it is soon ruptured as the group, caught in a spiraling wave of poverty and depressed opportunities, turn to crime and violence as a way to both construct their manhood and solve their most immediate problems. Determined to give their lives some sense of agency, the group moves from ripping off a record store to burglarizing a grocery market to the ruthless murder of the store owner and eventually each other. Caught in a world in which the ethics of the street are mirrored in the spectacle of TV violence, Bishop, Quincy, Raheem, and Steel (Tupac Shakur, Omar Epps, Kahalil Kain, and Jermaine Hopkins) decided, after watching James Cagney go up in a blaze of glory in *White Heat,* to take control of their lives by buying a gun and sticking up a neighborhood merchant who once chased them out of his store. Quincy is hesitant about participating in the stick-up because he is a talented disc jockey and is determined to enter a local deejay contest in order to take advantage of his love of rap music and find a place for himself in the world.

Quincy is the only Black youth in the film who models a sense of agency that is not completely caught in the confusion and despair exhibited by his three friends. Trapped within the loyalty codes of the street and in the protection it provides, Quincy reluctantly agrees to participate in the heist. Bad choices have major consequences in this typical big-city ghetto, and Quincy's sense of hope and independence is shattered as Bishop, the most violent of the group, kills the store owner and then proceeds to murder Raheem and hunt down Quincy and Steele, since they no longer see him as a respected member of the group. Quincy eventually buys a weapon to protect himself, and in the film's final scene, confronts Bishop on the roof. A struggle ensues, and Bishop plunges to his death. As the film ends, one onlooker tells Quincy,

"You got the juice," but Quincy rejects the accolade ascribing power and prestige to him and walks away.

Juice reasserts the importance of rap music as the cultural expression of imaginable possibilities in the daily lives of Black youth. Not only does rap music provide the musical score that frames the film, it also plays a pivotal role by socially contextualizing the desires, rage, and independent expression of Black male artists. For Quincy, rap music offers him the opportunity to claim some "juice" among his peers while simultaneously providing him with a context to construct an affirmative identity along with the chance for real employment. Music in this context becomes a major referent for understanding how identities and bodies come together in a hip-hop culture that at its most oppositional moment is testing the limits of the American dream. But *Juice* also gestures, through the direction of Ernest Dickerson, that if violence is endemic to the Black ghetto, its roots lie in a culture of violence that is daily transmitted through the medium of television. This is suggested in one powerful scene in which the group watch on television both the famed violent ending of James Cagney's *White Heat,* and the news bulletin announcing the death of a neighborhood friend as he attempted to rip off a local bar. In this scene, Dickerson draws a powerful relationship between what the four youth see on television and their impatience over their own lack of agency and need to take control of their lives. As Michael Dyson points out:

> Dickerson's aim is transparent: to highlight the link between violence and criminality fostered in the collective American imagination by television, the consumption of images through a medium that has replaced the Constitution and the Declaration of Independence as the unifying fiction of national citizenship and identity. It is also the daily and exclusive occupation of Bishop's listless father, a reminder that television's genealogy of influence unfolds from its dulling effects in one generation to its creation of lethal desires in the next, twin strategies of destruction when applied in the black male ghetto.[20]

While Dyson is right in pointing to Dickerson's critique of the media, he overestimates the importance given in *Juice* to the relationship between Black-on-Black violence and those larger social determinants that Black urban life both reflects and helps to produce. In fact, it could be argued that the violence portrayed in *Juice* and similar films, such as *Boyz N the Hood, New Jack City,* and especially *Menace II Society,* "feeds the racist national obsession that Black men and their community are the central locus of the American scene of violence."[21]

Although the violence in these films is traumatizing as part of the effort to promote an anti-violence message, it is also a violence that is hermetic, sutured, and sealed within the walls of the Black urban ghetto. While the counterpart of this type of violence, in controversial White films such as *Reservoir Dogs* is taken up by most critics as part of an avant garde aesthetic, the violence in the recent wave of Black youth films often reinforces for middle-class viewers the assumption that such violence is endemic to the Black community. The only salvation gained in portraying such inner-city hopelessness is that it be noticed so that it can be stopped from spreading like a disease into the adjoining suburbs and business zones that form a colonizing ring around Black ghettoes. Because films such as *Juice* do not self-consciously rupture dominant stereotypical assumptions that make race and crime synonymous, they often suggest a kind of nihilism that Cornel West describes as "the lived experience of coping with a life of horrifying meaninglessness, hopelessness and (most important) lovelessness."[22]

Unfortunately, West's notion of nihilism is too tightly drawn and while it may claim to pay sufficient attention to the loss of hope and meaning among Black youth, it fails to connect the specificity of Black nihilism to the nihilism of systemic inequality, calculated injustice, and moral indifference that operates daily as a regime of brutalization and oppression for so many poor youth and youth of color in this country. Itabari Njeri forcefully captures the failure of such an analysis and the problems that films such as *Juice*, in spite of the best intentions of their directors, often reproduce. Commenting on another coming-of-age Black youth film, *Menace II Society*, he writes:

> The nation cannot allow nearly 50% of black men to be unemployed, as is the case in many African American communities. It cannot let schools systematically brand normal black children as uneducable for racist reasons, or permit the continued brutalization of blacks by police, or have black adults take out their socially engendered frustrations on each other and their children and not yield despair and dysfunction. This kind of despair is the source of the nihilism Cornel West described. Unfortunately, the black male-as-menace film genre often fails to artfully tie this nihilism to its poisonous roots in America's system of inequality. And because it fails to do so, the effects of these toxic forces are seen as causes.[23]

In both pedagogical and political terms, the reigning films about Black youth that have appeared since 1990 may have gone too far in producing narratives that employ the commercial strategy of reproducing graphic violence and then moralizing about its effects. Violence in these films is tied to a self-destructiveness and senselessness that shocks but often fails to inform the audience about either its wider determinations or the audience's possible complicity in such violence. The effects of such films tend to reinforce for White middle-class America the comforting belief that nihilism as both a state of mind and a site of social relations is always somewhere else — in that strangely homogenized social formation known as "Black" youth.

Of course, it is important to note that *Juice* refrains from romanticizing violence, just as it suggests at the end of the film that Quincy does not want the juice if it means leading a life in which violence is the only capital that has any exchange value in African American communities. But these sentiments come late and are too underdeveloped. One pedagogical challenge presented by this film is for educators and students to theorize about why Hollywood is investing in films about Black youth that overlook the complex representations that structure African American communities. Such an inquiry can be taken up by looking at the work of Black feminist film makers such as Julie Dash, and the powerful and complex representations she offers Black women in *Daughters of the Dust,* or the work of Leslie Harris, whose film *Just Another Girl on the IRT* challenges the misogyny that structures the films currently being made about Black male youth. Another challenge involves trying to understand why large numbers of Black, urban, male youth readily identify with the wider social representations of sexism, homophobia, misogyny, and gaining respect at such a high cost to themselves and the communities in which they live. Films about Black youth are important to engage in order to understand both the pedagogies that silently structure their representations and how such representations pedagogically work to educate crossover White audiences. Most importantly, these films should not be dismissed because they are reductionist, sexist, or one dimensional in their portrayal of the rite of passage of Black male youth; at most, they become a marker for understanding how complex representations of Black youth get lost in racially coded films that point to serious problems in the urban centers, but do so in ways that erase any sense of viable hope, possibility, resistance, and struggle.

Contemporary films about Black youth offer a glimpse into the specificity of otherness; that is, they cross a cultural and racial border and in doing so perform a theoretical service in making visible what is often left out of the dominant politics of representations. And it is in the light of such an opening that the possibility exists for educators and other **cultural workers**[h] to take up the relationship among culture, power, and identity in ways that grapple with the complexity of youth and the intersection of race, class, and gender formations.

Combining cultural studies with pedagogical theory would suggest that students take these films seriously as legitimate forms of social knowledge that reveal different sets of struggles among youth within diverse cultural sites. For White youth, these films mimic a coming-of-age narrative that indicts the aimlessness and senselessness produced within a larger culture of commercial stupification; on the other hand, Black youth films posit a *not* coming-of-age narrative that serves as a powerful indictment of the violence being waged against and among African American youth. Clearly, educators can learn from these films and in doing so bring these different accounts of

---

[h] A **cultural worker** ("transformative intellectual" or "public intellectual"), in the best light, is an educator who critically engages learning (wherever it may take place) with the goal of working pedagogically and politically to ensure the development of a critical, multicultural democracy. However, in the negative sense, public figures, such as talk show hosts or movie directors, are also cultural workers in that their interpretations, by distorting the ways in which identities are depicted or "represented" in the mainstream, can shape the ways in which different cultural groups interact.

the cultural production of youth together within a common project that addresses the relationship between pedagogy and social justice, on the one hand, and democracy and the struggle for equality on the other. These films suggest that educators need to ask new questions, and develop new models and new ways of producing an oppositional pedagogy that is capable of understanding the different social, economic, and political contexts that produce youth differently within varied sets and relations of power.

Another pedagogical challenge offered by these films concerns how teachers can address the desires that different students bring to these popular cultural texts. In other words, what does it mean to mobilize the desires of students by using forms of social knowledge that constitute the contradictory field of popular culture? In part, it means recognizing that while students are familiar with such texts, they bring different beliefs, political understandings, and affective investments to such a learning process. Hence, pedagogy must proceed by acknowledging that conflict will emerge regarding the form and content of such films and how students address such issues. For such a pedagogy to work, Fabienne Worth argues that "students must become visible to themselves and to each other and valued in their differences."[24] This suggests giving students the opportunity to decenter the curriculum by structuring, in part, how the class should be organized and how such films can be addressed without putting any one student's identity on trial. It means recognizing the complexity of attempting to mobilize students' desires as part of a pedagogical project that directly addresses representations that affect certain parts of their lives, and to acknowledge the emotional problems that will emerge in such teaching.

At the same time, such a pedagogy must reverse the cycle of despair that often informs these accounts and address how the different postmodern conditions and contexts of youth can be changed in order to expand and deepen the promise of a substantive democracy. In part, this may mean using films about youth that capture the complexity, sense of struggle, and diversity that marks different segments of the current generation of young people. In this case, cultural studies and pedagogical practice can mutually inform each other by using popular cultural texts as serious objects of study. Such texts can be used to address the limits and possibilities that youth face in different social, cultural, and economic contexts. Equally important is the need to read popular cultural texts as part of a broader pedagogical effort to develop a sense of agency in students based on a commitment to changing oppressive contexts by understanding the relations of power that inform them.

The pedagogical challenge represented by the emergence of a postmodern generation of youth has not been lost on advertisers and market research analysts. According to a 1992 study by the Roper Organization, the current generation of 18- to 29-year-olds have an annual buying power of $125 billion. Addressing the interests and tastes of this generation, "McDonald's, for instance, has introduced hip-hop music and images to promote burgers and fries, ditto Coca-Cola, with its frenetic commercials touting Coca-Cola Classic."[25] Benetton, Esprit, The Gap, and other companies have followed suit in their attempts to identify and mobilize the desires, identities, and buying patterns of a new generation of youth.[26] What appears as a despairing expression of the postmodern condition to some theorists becomes for others a challenge to invent new market strategies for corporate interests. In this scenario, youth may be experiencing the indeterminacy, senselessness, and multiple conditions of postmodernism, but corporate advertisers are attempting to theorize a pedagogy of consumption as part of a new way of appropriating postmodern differences among youth in different sites and locations. The lesson here is that differences among youth matter politically and pedagogically, but not as a way of generating new markets or registering difference simply as a fashion niche.

What educators need to do is to make the pedagogical more political by addressing both the conditions through which they teach and what it means to learn from a generation that is experiencing life in a way that is vastly different from the representations offered in modernist versions of schooling. This is not to suggest that modernist schools do not attend to popular culture, but they do so on very problematic terms, which often confine it to the margins of the curriculum. Moreover, modernist schools cannot be rejected outright. As I have shown elsewhere, the political culture of modernism, with its emphasis on social equality, justice, freedom, and human agency, needs to be refigured within rather than outside of an emerging postmodern discourse.[27]

The emergence of the electronic media coupled with a diminishing faith in the power of human agency has undermined the traditional visions of schooling and the meaning of pedagogy. The language of lesson plans and upward mobility and the forms of teacher authority on which it was based has been radically delegitimated by the recognition that culture and power are central to the authority/knowledge relationship. Modernism's faith in the past has given way to a future for which traditional markers no longer make sense.

CULTURAL STUDIES AND YOUTH:
THE PEDAGOGICAL ISSUE

Educators and cultural critics need to address the effects of emerging postmodern conditions on a current generation of young people who appear hostage to the vicissitudes of a changing economic order, with its legacy of diminished hopes on the one hand, and a world of schizoid images, proliferating public spaces, and an increasing fragmentation, uncertainty, and randomness that structures postmodern daily life on the other. Central to this issue is whether educators are dealing with a new kind of student forged within organizing principles shaped by the intersection of the electronic image, popular culture, and a dire sense of indeterminacy.

What cultural studies offers educators is a theoretical framework for addressing the shifting attitudes, representations, and desires of this new generation of youth being produced within the current historical, economic, and cultural juncture. But it does more than simply provide a lens for resituating the construction of youth within a shifting and radically altered social, technological, and economic landscape: it also provides elements for rethinking the relationship between culture and power, knowledge and authority, learning and experience, and the role of teachers as public intellectuals. In what follows, I want to point to some of the theoretical elements that link cultural studies and critical pedagogy and speak briefly to their implications for cultural work.

First, cultural studies is premised on the belief that we have entered a period in which the traditional distinctions that separate and frame established academic disciplines cannot account for the great diversity of cultural and social phenomena that has come to characterize an increasingly hybridized, post-industrial world. The university has long been linked to a notion of national identity that is largely defined by and committed to transmitting traditional Western culture.[28] Traditionally, this has been a culture of exclusion, one that has ignored the multiple narratives, histories, and voices of culturally and politically subordinated groups. The emerging proliferation of diverse social movements arguing for a genuinely multicultural and multiracial society have challenged schools that use academic knowledge to license cultural differences in order to regulate and define who they are and how they might narrate themselves. Moreover, the spread of electronically mediated culture to all spheres of everyday intellectual and artistic life has shifted the ground of scholarship away from the traditional disciplines designed to preserve a "common culture" to the more hybridized fields of comparative and world literature, media studies, ecology, society and technology, and popular culture.

Second, advocates of cultural studies have argued strongly that the role of culture, including the power of the mass media with its massive apparatuses of representation and its regulation of meaning, is central to understanding how the dynamics of power, privilege, and social desire structure the daily life of a society.[29] This concern with culture and its connection to power has necessitated a critical interrogation of the relationship between knowledge and authority, the meaning of canonicity, and the historical and social contexts that deliberately shape students' understanding of accounts of the past, present, and future. But if a sea change in the development and reception of what counts as knowledge has taken place, it has been accompanied by an understanding of how we define and apprehend the range of texts that are open to critical interrogation and analysis. For instance, instead of connecting culture exclusively to the technology of print and the book as the only legitimate academic artifact, there is a great deal of academic work going on that analyzes how textual, aural, and visual representations are produced, organized, and distributed through a variety of cultural forms such as the media, popular culture, film, advertising, mass communications, and other modes of cultural production.[30]

At stake here is the attempt to produce new theoretical models and methodologies for addressing the production, structure, and exchange of knowledge. This approach to inter/post-disciplinary studies is valuable because it addresses the pedagogical issue of organizing dialogue across and outside of the disciplines in order to promote alternative approaches to research and teaching about culture and the newly emerging technologies and forms of knowledge. For instance, rather than organize courses around strictly disciplinary concerns arising out of English and social studies courses, it might be more useful and relevant for colleges of education to organize courses that broaden students' understanding of themselves and others by examining events that evoke a sense of social responsibility and moral accountability. A course on "Immigration and Politics in Fin de Siècle America" could provide a historical perspective on the demographic changes confronting the United States and how such changes are being felt within the shifting dynamics of education, economics, cultural identity, and urban development. A course on the Los Angeles uprisings could incorporate the related issues of race, politics, economics, and education to address the multiple conditions underlying the violence and despair that produced such a tragic event.

Third, in addition to broadening the terms and parameters of learning, cultural studies rejects the professionalization of educators and the alienating and often elitist discourse of professionalism and sanitized expertise. Instead, it argues for educators as public intellectuals. Stuart Hall is instructive on this issue when he argues that cultural studies provides two points of tension that intellectuals need to address:

> First, cultural studies constitutes one of the points of tension and change at the frontiers of intellectual and academic life, pushing for new questions, new models, and new ways of study, testing the fine lines between intellectual rigor and social relevance.... But secondly ... cultural studies insist on what I want to call the vocation of the intellectual life. That is to say, cultural studies insists on the necessity to address the central, urgent, and disturbing questions of a society and a culture in the most rigorous intellectual way we have available.[31]

In this view, intellectuals must be accountable in their teaching for the ways in which they address and respond to the problems of history, human agency, and the renewal of democratic civic life. Cultural studies strongly rejects the assumption that teachers are simply transmitters of existing configurations of knowledge. As public intellectuals, academics are always implicated in the dynamics of social power through the experiences they organize and provoke in their classrooms. In this perspective, intellectual work is incomplete unless it self-consciously assumes responsibility for its effects in the larger public culture while simultaneously addressing the most profoundly and deeply inhumane problems of the societies in which we live. Hence, cultural studies raises questions about what knowledge is produced in the university and how it is consequential in extending and deepening the possibilities for democratic public life. Equally important is the issue of how to democratize the schools so as to enable those groups who in large measure are divorced from or simply not represented in the curriculum to be able to produce their own representations, narrate their own stories, and engage in respectful dialogue with others. In this instance, cultural studies must address how dialogue is constructed in the classroom about other cultures and voices by critically addressing both the position of the theorists and the institutions in which such dialogues are produced. Peter Hitchcock argues forcefully that the governing principles of any such dialogic exchange should include some of the following elements:

> 1) attention to the specific institutional setting in which this activity takes place; 2) self-reflexivity regarding the particular identities of the teacher and students who collectively undertake this activity; 3) an awareness that the cultural identities at stake in "other" cultures are in the process-of-becoming in dialogic interaction and are not static as subjects; but 4) the knowledge produced through this activity is always already contestable and by definition is not the knowledge of the other as the other would know herself or himself.[32]

Fourth, another important contribution of cultural studies is its emphasis on studying the production, reception, and use of varied texts, and how they are used to define social relations, values, particular notions of community, the future, and diverse definitions of the self. Texts in this sense do not merely refer to the culture of print or the technology of the book, but to all those audio, visual, and electronically mediated forms of knowledge that have prompted a radical shift in the construction of knowledge and the ways in which knowledge is read, received, and consumed. It is worth repeating that contemporary youth increasingly rely less on the technology and culture of the book to construct and affirm their identities; instead, they are faced with the task of finding their way through a decentered cultural landscape no longer caught in the grip of a technology of print, closed narrative structures, or the certitude of a secure economic future. The new emerging technologies that construct and position youth represent interactive terrains that cut across "language and culture, without narrative requirements, without character complexities. . . . Narrative complexity [has given] way to design complexity; story [has given] way to a sensory environment."[33] Cultural studies is profoundly important for educators in that it focuses on media not merely in terms of how it distorts and misrepresents reality, but also on how media plays "a part in the formation, in the constitution, of the things they reflect. It is not that there is a world outside, 'out there,' which exists free of the discourse of representation. What is 'out there' is, in part, constituted by how it is represented."[34]

I don't believe that educators and schools of education can address the shifting attitudes, representations, and desires of this new generation of youth within the dominant disciplinary configurations of knowledge and practice. On the contrary, as youth are constituted within languages and new cultural forms that intersect differently across and within issues of race, class, gender, and sexual differences, the conditions through which youth attempt to narrate themselves must be understood in terms of both the context of their struggles and a shared language of agency that points to a project of hope and possibility. It is precisely this language of difference, specificity, and possibility that is lacking from most attempts at educational reform.

Fifth, it is important to stress that when critical pedagogy is established as one of the defining principles of cultural studies, it is possible to generate a new discourse for moving beyond a limited emphasis on the mastery of techniques and methodologies. Critical pedagogy represents a form of cultural production implicated in and critically attentive to how power and meaning are employed in the construction and organization of knowledge, desires, values, and identities. Critical pedagogy in this sense is not reduced to the mastering of skills or techniques, but is defined as a cultural practice that must be accountable ethically and politically for the stories it produces, the claims it makes on social memories, and the images of the future it deems legitimate. As both an object of critique and a method of cultural production, it refuses to hide behind claims of objectivity, and works effortlessly to link theory and practice to enabling the possibilities for human agency in a world of diminishing returns. It is important to make a distinction here that challenges the liberal and conservative criticism that, since critical pedagogy attempts both to politicize teaching and teach politics, it represents a species of indoctrination. By asserting that all teaching is profoundly political and that critical educators and cultural workers should operate out of a project of social transformation, I am arguing that as educators we need to make a distinction between what Peter Euben calls political and politicizing education.

Political education, which is central to critical pedagogy, refers to teaching "students how to think in ways that cultivate the capacity for judgment essential for the exercise of power and responsibility by a democratic citizenry. . . . A political, as distinct from a politicizing education would encourage students to become better citizens to challenge those with political and cultural power as well as to honor the critical traditions within the dominant culture that make such a critique possible and intelligible."[35] A political education means decentering power in the classroom and other pedagogical sites so the dynamics of those institutional and cultural inequalities that marginalize some groups, repress particular types of knowledge, and suppress critical dialogue can be addressed. On the other hand, politicizing education is a form of pedagogical terrorism in which the issue of what is taught, by whom, and under what conditions is determined by a doctrinaire political agenda that refuses to examine its own values, beliefs, and ideological construction. While refusing to recognize the social and historical character of its own claims to history, knowledge, and values, a politicizing education silences in the name of a specious universalism and denounces all transformative practices through an appeal to a timeless notion of truth and beauty. For those who practice a politicizing education, democracy and citizenship become dangerous in that the precondition for their realization demands critical inquiry, the taking of risks, and the responsibility to resist and say no in the face of dominant forms of power.

CONCLUSION

Given its challenge to the traditional notion of teachers as mere transmitters of information and its insistence that teachers are cultural producers deeply implicated in public issues, cultural studies provides a new and transformative language for educating teachers and administrators around the issue of civic leadership and public service. In this perspective, teacher education is fashioned not around a particular dogma, but through pedagogical practices that address changing contexts, creating the necessary conditions for students to be critically attentive to the historical and socially constructed nature of the locations they occupy within a shifting world of representations and values. Cultural studies requires that teachers be educated to be cultural producers, to treat culture as an activity, unfinished and incomplete. This suggests that teachers should be critically attentive to the operations of power as it is implicated in the production of knowledge and authority in particular and shifting contexts. This means learning how to be sensitive to considerations of power as it is inscribed on every facet of the schooling process.

The conditions and problems of contemporary youth will have to be engaged through a willingness to interrogate the world of public politics, while at the same time appropriating modernity's call for a better world but abandoning its linear narratives of Western history, unified culture, disciplinary order, and technological progress. In this case, the pedagogical importance of uncertainty and indeterminacy can be rethought through a modernist notion of the dream-world in which youth and others can shape, without the benefit of master narratives, the conditions for producing new ways of learning, engaging, and positing the possibilities for social struggle and solidarity. Critical educators cannot subscribe either to an apocalyptic emptiness or to a politics of refusal that celebrates the abandonment of authority or the immediacy of experience over the more profound dynamic of social memory and moral outrage forged within and against conditions of exploitation, oppression, and the abuse of power.

The intersection of cultural studies and critical pedagogy offers possibilities for educators to confront history as more than **simulacrum**[i] and ethics as something other than the casualty of incommensurable language games. Educators need to assert a politics that makes the relationship among authority, ethics, and power central to a pedagogy that expands rather than closes down the possibilities of a radical democratic society. Within this discourse, images do not dissolve reality into simply another text: on the contrary, representations become central to revealing the structures of power relations at work in the public, in schools, in society, and in the larger global order. Pedagogy does not succumb to the whims of the marketplace in this logic, nor to the latest form of educational chic; instead, critical pedagogy engages cultural studies as part of an ongoing movement towards a shared conception of justice and a radicalization of the social order. This is a task that not only recognizes the multiple relationships between culture and power, but also makes critical pedagogy one of its defining principles.

NOTES

1. Dick Hebdige, *Hiding in the Light* (New York: Routledge, 1988), pp. 17–18.
2. See the November 29, 1993, issue of *Newsweek*. Of course, the issue that is often overlooked in associating "gangsta rap" with violence is that "gangsta rap does not appear in a cultural vacuum, but, rather, is expressive of the cultural crossing, mixing, and engagement of black youth culture with the values, attitudes, and concerns of the white majority." bell hooks, "Sexism and Misogyny: Who Takes the Rap?" *Z Magazine*, February 1994, p. 26. See also Greg Tate's spirited defense of rap in Greg Tate, "Above and Beyond Rap's Decibels," *New York Times*, March 6, 1994, pp. 1, 36.
3. This is most evident in the popular media culture where analysis of crime in the United States is almost exclusively represented through images of Black youth. For example, in the May 1994 issue of *Atlantic Monthly*, the cover of the magazine shows a Black urban youth, without a shirt, with a gun in his hand, staring out at the reader. The story the image is highlighting is about inner-city violence. The flurry of articles, magazines, films, and news stories about crime produced in 1994 focuses almost exclusively on Black youth, both discursively and representationally.
4. Camille Colatosti, "Dealing Guns," *Z Magazine*, January 1994, p. 59.
5. Holly Sklar, "Young and Guilty by Stereotype," *Z Magazine*, July/August 1993, p. 52.
6. Stanley Aronowitz, "A Different Perspective on Educational Inequality," *The Review of Education/Pedagogy/Cultural Studies* (University Park, PA: Gordon & Breach, 1995), p. 15.
7. Aronowitz and Giroux, *Education Still Under Siege*, pp. 4–5.
8. These quotes and comments are taken from a stinging analysis of Kaus in Jonathan Kozol, "Speaking the Unspeakable," Unpublished manuscript (1993). The context for Kaus's remarks is developed in Mickey Kaus, *The End of Equality* (New York: Basic Books, 1992).
9. Paul Virilio, *Lost Dimension*, trans. Daniel Moshenberg (New York: Semiotext[e], 1991).

---

[i] Related to the word simulation, **simulacrum** refers to the idea that reality is seen simply as fleeting images, as a spectacle.

10. Andrew Ross and Tricia Rose, eds., *Microphone Fiends: Youth Music and Youth Culture* (New York: Routledge, 1994), and Jonathon Epstein, ed., *Adolescents and Their Music: If It's Too Loud, You're Too Old* (New York: Garland, 1994).
11. Theodor Adorno and Max Horkheimer, writing in the 1940s, argued that popular culture had no redeeming political or aesthetic possibilities. See Max Horkheimer and Theodor Adorno, *Dialectic of Enlightenment* (New York: Herder & Herder, 1944/1972), especially "The Culture Industry: Enlightenment as Mass Deception," pp. 120–167.
12. Walter Parkes, "Random Access, Remote Control," *Omni,* January 1994, p. 54.
13. This section of the paper draws from Henry A. Giroux, "Slacking Off: Border Youth and Postmodern Education," *Journal of Advanced Composition, 14,* No. 2 (1994), 347–366.
14. Carol Anshaw, "Days of Whine and Poses," *Village Voice,* November 10, 1992, p. 27.
15. For a critique of the so-called "twenty-something generation" as defined by *Time, U.S. News, Money, Newsweek,* and the *Utne Reader,* see Chris de Bellis, "From Slackers to Baby Busters," *Z Magazine,* December 1993, pp. 8–10.
16. Andrew Kopkind, "Slacking Toward Bethlehem," *Grand Street, 11,* No. 4 (1992), 183.
17. The contours of this type of criticism are captured in a comment by Andrew Kopkind, a keen observer of slacker culture, in "Slacking Toward Bethlehem," p. 187:

 > The domestic and economic relationships that have created the new consciousness are not likely to improve in the few years left in this century, or in the years of the next, when the young slackers will be middle-agers. The choices for young people will be increasingly constricted. In a few years, a steady job at a mall outlet or a food chain may be all that's left for the majority of college graduates. Life is more and more like a lottery — is a lottery — with nothing but the luck of the draw determining whether you get a recording contract, get your screenplay produced, or get a job with your M.B.A. Slacking is thus a rational response to casino capitalism, the randomization of success, and the utter arbitrariness of power. If no talent is still enough, why bother to hone your skills? If it is impossible to find a good job, why not slack out and enjoy life?

18. For an analysis of Black American cinema in the 1990s, see Ed Guerrero, "Framing Blackness: The African-American Image in the Cinema of the Nineties," *Cineaste, 20,* No. 2 (1993), 24–31.
19. Michael Dyson, "The Politics of Black Masculinity and the Ghetto in Black Film," in *The Subversive Imagination: Artists, Society, and Social Responsibility,* ed. Carol Becker (New York: Routledge, 1994), p. 155.
20. Dyson, "The Politics of Black Masculinity," p. 163.
21. Itabari Njeri, "Untangling the Roots of the Violence Around Us — On Screen and Off," *Los Angeles Times Magazine,* August 29, 1993, p. 33.
22. Cornel West, "Nihilism in Black America," in Dent, *Black Popular Culture,* p. 40.
23. Itabari Njeri, "Untangling the Roots," p. 34.
24. Fabienne Worth, "Postmodern Pedagogy in the Multicultural Classroom: For Inappropriate Teachers and Imperfect Spectators," *Cultural Critique,* No. 25 (Fall, 1993), 27.
25. Pierce Hollingsworth, "The New Generation Gaps: Graying Boomers, Golden Agers, and Generation X," Food Technology, 47, No. 10 (1993), 30.
26. I have called this elsewhere the pedagogy of commercialism. See Giroux, *Disturbing Pleasures.*
27. For an analysis of the relationship among modernist schooling, pedagogy, and popular culture, see Henry A. Giroux and Roger I. Simon, "Popular Culture as a Pedagogy of Pleasure and Meaning," in *Popular Culture, Schooling, and Everyday Life,* ed. Henry A. Giroux and Roger Simon (Granby, MA: Bergin & Garvey, 1989), pp. 1–30; Henry A. Giroux and Roger I. Simon, "Schooling, Popular Culture, and a Pedagogy of Possibility," in Giroux and Simon, *Popular Culture,* pp. 219–236.

28. Anyone who has been following the culture wars of the past eight years is well aware of the conservative agenda for reordering public and higher education around the commercial goal of promoting economic growth for the nation while simultaneously supporting the values of Western civilization as a common culture designed to undermine the ravages of calls for equity and multiculturalism. For a brilliant analysis of the conservative attack on higher education, see Ellen Messer-Davidow, "Manufacturing the Attack on Liberalized Higher Education," *Social Text, 11,* No. 3 (1993), 40–80.
29. This argument is especially powerful in the work of Edward Said, who frames the reach of culture as a determining pedagogical force against the backdrop of the imperatives of colonialism. See Edward Said, *Culture and Imperialism* (New York: Alfred A. Knopf, 1993); see also, Donaldo Macedo, *Literacies of Power* (Boulder, CO: Westview Press, 1994).
30. Selective examples of this work include: Carol Becker, ed., *The Subversive Imagination* (New York: Routledge, 1994); Giroux and McLaren, *Between Borders;* Simon, *Teaching Against the Grain;* David Trend, *Cultural Pedagogy: Art/Education/Politics* (Westport, CT: Bergin & Garvey, 1992); James Schwoch, Mimi White, and Susan Reilly, *Media Knowledge: Readings in Popular Culture, Pedagogy, and Critical Citizenship* (Albany: State University of New York Press, 1992); Lawrence Grossberg, *We Gotta Get Out of This Place: Popular Conservatism and Postmodern Culture* (New York: Routledge, 1992). See also, Douglas Kellner, *Media Culture* (New York: Routledge, 1995); Jeanne Brady, *Schooling Young Children* (Albany: State University of New York Press, 1995).
31. Stuart Hall, "Race, Culture, and Communications: Looking Backward and Forward at Cultural Studies," *Rethinking Marxism, 5,* No. 1 (1992), 11.
32. Peter Hitchcock, "The Othering of Cultural Studies," *Third Text, No. 25 (Winter, 1993–1994),* 12.
33. Walter Parkes, "Random Access, Remote Control: The Evolution of Story Telling," Omni, January 1994, p. 50.
34. Hall, "Race, Culture, and Communications," p. 14.
35. Peter Euben, "The Debate Over the Canon," *Civic Arts Review, 7,* No. 1 (1994), 14–15.

I would like to thank Susan Searls, Doug Kellner, and Stanley Aronowitz for their critical reading of this manuscript.

6

A Dialogue with Noam Chomsky

The following dialogue took place between Noam Chomsky and *Harvard Educational Review* Editors Pepi Leistyna and Stephen Sherblom in the fall of 1994, at Chomsky's office at the Massachusetts Institute of Technology. The purpose of the conversation was to frame the lives of youth in the United States, and the culture of violence that permeates much of U.S. society, within an interdisciplinary perspective that explores the historical, sociopolitical, economic, and cultural conditions of US. society, laying bare the ideologies that drive such conditions. While Chomsky's prolific work has accomplished this in many important respects, his political critiques and insights have been almost entirely excluded from national efforts to understand community disintegration and address issues of youth violence. By bringing Chomsky's critical perspectives, concerns, and outlooks to the center of educational debates, it is our belief that educators can better understand the complex roots and history of inequality and violence in this country, and thus better inform themselves of the current social context in which children live, as well as what tools they will need to become active, critical, and responsible citizens. "Critical" in this sense implies that both teachers and students will be able to understand, analyze, and work to affect the sociohistorical and economic realities that shape their lives.

Complementing Henry Giroux's analysis of how youth (as well as perceptions of youth) are manipulated through particular images in popular film, and his contention that the conditions within which many youth live are not critically understood in terms of their social and historical causes, this dialogue with Chomsky begins by confronting the dominant ideologies that have driven this nation's history of systemic inequalities, oppression, and sanctioned violence, all of which have contributed to the current culture of violence that youth experience on a daily basis. The concept of "dominant ideologies" refers to the body of ideas held by cultural groups that are politically, socially, and economically in positions of power. Through various social institutions and practices, such groups are able to impose on the greater society their values and interests, usually at the expense of others. Social institutions such as schools and the media (which Chomsky refers to as "systems of doctrinal control") function to indoctrinate, marginalize (that is, to force a person or a group out of mainstream society, limiting their access to political and economic power, or to push ideas and concepts that conflict with dominant views to the fringes of academic debate, labelling them as important only to special interest groups), or exclude people and perspectives that are not sanctioned by the dominant groups. This results in systemic inequalities that are built into our present society and that function to keep power from groups of people based on their differences in terms of class, gender, ethnicity, race, and sexual orientation.

Chomsky's sociohistorical perspective acknowledges that we all inherit, at some level, beliefs, values, and ideologies. He reveals the importance of critically examining those traditions, rather than simply passing them from generation to generation. However, as this dialogue points out, the United States has experienced a great deal of historical amnesia, in which only selective beliefs and cleansed histories are encouraged and transmitted by schools and other dominant institutions, while both oppressive practices and the inevitable resistance are virtually erased from public memory.

The central theme in this particular conversation is tracing back the culture of violence in our society to its roots. In particular, Chomsky focuses on how capitalism, as it has been practiced in the United States, has produced a set of social values and a culture that prioritize, at great social cost, individualism, the production and accumulation of wealth and material goods, and the wielding of power over others. Some of the effects of these cultural values are a lack of political awareness, community, caring, and democratic struggle. In fact, throughout the dialogue, Chomsky vividly illustrates how we, as a society, often work against the values that we publicly profess, such as the growth and health of children, the social and economic well-being of all people, and the basic tenets of democracy. The dialogue then dissects the relationship between the state and the business sector and exposes the ways in which the poor and middle-class in the United States subsidize the wealthy. Chomsky discusses how the media and public institutions often function (through the use of scapegoats, distortions of history, and propaganda) to manufacture consent; that is, to lead the public to internalize values and beliefs that result in the unequal distribution of privilege, wealth, and power. He shows this has happened with media coverage of "the problem of violence" by divorcing it from larger social causes and portraying it as a problem of "inner cities," "minority communities," and "poor families." This dialogue's interdisciplinary treatment of violence provides a concrete example of the power of critical pedagogy to help us see beyond the confines of what information we are fed. Chomsky concludes with a discussion of the possibilities for radical social change.

While the media portray violence as if it's a new epidemic in this country, your work has shown that historically the United States has been based on a "culture of violence." Could you elaborate as to what you feel are the actual ideological and systemic elements that inform the history of violence in our society?

The entire history of this country has been driven by violence. The whole power structure and economic system was based essentially on the extermination of the native populations and the bringing of slaves. The Industrial Revolution was based on cheap cotton, which wasn't kept cheap by market principles but by conquest. It was kept cheap by the use of land stolen from the indigenous populations and then by the cheap labor of those exploited in slavery. The subsequent conquest of the West was also very brutal. After reaching the end of the frontier, we just went on conquering more and more — the Philippines, Hawaii, Latin America, and so on. In fact, there is a continuous strain of violence in U.S. military history from "Indian fighting" right up through the war in Vietnam. The guys who were involved in "Indian fighting" are the guys who went to the Philippines, where they carried out a massive slaughter; and the same people who had just been tried for war crimes in the Philippines went on to Haiti, where they carried out another slaughter. This goes on right up through Vietnam. If you look at the popular literature on Vietnam, it's full of "We're chasing Indians." But that's only one strain of the institutionalized brutality in our history.

Internally, American society has also been very violent. Take the labor history. U.S. workers were very late in getting the kind of rights that were achieved in other industrial societies. It wasn't until the 1930s that U.S. workers got the minimal rights that were more or less standard in Europe decades earlier. But that period of development in the United States was also much more violent than Europe's. If I remember the numbers correctly, about seven hundred American workers were killed by security forces in the early part of this century. And even into the late 1930s, workers were still getting killed by the police and by the security forces during strikes. Nothing like that was happening in Europe; even the right-wing British press was appalled by the brutal treatment of American strikers.

There have been other sources of violence as well; for example, the ways that a large part of the population is systematically marginalized in this society. We're again different from other industrial societies in that we don't have much of a social contract. So if you compare us even with, say, Canada, Europe, or Japan, there is a kind of a social contract that was achieved in these industrial societies concerning public welfare, such as health care. European societies grew out of a social framework that included feudal structures, church structures, and all sorts of other things. And the business classes in Europe, as they came along, made various accommodations with these existing structures, resulting in a more complex society than we have here in the United States, where the business class just took over. It was kind of like we started afresh, creating a new society, and the only organized force was a very highly class-conscious business community. Because the United States is essentially a business-run society, much more so than others, we're the only industrial nation that doesn't have some sort of guaranteed health insurance. In many respects we're just off the spectrum, which is pretty striking considering we're also the richest society by far. Despite being the richest society we have twice the poverty rate of any other industrial nation, and much higher rates of incarceration. In fact, we're the highest in the world and both will continue to worsen in light of the Gingrich "Contract with America" and the new crime bill. Out of these sociohistorical and economic structures, which embrace conquest and an indifference to public welfare, comes a streak of violence.

From the very roots of this country we see that capitalism and so-called "free-market" practices have worked to benefit the prosperous few who manage the economy and dictate social policy. In your estimation, where on the spectrum of capitalist practices is the United States presently situated?

In a real capitalist society, the only rights you have would be the rights you get on the labor market. There are no other rights, certainly no human rights. In fact, it's classical economics, but no society could realistically survive that way, though we're closer to that than most others. However, in our system, there is a double standard. The poor, more than anyone, get the rights they can achieve on the labor market, but for the rich, there's powerful state protection. They've never been willing to accept market discipline. The United States has, from its origins, been a highly protectionist society with very high tariffs and massive subsidies for the rich. It's a huge welfare state for the rich, and society ends up being very polarized. Despite the New Deal, and the Great Society measures in the 1960s, which attempted to move the United States toward the social contracts of the other industrial nations, we still have the highest social and economic inequality, and such polarization is increasing very sharply. These factors — high polarization, a welfare state for the rich, and marginalization of parts of the population — have their effects.

One effect is a lot of crime. You have people who are cooped up in urban slums, which are basically concentration camps, while the rich protect themselves in affluent areas, which are often, in fact, subsidized by the poor. In the 1980s and the 1990s it's been quite striking how much the polarization has increased. A symbol of this is Newt Gingrich, who now is spearheading the "get the government off our backs" campaign. If you look carefully, it again is a double standard. He wants the government "off our backs" when its policies assist the poor, but he wants the government "on our backs" if it's benefitting rich people. In fact, his district, a very wealthy suburb of Atlanta, gets more federal subsidies — taxpayers' money — than any suburban county in the country, outside the federal system itself. This rich suburb is carefully insulated from the downtown, so you don't get any poor Blacks coming in there. And here's Gingrich saying, "Get the government off our backs." Well, that tells you exactly what it's all about. You get the government out of the business of helping poor people, but make sure it's in the business of helping the rich. And, in fact, once again, if you look at this Republican Contract with America, that's exactly what it says. It's cutting social spending for the poor, but increasing welfare for the rich. That's inevitably going to lead to increased polarization, resentment, brutality, and violence.

How does the money flow from the poor to the rich?

Here we are at MIT, which is part of the system whereby poor people fund high technology industries. We have offices and things because the whole system of public funding, meaning taxpayers, ends up supporting research and development. If it's profitable, the technology goes right off to the big corporations.

There sure are a lot of government license plates out in the parking lots.

Yeah, but it isn't just government license plates, they're simply part of the whole system by which the poor subsidize the rich. And in fact, it was perfectly, consciously designed that way. If you look back to the business press in the late 1940s, they are absolutely frank about it. They said, Look, advanced industry can't survive in an unsubsidized, competitive "free enterprise" economy, in a true market — the government has to be "the savior." And how do you do it? Well, they talked about various methods, but the obvious method was the Pentagon system, which largely functions as a way of subsidizing the rich. That's why it hasn't declined substantially with the end of the Cold War. There was all this talk about defending ourselves from the Russians. Okay, now that the Russians are no longer a threat, has the Pentagon system gone? No, the U.S. is still spending almost as much on the military as the rest of the world combined. And anyone in industry knows why. There's no other way to force people to pay the costs of high-tech industry.

Take Newt Gingrich, for example. The biggest employer in his district happens to be Lockheed. Well, what's Lockheed? That's a publicly subsidized corporation. Lockheed wouldn't exist for five minutes if it wasn't for the public subsidy under the pretext of defense, but that's just a joke. The United States hasn't faced a threat probably since the War of 1812. Certainly there's no threat now. We're not as threatened as the rest of the world combined. In fact, an awful lot of the production of arms is sold to other countries. If anything, that increases any threat. So the whole thing has nothing to do with threats and security; it's a joke. In fact, that was always known. If you go back to the late 1940s, the first Secretary of the Air Force, Stuart Symington, said publicly, I think in Congress, — Look, the word to use is not "subsidy," the word to use is "security." That's the way we'll make sure that the advanced industry gets going. That's how the aircraft industry works, that's how the computer and electronics industries work also. About 85 percent of research and development in electronics was funded by the government in the 1950s.

Take, as another example, the research and development of automation. The apologists for our system say that the creation of automation is the result of "market principles." That's just baloney. Automation was so inefficient that it had to be developed in the state system for several decades — it was developed by the Air Force. The same holds true for containerization; trade looks efficient because we have container ships. How were container ships developed? Not through the market; they were developed by the Navy, through a public subsidy. They don't have to worry about costs, because the public's paying. Now that it's profitable it's turned over to "private enterprise," and is used to undermine working people who funded it. Automation is now putting people out of work.

Can you elaborate on other ways that the privileged benefit from this enormous system of subsidies?

On top of the Pentagon system there are the straight welfare payments. If you have a home mortgage, you get a tax rebate. A tax rebate is exactly equivalent to a welfare payment. It's exactly the same if I don't give the government $100 or if the government does gives me $100. Well, who do home mortgage loans go to? These go overwhelmingly to the privileged. In fact, about 80 percent of them go to people with incomes over $50,000, and as you go into the higher tax brackets, it's skewed even more. Or take business expenses as tax write-offs, for example. If you take your friends out to a ballgame or something like that, for so-called business purposes, that's paid for by the taxpayer. If you look at that whole range of expenditures, which are the exact equivalent of welfare payments, they far outweigh welfare payments to the poor. And these expenditures are going to be increased, because the Republican Contract with America will increase military spending, and increase the regressive fiscal measures that amount to welfare for the rich. They want to give subsidies for business investment and cut back capital gains taxes. Those are subsidies to the wealthy.

So, as the society gets more polarized and more people are marginalized, and people are working harder just to stay where they are, social relations further crumble to a point where you get a lot of violence. Actually, it's amazing that despite all this, if you look at, say, FBI statistics, the level of violence hasn't changed very much. There's probably more violence among eleven-year-olds than there was, but there's less violence in other places. And the violence among the eleven-year-olds is a result of the Reagan and Gingrich war against families.

What are some of the central ways that these social and economic policies and practices affect the lives of youth in this country?

One aspect of this, specifically with regard to children, is something that isn't discussed much here in the United States. There's been a war against children and families for the last fifteen years, a real war. There's an interesting study of this by UNICEF, completed about a year ago, called "Child Neglect in Rich Societies," written by a well-known American economist, Sylvia Ann Hewlett. She compares what has happened to children and families in the last fifteen years in rich societies, and she finds that the results break pretty sharply into two models. The European/Japanese model was supportive of families, with day-care systems and prenatal care, and other such benefits. Whereas the Reagan/Thatcher model, which extended to some extent to the other English-speaking societies, tended to force families into using privatized child care without other support systems. One of the reasons child care was impossible to afford was because wages were being driven down. That means that there are plenty of families where you have to have a husband and a wife working fifty or sixty hours a week just to provide necessities. Perhaps much of one person's salary is going to pay day-care. With very little in the way of a public support system, they can't get such things as health insurance because it costs too much. Well, the effect of this, which Hewlett describes in this study, is quite obvious — kids are left on their own, unsupervised and unprotected much more in the Anglo-American model than in the European/Japanese model. There are a lot more latch-key children, T.V. as baby-sitter, and that sort of thing going on here in the United States. Actually, she reports that contact hours between parents and children in the United States decreased by about 40 percent since about 1960. High-quality contact, where you really pay attention to each other, has declined very, very sharply. The effects of all that are completely obvious — you get violence against children and violence by children. You also get substance abuse. All of these are obvious consequences of that social policy. If kids are neglected, with no care and guidance, they're going to be either watching television or wandering around the streets.

When you put this together with the effects of poverty, discrimination, and racism, and all the other unmet social needs such as quality schooling and economic opportunity, the violence being done to children will inevitably be a catalyst for a rise in violence by children. It's clear that this kind of monopolistic capitalism that you're talking about destroys community even at its most basic level — the family. Despite all the national attention on violence and youth, and a growing body of literature in the social sciences documenting the unmet needs of so many youth in this country, it is amazing how few links are made in the national debates, including those in the academy, between government policies that hurt children and families and the increasing violence involving youth. And we've only just started to see the beginning of it.

Oh yeah! It's going to get worse because now they want to extend the war against families in the name of "family values," and they will get away with it, just as Newt Gingrich got away with representing the most subsidized district in the country while he was claiming "we don't want federal subsidies." Now, how do they get away with it? Well, I think the explanation is pretty simple. The political opposition, though they could have made hay out of Gingrich or out of "family values," basically agrees with him. There's a class interest in common. They don't want to expose the fact that there are public subsidies for the rich because they're in favor of them. And they don't want to expose the fact that there's a war against families and children because they agree with it. So they're not exposing it. The Gingrich case is particularly interesting, because he is slaughtering the Democrats, but even their interest in political survival didn't override their class interest in not exposing what was going on. The two political parties are more or less united in subsidizing the rich.

The political right seeks to distract the public from these issues by preaching that a stimulated market will be the answer to our social problems. How could the state of the market possibly resolve the violence of racism, illiteracy, and poverty? It certainly didn't in the "prosperous" years following World War II. How can the market solve what it in fact creates?

Maybe people talk themselves into believing that the market is the solution, but the reason they believe it is because the actual system is going to enrich them. They refuse to accept market discipline for themselves, though they insist on imposing it on others. There's almost nobody who advocates market discipline for themselves; it's always for someone else. And that's not because they've figured out that the market is going to solve problems, it's because that double-edged policy is going to enrich them. Adam Smith talks about this; these are truisms.

One major detrimental result of capitalist social relations, which emphasizes money and acquisition over caring for people's basic needs and fostering community, is that it works to fashion children's identities, and the ways in which they interact socially, around the excesses of marketing and consumption.

One of the things that is indeed fostered, and has been for centuries, is mindless consumerism. It was understood a long time ago that you can't force people to work unless you trap them into wanting commodities. That goes right through the Industrial Revolution — from early England right up to today. So you have to put enormous amounts of effort into atomizing people, breaking down social relations, making sure there aren't other ways of realizing their interests and concerns, and optimally turning them into atoms of consumption and tools of production. That would be the perfect thing, and an enormous amount of effort goes into that. Take, for example, the information highway; it's probably going to end up being a home shopping service because that's a terrific way to atomize people and make them consume more. Therefore, consumers have got to work more, while they are making less pay, and for the business class trying to enrich themselves, this is perfect. And the propaganda that goes into this is extreme. The public relations industry spends billions of dollars a year, essentially, trying to convince people that they need things that they don't want. Those things are part of the technique of breaking down social relations, making people feel that the only thing that matters is getting more than your neighbor. This diminishes social interaction, feelings of solidarity, sympathy, and support. And, in fact, that provides a backdrop for violence.

Which most people don't seem to understand. If you are taught to believe that the meaning in life resides in getting status, power, and money, and not in the development of quality relationships with others, you're likely to hurt people to get what you want. When an eleven-year-old kills another kid for a pair of sneakers, people generally respond, "I can't imagine how this could happen."

Why not? We're telling this eleven-year-old through television, "You're not a real man unless you wear the sneakers that some basketball hero wears." And you also look around you and see who gets ahead — the guys who play by the rules of "get for yourself as much as you can" — so, here's the easy way to do it. Kids notice everybody else is robbing too, including the guys in the rich penthouses, so why shouldn't they? The rich guys do it their way and the eleven-year-old does it his way.

Well, look what they are telling the rest of the population! They're telling them that someone else, other than the rich, is responsible for the social demise. In fact, conservative mainstream arguments contend that violence and drug abuse are simply the result of the lack of family values. Such arguments contend that women working outside the home are responsible for the breakdown of families. Oppressed groups, portrayed as "lazy freeloaders," and those disgracefully referred to as "illegal aliens" are also targeted. Would you comment on the ability and purpose of those in power to create and punish scapegoats in this fashion?

Those are indeed the arguments, but every single one of them is utterly ludicrous. For instance, if women who want to stay home and take care of their children are being forced into the marketplace, that's because the Republicans' social policies drive down wages, so you can only survive by having two members of the family work. As I mentioned before, if there's no care for children, that's because we don't provide child support.

This building up of scapegoats and fear is standard. If you're stomping on people's faces, you don't want them to notice that; you want them to be afraid of somebody else — Jews, homosexuals, welfare queens, immigrants, whoever it is. That's how Hitler got to power, and in fact he became the most popular leader in German history. People are scared, they're upset, the world isn't working, and they don't like the way things are. You don't want people to look at the actual source of power, that's much too dangerous, so, therefore, you need to have them blame or be frightened of someone else.

So it not only justifies the violence against the scapegoats, but diverts attention from the other violence being done to the general population.

Diverts attention, sure. In fact you can see this very clearly in polls. People have repeatedly been asked to estimate how they think the federal budget is spent. In fact, of the discretionary funds, over half is military spending. But under a third of the population knows that. Many pick foreign aid — which is undetectable. And they very much overestimate the welfare that goes to, say, "Black mothers with Cadillacs." These are the things that people believe. They believe that they're working hard, and that their money is being taken and given to poor people overseas, and to Black women who refuse to work and just keep "breeding." The fact is that their money is going to Newt Gingrich's constituents through the Pentagon system. Scapegoating certainly serves that purpose.

It's just amazing how something like California Proposition 187 is so openly racist and, in a time of so-called "family values," actually contributes to the disintegration of families. While the cheap labor of "illegal immigrants" is a staple of the California economy, the state doesn't want to provide much-needed social services to that labor force, such as education and health-care for children. Pete Wilson's entire political platform was based on this scapegoating. Conservative media representations of "illegal aliens" continually work to convince the general public that they are somehow responsible for this country's multi-trillion dollar debt.

Which Reagan and Reaganites created. And did on purpose, because they wanted to cut back social spending.

Which is something we never hear from the Democrats.

Rarely, because they agree. Look, there was a Democratic Congress — they basically went along with the policies because they more or less agreed with them. And they all represent more or less the same class. There are, to be sure, important differences: Ted Kennedy isn't the same as Newt Gingrich. But there's enough commonality of interests that they're not going to expose each other very much, any more than they exposed Gingrich this time around. I mean, he was wiping them out on this big government business. I never saw one person point out, "You're the biggest exponent of the welfare state!"

One consequence of this unwillingness to speak the truth is that the present Republican emphasis on creating prisons and employing more police is falsely legitimized. You mentioned earlier the dramatic increase in incarceration. According to the U.S. Justice Department, there are well over a million people presently in prison. Increasing the number of prisons and police are certainly only short-term solutions that serve to divert attention from the real causes of drug abuse, crime, and violence. People being "criminalized" are being scapegoated and incarceration becomes the big business solution to "the problem."

Exactly, for example the drug war, which was almost completely phony, was simply used as a technique of incarceration. There was a huge increase in imprisonment during the Reagan years, and some enormous percentage of it, like two-thirds, was for drug use. And most of it isn't even crime — it's victimless crime, like catching somebody with a joint in their pocket. In fact, if you look in the federal prisons, you don't find many bankers and chemical corporation executives and so on, although they're involved in the drug racket. Banks are involved in money laundering, and government agencies pointed out years ago that the big chemical corporations are exporting chemicals to Latin America way beyond any industrial use. What they're exporting, in fact, is what's used for commercial production of drugs. But the idea is to go after the Black kid on the corner in the ghetto, because he's the one you want to get rid of. For example, take cocaine. The drug most often used in the ghettos is crack; in the White suburbs, it's powder. Well, you know, the way the laws are crafted, powdered cocaine gets much less of a sentence than crack cocaine. That's social policy. It's part of criminalizing the "irrelevant" population; even drugs are used for that purpose. Thus, incarceration is a technique for social control. It's the counterpart in a rich society of the death squads in a poor society. You throw them in jail if you can't figure out what else to do with them.

Wouldn't you say that the same is true of the "war on drugs" abroad?

Yes, it has little effect on the production and sale of drugs, but has lots of effect on controlling people. So, in Colombia, the counter-insurgency war has had no effect on drug production; it's had a huge effect on slaughter and controlling the population. In fact, Colombia's now the biggest human rights violator in the hemisphere, with a hideous record of atrocities. And it's also the biggest recipient of U.S. military aid, more than half for the entire hemisphere. Has that stopped the flow of drugs? Of course not. Although it's kind of interesting what has happened, if you look at the details. There were two big drug cartels in Columbia — the Medellin and Cali cartels. In this so-called "war on drugs," the Medellin cartel was more or less wiped out. The Cali cartel, however, was untouched, and, in fact, much enriched. There was a recent report by a Jesuit-based peace and justice group in Colombia about this matter. They point out that the Medellin cartel was kind of pre-capitalist. It's similar to the Mafia in Sicily. It had partially lower class origins, and the guys who were running it were like the city boss type. For example, Pablo Escobar, the head of the Medellin cartel, would build a soccer stadium for the poor people. In fact, they were very popular because of their social roots and because there was something of a Robin Hood quality to them. Not that they were nice guys or anything, but that was the kind of crime it was. Now Cali is different, that's just rich business — bankers, industrialists, and big business enterprises. So while the Medellin cartel was being wiped out, the Cali cartel was untouched and their power was increased.

Just to give you an example of what a joke the drug war is: in the mid-1980s, Colombia requested from the Reagan administration technical aid for a radar station to detect low-flying planes that were coming in from the Andean region, bringing in coca leaves, which were then processed. The Reagan administration agreed, and they built a radar station, but they built it on the part of Colombian territory that is as remote as possible from the drug routes. Namely, they built it out on an island, called San Andres, which happens to be off the coast of Nicaragua. If you think about the map, that's the opposite place from where the drug flights are coming. But it was very useful for surveillance of Nicaragua, and for sending terrorist forces to destroy health clinics and so forth. So that's the way they fought the drug war. And it just works across the board. It's an absolute farce, except that it's serving its purpose. Its purpose in this country is to criminalize Blacks and other marginalized groups, to treat them like a population under military occupation, to lock them up, in effect without constitutional rights, and race and class are closely enough correlated in the United States, so that this is also part of the class war.

A great deal of your work, including Media Propaganda, Necessary Illusions, Thought Control in Democratic Societies, *and* Manufacturing Consent, d*iscusses the role of the media in* **colonizing the psyche**[a] a*nd the social relations of the larger public sphere, in terms of getting people to buy into some of the malignant myths we've discussed. You state in your book,* What Uncle Sam Really Wants, *that*

> the sectors of the doctrinal system serve to divert the unwashed masses and reinforce the basic social values — passivity, submissiveness to authority, the overriding virtue of greed and personal gain, lack of concern for others, fear of real or imagined enemies, etc. The goal is to keep the bewildered herd bewildered. It's unnecessary for them to trouble themselves with what's happening in the world. In fact, it's undesirable. If they see too much of reality, they may set themselves to change it.

The Gulf War is a perfect illustration of how the state and the media worked to divert the masses. The strategy was to demonize and, thus, dehumanize the Iraqis in order to mobilize the U.S. population in support of what really were foreign economic adventures, shrouded in the idealistic rhetoric of defending democracy.

The public relations industry — a U.S. creation — is very aware that their job is controlling the population. But, we shouldn't overestimate its success. This is a very heavily polled society, and most of the polls are done for business because the public relations industry wants to know how to craft the propaganda. There's a ton of information on public attitudes. Take the Gulf War, for example. The polls that were taken two or three days before the bombing found the population to be two to one in favor of a negotiated

---

[a] **Colonizing the mind** (or psyche) refers to the process through which an individual or group internalizes certain values (or is indoctrinated), and thus conforms with particular practices, which are usually oppressive in nature.

settlement. Those two-thirds who came out in favor of negotiating a settlement did not, when they described their position, know that was also Iraq's position. Iraq had, in fact, put that position on the table, and the United States had simply rebuffed it because they didn't want to negotiate a withdrawal. If the population had known those facts, which were very carefully concealed — I believe they only appeared in one newspaper in the United States — the results wouldn't have been two to one, they probably would have been twenty to one. And the same is true on other issues. Take, say, the economic system. Over 80 percent of the population regard it as inherently unfair. In addition, the political system — everyone knows it's regarded as a joke. On issue after issue, the public is not in line with elite opinion, but the public is marginalized.

This business about "the bewildered herd" — I didn't make that phrase up — that's Walter Lippmann, the dean of American journalists, in his "progressive" essays on "democracy." He said that we have to protect ourselves from "the trampling and the roar of a bewildered herd," "we" being the smart guys who are supposed to run things; we've got to make sure the bewildered herd doesn't get in our way. Perhaps 90 percent of the population, "they're bewildered," and we're going to keep them bewildered because, as he put it pretty frankly, in a democracy, the public has the role of **"spectators"** but not **"participants"**.[b] "We," the elite 10 percent or so, are the participants. "We" are the "responsible men." And that's the "progressive" fringe; reactionaries are even worse. And that's understandable, because if people knew what was going on and they acted on their own motives, that would dismantle the system of privilege. Not many people would be happy to know that they're paying taxes so that the people in Newt Gingrich's rich suburb can get even richer. If they found that out, there would be changes.

How do schools and institutions of education — which play a significant role in the ongoing formative nature of culture, identity, and social relations by directly influencing children's ways of seeing themselves and others in the world — contribute to this colonizing of people's minds?

Well, every possible way. It starts in kindergarten: the school system tries to repress independence, it tries to teach obedience. Kids, and other people, are not induced to challenge and question, but the contrary. If you start questioning, you're a behavioral problem or something like that; you've got to be disciplined. You're supposed to repeat, obey, follow orders, and so on. When you get over to the more totalitarian end, like the Newt Gingriches,

---

[b] This idea of **spectators** and **participants** is often described by critical pedagogues as a person being an "object" and not a "subject" of history. That is, a person is treated as an entity that is acted upon, manipulated, and controlled as an object of history, rather than as an active and critical participant. A basic tenet of critical pedagogy is that only as active, critical subjects are we able to make substantive change. "Colonizing" the mind refers to the process through which an individual or group internalizes certain values (or is indoctrinated), and thus conforms with particular practices, which are usually oppressive in nature.

they actually want to do things like coerce kids into praying, and they call it voluntary. But you know, you have a six-year-old kid who's got a choice of praying like everyone else or walking out of the room, it's not voluntary and those demanding school prayer know it. Such forms of state coercion and imposing discipline would absolutely horrify the "founding fathers," not that Gingrich cares one way or the other.

How does this "manufacturing of consent" happen in the larger social and political spheres, and in business and corporate sectors?

When you talk about the state and the business community in the United States, it's extremely hard to separate them. The state is overwhelmingly penetrated and dominated by the corporate sector; the financial and corporate institutions have most of the top decisionmaking positions, so it's very hard to disentangle the corporate sector and the state. They're different manifestations of very closely related things. The media are another part of this. The media are big corporations that sell audiences to other businesses. An example of this manufacturing of consent was in yesterday's paper, where you'll find Elaine Sciolino, chief intellectual in the New York Times, describing Clinton's Indonesia trip, and she describes how his big achievement there was that he was able to get jobs for Americans. How did he get jobs for Americans? Well, by implementing a $35 billion deal whereby Exxon Corporation develops natural gas fields in Indonesia. Is that going to be jobs for Americans? A couple of American executives and some public relations firms, and maybe some corporate law firms, but it's going to give jobs to very few Americans. On the other hand, it's going to give profits to quite a lot of rich Americans; but you're not allowed to mention the word "profits." That's a dirty word. So, it can't be that Clinton was over there to get profits for rich Americans, it's got to be that he's getting jobs for poor Americans. The discipline on that topic approaches 100 percent. You just can't find the word "profits" — it's always "jobs" in the media and the political rhetoric. Remember when Bush went to Japan with a bevy of auto executives a couple of years ago? The big slogan was "Jobs, Jobs, Jobs." General Motors is trying to get jobs for Americans? Is that why they're closing down twenty-four plants here and have become the biggest employer in Mexico and are now moving to Poland — because they want jobs for Americans? No, they want profits for rich Americans, but you can't say that. And if you tried to say that, first of all, in elite circles, you probably wouldn't be understood.

What's amazing is that companies like General Motors will strategically shroud themselves in the American flag, and in a kind of baseball, hotdogs, and apple pie patriotism. And people generally buy into such representations.

Because there is so much indoctrination that many people can't even understand the word "profits." If you try using the word "profits" around Harvard, for example, in the Kennedy School of Government, if you say "Clinton's out there getting profits for rich Americans," then people would be appalled — "Is he some kind of conspiracy theorist? Marxist? anti-American? or crazed radical?" Even elementary truisms like this, which to someone like Adam Smith, are so obvious he scarcely even bothered to talk about them, are completely beaten out of heads of educated people. In fact, I think it's worse among the educated sectors than among the uneducated. I've talked to all sorts of people, and it would be harder to convince Harvard graduates that this deal with Exxon was for profits than it would be to convince guys on the street. They'd say "Yeah, obviously." And the reason is, if you've been really well educated, meaning well indoctrinated, you can't even think rational thoughts any longer. They can't come to you, the words can't come to you. So, I don't think Elaine Sciolino is lying, it's just that the conception of the state working to increase profits for wealthy Americans is inconceivable. You can't think that thought. If it's ever expressed, you have to designate it "unthinkable," with scare words like "conspiracy theory." And that's the process of "good education." People who don't internalize those values are weeded out along the way. By the time you get to the top, you've internalized them.

This phenomenon certainly carries over in the teaching of history, especially U.S. history. The possibility of thinking about the history of this country in terms of profit and greed, and the resulting violence and even genocide, is eliminated. Those words are seldom even in the textbooks.

Well, it's a little better than it used to be, but not much. Much of history is just wiped out. We just went through a war in Central America in which hundreds of thousands of people were slaughtered, and countries destroyed — huge terror. U.S. operations were condemned by the World Court as international terrorism. It's nevertheless described in this country as an effort to bring democracy to Central America. How do they get away with that? If you have a deeply indoctrinated educated sector, as we do, you're not going to get any dissent there, and among the general population who may not be so deeply indoctrinated, they're marginal. They're supposed to be afraid of welfare mothers and people coming to attack us, and busy watching football games and so on, so it doesn't matter what they think. And that's pretty much the way the educational system and the media work. So the *New York Times* and the *Washington Post,* they're for educated folk, and they sort of beat them on the head with the right ideology. Most of the rest of the media are there just to keep people's minds on something else.

This practice of constricting what's acceptable to think and to consider in the academy and public debate is certainly evident in your experiences as a social theorist. Your work has been recognized globally, and you're seen, historically, as one of the world's most brilliant intellectuals. However, at the same time, your political critique and insights, have been for the most part marginalized, if not ridiculed, in the United States.

True, but the respectable intellectual culture is not so dramatically different in most countries.

The idea of "public intellectual" in present-day politics is a contradiction. If people are honest in their critique of the system in the United States, they are either declared non-intellectual, or, as you state, derided as "anti-American, Marxist, or conspiracy theorists," and removed from the public media.

It's not really a contradiction; it's perfectly normal under this system of control. For one thing, I'm on the radio and television and writing articles all over the world — not here. And that's to be expected. If I started getting public media exposure here, I'd think I were doing something wrong. Why should any system of power offer opportunities to people who are trying to undermine it? That would be crazy. It's not that this is something new. The people who are called "intellectuals" are those who pretty much serve power. Others may be equally intellectual, but they're not called intellectuals. And that goes all the way back to the origins of recorded history. Go back to the Bible; who were the people who were respected, and who were the people who were reviled? Well, the people who were respected were the ones who, a thousand years later, were called false prophets. And the ones who were reviled and jailed and beaten and so on are the ones who years later were called prophets. And it goes right up until today. In the United States, people respected Soviet dissidents, but they weren't respected in Soviet society. There, they respected the commissars. So you are a respected intellectual if you do your job as a part of the system of doctrinal control. Raise questions about it and you're just not acceptable — you're anti-American or some sort of shrill and strident something or other. Why was Walter Lippmann one of the "responsible men," while Eugene Debs was in jail? Was it that Walter Lippmann was smarter than Eugene Debs? Not that I can see. Eugene Debs was just an American working-class leader who raised unacceptable questions, so he was in jail. And Walter Lippmann was a servant of the major powers, so he was respected. And it would be amazing if it was anything else.

But then what is the role of intellectuals, in terms of offering a public counter-discourse that links violence and social decay to structural flaws and undemocratic practices? And, in light of the recent Republican repositioning of power, what are the possibilities of such counter-discourses?

The job of the honest intellectual is to help out people who need help; to be part of the people who are struggling for rights and justice. That's what you should be doing. But of course, you don't expect to be rewarded for that.

In terms of teachers in this country who express the desire to work towards more democratic social change, what do you think they could do?

It's easy for me to talk, but the fact is, if you're in a classroom and you try to act like an honest independent person, you'd probably be thrown out.

The school board won't like it —especially if it's made up of wealthy parents, they're not going to like it. I remember in the 1960s when the student ferment began, we lived in Lexington, a professional, upper middle-class suburb outside Boston. The parents wanted the school to be run like the Marine Corps. They wanted their kids controlled. They didn't want them to think. Well, there were in those days, maybe more than now, young people coming out of the universities who believed in teaching kids to think, as a means of social transformation. They would do things like elementary school teaching, and some of them tried and they were very good. My son had one of these teachers for a while in elementary school. But it's very hard to live in the system and survive it. It's clear what you ought to do, but whether you can survive it is another question.

This question of teaching children to think critically, to better understand and participate in the transformation of the violence, racism, social control, and social disintegration around them, is taken up in critical pedagogy. While you certainly embrace critical education, what do you think are its realistic possibilities here in the United States?

It's just not going to be allowed, because it's too subversive. You can teach students to think for themselves in the sciences because you want people to be independent and creative, otherwise, you don't have science. But science and engineering students are not encouraged to be critical in terms of the political and social implications of their work. In most other fields you want students to be obedient and submissive, and that starts from childhood. Now, teachers can try, and do break out of that, but, they will surely find if they go too far, that as soon as it gets noticed there'll be pressures to stop them.

There is a problem with this fragmentation of knowledge into separate disciplines in the academy — this is science, that's politics, this is psychology. Even the word "discipline" is so ironic, alluding to constraint. When I try, in graduate school, to talk about moral development and its inherent connection with the sociohistorical and political structures that we've been speaking about, then some people immediately react by saying: "You're not talking about moral development anymore, now you're talking about politics, or some other discipline, and we don't deal with that." How can you talk about moral development and violence without talking about the larger social, cultural, and economic environments in which people live and develop?

You can't! On the other hand, if you simply talk about the world in the accepted ways, that would not be called politics, that would be being reasonable. It becomes "ideological" or extremist when it deviates from the accepted patterns. The term "ideological" is an interesting one. If you repeat the clichés of the propaganda system, that's not ideological. On the other hand, if you question them, that's ideological and very strident or anti-American. Anti-American is an interesting expression, because the accusation of being anti-nation is used typically in totalitarian societies, for example, the former Soviet Union accused dissidents of being anti-Soviet. But try "anti-Italian" or "anti-Belgian," people in Milan or Brussels would laugh.

The term "propaganda" is used in neither the media nor the academy in reference to this country's practices — as if propaganda only functions in places like the former Soviet Union or Nazi Germany.

Yeah, like the invasion of Haiti, or whatever you want to call that thing. The big thinkers in the press presented what they called "historical background." R. W. Apple over at the New York Times wrote an article on "perspectives" and explained that for hundreds of years, the benevolent Westerners have been trying to bring some order to Haitian society, where groups with homicidal tendencies are attacking one another and are heavily armed, like right now. So you've got two "homicidal gangs" attacking each other — the people who are getting murdered in the slums, and the troops whom we trained and armed who were killing them. Then he goes on about how, at different periods in history, both Napoleon and Woodrow Wilson tried to do "good things" for the Haitian people, which didn't work. We are used to the fact that the Wilson intervention, which was murderous and brutal, was regarded as sweet charity, but Napoleon? That was one of the most murderous invasions of a period that was not known for its gentility, but it must be that "good" Westerners were trying to bring order to this society. And David Broder of the *Washington Post* wrote the same thing. That's "history" — the idealistic Americans are trying to help out. But they're baffled by the violence of the society that has no experience with democracy, and so on and so forth. I mean the relation of that to history — it's 180 degrees off. But if you repeat that stuff, that's not ideological, that's being "responsible." David Landes, a well-known Harvard historian, wrote an article on Haiti some years back, in which he described the Marine invasion — the Wilson intervention — as very beneficial to Haiti. In fact, it had a devastating effect on the society, dismantling the Parliamentary system, and killing thousands of people, forcing them to accept laws that let U.S. corporations buy up the land and turn it into plantations, reintroducing virtual slavery. It also left a military force to attack the people — it was monstrous. This from a leading historian — but that's not ideological. On the other hand, if you tell the truth, that's ideological. That makes sense, in some strange way.

Fostering historical amnesia and refusing to acknowledge the violent and **hegemonic**[c] *nature of their own ideology allow those who have historically run this country to perpetuate the myth that this is a democratic society. Your work has shown that U.S.*

---

[c] **Hegemony**, as derived from the work of Italian theorist Antonio Gramsci, is used to express how certain groups manage to dominate others. An analysis of hegemony is especially concerned with how the imposition of particular ideologies and forms of authority results in the reproduction of social and institutional practices through which dominant groups maintain not only their positions of privilege and control, but also the consensual support of other members of society.

international political and economic practices have actually destroyed what you refer to as "good examples — prospects for real progress towards meaningful democracy and meeting human needs" in "third-world" countries. Such examples are falsely represented to the American public as posing a threat to our security and well-being, and people generally buy into that. They actually believe that they live in a truly democratic society.

I suppose that around Harvard they do! But if you look at the polls, half the population thinks that both political parties should be dismantled. Is that living in democracy? What you get in off-year elections is about a third of the population voting — this year, around 39 percent. That's because people just regard the whole electoral process as a farce. In fact, there are regular Gallup polls in which people are asked, "Who do you think runs the government?" And about 50 percent regularly say that the government is run by a few big interests looking out for themselves. Try that in the Harvard Faculty Club. The official story is that the political system is pluralistic, everyone's part of some different interest or pressure group. It's not a few big interests looking out for themselves. You have to be uneducated to be able to see that.

Given the implications of your work and what we've said in the last hour, what are the possibilities for fulfilling a progressive vision of a future social order — one that actively incorporates the majority of the population in nonviolent political struggle, resistance, and social transformation?

As everyone has always known, the best way to defend civil liberties is to collectively build a movement for social change that has broad-based appeal, that encourages free and open discussion, and offers a wide range of possibilities for social agency. The potential for such a movement surely exists. Many positive changes have taken place in the last thirty years as the result of popular movements organized around such issues as civil rights, peace, feminism, and the environment. If this struggle ever becomes a mass movement of the oppressed and exploited on an international level, the impulse to contribute to it may intensify, growing both from moral pressure and the desire for self-fulfillment in a decent and humane society. One immediate concern of industrial democracies is the rational and humane use of the Earth's resources, on which the United States continues to do very poorly, and which, as exploitation, is another form of violence. "Broad-based" also implies that along with the general public, scientists, engineers, technicians, and skilled workers, educators, writers, and artists also need to be deeply involved in the development of the intellectual resources necessary for providing plausible, concrete, short- and long-term solutions to the problems of our advanced industrial society.

You have stated in the past that any system of power, even a fascist dictatorship, is responsive to public dissidence. In the context of everyday life in this country, where does such dissention begin when the deck is so clearly stacked against popular struggle?

The general population has lots of cards. People can organize, initiate demonstrations, write letters, and vote. They can form unions and other grassroots organizations, political clubs, even an opposition political party so that we'll at least have a two-party system. Citizens can organize to press a position and pressure their representatives about it. Elections can also matter. The systems of private tyranny — totalitarian in character — are also not there by natural law, but by human decisions. They can be dismantled and democratized. What concentrated privilege can't live with is sustained pressure that keeps building, organizations that keep doing things, people that keep learning lessons from the last time and doing it better the next time. Students and others with similar privilege — and it is privilege — can also do their own research by going back to original sources in public libraries. Real research and inquiry is always a collective activity. Such efforts can make a large contribution to changing consciousness, increasing insight and understanding, and leading to constructive action.

Well, as you conclude in What Uncle Sam Really Wants, *"We don't know that honest and dedicated effort will be enough to solve or even mitigate our problems; however, we can be quite confident that the lack of such efforts will spell disaster."*

We would like to take this opportunity to express our gratitude for your generous contribution to this special issue on violence and youth, and also to recognize and celebrate your lifelong commitment to the struggle for justice and the possibilities for human liberation.

7

Academic Freedom and the Parameters of Knowledge

WILLIAM G. TIERNEY

As all of the previous authors have argued, William Tierney reaffirms the view that knowledge is not neutral, but, rather, that it reflects the human interests and the social and power relationships within society. Illustrating ways in which knowledge is a social construction that has inevitable political ramifications (refuting the conservative assertion that politics has corrupted the academic environment), Tierney explores the issue of academic freedom as it pertains to the contemporary constraints placed on "permissible" fields of study, multiple perspectives, and modes of communication and interaction. Using a case study of a large university, he addresses the ideological restraints — the overt and covert limitations — that have been placed on study and discussion of gay, lesbian, and bisexual issues on the college campus. For example, he reveals how gay and lesbian issues are studied only in relation to deviance, thus constructing a particular notion (what often becomes socially accepted "knowledge") of sexual orientations "outside" of heterosexuality.

Tierney's findings reveal a paradox: at a university committed to the advancement of human understanding and academic openness, lesbian, gay, and bisexual faculty, staff, and students feel that their civil rights are threatened, which both implicitly and explicitly limits research pertaining to these issues. Throughout the analysis of this case study, he raises new questions and presents his own understanding of academic freedom.

Over the last decade, conservative critics of the academy have attacked what they see as the radical orientation that currently resides on college campuses. Allan Bloom (1987), Roger Kimball (1990), Diane Ravitch (1990), Dinesh

D'Souza (1991) and others decry the politicization of virtually all aspects of academic life — from the construction of the curriculum to admission requirements, from hiring quotas for faculty to the selection of college presidents. The traditional notion of the academy as a monastery where truth is pursued to advance knowledge for the common good has, in the eyes of the conservatives, been shattered. They argue that, instead of academics who struggle with life's great truths, we now have a radical cadre of intellectuals who seek to impose their own values and doctrines on college and university campuses. Most importantly, conservative critics assert that radical faculty seek to corrupt the young by the bastardization of traditional notions of the curriculum. As Kimball notes, "Their object is nothing less than the destruction of the values, methods, and goals of traditional humanistic study" (1990, p. xi).

Given the apocalyptic nature of their argument, one should not be surprised that conservatives also feel that the heart of academic life — academic freedom — is also under attack. They contend that demands for ideological conformity, or "political correctness," have encroached on basic academic freedoms to such an extent that the free expression of ideas no longer exists on college campuses. Indeed, the conservatives believe that the curtailment of free speech has so poisoned the atmosphere in the academy that if one disagrees with a "politically correct" position, one will not merely be labeled a racist, sexist, or some other epithet; the recalcitrant will also face severe reprimands, such as administrative sanctions.

In this article, I take issue with the conservative critique and subsequent call to arms. I argue that knowledge is a social construction that always has had inevitable political ramifications. As I will discuss, when I speak of knowledge in this manner, I am suggesting that what we come to know is in part determined by the multiple contexts in which we come to learn and are situated. A concept such as academic freedom has never existed in a political vacuum; rather, the parameters of knowledge define what we mean by academic freedom, which, in turn, allows some topics to be worthy of investigation and others to be unworthy of study. The parameters of knowledge are those acceptable definitions of an idea or concept; as we shall see, the central focus of this text is to consider how such definitions gain acceptance. Conversely, we also will see how other definitions lose credence, or, as discussed here, never even gain consideration.

I highlight my argument with a case study pertaining to gay, lesbian, and bisexual issues on one campus. I offer data from unstructured interviews and two surveys of attitudes pertaining to sexual orientation that underscore how individuals come to define what are legitimate forms of knowledge. In doing so, I suggest that, rather than return to the conservative ideal of the academy that is based on a singular notion of truth, we need to reconceptualize our idea of community so that we become capable of building academic communities of difference. My selection of a case study about gay, lesbian, and bisexual issues is purposeful, for, as we shall see, an area of investigation such as lesbian and gay studies has never been considered acceptable unless one has studied the topic from the perspective of deviance. I will argue that as a contested and political concept, academic freedom often gets defined by social constructs such as gender, class, and race. In the case presented here, we see how a specific academic community has defined knowledge in a manner that denies any validity to gay, lesbian, and bisexual issues. A community of difference, in contrast, is one that enables those individuals and groups who have been silenced to gain voice, which, in turn, alters communal definitions of knowledge and academic freedom. By "voice" I mean that individuals and groups are able to seize the conditions for speaking and acting on their own, rather than having those in power set the terms on which they may speak, or be silent.

The article has three sections. First, I entertain a discussion about how writers have defined academic freedom; I analyze the underlying epistemological assumptions of these positions to demonstrate how previous interpretations of academic freedom have relied on a singular notion of truth that has privileged some individuals and silenced others. I then offer a case study of Normal State University (a pseudonym), which recently has implemented a sexual orientation clause in its statement of nondiscrimination. A conservative interpretation of this action is in keeping with the assertion that politics has corrupted the academic environment. I call upon the work of Michel Foucault (1980), Henry Giroux (1988), and Peter McLaren (1989) to offer an alternative analysis based on a postmodern perspective that utilizes critical theory. The article concludes with a discussion of how one might simultaneously deal with conservative attacks on "political correctness" and construct academic communities of difference.

ACADEMIC FREEDOM AND THE CULTURE OF KNOWLEDGE

Defining Academic Freedom

Throughout this century we have assumed that academic freedom is the basic right of faculty freely to pursue and disseminate knowledge. Although the idea certainly has a sociological base in the religious and civil rights that formed the cornerstone of U.S. society, in general, historians of education point out that the roots of the concept derive from the turn-of-the-century German ideal of *Lehrfreiheit*. The initial idea of *Lehrfreiheit* pertained to "the right of the university professor to freedom of inquiry and to freedom of teaching, the right to study and to report on his findings in an atmosphere of consent" (Rudolph, 1962, p. 412). Previous authors have shown that U.S. faculty who returned from study in Germany were significantly influenced by the ideal of "academic freedom" and struggled to implement the concept in U.S. institutions (Hofstadter & Metzger, 1955; Veysey, 1965).

To define academic freedom, authors often have provided examples of individuals from academe's past whose academic freedom was abridged; in other words, academic freedom is often defined by its absence. Ellen

Schrecker, for example, begins her discussion of academic freedom by telling the story of Richard Ely, a liberal economist at the University of Wisconsin, who in 1894 was tried by a committee of Regents for his support of unions and lost his job (1983, p. 27). Carol McCart stretches back to the 1820s to discuss the case of Thomas Cooper, a college president whose opposition to Calvinism placed his job in jeopardy (1991, p. 12). Richard Hofstadter relates the case of Wilcott Gibbs, who in 1853 was not hired for a job at Columbia College because he was a Unitarian (1955, p. 273). Previously, I considered the case of a liberal economics professor, Edward Ross of Stanford University, who spoke out against private ownership of railroads and ran into trouble with the railroad baron, Leland Stanford, who in 1890 demanded his removal (Tierney, 1983).

Moving into this century, Sheila Slaughter relates how Scott Nearing was fired in 1915 from the University of Pennsylvania because he opposed the use of child labor in coal mines (1980, p. 52). Walter Metzger tells the tale of John Mecklin, an outspoken liberal professor at Lafayette College, who was forced to resign in 1913 because of his philosophical relativism, interest in pragmaticism, and teaching of evolution (1955, p. 201). In more contemporary times, Bertell Ollman outlines the Joel Samoff case in which a well-respected political science professor was denied tenure because he used a "Marxist approach to his subject matter" (1983, p. 46). In a previous work, I discuss the Bruce Franklin case in which a professor's tenure was revoked because of his vociferous opposition to Stanford University's involvement with activities concerned with the Vietnam War (Tierney, 1983). Slaughter points out how George Murray and Staughton Lynd also had to face "wholesale attacks on [their] academic freedom. . . . As always, [they] were political activists, often using their academic expertise to challenge **dominant ideologies**"[a] (1980, p. 60).

Presumably, all of these violations of an individual's ability to conduct teaching and research without interference has led to the codification of the concept of academic freedom. By 1940, the conditions in U.S. higher education had matured to the point where the American Association of University Professors (AAUP) was able to offer the following definition:

> The purpose of this statement is to promote public understanding and support of academic freedom and tenure and agreement upon procedures to assure them in colleges and universities. Institutions of higher education are conducted for the common good and not to further interest of either individual teacher or the institution as a whole. The common good depends upon the free search for truth and its free exposition. Academic freedom is essential to these purposes. (AAUP, 1940/1977)

---

[a] **Dominant ideologies** are bodies of ideas held by cultural groups that are politically, socially, and economically in positions of power and are therefore able to impose on the greater society, through various social institutions and practices, particular traditions, bodies of knowledge, discourse styles, language uses, values, norms, and beliefs, usually at the expense of others.

In a contemporary vein, Howard Bowen and Jack Schuster add that academic freedom

> includes the right of faculty members to substantial autonomy in the conduct of their work, and to freedom of thought and expression as they discover and disseminate learning. This freedom is held to be essential to the advancement of learning. To ensure this freedom, faculty members should be evaluated by their peers who may include local colleagues and sometimes outside specialists. To reinforce academic freedom, faculty members should be given lifetime tenure subject to safeguards relating to a probationary period, dismissal for cause, and financial exigency on the part of the employing institution. (1986, p. 53)

Recent research efforts demonstrate that virtually all individuals in academe are in favor of academic freedom, although differences exist with regard to type of institution, discipline, research productivity, age, and rank (Clark, 1987; Ladd & Lipset, 1977; Lazarsfeld & Theilens, 1958; Lewis, 1966; McCart, 1991; Olswang & Lee, 1984; Wences & Abramson, 1971). As Burton Clark has noted, academic freedom is "a totem for the vast majority of respondents across disciplines and up and down the line of the institutional hierarchy" (1987, p. 135).

These descriptions portray an understanding of academic freedom as a concept that is in general defined by when it is limited. Regardless of one's political persuasion, academic freedom remains a mythic symbol pertaining to the underlying purpose of academe. Indeed, radical scholars such as Slaughter and Ollman and conservatives such as Kimball and William Bennett are united in little else other than their defense of academic freedom. To be sure, how radicals and conservatives operationalize academic freedom differs dramatically, yet their epistemological suppositions are generally quite similar, and to this I now turn.

The Cultural Politics of Academic Freedom

Hofstadter and Metzger have argued that modern academic freedom befits our belief in modern science and the assumption that knowledge exists as a free market where we see "free competition among ideas" (1955, p. 61). From this perspective, knowledge is reified as a social product that scholars study and investigate from any number of different theoretical angles. The modernist concept of science assumes that facts exist and scholars function to uncover the meanings and patterns of those facts.

Knowledge production occurs independent of the researcher; that is, the researcher's biases or beliefs are not supposed to enter into either the research topic chosen or the theoretical orientation employed. In essence, social scientists have tried throughout the twentieth century to mirror the objectivity of the natural scientist's laboratory. Scientific inquiry is to be bereft of ideology, and objectivity is the sine qua non of inquiry. I have previously pointed out that the portrait this assumption presents is of knowledge as a "jigsaw puzzle that can be shaped into multiple [images]; even though different representations can be drawn, the pieces of the puzzle are the same to all" (Tierney, 1989, p. 73).

The implications for academic freedom are that we need to protect the manner in which someone studies the "puzzle." A conservative or a radical must be free to investigate the same pieces and interpret them differently. As observed above, in previous discussions we find examples of individuals whose academic freedom was violated because of the manner in which they explained a particular puzzle. Those individuals often were liberals such as Ely or Ross, who interpreted economics from a particular point of view. The point, of course, is not simply that someone was liberal or conservative, but that their ideas represented a particular point of view that fell outside the accepted definitions of the academy. However, we now find conservatives who claim that their academic freedom is violated because they offer a different representation from that which is "politically correct." Ultimately, the assumption is that, in the rarefied atmosphere of a university where political intrigue is supposed to be absent, a single true interpretation of the particular puzzle will prevail. The battle of opposing ideas must occur so that an objective analysis and persuasive solution can be found for whatever particular puzzle is being studied.

As the AAUP statement pointed out, academic freedom exists so that individuals may function in an institution "conducted for the common good." And tautologically, the "common good" depends upon the free search for truth. From a critical or postmodern perspective, the problem begins here. When we assume a singular interpretation of modernist concepts such as the "common good" or "truth," we are overlooking that communal life is rarely organized around a single substantive idea (Mouffe, 1990, p. 62). Different individuals and groups will constantly be in conflict with one another due to relations of power. Some individuals are silenced and others are given voice according to how they fit within an organization's or system's cultural borders. Issues such as race, class, and gender come into play so that "common good" and "truth" get defined in terms of dominant community values and mores.

A critical perspective argues that the production of knowledge is socially constructed and incorporates the manifold perspectives that account for the "common good" (Tierney, 1991, p. 204). Participants define knowledge according to their social and historical contexts. In this light, how we have come to think about gender in the late twentieth century, for example, is not simply a result of the accretionary advances in knowledge, but is, rather, specifically tied to the social and cultural contexts in which we have lived over the past thirty years. Thus, knowledge is not something abstract and reified, divorced from any relationship to the researcher. Instead, following Foucault (1972), I am arguing that institutions, individuals, and the constantly shifting social forces of society combine to determine what accounts for knowledge at a particular moment in history.

The suggestion advanced here is that a cultural politics surrounds how knowledge gets defined, studied, and enacted, which in turn structures how we have thought about academic freedom. By cultural politics I mean that concepts such as "knowledge" are inevitably related to power and ideology, and that to speak of knowledge as if it is a reified object is to overlook the theoretical scaffolding upon which it rests. Thus, we see how a traditional definition of an academic area such as English or History has not merely represented a reified idea, but also reflected the interests, for example, of men or the upper class.

Culture includes the symbolic expressive acts of human beings that occur within organizational landscapes; the manner in which these acts take place gets defined as cultural politics. The challenge is to develop a **nonessentialist**[b] view of knowledge and academic freedom that acknowledges the impossibility of a fully realized definition of community. In turn, such a definition will struggle to come to terms with how to enable those who have been silenced to gain voice. Rather than assume that one definition exists, which suggests that the community operates on a consensual model, we operate from the perspective of a conflict model in which we assume that competing interests will always exist. The paradox, of course, is how a community may simultaneously exist so that definitions of "common good" are not all enveloping, yet at the same time some bonds of social obligation and affiliation operate to tie the group together.

Thus, what counts as knowledge inevitably concerns our assumptions about the nature of knowledge. I need to be clear here. I am not merely suggesting that different individuals will interpret ideas, objects, or events in various ways, for that is precisely the modernist conception I am struggling to bring into question. Rather, I am arguing that what we define as knowledge constantly undergoes reinterpretation. If we return to the example of knowledge as a "puzzle," the modernist assumption is that everyone begins their study with the same pieces of a puzzle but their interpretations may differ. Ultimately, however, the modernist assumption is that an objective view will enable one singular picture to develop. The postmodern stance is that researchers do not even begin with similar puzzle pieces, and that no amount of scientific objectivity will enable researchers to construct the same puzzle. The argument pertains more to how we produce, define, and interpret knowledge than how knowledge accumulates (Sedgwick, 1990). Clearly, knowledge is a social product with political roots. Such a view of knowledge requires us to analyze how the various actors define "the common good."

---

[b] **Essentialism** ascribes a fundamental nature or a biological determinism to humans (i.e., men are naturally aggressive, and women are naturally nurturing) through attitudes about identity, experience, knowledge, and cognitive development. Within this monolithic and homogenizing view, categories such as race and gender become gross generalizations and single-cause explanations about individual character. Tierney's use of "nonessentialist" points to the idea that universal knowledge, a realm of pure thought and reason, does not exist. Instead, knowledge is a sociohistorical construction that reflects certain values and interests.

Knowledge has political consequences tied to the context in which the investigation resides and to the researcher who undertakes the analysis, regardless of his or her political orientation.

Academic freedom, then, needs to be investigated not simply by examples of those who had a particular point of view and were penalized, but by undertaking an analysis of conceptual modes of thought that are not allowed or countenanced or even seen as knowledge. Such an analysis underscores how knowledge is socially constructed and how the organizational context in which it resides helps define the parameters of knowledge.

To demonstrate what I mean, in the next section I detail a case study of Normal State University and the discourse surrounding lesbian, gay, and bisexual issues. I argue that the parameters of knowledge have been set at Normal State so that individuals are not able even to conceive of studying certain ideas such as lesbian and gay studies, which in turn makes academic freedom a concept that demands reanalysis and conceptual clarity from a postmodern perspective. The issue here is not whether or not we might interpret the pieces of the puzzle differently, but instead, the issue relates to what puzzles we might be free to examine.

NORMAL STATE AND THE COMMON GOOD: REDEFINING KNOWLEDGE

My objectives in this section are two-fold. First, I provide a case history of Normal State University's efforts at implementing a sexual orientation clause in their statement of nondiscrimination. In addition to the data collected for the case history, I also analyze findings from two surveys conducted at Normal State during the 1990–1991 academic year. One survey was geared towards students and the other towards faculty and staff. As we shall see, the case history and surveys reveal a variety of opinions about homosexuality, which in turn influences an individual's ability to investigate issues such as lesbian and gay studies. My goal here is to underscore how a particular issue — in this instance, gay and lesbian studies — gets contextually defined, which in turn highlights the shortcomings of present conceptualizations of academic freedom. In this present case, the ideology at this University defines homosexuality as aberrant and seeks to silence those who think otherwise.

For example, one young man commented, "Since I've been here at Normal State, I've learned a lot about homosexuality. I am a gay male, but nobody knows. I've been 'in the closet' far too long, but I'm terrified to open the door and come out." Presumably, the young man's terror derives from the context in which he resides and how homosexuality has been defined both at Normal State and beyond its borders. A second individual, an untenured gay assistant professor at Normal State, added, "The reason I chose a liberal arts department instead of something like a College of Education is that I thought liberal arts would be less homophobic than a School of Education. That was a conscious choice; I thought about it." Another gay untenured professor said, "You feel the pain of oppression, of knowing, of having mirrored back to you every day that you're different and that there are people who want to hurt you, and deny you basic human rights." A lesbian faculty member said, "This is not an easy community to be in. . . . You have to be very cautious about 'coming out' to the wrong people. It is hard to know when it is safe to be who you are." And another lesbian faculty member summarized: "Professionally I would be frightened to be open about my lifestyle. Having a president who doesn't want to include a sexual orientation clause makes me fearful of being found out. What concerns me most right now is my career. I must protect it."

Each individual paints a picture of fear about being discovered as a gay, lesbian, or bisexual person. Certainly, their fears may not be well-founded; perhaps their perceptions are ill-conceived. Such a suggestion underscores two points that return us to a discussion about defining knowledge and academic freedom. First, one needs to contextualize those perceptions and come to terms with how well-founded they are. Second, we need to consider how homosexuality is a constructed social product in this community and decide how individuals connect their notions of homosexuality to their definitions of academic freedom. How does the "common good" at Normal State silence or give voice to such an issue and to the individuals who define themselves as lesbian or gay?

Implementing a Sexual Orientation Clause at Normal State

Normal State University is a large, public, land-grant university situated in a rural area several hours away from any major city. Although many individuals describe the area as "very conservative," their interpretation is more toward a Bush-style conservatism than that of the Ku Klux Klan. The Board of Trustees is generally viewed as a conservative and powerful influence on campus. The institution also has several vocal, well-organized student groups. An extensive fraternity and sorority system is seen as relatively conservative, while the student government has traditionally been liberal. The most vocal student groups have come together under one banner tentatively called, "The Council of Underrepresented Peoples" (COUP). The COUP is composed of different constituencies of underrepresented students, such as African Americans, Hispanics, and Native Americans. One of these groups is the Lesbian, Gay, and Bisexual Student Alliance (LGBSA). During the last five years, LGBSA has received extensive coverage in the student newspaper, and they have forced a discussion of lesbian, gay, and bisexual issues on campus.

LGBSA has had a somewhat stormy twenty-year history. When they first surfaced (under another acronym) in 1971, the Vice President for Student Affairs informed the organization that they would be denied access to campus facilities and that the University's lawyers had begun an investigation of the group. Eventually, the charter of the group was revoked. A gay student in the 1970s became a celebrity because he was open about his sexuality and about his desire to be a school teacher. Although he had been rated a superb student teacher, his school district fired him; in general, Normal State's College of Education faculty supported the removal.

By 1985, LGBSA was allowed to exist on campus, but they were officially ignored. Unlike other student groups, they received no office space and had no voting rights in the student government. Since that time, the group has worked tirelessly at advocating change. They have gained seats on the student government and have developed a wide array of services for lesbian, gay, and bisexual students. Perhaps more than any other activity, they have lobbied to change the University's statement of nondiscrimination.

When a new president arrived at Normal State in the fall of 1990, one of the first issues with which he was hit was the demand from LGBSA to enact a sexual orientation clause in the University's statement of nondiscrimination. Essentially, all the students wanted were the words "sexual orientation" added to the University's nondiscrimination statement so that lesbians, gays, and bisexuals would be protected from discrimination in the same manner that one is protected on the basis of race, gender, age, and the like. Over time, different groups spoke up to support "the clause," as the issue came to be known. First the student government and then the COUP spoke out on behalf of LGBSA's push for such a clause. The student newspaper was a central vehicle that individuals used to publish columns and letters in support of the clause.

In the fall of 1990, a loosely affiliated group formed that called itself "Gay and Lesbian Faculty and Staff." Unlike their counterparts in the student body, Normal State's faculty and staff had been entirely silent as a group about the discrimination and harassment gay, lesbian, and bisexual people faced on campus. On occasion, one or two lone faculty members spoke up, but they were seen as individuals and not part of any united constituency. While social activities occurred in the gay community, such as occasional potlucks at one another's houses or picnics, any sense of united political action was absent and, indeed, feared. Gradually, for a whole complex of reasons I explore elsewhere (Tierney, 1993), different faculty began to speak up and "come out" — a process of telling one's sexual orientation to family, friends, and colleagues. During the course of the academic year, about thirty gay, lesbian, and bisexual faculty and staff participated in informal meetings, two-thirds of whom still would not identify themselves to the university community as lesbian or gay. However, ten individuals who did "come out" sent a letter to the President requesting a meeting.

The President agreed to the meeting, but little came of it except acrimony. The President refused to consider implementing a sexual orientation clause, although he said he was sympathetic to the concerns of homosexuals. During the year, different administrators commented on how the Board of Trustees had made their displeasure over this issue obvious to the new President when he interviewed for the job. Privately, these administrators commented that if the President were entirely free to act on his own he would implement the clause, but he had to gain approval from the Board of Trustees; the President thought it was impossible that the Board would approve the measure, and that it would be political suicide for him to bring the issue before the Board.

A few weeks after the meeting with the President in the fall of 1990, when the students felt that no positive change was going to occur, they planned a demonstration that was supported by all of the University's underrepresented groups and the student government. A senior administrator heard about the plans and asked for a secret meeting off campus with an LGBSA student leader, the student government president, and a faculty member of the newly formed group. The senior administrator wanted, in his words, to "cut a deal." In return for avoiding demonstrations or takeovers of buildings, the administration would agree to two actions. First, the President would refer to the Faculty Senate the matter of whether to include a sexual orientation clause in the policy of nondiscrimination. Second, the administration would create a Committee of Lesbian and Gay Concerns whose charge was to investigate the climate, problems, and potential solutions for the lesbian, gay, and bisexual community. The group agreed to the "deal" and the building takeover did not take place.

After a semester's worth of heated discussion in the spring of 1991, the Faculty Senate voted 93–12 to include sexual orientation in the nondiscrimination statement. Over two hundred letters were sent in support of the clause, and LGBSA put together a four-hundred-page document that pertained to the harassment and discrimination lesbian, gay, and bisexual individuals have faced at Normal State. In informal discussions with prominent members of a major administrative group on campus, the Deans' Council, individuals commented how the group supported the clause quietly because they did not want to embarrass the new President, but they also feared that this issue was a topic that would consume much energy if it was not passed.

The newly elected Chair of the Board of Trustees worked tirelessly on behalf of the clause. Politically astute and also morally in support of such a clause, the Chair met unofficially with a small group of gay, lesbian, and bisexual students and faculty early in the year. She came away from the meeting convinced that if the Board did not pass the clause, the University would remain mired in an uproar and the Board would become severely divided. Some years previously, a similar issue had come to the Board concerning divestment of stock in companies that did business with South Africa. The issue turned out to be tremendously divisive and the Board was unable to concur on several other topics because of anger at one another over divestment; the Chair did not want a repetition with this issue. Thus, the Board of Trustees reluctantly agreed to the measure at their final meeting of the academic year and the sexual orientation clause was implemented.

The preceding pages highlight both the steps leading up to the passage of the sexual orientation clause and the general process by which gay, lesbian, and bisexual students, staff, and faculty overcame resistance at Normal State. In addition to the political maneuvering taking place, there was also a broad research effort designed to better understand the campus environment in relation to lesbian, gay, and bisexual issues. This effort was led by the Committee on Lesbian and Gay Concerns formed at the start of second semester. In the next section, I discuss the role of this committee and their investigation of the campus climate at Normal State during the spring semester.

Context and Analysis of Survey Responses about Homosexuality

In keeping with the terms of the deal made to avert a demonstration, the Committee on Lesbian and Gay Concerns was created at the end of the fall semester and had their first meeting at the start of the second semester. This committee, composed of students, faculty, administrators, and staff, conducted three activities. First, they collected diversity-related documents from University departments and services to see whether lesbian or gay issues were included and studied documents from other universities. Second, they interviewed lesbian, gay, and bisexual faculty and staff to better understand the problems they faced. Third, they conducted two surveys on gay and lesbian issues during the spring. The goals of the surveys were to gauge the community's understandings and tolerance of lesbian, gay, and bisexual issues. The surveys essentially asked the same questions, but they were geared to two different groups. One survey went to a random sample of 4,500 faculty and staff; the other was sent to a random sample of 2,000 of the 30,000 undergraduate students. The response rates were 23 percent for the student survey and 45 percent for the faculty and staff. On the final page of the anonymous, confidential surveys, individuals were invited to offer any comments they felt appropriate. Two-hundred-sixty-two students and 564 faculty/staff offered comments. Over 250 individuals also requested a confidential interview.

Much commotion occurred when the surveys were distributed throughout the campus community in the late spring. The President and Vice Provost received letters and phone calls denouncing the University's efforts to better understand the problems that lesbians and gays face. In many people's eyes, homosexuality was immoral, and the University was spending money improperly because of a vocal minority. The Committee on Lesbian and Gay Concerns also received letters and complaints about the surveys. Most importantly, the Institutional Review Board (IRB) of the University demanded to review the surveys to see if the University had been adequately protected. Interestingly, the rationale for the review stemmed not from anyone who had felt that his or her confidentiality had been compromised, but from one individual who was upset at the questions and another individual who disagreed with the surveys' design. When the IRB met, they agreed that nothing had been done that was wrong, but they still commented that they should have been consulted.

The findings from the surveys highlight a community divided. The results showed that half of the faculty and staff felt that "homosexual behavior is immoral." Eighty-seven percent of the faculty and staff said they did not know

Table 1. Breakdown of Comments by Faculty, Staff, and Students

Type of Comment	Frequency of Response
Gay-affirming	12 percent
Homosexuality as a private act	43 percent
Homosexuality as immoral	31 percent
Ethno-violence and hatred	14 percent

anyone who is gay, and 65 percent of the male students responded that they would feel unsettled if their best friend were gay or lesbian. Over half the students felt that lesbians or gays faced discrimination or harassment. More revealing, perhaps, were the 826 comments generated from the surveys. One-hundred-forty-five of these comments were neutral in that the individual offered some suggestion or criticism of the survey, but did not indicate support or opposition to lesbian, gay or bisexual issues. Of the remaining 681 comments, four general attitudes were taken towards homosexuality, which I categorize as: gay-affirming, homosexuality as a private act, homosexuality as immoral, and ethno-violence (in this case, the acceptibity of violence against lesbians, gays, and bisexuals as a cultural group) and hatred. I created these categories as a means of delineating differences of the respondents. Because such little research has been done on lesbian, gay, and bisexual issues, there were not pre-formed terms to which we could place these comments. Accordingly, four individuals independently sifted through the comments and placed them in the categories. When there was a disagreement about in which category a specific comment should be placed, the group discussed the statement and eventually reached consensus. Table 1 provides a percentage breakdown of the comments.

Gay-Affirming The smallest percentage of individuals were those who felt positively about a lesbian, gay, or bisexual lifestyle, and felt that lesbians and gays faced specific problems that needed to be overcome. One individual wrote, "Homophobia is still a problem at this campus. The greatest insult is to suggest that another student is gay. I am dismayed and shocked." Another individual added, "I believe there is a clear need for the addition of a sexual orientation clause." A third person wrote, "I am very pleased we are finally dealing proactively with this issue."

Homosexuality as a Private Act A larger group was disturbed that such an issue was discussed publicly. Although most of these people felt that the gay community did not deserve any specific rights or protection, their responses pertained more to the belief that what an individual does in his or her bedroom should not be of anyone's concern. "I can't believe we are making a sexual issue a moral or political issue," commented one individual. A second person said, "I feel too much emphasis is placed on the issue of sexual orientation at Normal State. Although I personally believe homosexuality is morally wrong, it is a personal issue." A third person argued, "I'm not interested in knowing someone's sexual orientation." Another person continued, "I feel that homosexuality is a problem at Normal State because it is always thrown in our face with articles in the student newspaper."

Thus, these individuals wanted the issue of gay and lesbian rights to go away; they did not feel themselves to be "homophobic" or unjust. Rather, they believed that the University should not be a place that concerns itself with issues of sexual orientation. To be sure, if someone was harassed or discriminated against he or she should have protection, but that was true for every individual. There was no need for naming specific constituencies such as lesbians, gays, or bisexuals. Some individuals went one step further and were angered that lesbians, gays, and bisexuals were equated with other minority groups such as Blacks. As one person commented, "Gay/lesbian individuals have made their sexual choices. They must live with that as I do mine." In general, this perception was that one's sexual orientation was a matter of choice, and what one chose to do should not be afforded any specific privileges. Further, the definition of one's sexual orientation revolved around a sexual act; one was gay or lesbian by what took place in the bedroom.

Homosexuality as Immoral Most of these individuals based their opinion on their religious beliefs. "Homosexuality is a sin," said one individual. A second person added, "I think gay is wrong. God put a man and woman on this earth together." A third writer concluded, "I think homosexuality is morally wrong and unnatural and should NOT be acceptable in our society. There should be laws against it." A fourth person agreed, "It is a grave mistake to accept homosexual behavior as just another sexual lifestyle. It is sinful behavior and by condoning it we jeopardize ourselves and our society."

Some individuals believed that homosexuals should be viewed with compassion, but the "homosexual act" should be condemned. These people were against discrimination, but feared that policies that sought to protect such individuals would "bring homosexual relationships out of the closet (and) ask for real problems." Other individuals felt that homosexuality was immoral, and that the beliefs of the majority of the country and the University should be upheld. As one individual commented, "Please don't ask the normal majority to put up with this public display." Still other individuals felt that homosexuality was not only immoral, but was also a medical problem. One writer opined:

> Homosexuality is perverted sexual behavior and it is also sinful. Instead of just accepting this type of behavior it needs to be dealt with just like other physiological problems such as alcoholism, drug addiction, child molestation, or any of our other social diseases. This issue caused the destruction of biblical Sodom and Gomorrah, contributed to the fall of Rome, and I

believe if it is allowed to run rampant in this country, it will contribute to its demise.

By far, most of the comments fell into the second and third categories. That is, the vast majority of respondents felt either that homosexuality was an issue that should not be talked about in public, or that homosexuality was immoral. The fourth general attitude was not as prevalent as the second and third categories, but nonetheless offers insight into the reasons that lesbian, gay, and bisexual students, faculty, and staff experience fear at Normal State University.

Ethno-Violence and Hatred "Inject everyone of them with the AIDS virus," said one individual. "All gay people should be taken out and shot in the head," wrote another. "I believe all fags should be quarantined," added a third. Continued another, "One day there was a gay/lesbian rally on campus and I stayed as far away from it as I could. I think the whole idea is sick." "I think we should burn all of you faggots for the amount of paper you used to send this shit and wasted my tuition money!" wrote a fifth. Finally, one person added, "If I knew any gays I would NOT hesitate one minute to smash their faces in if I could get away with it."

DISCUSSION

In the first section of this paper, I discussed different outlooks on academic freedom and I suggested an alternative view — a critical perspective. It will be helpful here to tie these differing perspectives to the situation at Normal State University. One view subscribes to the idea that if someone conducted research or taught a course on lesbian or gay studies, then that person's academic freedom should not be restricted. This is the notion of those scholars who have pointed out how previous individuals such as Ross at Stanford or Ely at Wisconsin had their academic freedom taken away by espousing unpopular opinions.

Indeed, in a related study, McCart quoted a senior professor of chemical engineering at Normal State. When asked if "controversial" faculty members would be supported and their academic freedom upheld, the individual commented, "By and large, the Department would support them. I would hate to try to debate the situation where we had an openly avowed homosexual in the classroom" (1991, p. 229). Presumably, then, if the University or College of Engineering at Normal State had a professor who was openly gay, then the individual's academic freedom might be placed in jeopardy. Thus, the first perspective of academic freedom is that its purpose is precisely to protect such an individual.

A second interpretation of academic freedom comes from present-day conservatives. This view is concerned with the comments made on the surveys administered at Normal State University. Authors such as Dinesh D'Souza

(1991) and Chester Finn (1989) would decry the attempt to stifle any of the opinions stated above. They would argue that a "politically correct" stance has been taken by Normal State that does not allow alternative notions about homosexuality to be voiced and debated. They would want to ensure that individuals who believe that one's sexual orientation must not be discussed in public, or those who believe that being gay is immoral, are able to speak publicly. Presumably, conservative critics also want to ensure the rights of those who espouse ethno-violence and hatred. In other words, the conservative orientation is that whatever one says — however ill-informed or hateful — should not be silenced or penalized. In general, the limits of free speech extend to the point where someone calls for a specific act against a specific individual. This view holds that to say "gays should have their faces smashed in" is permissible; to say, however, "I'm going to smash your face in, John," is not.

There are distinct problems with both perspectives with regard to lesbian and gay issues. The first interpretation assumes that academic freedom exists at Normal State because no challenges have occurred where someone has had, for example, his or her tenure revoked because of conducting research or teaching about lesbian and gay studies. Again, academic freedom is defined by when it is abridged.

The second view assumes that academic freedom exists if an individual may state whatever he or she feels. Conservatives would say that academic freedom does not exist at Normal State because those who are against homosexuality do not feel that they can speak openly on this issue. Parenthetically, it is ironic how conservatives have twisted the concept of "political correctness" and academic freedom. No one at Normal State who thinks homosexuality is immoral, or a private matter, or even worthy of murder, has been threatened. No one has faced the loss of his or her job or a chance at a promotion because he or she has said something negative or hateful about lesbians, gays, and bisexuals. To be sure, on occasion, a student letter in the newspaper has labeled someone with any of those viewpoints "homophobic." Presumably, such labeling is what creates the "politically correct" environment and stifles an individual's academic freedom.

A third interpretation returns us to the cultural politics of academic freedom. The assumption advanced here is that academic freedom is most assuredly threatened at Normal State, but not in the manner considered by the previous two opinions. Rather, the cultural politics of Normal State actively works against anyone presuming that lesbian and gay studies is a viable object of knowledge, which in turn limits an individual's academic freedom. I am suggesting that we need to think about academic freedom in a fundamentally different manner from previous interpretations. This new way incorporates the first interpretation: when someone loses his or her job or is sanctioned because of an unpopular opinion, then he or she must be protected. And to a certain extent, the second interpretation is also included;

dialogue[c] must occur and flourish in academic institutions. However, it is naive to say that simply because a student writes letters of complaint to a newspaper, a professor's academic freedom is in jeopardy. In large part, the argument about "political correctness" is little more than a mask for authors who are upset that they no longer control the discourse of the University.

The first two views highlight my point concerning the relationship of academic freedom to knowledge and societal contexts. For when we suggest that the academy absent itself from the political battles of society, we have wrongfully assumed that all individuals are allowed to investigate any issue irrespective of political persuasion. When we argue that politics must not exist on campus because to do so jeopardizes the search for truth, we also mistakenly believe that the absence of political dialogue enables academic freedom to occur. As we have seen, such was not the case at Normal State.

To conceive of knowledge as a social construct with political consequences alters one's thinking about academic freedom. As I have described, the culture of Normal State presupposes a definition of homosexuality as aberrant behavior; 45 percent of respondents to the survey felt that it was immoral and/or deserving of punishment. Thus, the majority of survey respondents have defined the "common good" and "truth" in relation to sexual orientation and placed lesbians, gays, and bisexuals on the opposite side. Given the overarching pervasiveness of the hostility directed towards lesbians, gays, and bisexuals, virtually no one considers speaking up about lesbian, gay, and bisexual studies. Again, I need to be clear here. A postmodern view of the world rejects the assumption that everyone will arrive at similar conclusions; we have seen from the surveys' comments that people held a variety of opinions about why homosexuality should not be condoned. Yet the climate that has been created at Normal State sends a clear message to anyone concerned about lesbian, gay, and bisexual issues — it is wrong. One may face disapproval, or sanction, or perhaps even physical harm if he or she speaks out. To be sure, anyone — gay or straight — who speaks up in support of lesbian and gay rights may face severe challenges. Further, if an individual is lesbian or gay, then he or she is at greater risk than someone who is gay/lesbian supportive, but straight. Any number of surveys have pointed out how gay, lesbian, and bisexual individuals have faced physical harm in the society at large over the last few years, as well as on campuses that have looked at the issue (D'Augelli, 1989; Herek, 1989).

Further, simply because ten individuals are open about their sexual orientation, or merely because one professor or another writes a paper that investigates some aspect of lesbian and gay studies, does not mean that aca-

---

[c] As defined by Donaldo Macedo and Paulo Freire in this book, "**dialogue** as a process of learning and knowing must always involve a political project with the objective of dismantling oppressive structures and mechanisms prevalent both in education and society" (p. 203). Therefore, the sharing of experiences should not be isolated in the realm of psychology, but, rather, requires a political and ideological analysis as well.

demic freedom exists. To come to terms with academic freedom, one must investigate the climate and culture in which a specific topic resides and ask a series of questions: How is knowledge conceived? Whose interests have been advanced by these forms of knowledge? How has what we defined as knowledge changed over time? How does the organization's culture promote or silence some individuals? How are some topics marginalized and others promoted? (Tierney, 1989).

When we ask such questions of the Normal State situation, we find that the definitions of knowledge excluded issues pertaining to lesbian and gay themes unless they were defined as "deviant." We see that the interests of the lesbian and gay communities were rendered voiceless, and those who sought to insert traditional definitions of "community" were powerful. In doing so, the vast majority of individuals in the fabric of the investigation either explicitly avoided or never assumed that a topic such as lesbian and gay issues was worthy of investigation.

The purpose of such questions is to ensure that individual rights are tied to the promotion of social justice based on the ideal of a community founded on difference rather than similarity. The original perspectives on academic freedom have functioned at an epistemological level that assumes that knowledge is a concrete entity to be interpreted based on common notions of truth, as if academic communities are organized around single ideas of the common good. The argument advanced here has been that knowledge is socially constructed, and that the act of its construction privileges some and silences others.

Our challenge is to investigate those silences and to develop ways that ensure protection of all individuals and of all groups, so that they are no longer invisible and silent. As we have seen, one group that has been voiceless is the lesbian and gay community at Normal State University. The overwhelming sentiment of the University community is to condemn, ignore, or harass anyone who is lesbian, gay, or bisexual. A climate of intolerance exists that forces the group to be silent, as if they have no right to have a voice. To be sure, changes have occurred. Thirty years ago, such a topic was not even countenanced as a legitimate form of discussion. Ten years ago, a discussion about a "clause" was merely an idea among a few individuals. My point here is two-fold. First, social constructionist interpretations far too often have the tendency to point out that change does not occur, but as we have seen in this text, it does. People's struggles do make a difference and can effectively alter the parameters of knowledge and reframe issues of social justice and equity. Second, however, is that one change is but a step in a process, and those in power, as Foucault has pointed out so well, are consistently in movement to incorporate challenges so that norms become reintroduced.

Finally, I reiterate that the "challenge" I stated above is not merely to investigate silences; rather, we must develop ways to extend our analyses and research one step further. We must undertake **praxis**[d]-oriented efforts that work to enable those who are voiceless to gain voice. Ultimately, the meaning of academic freedom should not merely be judged on when it is curtailed, but on how well it protects the rights of the silent and marginalized and enables them to gain voice.

REFERENCES

American Association of University Professors (AAUP). (1940/1977). Academic freedom and tenure: 1940 statement of principles and interpretive comments. In *AAUP Policy Documents and Reports.* Washington, DC: Author.

Bloom, A. (1987). *The closing of the American mind.* New York: Simon & Schuster.

Bowen, H. R., & Schuster, J. H. (1986). *American professors: A national resource imperiled.* New York: Oxford University Press.

Clark, B. R. (1987). *The academic life.* Princeton, NJ: Carnegie Foundation for the Advancement of Teaching.

D'Augelli, A. R. (1989). Lesbians' and gay men's experiences of discrimination and harassment in a university community. *American Journal of Community Psychology, 17,* 317–321.

D'Souza, D. (1991). *Illiberal education: The politics of race and sex on campus.* New York: Free Press.

Finn, C. E., Jr. (1989). The campus: "An island of repression in a sea of freedom." *Commentary, 88*(3), 17–23.

Foucault, M. (1972). *The archaeology of knowledge* (A. M. Sheridan Smith, Trans.). New York: Pantheon Books.

Foucault, M. (1980). *Power/knowledge: Selected interviews & other writings 1972–1977.* New York: Pantheon Books.

Giroux, H. A. (1988). *Teachers as intellectuals: Toward a critical pedagogy of learning.* Granby, MA: Bergin & Garvey.

Herek, G. M. (1989). Hate crimes against lesbians and gay men: Issues in research and social policy. *American Psychologist, 44,* 933–940.

Hofstadter, R. (1955). *Academic freedom in the age of the college.* New York: Columbia University Press.

Hofstadter, R., & Metzger, W. (1955). *The development of academic freedom in the United States.* New York: Columbia University Press.

Kimball, R. (1990). *Tenured radicals.* New York: Harper & Row.

Ladd, E. C., Jr., & Lipset, S. M. (1977). *Survey of the American professoriate.* Storrs: University of Connecticut Press.

Lazersfeld, P., & Theilens, W. (1958). *The academic mind.* Glencoe, IL: Free Press.

Lewis, L. S. (1966). Faculty support of academic freedom and self-government. *Social Problems, 13,* 456–461.

McCart, C. L. (1991). *Using a cultural lens to explore faculty perceptions of academic freedom.* Unpublished doctoral dissertation, Pennsylvania State University, University Park.

McLaren, P. (1989). *Life in schools: An introduction to critical pedagogy in the foundations of education.* New York: Longman.

---

[d] **Praxis** is the relationship between theoretical understanding and critique of society (that is, its historical, ideological, sociopolitical, and economic influences and structures) and action that seeks to transform individuals and their environments. Arguing that people cannot transform a given situation simply through awareness or the best of intentions, nor through unguided action, Paulo Freire defines "praxis" throughout his work as a dialectical movement that goes from action to reflection and from reflection upon action to a new action.

Metzger, W. (1955). *Academic freedom in the age of the university.* New York: Columbia University Press.
Mouffe, C. (1990). Radical democracy or liberal democracy? *Socialist Review, 2,* 57–66.
Ollman, B. (1983). Academic freedom in America today: A Marxist view. In C. Kaplan & E. Schrecker (Eds.), *Regulating the intellectuals* (pp. 45–59). New York: Praeger.
Olswang, S. G., & Lee, B. A. (1984). *Faculty freedoms and institutional accountability: Interactions and conflicts* (ASHE-ERIC Higher Education Research Report No. 5). Washington, DC: Association for the Study of Higher Education.
Ravitch, D. (1990). Multiculturalism. *The American Scholar, 59,* 337–355.
Rudolph, F. (1962). *The American college and university: A history.* New York: Vintage Books.
Schrecker, E. (1983). Academic freedom: The historical view. In C. Kaplan & E. Schrecker (Eds.), *Regulating the intellectuals* (pp. 25–43). New York: Praeger.
Sedgwick, E. K. (1990). *Epistemology of the closet.* Berkeley: University of California Press.
Slaughter, S. (1980). The danger zone: Academic freedom and civil liberties. *The ANNALS of The American Academy of Political and Social Science, 448,* 4661.
Tierney, W. G. (1983, October). *The tenure drum: An investigation of rituals in the modern university.* Paper presented at the meeting of the Ethnography in Education Conference, Philadelphia.
Tierney, W. G. (1989). Cultural politics and the curriculum in postsecondary education. *Journal of Education, 171*(3), 72–88.
Tierney, W. G. (1991). Academic work and institutional culture: Constructing knowledge. *The Review of Higher Education, 14*(2), 199–216.
Tierney, W. G. (1993). *Building communities of difference: Higher education in the 21st century.* Granby, MA: Bergin & Garvey.
Wences, R., & Abramson, H. J. (1971). Faculty opinion on the issues of job placement and dissent in the university. *Social Problems, 18,* 2738.
Veysey, L. R. (1965). *The emergence of the American university.* Chicago: University of Chicago Press.

8

Rethinking Liberal and Radical Perspectives on Racial Inequality in Schooling: Making the Case for Nonsynchrony

CAMERON McCARTHY

In the spirit of *Breaking Free*'s call for the development of multiple literacies, Cameron McCarthy analyzes mainstream and radical socioeconomic explanations of racial inequality in schools, and argues that the theoretical stance of the former depicts racial factors as manipulable variables tied to beliefs, values, and psychological differences; the latter position subsumes issues of race relations into socioeconomic interests. Instead, this author presents a theory of identity based on what he refers to as "nonsynchrony," which is an attempt to understand the dynamic, complex, and often contradicting interrelations that begins to explain the interaction of race, gender, and class within the economic, political, and social environments as they differentially function within the daily practices of schooling.

> It is not altogether surprising to find a certain uneven development within the various branches of the social science disciplines.... It could be argued that race analysis is surprisingly backward in this respect, far more so, for instance, than recent debates within the feminist movement. (Ben-Tovim, Gabriel, Law, & Stredder, 1981, p. 155)

Marxist and other progressive writers on Africa generally approach the issue of "tribalism" as one would approach a minefield. (Saul, 1979, p. 391)

Despite comprehensive evidence of glaring disparities in education in the United States, rigorous, durable, and compelling explanations of the **reproduction**[a] and persistence of racial inequality in schooling have been slow in coming. In sharp contrast, American curriculum theorists and sociologists of education have been far more forthcoming in their examination of how the variables of class and, more recently, those of gender, have informed the organization and selection of school youth (Anyon, 1979; Apple, 1982; Apple & Weis, 1983; Bowles & Gintis, 1976; Everhart, 1983). As Black sociologists such as Mullard (1985) and Sarup (1986) have pointed out, both mainstream and radical educational researchers have tended to under-theorize and marginalize phenomena associated with racial inequality.

This essay seeks to fulfill three objectives. First, I situate the issue of racial inequality within the context of current data on the status of racial minorities vis-à-vis Whites in U.S. schools and society. Second, I examine how the topic of race is treated in contemporary mainstream and neo-Marxist curriculum and educational research, paying particular attention to the limits and possibilities of the value-oriented thesis of multiculturalism that mainstream liberal educators have championed over the last fifteen years or so as a panacea for racial inequality in schooling. I also offer a critique of neo-Marxist subordination of racial inequality in education to working-class exploitation and the structural requirements of the economy. Third, I present an alternative approach, what I call a nonsynchronous theory of race relations in schooling, in which I argue against the **"essentialist"**[b] or single-cause explanations of the persistence of racial inequality in education currently offered in both mainstream and radical curriculum and educational literatures. Instead, I direct attention to the complex and contradictory nature of race relations in the institutional life of social organizations such as schools. In addition, this nonsynchronous approach attempts to dissolve the unwarranted separation of "values" from considerations of structural constraints

---

[a] Critical social theorists argue that dominant ideologies and knowledge are built into social institutions that both privilege and exclude particular perspectives, voices, authorities, and representations. Within theories of **cultural reproduction**, schools, educators, and curricula are generally viewed as mechanisms of ideological control that work to reproduce and maintain dominant beliefs, values, norms, and oppressive practices. This reproductive process is mediated, in part, through the "hidden curriculum" — the hidden agenda of maintaining the status quo through specific schooling practices.

[b] **Essentialism** ascribes a fundamental nature or a biological determinism to humans (i.e., men are naturally aggressive, and women are naturally nurturing) through attitudes about identity, experience, knowledge, and cognitive development. Within this monolithic and homogenizing view, categories such as race and gender become gross generalizations and single-cause explanations about individual character. However, critical feminists have argued that gender is not the only determinant of a woman's identity, and that one must also look at the multiple and interconnecting relationships such as race, class, and sexual orientation in order to understand experience.

on human actions in current accounts of the race/education couplet. I emphasize the materiality of ideology and argue for the codetermination of culture and politics, along with the economy, in radical accounts of the elaboration of the racial character of schooling. Ideology, culture, and politics are as important determinants in shaping race relations in schooling as is the economy. Typically, neo-Marxists emphasize the last of these realms. Racist ideology as a specific set of linked but contradictory ideas manifests itself unevenly in educational structures and the formal and informal practices of school life. In this sense, curricula and programs that seek to address racial antagonism in schooling must take into account, for example, the discriminatory effects of what Kevin Brown (1985) calls "White non-racism" (p. 670). "Non-racism" refers to the covert use of racial evaluation, "apparently" neutral but coded rhetoric or criteria to discuss minorities — for example, the use of code words such as "over-crowding," "welfare mothers," "the lack of experience," or "strain on current resources."

Mounting statistical evidence supplied in government commission reports, census data, and academic journals documents persistent and glaring disparities in the relative economic, social, and educational status of racial minorities and Whites in the United States (Editors, 1986). For instance, unemployment among Black women and men is currently more than twice the level of that among Whites. For Black families, the median income remains at about 56 percent of White families' median income — roughly what it was three decades ago. The Alliance Against Women's Oppression (1983) contends that Black mothers are four times as likely to die in childbirth as White mothers. Black and Native American infant mortality rates are currently higher than those of such Third World countries as Trinidad and Tobago and Costa Rica.

Current data on schooling also present an alarming picture of minority disadvantage. Data from the 1979 Census Bureau study showed that 35 percent of Hispanic and 26 percent of Black youth, ages 18 through 21, had dropped out of school, compared with 15 percent of all Whites of similar ages. Black and Hispanic youth who graduate from high school are less likely than White graduates to enroll in college. At the university level, the percentage of degrees awarded to minority students is also declining. Black students earned only 6.5 percent of all bachelor's degrees awarded in 1981 compared with 10 percent in 1976 (Editors, 1986). These statistics trenchantly underscore the intractability of racial inequality in school and society in the United States. But racial inequality of this sort is by no means peculiar to America; in other urban industrialized societies, such as England, Japan, Canada, and Australia, research has shown that minority youth fare poorly in school and in the labor market (Ogbu, 1978).

Over the years, mainstream and radical sociologists of curriculum and education have provided contrasting explanations for the persistence of racial inequality in schooling. Neo-Marxist sociologists of education such as Berlowitz (1984), Bowles and Gintis (1976), Carnoy (1974), Jakubowicz

(1985), and Nkomo (1984) locate the roots of racial domination within the structural properties of capitalism and its elaboration as a world system. In these accounts, racial antagonism is seen as a by-product of the major class contradiction between labor and capital. These radical critics of schooling subsume the problem of racial inequality under the general rubric of working-class oppression. They argue that there is a structural relationship between a racially differentiated school curriculum and a discontinuous labor market. Schools in this view follow the pattern of the economy and serve a narrow reproductive function. As a result, neo-Marxist sociologists of education offer no satisfactory theoretical explanation and no programmatic solution to the problem of racial inequality — the racial dimension is seen as of secondary import, and the inequality is expected to disappear with the abolition of capitalism.

Conversely, mainstream sociologists of schooling reduce the complexities associated with racial inequality to one overwhelming theoretical and programmatic concern: *the issue of educability of minorities.* Their central task has been to explain perceived differences between Black and White students as reflected in differential achievement scores on standardized tests, high school dropout rates, and so on. Their explanations of Black "underachievement" consequently depend upon pathological constructions of minority cognitive capacities (Jensen, 1981), child-rearing practices (Bell, 1975), family structures (Moynihan, 1965), and linguistic styles (Hess & Shipman, 1975). (For an extended discussion of these constructions see Henriques, 1984.) Mainstream theorists have in this sense tended to "blame the victim." Interventions and curriculum practices predicated on these approaches attempt to improve minority school performance through the manipulation of specific school variables, such as teacher behavior, methods of testing, placement, and so on (Atkinson, Morten, & Sue, 1979; Banks, 1981; Ogbu, 1978). As we shall see, multiculturalism represents an important but contradictory inflection on mainstream approaches to racial inequality in schooling.

THE MULTICULTURAL SOLUTION

Multiculturalism is a body of thought which originates in the liberal pluralist approaches to education and society. Multicultural education, specifically, must be understood as part of a curricular truce, the fallout of a political project to deluge and neutralize Black rejection of the conformist and assimilationist curriculum models solidly in place in the 1960s. Gwendolyn Baker (1977), for instance, cites Black "discontent" as the "catalyst" for the multicultural education movement in the United States: "The school district in Ann Arbor, Michigan, was much like other school districts throughout the country in the late 1960s. Students, particularly Black students, were involved in and responded to the civil rights and ethnic awareness activities of that decade" (p. 163). Barry Troyna (1984) makes similar claims with respect to the origins of multicultural education policies in England: "It is no coincidence that this flurry of [multicultural] activity has taken place in the period since the civil disturbances rocked virtually every major English city in the summer of 1981. . . . Broadly speaking, this educational response parallels what took place in the U.S.A. after the 1965 riots" (p. 76).

Multicultural education as a "new" curricular form attempted to absorb Black radical demands for the restructuring of school knowledge and pedagogical practices and rearticulated them into a reformist discourse of "nonracism." The discourse of nonracism was explicitly aimed at sensitizing White teachers and school administrators to minority "differences" as part of the plurality of differences that percolated throughout the educational system. At the same time, multiculturalism represented an ameliorative advance over rigidly coercive policies and Anglo conformity that had stabilized in American education during the first half of the century. The early twentieth-century educator Ellwood P. Cubberley summarized the curriculum and policy objectives of the American education system in these terms:

> Our task is to assimilate these people [racial minorities and immigrants] as part of the American race, and to implant in their children so far as can be done the Anglo-Saxon conceptions of righteousness, law, order, and popular government, and to awaken in them reverence for our democratic institutions and for those things which we as a people hold to be of abiding worth. (quoted in Grant, Boyle, & Sleeter, 1980, p. 11)

Proponents of multicultural education explicitly challenge this assimilationist stance, and urge that we draw more closely to the democratic pulse of egalitarianism and pluralism (Banks, 1981). Grant (1975), for example, argues that "multicultural education assigns a positive value to pluralism" (p. 4). The ideological and professional stance of multiculturalism therefore espouses an emancipatory program with respect to racial inequality in school. First, proponents of multicultural education suggest that the fostering of universal respect for the various ethnic histories, cultures, and languages of the students in American schools will have a positive effect on individual minority student self-concepts. Positive self-concepts should in turn help to boost academic achievement among minority youth. Second, proponents suggest that through achieving, minority students could break the cycle of "missed opportunity" created by a previous biography of **cultural deprivation**.[c] The labor market is expected to verify multicultural programs by absorbing large numbers of qualified minority youth. This thesis of a

---

[c] The deficit model is used to explain the low academic achievement of students from oppressed groups as being due to individual or group pathology, **cultural deprivation**, or genetic limitations (e.g., cognitive and linguistic deficiencies, poor motivation). As Lilia Bartolomé describes in "Beyond the Methods Fetish," students perceived in this fashion are "in need of fixing (if we could only identify the right recipe!), or, at worst, culturally or genetically deficient and beyond fixing" (p. 237).

"tightening bond" between multicultural education and the economy is suggested in the following claim by James Rushton (1981):

> The curriculum in the multicultural school should encourage each pupil to succeed wherever he or she can and strive for competence in what he or she tries. Cultural taboos should be lessened by mutual experience and understandings. The curriculum in the multicultural school should allow these experiences to happen. If it does, it need have no fear about the future careers of its pupils. (p. 169)

But, as asserted by Rushton and other multicultural proponents, this linear connection between educational credentials and the economy is problematic. The assumption that a more sensitive curriculum will necessarily lead to higher educational attainment and achievement and to jobs for Black and minority youth, is frustrated by the existence of racial practices in the job market itself. Troyna (1984) and Blackburn and Mann (1979), in their incisive analyses of the British job market, explode the myth of a necessary "tightening bond" between education and the economy. In his investigation of the fortunes of "educated" Black and White youth in the job market, Troyna concludes that racial and social connections, rather than educational qualifications per se, "determined" the phenomenon of better job chances for White youth even when Black youth had higher qualifications than their White counterparts (1984). The tendency of employers to rely on informal channels or "word of mouth" networks, together represent some of the systematic ways in which the potential for success of qualified Black youth in the labor market is undermined. Carmichael and Hamilton (1967) and Marable (1983) have made a similar argument with respect to the racial obstacles to the employment of qualified Black youth in the job market in the United States. In an analysis of Black unemployment in the 1980s, Chrichlow (1985) concludes that there is no "good fit" between Black educational achievement and the job market. Expanding this argument, he makes the following claim:

> In combination with subtle forms of discrimination, job relocation, and increasing competition among workers for smaller numbers of "good" jobs, rising entry level job requirements clearly underscore the present employment difficulties experienced by young Black workers. Whether they possess a high school diploma or not. Blacks, in this instance, continue to experience high rates of unemployment despite possessing sound educational backgrounds and potential (**capital**[d]) to be productive workers. (p. 6).

---

[d] **Cultural capital** refers to Pierre Bourdieu's concept that different forms of cultural knowledge, such as language, modes of social interaction, and meaning, are valued hierarchically in society. Critical pedagogues argue that only those characteristics and practices (i.e., cultural wealth) of the dominant paradigm will facilitate academic achievement within mainstream schools that reflect that dominant and exclusionary ideology.

Besides this particular naiveté about the racial character of the job market, a further criticism can be made of the multicultural reformist thesis. As Berlowitz (1984), Carby (1982), and Mullard (1985) have all contended, the underlying assumptions of multicultural education are fundamentally idealistic. As such, the structural and material relations in which racial domination is embedded are underemphasized. This has a costly result. By focusing on sensitivity training and on individual differences, multicultural proponents typically skirt the very problem which multicultural education seeks to address: WHITE RACISM. The A.L.T.A.R.F. (All London Teachers Against Racism and Fascism), in their volume *Challenging Racism* (1984), berate the multicultural education program in London on precisely these grounds:

> These years have witnessed the growing acceptance by LEAs [local educational agencies] of a bland and totally depoliticized form of multicultural education alongside the intensification of state racism in the form of ever increasing deportations, police brutality against Black people, discrimination in employment and harassment in unemployment. (p. 1)

Despite these problems, multicultural education offers a range of ameliorative possibilities to the school curriculum that are not present within an assimilationist framework of Anglo-conformity. For example, in terms of what should be included in the school curriculum, multiculturalism raises the possibility that the plurality of experiences of racial minorities, women, and the socially disadvantaged classes would be taken seriously within a new core curriculum (Banks, 1981). In this sense, multicultural proponents strain their relationship to more mainstream notions of "what every American school child ought to know." This strategic challenge to liberal frameworks over what should constitute the core curriculum represents an important political space within current educational discourses — a political space that must be used to develop more creative and sustained challenges to racial inequality in schooling.

NEO-MARXIST APPROACHES TO RACE AND EDUCATION

> Left critics provided theoretical arguments and enormous amounts of empirical evidence to suggest that schools were in fact, agencies of social, economic and cultural reproduction. (Giroux, 1985, p. xv)

On the subject of racial inequality in schooling neo-Marxist and radical formulations stand in sharp relief to the formulations of mainstream educational theorists. Neo-Marxist sociologists of education critique mainstream frameworks which depict the relationship between education and social differences and inequality. These radical theorists maintain that attempts to cast the problem of racial oppression in American schooling in terms of attitudes, values, and psychological differences are grossly inadequate. They argue further that liberal emphasis on the domain of values serves to divert our attention from the relationship of schooling to political economy and political power.

Radical educational theorists such as Berlowitz (1984), Bowles and Gintis (1976), and Nkomo (1984) have asserted instead that problems of social difference and inequality are more firmly rooted in the socioeconomic relations and structures generated within capitalist societies such as the United States. Education plays an essentially reproductive role in this story, insofar as it functions to legitimize social disparity and social differences through its selection process and its propagation of **dominant values.**[e] But in these analyses, racial domination occurs as a tangential distraction to the main drama of class conflict. The whole structure of this radical theoretical framework ultimately rests upon an economic base, from which class relations are derived. All that is non-economic exists in the firmament of the superstructures, namely, the arenas of ideology, culture, consciousness, and so on. Schooling and ethnicity or race are thus dependent variables — epiphenomena relegated to the superstructures.

As C. L. R. James (1980) maintains, neo-Marxist sociologists and educational theorists tend to conceptualize race and racial struggles as episodic rather than determinant. Race, defined as the **"otherness"**[f] of **subordinate groups,**[g] manifests itself in neo-Marxist sociological theories only through a proliferation of negatives — "superexploitation" (Blauner, 1972), "split/labor market" (Bonacich, 1980), and the "divide and conquer" strategies of individual capitalist employers (Roemer, 1979). This emphasis on the negative features of racial dynamics is reproduced in neo-Marxist theories of education. Berlowitz (1984) and Edari (1984), for example, explore the relationship of race to schooling through such taken-for-granted concepts as "minority failure," "underachievement," and "drop-out" rates. But for Berlowitz (1984), Jakubowicz (1985), and others, racial inequality in schooling is at best symptomatic of more powerful class-related dynamics operating

---

[e] **Dominant values/ideologies** are bodies of ideas of cultural groups that are politically, socially, and economically in positions of power and are therefore able to impose on the greater society, through various social institutions and practices, particular traditions, bodies of knowledge, discourse styles, language uses, values, norms, and beliefs, usually at the expense of others.

[f] In a society in which the dominant referent for defining "difference" is based on White, middle-class, heterosexual male characteristics, **otherness** refers to anybody that falls outside of, or is excluded from, this prevailing paradigm. In the literature, one often finds the use of the term "decentering." This refers to an attempt to rupture the undemocratic hierarchy (or centrality) of the dominant beliefs, values, and practices.

[g] **Subordinate groups** refers to groups that have been historically, politically, socially, and economically disempowered in the greater society. As Lilia Bartolomé states, "While individual members of these groups may not consider themselves subordinate in any manner to the White 'mainstream,' they nevertheless are members of a greater collective that historically has been perceived and treated as subordinate and inferior by the dominant society. Thus it is not entirely accurate to describe these students as 'minority' students, since the term connotes numerical minority rather than the general low status (economic, political, and social) these groups have held" (p. 230).

within the economy. Edari (1984) summarizes the structuralist definition of race within the neo-Marxist framework: "For this purpose, ethnicity, racism and sexism must be understood in the proper perspective as forms of ideological mystification designed to facilitate exploitation and weaken the collective power of the laboring classes" (p. 8).

In summary, then, neo-Marxist educational theorists explain the specificity of racial domination within the evolution of capitalism in terms of a "structurally convenient form of ideology" (Mullard, 1985, p. 66). Racism as an ideology fulfills capitalism's economic requirements for superexploitation and the creation of a vast reserve army of labor. Racial strife disorganizes the working class and hence weakens working-class resistance to capitalist domination. Schools, as apparatuses of the state, both legitimize racial differences in society and reproduce the kind of racially subordinate subjects who are tracked into the secondary labor market.

But there are significant weaknesses in neo-Marxist theories of racial inequality in general and racial inequality in schooling in particular. First, the specification of the origins of racism within the origins of capitalism seems theoretically and empirically dubious. As both West (1982) and Mullard (1985) have noted, forms of racism existed prior to capitalism in pre-Columbian Latin America, ancient Greece, and elsewhere.

Second, there appears to be neither historical nor contemporary evidence to substantiate that relations established and legitimized on the basis of race were or are identical to those established and legitimized on the basis of class. Historically, for instance, slave labor was constituted by fundamentally different forms of economic, political, and ideological relations from those of wage labor (West, 1982). Slavery involved the exploitation of unfree and politically disenfranchised labor (the slave was the property of her or his employer). On the other hand, the wage-earning worker has the "freedom" within the capitalistic society to sell her or his labor power and the political civil right of mobility — the right to choose employers. It would be very difficult to explain the current incidences of racism against minorities on college campuses across the United States as an effect solely of class differences between different groups of students (Lord, 1987). These examples underscore the fact that the logic and fortunes of race relations are not at all coterminous with those of capitalism, as the persistence of racial antagonism in post-capitalist societies demonstrates (Greenberg, 1980).

Third, the neo-Marxist overemphasis on structural factors associated with the economy underrates the school's role in the production and reproduction of cultural identities and social differences. As such, these formulations trivialize the role of schooling in their accounts of the reproduction and transformation of race relations. In this sense, too, these school critics have ignored or minimized the importance of Black struggles, particularly those struggles conducted on the terrain of education. Black struggles have encouraged and intensified similar efforts with respect to class and gender struggles for political participation and inclusion, and for social and economic amelioration within the United States and in the Third World (McCarthy & Apple, 1988).

Fourth, both neo-Marxist and mainstream educational theorists treat racial groups as monolithic entities, disregarding both differences within groups and the interrelated dynamics of class and gender. As Marable (1985) has insisted, with respect to class dynamics among Black Americans, and Fuller (1980) has maintained, in relation to gender-based forms of **resistance**[h] within West Indian subcultures in England, the characterization of minority groups in monolithic terms leads to unwarranted generalizations about the social, political, and cultural behavior of racially oppressed groups.

PARALLELISM AND NONSYNCHRONY: TOWARD AN ALTERNATIVE APPROACH TO RACE AND EDUCATION

The traditional literature on race and education has failed to reconcile an unwarranted bifurcation. On the one hand, mainstream educational theories assign racial phenomena to the realm of values, beliefs, individual preferences, tastes, and so on; thereby forfeiting a consideration of the structural constraints that limit and regulate human action, and denying the power and materiality of ideology. On the other hand, orthodox and neo-Marxist formulations customarily subordinate human agency and consciousness in their discussion of racial inequality. In significant ways, then, both mainstream and neo-Marxist approaches to racial inequality are "essentialist" in that they eliminate the "noise" of multidimensionality, historical variability, and subjectivity from their explanations of educational differences (Omi & Winant, 1986). The theoretical and practical insights gained from a more relational analysis of racial domination in schooling — one that attempts to show the links between existing social structures (whether economic, political, or ideological) and what real people such as teachers do — have been forfeited.

In recent years, we have witnessed the appearance of more subtle cultural theories and ethnographies of inequality and schooling within Marxist sociology of education paradigms. The work of Apple and Weis (1983), Carby (1982), Giroux (1985), Omi and Winant (1986), Troyna and Williams (1986), and Weis (1985) represents the emergence of a culturalist Marxism that has begun to awaken the radical and liberal school theories with respect to racial and sexual inequality. These educators have drawn attention to the

---

[h] **Resistance** (oppositional identity) has traditionally been attributed to deviant behavior, individual pathology, learned helplessness, cultural deprivation, and genetic flaws. Critical pedagogy, on the other hand, sees resistance as a legitimate response to domination, used to help individuals or groups deal with oppression. From this perspective, resistance in any form should be part of a larger political project that is working towards change.

autonomous logics and effects of racial and sexual dynamics in schooling, and to their necessary interaction with class, in lived social and cultural practices in the organization, reproduction, and transformation of social life. These cultural-studies approaches to schooling also call into question the base-superstructure model of society traditionally used by neo-Marxist theorists to explain the relationship between education and the economy and between race and class.

Marxist cultural theorists have therefore argued for a more integrated and synthetic conceptual framework as the basis for researching inequality in schooling. This framework — one that directs our attention to the interrelationships among a number of dynamics and that attempts to illuminate complexity, not wish it away — is known as the *parallelist* position. The case for the parallelist approach to race and schooling is very effectively presented by Michael W. Apple and Lois Weis (1983). Apple and Weis criticize the tendency of mainstream and radical theorists to divide society into separate domains of structure and culture. They argue that this arbitrary bifurcation directly promotes tendencies toward essentialism (single-cause explanations) in contemporary thinking about race. Researchers often "locate the fundamental elements of race, not surprisingly, on their home ground" (Omi & Winant, 1986, p. 52). For neo-Marxists, then, one must first understand the class basis of racial inequality; and for liberal theorists, cultural and social values and prejudices are the primary sources of racial antagonism. In contrast, Apple and Weis contend that race is not a "category" or a "thing-in-itself" (Thompson, 1966) but a vital social process which is integrally linked to other social processes and dynamics operating in education and society. These proponents of the parallelist position therefore hold that at least *three* dynamics — race, class, and gender — are essential in understanding schools and other institutions. None are reducible to the others, and class is not necessarily primary:

> [A] number of elements or *dynamics* are usually present at the same time in any one instance. This is important. Ideological form is not reducible to class. Processes of gender, age, and race enter directly into the ideological moment. . . . It is actually out of the articulation with, clash among, or contradictions among and within, say, class, race, and sex that ideologies are lived in one's day-to-day life. (Apple & Weis, 1983, p. 24)

In addition to this critique of class essentialism, these writers also offer a re-evaluation of economically reductive explanations of unequal social relations. It is acknowledged that the economy plays a powerful role in determining the structure of opportunities and positions in capitalist society. But "the" economy does not exhaust all existing social relations in society. Rather than using the economy to explain everything, theorists of the parallelist position have argued for an expanded view of the social formation in which the role of ideology and culture is recognized as integral to the shaping of unequal social relations and life chances. Apple and Weis (1983) maintain that there are three spheres of social life: economic, political, and cultural. The dynamics of class, race, and gender operate within each sphere while the spheres themselves continually interact. Unlike base-superstructure models, proponents of parallelist theory assume that action in one sphere can have an effect on action in another (Omi & Winant, 1986). The parallelist position therefore presents us with a theory of *overdetermination* in which the unequal processes and outcomes of teaching and learning and of schooling in general are produced by the constant interactions among three dynamics (race, gender, and class) and in three spheres (economic, political, and cultural). The parallelist model is presented in Figure 1.

The proposition that "each sphere of social life is constituted by the dynamics of class, race, and gender" (Apple & Weis, 1983, p. 25) has broad theoretical and practical merit. For example, it is impossible to understand fully the problem of the phenomenal high dropout rate among Black and Hispanic school youth without taking into account the interrelated race, class, and gender oppressions in U.S. urban centers and the ways in which the intersections of these social dynamics work to systematically "disqualify" inner-city minority youth in educational institutions and in the job market. In a similar manner, theoretical emphasis on gender dynamics complements our understanding of the unequal division of labor in schools and society and directs our attention to the way in which capitalism uses patriarchal relations to depress the wage scale and the social value of women's labor.

At a time when class and economic **reductionism**[i] still play important roles in our explanations, the thesis of parallelism holds promise. This does not mean, however, that the movement toward a parallelist position is without problems. Its basic drawback is that parallelism has been construed in terms of static, additive models of double and triple oppression in which racial oppression is simply added to class and gender oppression.

Attempts to specify the dynamics of race, class, and gender phenomena in education have often been formulated in terms of a system of linear "additions" or gradations of oppression. Thus, for example, Spencer (1984), in her insightful case study of women schoolteachers, draws attention to their double oppression. Simply stated, these women perform onerous tasks with respect to both their domestic and emotional labor in the home and their instructional labor in the classroom (pp. 283–296). In Spencer's analysis, the oppression of these women in the home is "added" to their oppression as teachers working in the classroom. No attempt is made here to represent the *qualitatively* different experiences of Black women both in the context of the domestic sphere and within the teaching profession itself. In this essentially

---

[i] To be **reductionistic** is to simplify a particular phenomenon so as to mask its complexity. For example, arguing that social reality is shaped solely by socioeconomic status and class conflict obscures the multiple and interconnecting relationships of other significant human experiences (such as race, gender, and sexual orientation) and their effects on perception and struggle.

Figure 1. The Parallelist Position

		Spheres		
		Economic	*Cultural*	*Political*
	Class			
Dynamics	*Race*			
	Gender			

Taken from Michael W. Apple and Lois Weis, eds., *Ideology and Practice in Schooling* (Philadelphia: Temple University Press, 1983), p. 25. Reprinted with permission.

incremental model of oppression, patriarchal and class forms of oppression unproblematically reproduce each other. Accounts of the intersection of race, class, and gender such as these overlook instances of tension, contradiction, and discontinuity in the institutional life of the school setting (McCarthy & Apple, 1988). Dynamics of race, class, and gender are thus conceptualized as having individual and uninterrupted effects.

Notions of double and triple oppression are not wholly inaccurate. Nevertheless, we need to see these relations as far more complex, problematic, and contradictory than parallelist theory suggests. One of the most useful attempts to conceptualize the interconnections between race, class, and gender has been formulated by Emily Hicks (1981). She cautions critical researchers against the tendency to theorize about the interrelations between social dynamics as "parallel," "reciprocal," or "symmetrical." Instead, Hicks offers the thesis that the operation of race, class, and gender relations at the level of daily practices in schools, workplaces, and so forth, is systematically *contradictory or nonsynchronous.* Hicks's emphasis on nonsynchrony (the production of difference) helps to lay the basis for an alternative approach to thinking about the operation of these social relations and dynamics at the institutional level.

By invoking the concept of nonsynchrony, I wish to advance the position that individuals or groups in their relation to economic, political, and cultural institutions such as schools do not share an identical consciousness and express the same interests, needs, or desires "at the same point in time" (Hicks, 1982, p. 221). In this connection , it is also necessary to attach great importance to the organizing principles of selection, inclusion, and exclusion. These principles operate in ways that affect how marginalized minority youth are positioned in dominant social and educational policies and agendas. Schooling, in this sense, constitutes a site for the production of the politics of difference. The politics of difference or nonsynchrony in the material context of the school expresses "culturally sanctioned, rational responses to struggles over scarce [or unequal] resources" (Wellman, 1977, p. 4).

The concept of nonsynchrony begins to untangle the complexity of causal motion and effects "on the ground," as it were. It also raises questions about the nature, exercise, and multiple determination of power within the middle ground of everyday practices in schooling. The fact is that, as Hicks (1981) suggests, dynamic relations of race, class, or gender do not unproblematically reproduce each other. These relations are complex and often have contradictory effects even in similar institutional settings. It is, therefore, important that we begin to understand the dynamics of the interaction of race, class, and gender in settings inside and outside of schools. The patterns of the social stratification by race, class, and gender emerge not as static variables but as efficacious structuring principles that shape minority/majority relations in everyday life.

In their discussion of educational and political institutions, Gilroy (1982), Omi and Winant (1986), and Sarup (1986) have emphasized the fact that racial and sexual antagonism can, at times, "cut at right angles" to class solidarity. The work of Gilroy (1982) and others directs our attention to the issues of nonsynchrony and contradiction in minority/majority relations in institutional settings, and suggests not only their complexity, but the impossibility of predicting these dynamics in any formulaic way based on a monolithic view of race. For instance, both Omi and Winant (1986) and Sarup (1986) point to examples of the diminution of working-class solidarity outside education, in the context of racial antagonism within North American and British White-dominated labor unions. These unions have had a long history of hostility to minorities and minority causes. On the other hand, Nkomo (1984), in his discussion of the dynamics of race/class relations in South African educational institutions, cites examples of the augmentation of racial solidarity across class lines. He argues that the high levels of cultural alienation experienced in South African Bantu universities by both Black students from urban, professional, middle-class backgrounds and working-class students from the Bantustans heightens the bonds of racial solidarity between these youth of different class backgrounds. Burawoy (1981) has identified the opposite effect of the intersection of race and class in the South African context. In this case, the operation of class contradictions as expressed in the differing material interests and aspirations of middle-class Black teachers, nurses, state bureaucrats, and their racial counterparts — the Black proletariat from the Bantustans — undermines racial solidarity between these radically opposed socioeconomic groups. Mary Fuller (1980) points to other contradictions in her study of the subculture of West Indian girls at a British working-class high school. These students exist in a nonsynchronous relationship with both their West Indian male counterparts and White working-class girls. While West Indian male youth reject the British school curriculum, the West Indian girls in Fuller's study were among the school's high achievers. However, their apparent compliance with school values of academic success paradoxically constituted the ideological basis for their assertion of their "independence" from West Indian boys as well as their rejection of the racial "underachievement" label that the British school system applies to West Indian youth as a whole.

It is to this literature — literature on the tensions and contradictions among raced, classed, and gendered forms of domination both inside and outside education — that critical scholarship in education should now turn. The key concepts of nonsynchrony and contradiction need to be fully integrated into current research on racial domination in schooling. At the same time, though, we need to be careful not to revert to a totally structural reading of these issues. That is, we need to emphasize the symbolic, signifying, and language dimensions of social interactions and their integral relationship both to systems of control and to strategies for emancipation.

This emphasis on symbols, signs, and representations has been particularly important for advancing our theoretical understanding of the ways racial and sexual antagonisms operate within cultural, political, and economic institutions such as schools (Carby, 1982). Indeed, we must remember that for a long time Black and feminist writers have argued (much against the tide of dominant research) that racial antagonism and sexual oppression are mediated through ideology, culture, political and social theories themselves. While neo-Marxist researchers maintained that it was economic exploitation and capitalist need for surplus value that explained the oppression of the socially disadvantaged, Black and feminist writers drew attention to modes of devaluation of self-image, culture, and identity. For writers such as James Baldwin (1986), Ntozake Shange (1983), June Jordan (1980), and Audre Lorde (1982), American schools are principal sites for the production and naturalization of myths and ideologies that systematically disorganize and neutralize minority cultural identities. With the full acknowledgment of the persuasiveness of these claims, race relations theorists such as Cornel West (1982) have argued that it is precisely in these "non-economic" sites of self-production and identity formation, such as the school and the church, that African Americans have sought to struggle against White oppression.

The issues of culture and identity must be seriously incorporated into a nonsynchronous approach to racial domination in schooling — not in the sense of an easy reduction to beliefs and values or the benign pluralism ("We are all the same because we are different.") of the multicultural paradigm, but in terms of a politic that recognizes the strategic importance of the historical struggles over the production of knowledge and the positioning of minorities in social theories and educational policies. Only by taking these issues seriously can we overcome the past and present tendencies in radical scholarship, which, as cultural critics such as Edward Said (1986) argue, obliterate the specific histories and struggles of the oppressed. This, of course, must be done with a full recognition that culture and identity are produced in a material context — one that is completely racial, gendered, and class-defined. The fact that the principles of selection, inclusion, and exclusion that inform the organization of school life have been hitherto understood primarily through class and socioeconomic paradigms says more about the biographies of mainstream and radical neo-Marxist school theorists than about the necessary character of schooling. Critical analysis of inequality in schooling must involve some sober reflection on the racist and sexist character of the production and reproduction of curriculum research itself.

Theories of how race, class, and gender interact, and of how economic, political, and cultural power act in education, need to become increasingly subtle. A non-synchronous theoretical framework remains to be fully articulated. But we need to remember what all of this theoretical labor is about — the political, economic, and cultural lives of real people. Oppressed women and men and children of color are subject to relations of differential power. These relations are not abstract, but are experienced in ways that now help or hurt identifiable groups of people in all-too visible ways.

REFERENCES

All London Teachers Against Racism and Fascism. (1984). *Challenging racism*. London: Author.

Alliance Against Women's Oppression. (September, 1983). Poverty not for women only: A critique of the "feminization of poverty." *Discussion Paper 3*. San Francisco: Author.

Anyon, J. (1979). Ideology and the United States history textbooks. *Harvard Educational Review, 49*, 361–386.

Apple, M. (1982). *Cultural and economic reproduction in education*. Boston: Routledge & Kegan Paul.

Apple, M., & Weis, L. (Eds.). (1983). *Ideology and practice in schooling*. Philadelphia: Temple University Press.

Atkinson, D., Morten, G., & Sue, D.W. (Eds.). (1979). *Counseling American minorities: A cross-cultural perspective*. Dubuque, IA: William C. Brown.

Baker, G. (1977). Development of the multicultural program: School of Education, University of Michigan. In F. H. Klassen & D. M. Gollnick (Eds.), *Pluralism and the American teacher: Issues and case studies* (pp. 163–169). Washington, DC: Ethnic Heritage Center for Teacher Education of the American Association of Colleges for Teacher Education.

Baldwin, J. (1961). *Nobody knows my name*. New York: Dial.

Banks, J. (1981). *Multiethnic education: Theory and practice*. Boston: Allyn & Bacon.

Bell, R. (1975). Lower class Negro mothers' aspirations for their children. In H. R. Stub (Ed.), *The sociology of education: A sourcebook* (pp. 125–136). Homewood, IL: Dorsey Press.

Ben-Tovim, G., Gabriel, J., Law, I., & Stredder, K. (1981). Race, left strategies and the state. In D. Adlam et al. (Eds.), *Politics and power three: Sexual politics, feminism, and socialism* (pp. 153–181). London: Routledge & Kegan Paul.

Berlowitz, M. (1984). Multicultural education: Fallacies and alternatives. In M. Berlowitz & R. Edari (Eds.), *Racism and the denial of human rights: Beyond ethnicity* (pp. 129–136). Minneapolis: Marxist Educational Press.

Blackburn, R. M., & Mann, M. (1979). *The working class in the labour market*. London: Macmillan.

Blauner, R. (1972). *Racial oppression in America*. New York: Harper & Row.

Bonacich, E. (1980). Class approaches to ethnicity and race. *Insurgent Sociologist, 10*, 9–24.

Bowles, S., & Gintis, H. (1976). *Schooling in capitalist America*. New York: Basic Books.

Brown, K. (1985). Turning a blind eye: Racial oppression and the unintended consequences of white "non-racism." *Sociological Review, 33,* 670–690.
Burawoy, M. (1981). The capitalist state in South Africa: Marxist and sociological perspectives on race and class. In M. Zeitlin (Ed.), *Political power and social theory* (vol. 2, pp. 279–335). Greenwich, CT: JAI Press.
Carby, H. (1982). Schooling in Babylon. In Centre for Contemporary Cultural Studies (Ed.), *The empire strikes back: Race and racism in 70s Britain* (pp. 183–211). London: Hutchinson.
Carmichael, S., & Hamilton, C. (1967). *Black power.* New York: Vintage.
Carnoy, M. (1974). *Education as cultural imperialism.* New York: Longman.
Carnoy, M., & Levin, H. (1985). *Schooling and work in the democratic state.* Stanford: Stanford University Press.
Chrichlow, W. (1985). *Urban crisis, schooling, and black youth unemployment: Case study.* Unpublished manuscript.
Edari, R. (1984). Racial minorities and forms of ideological mystification. In M. Berlowitz & R. Edari (Eds.), *Racism and the denial of human rights: Beyond ethnicity* (pp. 7–18). Minneapolis: Marxist Educational Press.
Editors. (1986, May 14). Here they come ready or not: An *Education Week* special report on the ways in which America's population in motion is changing the outlook for schools and society. *Education Week,* p. 28.
Everhart, R. (1983). *Reading, writing and resistance.* London: Routledge & Kegan Paul.
Fuller, M. (1980). Black girls in a London comprehensive school. In R. Deem (Ed.), *Schooling for women's work* (pp. 52–65). London: Routledge & Kegan Paul.
Gilroy, P. (1982). Steppin' out of Babylon: Race, class, and autonomy. In Centre for Contemporary Cultural Studies (Ed.), *The empire strikes back: Race and racism in 70s Britain* (pp. 278–314). London: Hutchinson.
Giroux, H. A. (1985). Introduction. In P. Freire (Ed.), *The politics of education.* South Hadley, MA: Bergin & Garvey.
Grant, C. (1975). Exploring the contours of a multicultural education. In C. Grant (Ed.), *Sifting and winnowing: An exploration of the relationship between CBTE and multicultural education* (pp. 1–11). Madison: University of Wisconsin-Madison, Teacher Corps Associates.
Grant, C., Boyle, M., & Sleeter, C. (1980). *The public school and the challenge of ethnic pluralism.* New York: Pilgrim Press.
Greenberg, S. (1980). *Race and state in capitalist development: Comparative perspectives.* New Haven: Yale University Press.
Henriques, J. (1984). Social psychology and the politics of racism. In J. Henriques (Ed.), *Changing the subject* (pp. 60–89). London: Methuen.
Hess, R., & Shipman, V. (1975). Early experience and socialization of cognitive modes in children. In H. R. Stub (Ed.), *The sociology of education: A source book* (pp. 96–113). Homewood, IL: Dorsey Press.
Hicks, E. (1981). Cultural Marxism: Non-synchrony and feminist practice. In L. Sargeant (Ed.), *Women and revolution* (pp. 219–238). Boston: South End Press.
Jakubowicz, A. (1985). State and ethnicity: Multiculturalism as ideology. In F. Rizvi (Ed.), *Multiculturalism as an educational policy.* Geelong, Victoria: Deakin University Press.
James, C. L. R. (1980). *Spheres of existence: Selected writings.* Westport, CT: Hill & Co.
Jensen, A. (1981). *Straight talk about mental tests.* New York: Free Press.
Jordan, J. (1980). *Passion.* Boston: Beacon Press.
Lamar, J. V., Jr. (1986, December 1). Today's native sons. *Time,* p. 27.
Lord, M. (1987). Frats and sororities: The Greek rites of exclusion. *The Nation, 245* (1).
Lorde, A. (1982). *Zami: A new spelling of my name.* New York: Crossing Press.
Marable, M. (1985). *Black American politics.* London: Verso.

McCarthy, C. *Beyond intervention: Neo-Marxist theories of racial domination and the state.* Unpublished manuscript.

McCarthy, C., & Apple, M. W. (1988). Race, class, and gender in American educational research: Toward a Nonsynchronous Parallelist Position. In L. Weis (Ed.), *Class, Race, and Gender in American Education.* Albany: State University of New York Press.

Moynihan, D. (1965). *The Negro family: The case for national action.* Washington, DC: U. S. Department of Labor, Office of Policy, Planning, and Research.

Mullard, C. (1985). Racism in society and schools: History, policy, and practice. In F. Rizvi (Ed.), *Multiculturalism as an educational policy* (pp. 64–81). Geelong, Victoria: Deakin University Press.

Nkomo, M. (1984). *Student culture and activism in black South African universities.* Westport, CT: Greenwood Press.

Ogbu, J. (1978). *Minority education and caste.* New York: Academic Press.

Omi, M., & Winant, H. (1986). *Racial formation in the United States.* New York: Routledge & Kegan Paul.

Roemer, J. (1979, Autumn). Divide and conquer: Microfoundations of Marxian theory of wage discrimination. *Bell Journal of Economics, 10,* 695–705.

Rushton, J. (1981). Careers and the multicultural curriculum. In J. Lynch (Ed.), *Teaching in the multicultural school* (pp. 163–170). London: Ward Lock.

Said, E. (1986). Intellectuals in the post-colonial world. *Salmagundi, 70/71,* 44–64.

Sarup, M. (1986). *The politics of multiracial education.* London: Routledge & Kegan Paul.

Saul, J. (1979). *The state and revolution in Eastern Africa.* New York: Monthly Review Press.

Shange, N. (1983). *A daughter's geography.* New York: St. Martin's Press.

Spencer, D. (1984). The home and school lives of women teachers. *Elementary School Journal, 84,* 283–298.

Thompson, E. P. (1966). *The making of the English working class.* New York: Vintage Books.

Troyna, B. (1984). Multicultural education: Emancipation or containment? In L. Barton & S. Walker (Eds.), *Social crisis and educational research* (pp. 75–97). London: Croom Helm.

Troyna, B., & Williams, J. (1986). *Racism, education and the state.* London: Croom Helm.

Weis, L. (1985). *Between two worlds.* Boston: Routledge & Kegan Paul.

Wellman, D. (1977). *Portraits of White racism.* Cambridge, Eng.: Cambridge University Press.

West, C. (1982). *Prophecy and deliverance! Toward a revolutionary Afro-American Christianity.* Philadelphia: Westminster.

I would like to thank the following people for their critical support and comments on the various drafts of this article: Michael W. Apple, Marie Brennan, Ron Good, Stuart Hall, Maria Soledad Martinez, Avanthia Milingou, Laura Stempel Mumford, Bill Pinar, Leslie Roman, Fran Schrag, Odaipaul Singh, Ahmad Moruzso Sultan, Tony Whitson, Erik O. Wright, Osvaldo Vazquez, and all the members of the U.W./C.I. Friday Sessions.

9

A Tentative Description of Post-Formal Thinking: The Critical Confrontation with Cognitive Theory

JOE L. KINCHELOE and SHIRLEY R. STEINBERG

All of the essays in Part One of this book have theorized about the importance of recognizing and engaging the sociohistorical, economic, and ideological effects on knowledge construction, consciousness, and pedagogy. Nonetheless, Shirley Steinberg and Joe Kincheloe illustrate how, for the most part, educational research and pedagogical theories and practices are still overwhelmingly obsessed with "innate" cognitive explorations.

Contesting such limited analysis of learning and teaching, Steinberg and Kincheloe critique and challenge prominent conceptions of intelligence that underlie cognitive developmental theory. Working from the premise that traditional boundaries of thinking and creativity separate logic, emotion, and context, these authors contend that educational institutions function to suppress diversity, the development of critical consciousness, and social agency. They argue in fact that schools operate and evaluate on the lowest level of human thinking — the mere ability to memorize without contextualization and understanding. Recognizing the relationship among ideology, power, and knowledge, Kincheloe and Steinberg delineate the features of a socio-cognitive theory, what they refer to as a post-formal way of thinking, and provide practitioners with a critical framework for reconsidering both curricular and pedagogical practices.

We recommend that readers not familiar with the debates over "modernity" and "postmodernity" check the glossary under "postmodernism" before reading this chapter.

Postmodern analysis, though diverse in the ways it is conceptualized, has consistently laid bare the assumptions of Cartesian logic by exposing the ways that the structure of traditional science constructs imaginary worlds. Science, like a novel, is "written"; both the novel and science operate according to the arbitrary rules of a language game. Such postmodern understandings confront us with a dramatic socio-educational dilemma: how do we function in the midst of such uncertainty?

The contemporary debate over postmodernism is often framed in all-or-nothing terms — we can either completely accept or completely reject Western modernism. In our work, we have sought a middle ground that attempts to hold onto the progressive and democratic features of modernism while drawing upon the insights postmodernism provides concerning the failure of reason, the tyranny of **grand narratives,**[a] the limitations of science, and the repositioning of relationships between dominant and **subordinate cultural groups.**[b] In such complex and changing times, we, as critical educators, turn to our emancipatory system of meaning, grounded as it is in feminist notions of passionate knowing, African American epistemologies, **subjugated knowledges**[c] (ways of knowing that have been traditionally excluded from the conversation of mainstream educators), liberation-theological ethics, and the progressive modernist concerns with justice, liberty, and equality. As we temper our system of meaning with a dose of postmodern self-analysis and epistemological (or maybe post-epistemological) humility, we move to a new zone of cognition — a *post-formal* way of thinking.

Formal thinking à la Piaget implies an acceptance of a Cartesian-Newtonian mechanistic worldview that is caught in a cause-effect, hypothetico-deductive system of reasoning. Unconcerned with questions of power relations and the way they structure our consciousness, formal operational thinkers accept an objectified, unpoliticized way of knowing that breaks a social or

---

[a] **Grand narratives** represent any macro-theories that attempt to explain social reality in its entirety. Such explanations, by subsuming every aspect into one narrowly defined lens, are overly simplistic in that they suppress differences into homogenizing schemes. For example, the Marxist notion that class struggle is the unifying principle of human history, are totalizing narratives. In the case where there is a monopoly on the power structure in a particular social order, some of these theories *(master narratives)*, such as the modernist claim to universality, have a large impact on the structure of society and generally go unquestioned and unchallenged.

[b] **Subordinate cultural groups** refers to groups that are politically, socially, and economically disempowered in the greater society. As Lilia Bartolomé describes, "While individual members of these groups may not consider themselves subordinate in any manner to the White 'mainstream,' they nevertheless are members of a greater collective that historically has been perceived and treated as subordinate and inferior by the dominant society. Thus it is not entirely accurate to describe these students as 'minority' students, since the term connotes numerical minority rather than the general low status (economic, political, and social) these groups have held" (p. 230).

[c] **Subjugated knowledges** are the excluded, silenced, or marginalized histories, memories, and experiences of subordinated populations. Critical pedagogy calls for learners to become active participants in the reconstruction and transformation of their own identities and histories.

educational system down into its basic parts in order to understand how it works. Emphasizing certainty and prediction, formal thinking organizes verified facts into a theory. The facts that do not fit into the theory are eliminated, and the theory developed is the one best suited to limit contradictions in knowledge. Thus, formal thought operates on the assumption that resolution must be found for all contradictions. Schools and standardized testmakers, assuming that formal operational thought represents the highest level of human cognition, focus their efforts on its cultivation and measurement. Students and teachers who move beyond formality are often unrewarded and sometimes even punished in educational contexts.

This article attempts to define the type of thinking that might occur when individuals, and teachers in particular, move beyond the boundaries of Piagetian formality. Many theorists (Lave, 1988; Walkerdine, 1984, 1988) over the last two decades have sought to formulate a post-Piagetian cognitive theory. Too often, however, they have not used a social theoretical analysis to construct a critique and a new vision of cognitive theory. In some ways, Piaget anticipated our theoretical project as he and Rolando Garcia (Piaget & Garcia, 1989) discussed the impact of social and epistemic paradigms in shaping cognitive systems. Unfamiliar, however, with critical postmodern analysis of subjectivity and power, Piaget was limited as to how far his intuitions could take him. Even with such limitations, Piaget often understood far more than many of his students about the situated nature of cognition (Walkerdine, 1984, 1992). Nevertheless, he did not connect this situatedness with any effort to break the confines imposed by the abstract rationality of the formal stage. Grounded in an understanding of critical and postmodern advances in social theory, we attempt to develop a *socio*-cognitive theory that draws upon these evolving discourses and moves beyond the monolithic **essentialism**[d] of the past.

Moving to post-formality, critical educators politicize cognition; they attempt to disengage themselves from socio-interpersonal norms and ideological expectations. The post-formal concern with questions of meaning, emancipation via ideological **disembedding**,[e] and attention to the process of self-production rises above the formal operational level of thought and its devotion to proper procedure. Post-formalism grapples with purpose, devot-

---

[d] **Essentialism** ascribes a fundamental nature or a biological determinism to humans (i.e., men are naturally aggressive, and women are naturally nurturing) through attitudes about identity, experience, knowledge, and cognitive development. Within this monolithic and homogenizing view, categories such as race and gender become gross generalizations and single-cause explanations about individual character. These authors point out that cognitive development is not simply an innate dimension of human beings, but, rather, is motivated by sociohistorical, ideological, and other environmental influences.

[e] **Disembedding** in this sense refers to the process of identifying, challenging, and transforming the ideologies that structure particular bodies of knowledge and social practices. "Knowledge" in the modernist sense is seen as "objective." Critical pedagogues argue that buried (embedded) in all social constructions are values and interests. Kincheloe and Steinberg are calling for a process of extracting such ideologies so that they can be engaged.

ing attention to issues of human dignity, freedom, authority, and social responsibility. Many will argue that a post-formal mode of thinking with its emphasis on multiple perspectives will necessitate an ethical relativism that paralyzes social action. A more critical post-formality grounded in our emancipatory system of meaning does not cave in to relativistic social paralysis. Instead, it initiates reflective dialogue between critical theory and postmodernism — a dialogue that is always concerned with the expansion of self-awareness and consciousness, never certain of emancipation's definition, and perpetually reconceptualizing the system of meaning. Critical theory, in brief, refers to the tradition developed by the **Frankfurt School**[f] in Germany in the 1920s. Max Horkheimer, Theodor Adorno, and others attempted to rethink the meaning of human self-direction or emancipation, to develop a theory of non-dogmatic social transformation, to expose the hidden social relationships of the everyday world, and to analyze the problems of social theories that celebrated social harmony without questioning the assumptions of the larger society. In a sense, the dialogue between critical theory and postmodernism produces a theoretical hesitation, a theoretical stutter.

One of the main features of post-formal thinking is that it expands the boundaries of what can be labeled sophisticated thinking. When we begin to expand these boundaries, we find that those who were excluded from the community of the intelligent seem to cluster around exclusions based on race (the non-White), class (the poor), and gender (the feminine). The modernist conception of intelligence is an exclusionary system based on the premise that some people are intelligent and others aren't (Case, 1985; Klahr & Wallace, 1976). Intelligence and creativity are thought of as fixed and innate, while at the same time mysterious qualities found only in the privileged few. The modernist grand narrative of intelligence has stressed biological fixities that can be altered only by surgical means. Such an essentialism is a psychology of nihilism that locks people into rigid categories that follow them throughout life (Bozik, 1987; Lawler, 1975; Maher & Rathbone, 1986). Howard Gardner's work, though not situated in the postmodernist tradition, has criticized this type of rigid modernism. This article positively draws from Gardner's critiques and theories. At the same time, it attempts to move beyond some of Gardner's ideas by connecting the political realm to the cognitive (Gardner, 1983, 1989, 1991).

The developmentalism of Piaget, while claiming a **dialectical**[g] interaction between mind and environment, still falls captive to the grand narrative of

---

[f] This German institute of social research, frequented by the likes of Marcuse, Fromm, Horkheimer, Adorno, Habermas, Arendt, Brecht, Lukacs, and a great many others, had an enormous impact on the sociological, political, and cultural thought of this century. It was from this institute that the term "critical theory," and its ideas evolved.

[g] While there are a number of definitions and interpretations of **dialectics**, for the general purposes of critical pedagogy, this concept refers to the interconnecting and contradicting relationships that constitute a particular phenomenon, for example, among the economic, political, social, and cultural dimensions of society. A dialectical analysis is also often used to show

intelligence. The theory walks into its own captivity because it views intelligence as a process that culminates in an individual's mastery of formal logical categories. The development of thinking seems to come from thinking itself, separate from the external environment. This reflects the innate fixity of earlier Cartesian-Newtonian views of intelligence as a specter emerging from innate inner structures. The early Piaget, in particular, maintained that the desired pedagogical course was to move students' development away from the emotions so that rationality could dominate the progress of the mind. Stages were thus constructed around this logocentrism — stages that would become key supports in the commonsense, unquestioned knowledge about intelligence (Piaget, 1970, 1977; Piaget & Inhelder, 1968).

Feminist theory challenges this **meta-narrative**,[h] arguing that cognizance of social construction of individuals and the inseparability of rationality and emotion causes us to question essential categories of human development. Feminists ask us to examine the difference between masculine and feminine ways of knowing (Belenky, Clinchy, Goldberger, & Tarule, 1986). The masculine, of course, represents the "proper" path for human cognitive development. Proposing that intelligence be reconceptualized in a manner that makes use of various ways of thinking, feminist theorists teach us that intelligence is not an innate quality of a particular individual, but, rather, something related to the interrelationship among ideas, behaviors, contexts, and outcomes (Bozik, 1987; Lawler, 1975; Walkerdine, 1984).

Developmental psychological principles have become so much a part of teacher education programs that it is hard to see where questions about them might arise. Not understanding the etymology of cognitive developmentalism, educators are unable to see it as a system of scientific classification. Developmentalism hides behind its claim of "freeing the child" from traditional methods of instruction, protecting its identity as an order of regulation on which child-centered pedagogy has been established. Critical constructivism (a constructivism grounded on an understanding of critical theory and postmodernism) along with post-formal thinking seeks to expose developmentalism as a specific socio-historical construction grounded in a specific set of assumptions about the mind. Developmentalism is not the only way to view intelligence. As we have come to see individualized instruction and child-centered pedagogy as a set of regulated and normalized progressive stages, we have missed the rather obvious point that individuals operate simultaneously at divergent cognitive stages. For example, an eight-year-old may employ particular skills with a computer that certainly reflect a formal-like thinking, while his or her understanding of U.S. politics reflects a more

---

how every idea or force has its opposite/contradiction. For example, the dialectic of "oppressor" is the reality of the "oppressed." Such an analysis holds both "opposing" concepts together at once to see how they interconnect and play off each other.

[h] A **meta-narrative** analyzes the body of ideas and insights of social theories that attempt to understand and make understood a complex diversity of phenomena and their interrelations.

concrete-like cognitive stage. Indeed, is what Piaget described as formal thinking a "universal" stage in cognitive development? When we examine the percentage of adults who "fail" when assessed by this formal standard, its universality is brought into question. The irony in the twentieth century's history of developmental psychology is that in its concern with individual freedom and the production of a rationality that could save human beings in their struggle for survival, it produced a system of cognitive and pedagogical apparatuses that delimited and rigidly defined the normalized individual. The biological capacities developmentalism has designated have ensured that even *progressive* teachers often view the child as an object of scientific pronouncement and, in the process, have undermined the liberation promised (Maher & Rathbone, 1986; Riegal, 1973; Walkerdine, 1984).

Indeed, the child in the developmentalist discourse is often viewed, within an ethic of Lockean individualism, as an isolated entity. Critical studies (Bourdieu & Passeron, 1977; McLaren, 1986; McLeod, 1987) have long maintained that children come to school with disparate amounts of **cultural capital**[i] or awareness that can be traded in for advantage in the school microcosm. Knowledge of White middle-class language, concern for academic success, and the ability to deport oneself in a "courteous" manner all contribute to one's advantage at school. Metaphorical constructs and meaning-making frameworks brought to school by African American, Latino, or other children who do not come from White middle-class backgrounds are often dismissed as developmentally inappropriate. Because developmentalism fails to ground itself within a critical understanding of the power relationships of dominant and subordinate cultures, it has often privileged White middle-class notions of meaning and success (O'Loughlin, 1992). Liberatory outcomes are far from the consciousness of many curriculum makers who ground their work in the discourse of child development.

Liberatory intent is also betrayed when we fail to address the critical constructivist concern with the social construction of mind. In the same way that Cartesian-Newtonian science strips away the layers of the social from our analysis, cognitive development is essentialized. The social features (race, class, gender, place) that influence patterns and definitions of development are ignored, allowing what are actually social constructions to be seen as natural processes. Here rests the practical value of the postmodern critique with its **decentering**[j] of the subject. Not allowing for a pre-existent essence of self, postmodernism denies the existence of men and women outside of the socio-historical process. The grand narrative of liberal individualism is

---

[i] **Cultural capital** refers to Pierre Bourdieu's concept that different forms of cultural knowledge, such as language, modes of social interaction, and meaning, are valued hierarchically in society. Critical pedagogues argue that only those characteristics and practices (i.e., cultural wealth) of the dominant paradigm will facilitate academic achievement within mainstream schools that reflect that dominant and exclusionary ideology.

[j] This notion of **decentering** is a rebuttal to the modernist (central) notion that the autonomous self (the individual being outside of social and historical influences) exists.

thus subverted, for objects of any type (especially knower and known, self and world) cannot be defined in isolation to one another. Cognitive development, then, is not a static, innate dimension of human beings; it is always interactive with the environment, always in the process of being reshaped and reformed. We are not simply victims of genetically determined, cognitive predispositions (Lawler, 1975; Walkerdine, 1984).

The postmodern critique not only undermines cognitive essentialism, it also subverts socio-cognitive **reductionism**.[k] The normalization of social control along the lines of scientifically validated norms of development and conduct implicit within developmentalism is not the outcome of some repressive power broker determined to keep individuals in their place. Power manifests itself not through some explicit form of oppression, but via the implicit reproduction of the self. Thus, advocates of critical thinking will operate within the boundaries of developmentalism with its predetermined definitions of normality; these advocates teach and learn within its gravitational field. The task of those who understand both the social contextualization of thinking and the postmodern critique of its discursive practices is to overthrow these reductionistic views of the way power works. When we view the effect of power on the way we define intelligence, or when we construct consciousness as some simple cause-effect process, we forfeit our grasp on reality and lose our connection to the rhythms of social life (de Lauretis, 1986; Walkerdine, 1984). Post-formal thinking attempts to conceive cognition in a manner that transcends the essentialist and reductionist tendencies within developmentalism, coupling an appreciation of the complexity of self-production and the role of power with some ideas about what it means to cross the borders of modernist thinking.

Since one of the most important features of post-formal thinking involves the production of one's own knowledge, it becomes important to note in any discussion of the characteristics of post-formality that few boundaries exist to limit what may be considered post-formal thinking. Post-formal thinking and post-formal teaching become whatever an individual, a student, or a teacher can produce in the realm of new understandings and knowledge within the confines of a critical system of meaning. Much of what cognitive science, and in turn the schools, have measured as intelligence consists of an external body of information. The frontier where the information of the disciplines intersects with the understandings and experience that individuals carry with them to school is the point where knowledge is created (constructed). The post-formal teacher facilitates this interaction, helping students to reinterpret their own lives and uncover new talents as a result of their encounter with school knowledge.

---

[k] To be **reductionistic** is to simplify a particular phenomenon so as to mask its complexity. For example, arguing that social reality is shaped solely by socioeconomic status and class conflict obscures the multiple and interconnecting relationships of other significant human experiences (such as race, gender, and sexual orientation) and their effects on perception and struggle.

Viewing cognition as a process of knowledge production presages profound pedagogical changes. Teachers who frame cognition in this way see their role as creators of situations where student experiences could intersect with information gleaned from the academic disciplines. In contrast, if knowledge is viewed as simply an external body of information independent of human beings, then the role of the teacher is to take this knowledge and insert it into the minds of students. Evaluation procedures that emphasize retention of isolated bits and pieces of data are intimately tied to this view of knowledge. Conceptual thinking is discouraged, as schooling trivializes learning. Students are evaluated on the lowest level of human thinking — the ability to memorize without contextualization. Thus, unless students are moved to incorporate school information into their own lives, schooling will remain merely an unengaging rite of passage into adulthood.

The point is clear; the way we define thinking exerts a profound impact on the nature of our schools, the role that teachers play in the world, and the shape that society will ultimately take. As we delineate the following characteristics of post-formal thinking, each feature contains profound implications for the future of teaching. Indeed, the post-formal thinking described in the following section can change both the tenor of schools and the future of teaching. Self-reflection would become a priority with teachers and students, as post-formal educators attend to the impact of school and society on the shaping of the self. In such a context, teaching and learning would be considered acts of meaning-making that subvert the **technicist**[1] view of teaching as the mastering of a set of techniques. Teacher education could no longer separate technique from purpose, reducing teaching to a deskilled act of rule-following and concern with methodological format. A school guided by empowered post-formal thinkers would no longer privilege White male experience as the standard by which all other experiences are measured. Such realizations would point out a guiding concern with social justice and the way unequal power relations in school and society destroy the promise of democratic life. Post-formal teachers would no longer passively accept the pronouncements of standardized-test and curriculum makers without examining the social contexts in which their students live and the ways those contexts help shape student performance. Lessons would be reconceptualized in light of a critical notion of student understanding. Post-formal teachers would ask if their classroom experiences promote, as Howard Gardner puts it, the highest level of understanding that is possible (Gardner, 1991).

Our search for such understanding is enhanced by a delineation of the following four features of post-formal thinking: *etymology* — the exploration

---

[1] Emanating from the positivist tradition, technocratic models, which conceptualize teaching and learning as a discrete and scientific undertaking, embrace depersonalized methods for educating students that often translate into the regulation and standardization of teacher practices and curricula, and rote memorization of selected "facts" that can easily be measured through standardized testing. As such, the role of the teacher is reduced to that of a **technician** — an uncritical, "objective," and "efficient" distributor of information.

of the forces that produce what the culture validates as knowledge; *pattern* — the understanding of the connecting patterns and relationships that undergird the lived world; *process* — the cultivation of new ways of reading the world that attempt to make sense of both ourselves and contemporary society; and *contextualization* — the appreciation that knowledge can never stand alone or be complete in and of itself.

ETYMOLOGY

The Origins of Knowledge Many descriptions of higher order thinking induce us to ask questions that analyze what we know, how we come to know it, why we believe it or reject it, and how we evaluate the credibility of the evidence. Post-formal thinking shares this characteristic of other descriptions of higher order thinking, but adds a critical **hermeneutic**[m] and historical epistemological dimension to the idea. In order to transcend formality, we must become critically exposed to our own tradition (and other traditions as well) so that we may understand the etymology of the cultural forms embedded within us. Antonio Gramsci (1988) noted that philosophy cannot be understood apart from the history of philosophy, nor can culture be grasped outside the history of culture. Our conception of self and world, therefore, can only become critical when we appreciate the historicity of its formation. We are never independent of the social and historical forces that surround us — we are all caught at a particular point in the web of reality. The post-formal project is to understand what that point in the web is, how it constructs our vantage point, and the ways it insidiously restricts our vision. Post-formal teachers struggle to become aware of their own ideological inheritance and its relationship to their own beliefs and value structures, interests, and questions about their professional lives (Cherryholmes, 1988; Codd, 1984; Daines, 1987; Greene, 1988).

As historical epistemologists, post-formal thinkers understand the etymology of knowledge, the way that knowledge is produced and the specific forces that contribute to its production. The *Zeitgeist* influences knowledge production as it directs our attention to certain problems and potentialities —, for example, the questions of equity emerging from the civil rights movement, or the nature of religious fundamentalism coming from the rise of the New Right, or of gender bias growing out of the women's movement. As the *Zeitgeist* changes or as multiple *Zeitgeists* compete in the same era, some bodies of information go out of fashion and are forgotten for the time being. Other bodies of knowledge are shelved because they seem to be tied to one particular research methodology and are not amenable to extension into different contexts. Thus, social and educational knowledge is vulnerable to

---

[m] **Hermeneutics** refers to the ongoing process of interpreting text for understanding the significance of lived experience, as opposed to believing that meaning is evident or understandable without need of interpretation.

the ebb and flow of time and the changing concerns and emotional swings of different eras. This vulnerability to the temporal will probably continue, for social science shows no sign of developing consistent universal strategies for evaluating the validity of these various forms of knowledge. Indeed, such a strategy would be **positivistic**[n] and suggest regression to a more formalistic mode of thinking (Fiske, 1986).

Post-formal thinkers concerned with epistemological etymology and their own subjective etymology have identified with Michel Foucault's (1984) notion of genealogy. By epistemological and subjective etymology, we are referring to: 1) the process by which social forces shape our understanding of what constitutes knowledge (is it a scientific process or are there other legitimate ways of knowing?); and 2) the process by which social forces shape our subjectivities or, less subtly, our identities. Foucault uses the term genealogy to describe the process of tracing the formation of our own subjectivities. By recognizing the ambiguities and contradictions in the construction of their own subjectivities, post-formal teachers can better understand the complexities of their students' consciousnesses. As they engage in self-critical genealogy, draw on our critical system of meaning, and employ action-research techniques, post-formal teachers become "ungrounded" and "unrigorous" from the perspective of the technicists who wag their fingers at their lack of technical procedure and formal systemization. Indeed, the self-critical genealogy and the critical action research that grows out of it constitute an emancipatory "rite of post-formal passage," as teachers leave behind their cognitive past (Kincheloe, 1991). Exercising new insights, they come to formulate more penetrating questions about their professional practice, see new levels of activity and meaning in their classrooms, decipher connections between sociocultural meanings and the everyday life of school, and reconceptualize what they already "know." As post-formal teachers grow to understand the etymology of the race, class, and gender locations of the students and others they study, they come to appreciate their own etymology, their location, and the social relationships such locations produce (Aronowitz, 1992; Miller, 1990; Reinharz, 1982).

Thinking about Thinking — Exploring the Uncertain Play of the Imagination Like William Pinar's notion of *currere* (the Latin root of the word "curriculum,"

---

[n] Associated with the Enlightenment and modernism, **positivism** refers to a belief system or paradigm that makes claims to objectivity, truth, and certainty in defense of a scientific basis for the study of culture. As such, knowledge and reason are seen as neutral and universal, rather than as social constructions that reflect particular interests and ideologies. This uncritical call to science has resulted in an obsession with finding and using the "right" technique to understand a phenomenon or solve a problem. For example, "technocratic" models, which conceptualize teaching as a discrete and scientific undertaking, embrace depersonalized methods for educating students that often translate into the regulation and standardization of teacher practices and curricula, and rote memorization of selected "facts" that can easily be measured through standardized testing. As such, the role of the teacher is reduced to that of an uncritical, "objective," and "efficient" distributor of information.

meaning the investigation of the nature of the individual experience of the public), post-formal thinking about thinking allows us to move to our own inner world of psychological experience. The effort involves our ability to bring to conscious view our culturally created, and therefore limited, concept of both self and reality, thus revealing portions of ourselves previously hidden (Pinar, 1975). Indeed, we are again involved in an etymological exploration, the explanation of the origins of our consciousness. To think about one's own thinking in a post-formal manner involves understanding the way our consciousness is constructed and appreciating the forces that facilitate or impede our accommodations. Post-formal thinking about thinking involves our ability to engage in ideological disembedding, the ability to remove ourselves from socio-interpersonal norms and expectations. This post-formal concern with questions of meaning and attention to the process of self-production rises above the formal level of thought and its concern with proper procedure. Our conception of post-formal thinking about thinking never allows us to be content with what we have cognitively constructed. Never certain of the appropriateness of our ways of seeing and always concerned with the expansion of self-awareness and consciousness, post-formal thinkers engage in a running meta-dialogue, a constant conversation with self (Codd, 1984; Kegan, 1982).

Ancient Greeks mythologically portrayed this dialogue with self. They were fascinated by the lulls of profound silence that periodically spread across a room filled with conversation. The Greeks postulated that at such moments Hermes had entered the room. By silencing the everyday babble, Hermes allowed the Greeks to tap their imaginations, fears, hopes, and passions. Through this awareness they were freed from acting out socially constructed expectations they really didn't understand. Hermes came to symbolize the penetration of boundaries — boundaries that separated one culture from another, work from play, fantasy from reality, and consciousness from unconsciousness. As he connects us with the unconscious, Hermes becomes another in a long line of trickster gods whom ancients associated with the power of the imagination.

Post-formal thinking about thinking draws upon the boundary trespasses of Hermes and the playful parody of postmodernism to transgress the official constraints of our consciousness construction, to transcend modern convention by exposing its etymology and its ironic contradictions (Bohm & Peat, 1987; Combs & Holland, 1990; Hutcheon, 1988; Kramer, 1983; Van Hesteran, 1986). As Peter McLaren explains the postmodern double reading of the social world, he writes of a teaching disposition that encourages students to think about their thinking in a post-formal manner. Students learn to construct their identities in a way that parodies the rigid conventions of modernism, thus assuming the role of postmodern stand-up comics, social satirists (McLaren, forthcoming). Hermes, the playful trickster, mysteriously pops up everywhere with his fantasies, surprise inspirations, and other gifts of the imagination; they are ours for the taking if we can hold onto the silence long enough to listen to him, if we have not let social expectations crush our propensity for play (Kristeva, 1980).

Asking Unique Questions — Problem Detection   The technical rationality of modernism has long ignored the ability to ask unique questions and to detect problems as important aspects of higher order intelligence. This modernist tradition has often reduced intelligence, and in turn the work of teachers, to problem-solving. Such cognitive reductionism restricts teaching to the level of formal thinking and captures practitioners in a culture of bureaucratic technicalization where they simply seek solutions to problems defined by their superiors (Munby & Russell, 1989; Schön, 1983). When the work of teachers is reduced to mere problem-solving, a practitioner's ability to identify the problems of the classroom and to ask unique questions about them is neglected. Indeed, pedagogies of problem-solving and tests of intelligence that focus upon problem-solving ignore the initial steps of questioning and problem detecting, which are prerequisites to creative acts of learning and post-formal thinking (Courtney, 1988). Problem detecting is a far more holistic act than problem-solving, in that problem detecting demands understanding of the goals of social justice and the etymology of those forces that undermine them. Such etymological appreciations shape our post-formal ability to detect contradictions, conflicts in the social order.

Problem detecting is undoubtedly a necessary precondition for technical problem-solving, although problem detecting is not itself a technical problem — it cannot be approached in a formalist procedural (technical) way. As a problem is detected, questions are formulated about a situation. In the process, a coherence is imposed on the situation that exposes asymmetries and helps cultivate an intuition for what might need to be changed about the situation. The context is framed in which an observation will be made. A body of past experiences and understandings is applied in this framing process to the situation in question. Problem detecting and the questioning that accompanies it become a form of world making in that the way these operations are conducted is contingent on the system of meaning employed. For example, a teacher in a multicultural education classroom may find that the texts recommended and the conception of the classroom conveyed by the course description encourage students to ask questions about the cultural identity of a variety of minority groups. Though it is not framed as a problem in the traditional conversation about multicultural education, the post-formal teacher might detect a problem in the discourse's erasure of "Whiteness" as an ethnicity — indeed, an ethnicity with a cultural identity. Raising this issue as a problem might open a new window of insight into the ways that White ethnocentrism is constructed and how the power of dominant culture reveals itself. Such problem detecting exposes the ways White people are sometimes shielded from forms of self-reflection that might reveal the origins of condescending views of "the other." With their focus on meta-awareness, post-formal thinkers are cognizant of the relationship between the way they themselves and others frame problems and ask questions about the nature of the system of meaning they employ. They possess an understanding of the etymology of frames, even when the individual involved fails to recognize the origin of a question or a problem.

Without this meta-awareness of a system of meaning, we, as teachers and administrators, may learn how to construct schools but not how to determine what types of schools to construct. We will not grasp the connection between political disposition and the types of education that are developed. Grounded on an understanding of such connections, post-formal teachers, administrators, and teacher educators realize that school problems are not generic or innate. They are constructed by social conditions, cognitive assumptions, and power relations, and are uncovered by insightful educators who possess the ability to ask questions never before asked, questions that may lead to innovations that promote student insight, sophisticated thinking, and social justice (Munby & Russell, 1989; Ponzio, 1985; Schön, 1987).

PATTERN

Exploring Deep Patterns and Structures — Uncovering the Tacit Forces, the Hidden Assumptions that Shape Perceptions of the World Physicist David Bohm helps us conceptualize this aspect of post-formal thinking with his notion of the "explicate" and "implicate" orders of reality (Bohm & Edwards, 1991; Bohm & Peat, 1987). The explicate order involves simple patterns and invariants in time — that is, characteristics of the world that repeat themselves in similar ways and have recognizable locations in space. Being associated with comparatively humble orders of similarities and differences, explicate orders are often what is identified by the categorization and generalization function of formal thought. The implicate order is a much deeper structure of reality. It is the level at which ostensible separateness vanishes and all things seem to become a part of a larger unified structure. The implicate order is a process, an enfolded sequence of events like the process of becoming an oak embedded in an acorn. The totality of these levels of enfolding cannot be made explicit as a whole. They can be exposed only in the emergence of a series of enfoldings. In contrast to the explicate order (which is an unfolded order) where similar differences are all present together and can be described in Cartesian-Newtonian terms, the implicate order has to be studied as a hidden pattern, sometimes impenetrable to empirical methods of inquiry (Bohm & Peat, 1987).

Post-formal thinking's concern with deep structures is, of course, informed by an understanding of the implicate order. Many have speculated that at higher levels of human consciousness, we often peek at the implicate pattern. Profound insight in any field of study may involve the apprehension of structures not attainable at the explicate order of reality. At these points we transcend common sense — we cut patterns out of the cosmic fabric (Combs & Holland, 1990). "Artists don't reproduce the visible," Paul Klee wrote; instead they "make things visible" (Leshan & Margenau, 1982). Similarly, Albert Einstein often referred to his physics as based on a process of questioning unconscious assumptions so as to reveal the deep structures of the universe. The theory of relativity itself emerged from his probing of the tacit assumptions underlying classical physics, in particular, absolute conceptions of time and space (Reynolds, 1987). As Einstein exposed deep physical structures of the shape of space, he was at least approaching an implicate order of the physical universe.

Post-formal thinking works to get behind the curtain of ostensible normality. Post-formal teachers work to create situations that bring hidden assumptions to our attention and make the tacit visible. For example, an American history teacher can create a hermeneutic atmosphere, a safe learning situation where students are encouraged to seek meaning, to interpret, even to be wrong at times. In this context, the teacher could point out the implicate patriarchal order of the required U.S. history text. Predominantly a story of male triumph in the political and military spheres, the book is arranged as a story of exploration, conquest, consolidation of power, and the problems of ruling the expanding empire. Questions of women's history, the history of poverty, racial justice, moral self-reflection, the history of ideas and culture, if addressed at all, are secondary. What may be the most important dimension of such a classroom may involve the post-formal uncovering of hidden assumptions of U.S. textbook publishers. Post-formal students may come to recognize patterns of exclusion, identifying historical themes or events that are typically erased from the "American Pageant." Virginia Woolf argued that artists possess many of these same abilities: they uncover hidden realities and communicate them to their readers. These hidden realities are inseparable from implicate orders that ultimately are to be found at the base of all experience. Formal thinking has not been attuned to such a reality, possibly because the expansionist, conquest-oriented goals of the Cartesian-Newtonian paradigm emphasized the explicate order of things. The social world is in many ways like an onion — as we peel off one layer, we find another beneath. An outside layer of socio-educational reality is the standardized test performance of a school. A second layer is the assumptions behind the language that is used in discussing the curriculum. A third layer is the unspoken epistemological assumptions of the curricular reforms. A fourth layer is the body of assumptions about learning that students bring to school, ad infinitum (Bohm & Peat, 1987; Briggs, 1990; Greene, 1988).

Unfortunately, the formalist analysis of school is grounded in the explicate order in which deep structures remain enfolded and out of sight. The dominant culture's conversation, not only about education but also about the political process, racism, sexism, and social-class bias, is formalist and focuses on the explicate order. Educators come to understand, for example, that the most damaging form of racism is not an explicate "George Wallace in 1963" variety, but an institutional racism built into the enfolded structure of schools, corporations, professional sports, and other institutions. Critical postmodern theory has taught us that little is as it appears on the surface (Giroux, 1992; Kanpol, 1992; McLaren, 1989; Pagano, 1990). When post-formal observers search for the deep structures that are there to be uncovered in any classroom, they discover a universe of hidden meanings constructed by a variety of socio-political forces. These meanings often have little to do with the intended (explicate) meanings of the official curriculum. A post-formal analysis of curriculum is grounded on the recognition that there are implicate orders of forces that shape what happens in schools — some complimentary, others contradictory, some emancipatory, others repressive. When this post-formal analysis of deep structures is applied to education, the implications for change are infinite. Imagine the way we might post-formally reconceptualize evaluation, supervision, administration, and so on. The reductionism of the explicate approach to these areas would be overthrown.

Seeing Relationships between Ostensibly Different Things — Metaphoric Cognition
Post-formal thinking draws heavily on the concept of the metaphor. Metaphoric cognition is basic to all scientific and creative thinking and involves the fusion of previously disparate concepts in unanticipated ways. The mutual interrelationships of the components of a metaphor, not the components themselves, are the most important aspects of a metaphor. Indeed, many have argued that patterns of relationships, not objects, should be the basis of scientific thinking (Gordon, Miller, & Rollock, 1990; Grumet, 1992; Rifkin, 1989). When thinking of the concept of mind, the same thoughts are relevant. We might be better served to think of mind not in terms of parts, but in terms of the connecting patterns, the dance of the interacting parts. The initial consciousness of the "poetic" recognition of this dance involves a non-verbal mental vibration, an increased energy state. From this creative tension emerges a perception of the meaning of the metaphor and the heightened consciousness that accompanies it. Post-formal teachers can model such metaphoric perception for their students. Such perception is not simply innate, it can be learned (Bohm & Peat, 1987; Fosnot, 1988; Talbot, 1986).

Pondering the question of what is basic in education, Madeleine Grumet (1992) argues that the concept of relation, of connecting pattern, is fundamental. Ironically, she argues, it is relation that we ignore when asked to enumerate the basics. Education involves introducing a student to modes of being and acting in the world that are new to his or her experience. Grumet concludes that it is the relation, the dance between the student's experience and knowledge, that separates education from training or indoctrination (Grumet, 1992). Post-formal thinkers recognize that relationships, not discrete objects, should be the basis for definitions in the sciences and humanities. From this perspective, the physical and social worlds are seen as dynamic webs of interconnected components. None of the parts of the webs are fundamental, for they follow the dance of their relationship with the other parts. The nature of their interconnections shapes the form the larger web takes. The educational implications of such a realization are revolutionary. The uncovering and interpretation of the dance becomes a central concern of teachers and students. Curricular organization, evaluation techniques, teacher education, and definitions of student and teacher success cannot remain the same if this post-formal characteristic is taken seriously (Capra, 1982; Fosnot, 1988; Talbot, 1986).

In the attempt to understand more than the explicate order of school, post-formal thinkers might draw upon the perspectives of oppressed peoples (Welch, 1991). Taking a cue from liberation theologians in Latin America, post-formal analysts begin the cognitive process of understanding the way an institution works by listening to those who have suffered most as the result of its existence. These subjugated knowledges allow post-formal thinkers to gain the cognitive power of empathy — a power that enables them to take a picture of reality from different angles, to analyze the deep patterns and structures of oppression. The intersection of these angles and the connections of these deep patterns allow for a form of analysis that moves beyond the isolated, fragmented analysis of modernity. With these ideas in mind, post-formal thinkers seek a multicultural dialogue between eastern cultures and western cultures, as well as a conversation between the relatively wealthy northern cultures and the impoverished southern cultures (Bohm & Peat, 1987). In this way, forms of knowing that have traditionally been excluded by the modernist West move post-formal teachers to new vantage points and unexplored planetary perspectives. Understanding derived from the perspective of the excluded or the culturally different allows for an appreciation of the nature of justice, the invisibility of the process of oppression, and a recognition of difference that highlights our own social construction as individuals.

In this spirit, post-formal teachers begin to look at their lessons from the perspectives of their Asian students, their Black students, their Latino students, their White students, their poor students, their middle- and upper-middle-class students, their traditionally successful students, their unsuccessful students. They examine their teaching from the vantage points of their colleagues or outside lay observers, which helps them reveal the hidden patterns and assumptions that shape their approaches. Thus, they step out of their teacher bodies and look down on themselves and their students as outsiders. As they hover above themselves, they examine their technicist teacher education with its emphasis on bulletin board construction, behavioral objective writing, discussion skill development, and classroom management. They begin to understand that such technicist training reflects a limited formality, as it assumes that professional actions can be taught as a set of procedures (Nixon, 1981).

Uncovering Various Levels of Connection between Mind and Ecosystem — Revealing Larger Patterns of Life Forces As a result of a dinner conversation with Albert Einstein, Carl Jung theorized his notion of synchronicity, the meaningful connection between causally unconnected events (Combs & Holland, 1990). Jung maintained that at the center of the mind a level of consciousness existed that connected the inner world of the psyche with the outer world of physical reality. The inner world of the psyche, Jung argued, is a mirror of the outer world — thus, the origin of his notion of the collective consciousness or deep unconsciousness as a collective mirror of the universe. Such a theory implies a level of connection between mind and reality or ecosystem that opens a realm of cognition untouched by cognitive science. Peter McLaren (forthcoming) taps this post-formal level of cognition when he writes of the realm of "impossible possibility" where teaching begins to search for connections between causally unconnected phenomena. As we move beyond the Cartesian-Newtonian borders in the explosion of our post-modern cognitive revolution, we begin to transcend our current disposition of being-in-the-world, our acceptance of boredom, alienation, and injustice. In a way, we become the science fiction writers of education, imagining what is admittedly not yet possible; but because of the fact that we can conceive of it, like sci-fi writers who imagined trips to the Moon, it becomes possible (Combs & Holland, 1990).

Post-formality is life-affirming as it transcends modernism's disdain and devaluation of the spiritual. Post-formalism, in its postmodern deconstructive manner, contests the "meaning of life" — that is, the actual definition of life. In the process of the deconstruction, it begins the task of reshaping on multiple, possibly contradictory levels, the definition of living. Transcending Cartesian-Newtonian fragmentation, post-formal thinkers understand that life may have less to do with the parts of a living thing than with patterns of information, the "no-thing" of the *relations* between parts, the "dance" of a living process — that is, life as synchronicity. Postmodernism is the consummate boundary crosser, ignoring the no-trespassing signs posted at modernism's property line of certainty. It is possible that postmodernism and its socio-cognitive expression, post-formality, will lead us across the boundary dividing living and non-living. Those characteristics that modernism defined as basic to life are present in many phenomena in the universe — from sub-atomic particles to weather to seahorses. Because all life on the planet is so multi-dimensionally entwined, it is extremely hard to separate life from non-life. Indeed, some scientists have already begun to argue that the best definition of life is the entire Earth. Seen from this perspective, modernism's lack of concern with ecological balance is suicidal on many levels (Talbot, 1986). Post-formal teachers can design lessons that illustrate the physical and spiritual connections between self and ecosystem. For example, a post-formal biology teacher might design a research project that seeks to define where animate objects end and inanimate objects begin. Students would be encouraged to define "life-force" and to develop an alternative taxonomy of living entities.

The world around us (maybe more precisely, the world, an extension of us) is more like an idea than a machine. Post-formality's concern with etymology, pattern, process, and contextualization expresses a similar thought on the social level. Human beings cannot be simply separated from the contexts that have produced them. Post-formality assumes the role of the outlaw, as it points out modernism's tendency to fragment the world. Indeed, post-formality recognizes none of the official boundaries that define our separateness. This post-formal transgression of boundaries is the feminist concept of connectedness writ large (Belenky, Clinchy, Goldberger, & Tarule, 1986), a holistic connectedness that opens cognitive possibilities previously imaginable only by the dreamers. As a hologram, the brain may interpret a holographic universe on a frequency beyond Newtonian time and space (Ferguson, 1980). The only definition left for life in the postmodern world is not some secret substance or life-force, but an information pattern. This definition of life as an information pattern elevates the recognition of relationship from the cognitive to the spiritual realm, for it is the relationship that is us. The same is true for consciousness; that is, sensitive intelligence is present wherever an entity can tune into the woven mesh of cosmic information, the enchanting pattern, the implicate order of the universe. From this definition, then, the ecosystem is conscious — the "nothing" of perceived pattern is the very basis of life and mind. Post-formal thinkers thus become ambassadors to the domain of the *pattern*. The cognitive revolution initiated by post-formality reshapes the school in a way in which life and its multi-dimensional connectedness resides at the center of the curriculum. Thinking is thus conceived as a life-sustaining process undertaken in connection with other parts of the life force.

PROCESS

Deconstruction — Seeing the World as a Text to be Read The post-formal thinker reads between the lines of a text, whether the text be, as with a physical scientist, physical reality or, for a teacher, the classroom and students. Thus, a text is more than printed material, as it involves any aspect of reality that contains encoded meaning to be deconstructed (Scholes, 1982; Whitson, 1991). Deconstruction can be defined in many ways — as a method of reading, as an interpretive process, and as a philosophical strategy. For post-formality, it involves all three of these definitions since it views the world as full of texts to be decoded, to be explored for unintended meanings. Jacques Derrida (1976) has employed deconstruction to question the integrity of texts, meaning that he refuses to accept the authority of traditional, established interpretations of the world. He has characteristically focused on elements that others find insignificant. His purpose is not to reveal what the text really means or what the author intended, but to expose an unintended current, an unnoticed contradiction within it (Culler, 1981, 1982).

When post-formal teachers view the world as a text, deconstruction can revolutionize education. No longer can the reader be passive, a pawn of text producers. Whether the text is produced by an author or by tradition, "areas of blindness" are embedded within it. When these areas are exposed, they reveal insight into the nature of how our consciousness is constructed. All texts are silent on certain points, and the task of deconstruction is to reveal the meanings of such silences (Scholes, 1982). Operating in the spirit of deconstructionism, post-formal thinkers come to realize that what is absent is often as important, or maybe more important, than what is present in a text. Employing the deconstructive process, post-formal teachers and students gain a creative role that transcends the attempt to answer correctly questions about what the author meant. After deconstruction, we can never again be so certain and comfortable with the stability of the world's meanings. Here rests a key element of post-formal thinking. Aware of the instability of meaning, post-formal thinkers abandon the quest for certainty, for closed texts. Unlike more formal thinkers in search of solutions to logical problems, post-formal thinkers are not uncomfortable with ill-structured problems with ambiguous answers.

Deconstruction represents the contemporary postmodern extension of a century of attempts in art, literature, psychology, and physics to penetrate surface appearances, to transcend the tyranny of common sense, to expose the unconsciousness of a culture. Within a deconstructive framework, consider what has happened to the Cartesian-Newtonian concept of reality in the twentieth century. The work of Albert Einstein, Werner Heisenberg, Sigmund Freud, and Carl Jung planted mines in the sea of modernity. Lying dormant until armed by the postmodernists, the mines were detonated by the ships of absolute truth. In the explosions, certainty was destroyed. In the wake of the destruction, the postmodern critique has taught us that, like fiction, science is a text. It produces "truth" no more absolute than the truth of Mozart or Dickens — it is an inventive act, a creative cognitive process.

Connecting Logic and Emotion — Stretching the Boundaries of Consciousness Feminist theory, Afrocentrism, and Native American ways of knowing have raised our consciousness concerning the role of emotion in learning and knowing (Jensen, 1984; Myers, 1987; Nyang & Vandi, 1980). In Afrocentric and Native American epistemologies, reality has never been divided into spiritual and material segments. Self-knowledge lays the foundation for all knowledge in these traditions, and a unified process of thinking has moved these traditions to appreciate the continuum of logic and emotion, mind and body, individual and nature, and self and other. Such appreciations have often caused great historical problems. It is only in the last thirty years that some European peoples have begun to recognize the epistemological sophistication of the African and Native American paradigms, with their recognition of unity in all things. Thus, from the post-formal perspective, that which is deemed primitive by Western observers becomes a valuable source of insight in the attempt to attain higher levels of understanding (Kincheloe, 1991).

Feminist constructivists have maintained that emotional intensity precedes cognitive transformation to a new way of seeing. Knowing, they argue, involves emotional as well as cognitive states of mind. As such, emotions are seen as powerful knowing processes that ground cognition (Mahoney & Lyddon, 1988). Formal thinkers in the Cartesian-Newtonian lineage are procedural knowers who unemotionally pay allegiance to a system of inquiry — indeed, they often see emotion as a pollutant in reason. Post-formal thinkers grounded in feminist theory unite logic and emotion, making use of what the emotions can understand that logic cannot. Emotionally committed to their thoughts, post-formal thinkers tap into a passion for knowing that motivates, extends, and leads them to a union with all that is to be known. Feminist scholar Barbara DuBois describes passionate scholarship as "sciencemaking, [which is] rooted in, animated by and expressive of our values" (cited in Belenky, Clinchy, Goldberger, & Tarule, 1986, p. 141).

Using a cognitive process created by the union of reason and emotion, feminist thinkers have revealed unanticipated insights gleaned from the mundane, the everyday lived world. They have exposed the existence of silences and erasures where formal thinkers had seen only "what was there." Such absences were revealed by the application of women's lived experience to the process of analysis, thus forging new connections between knower and known. Cartesian-Newtonian formalists had weeded out the self, denied their emotions and inner voices, and in the process produced restricted and object-like interpretations of social and educational situations. Using empirical definitions, these formalist object-like interpretations were certain and scientific; feminist self-grounded interpretations were inferior, merely impressionistic, and journalistic. Feminist theorists came to realize that the objective cognitive process described by Piagetian formality was released from any social embeddedness or ethical responsibility. Objectivity in this sense became a signifier for ideological passivity and an acceptance of a privileged socioeconomic position. Thus, formalist objectivity came to demand a separation of logic and emotion, the devaluation of any perspective maintained with emotional conviction. Feeling is designated as an inferior form of human consciousness — those who rely on logical forms of thinking and operate within this framework can justify their repression of those associated with emotion or feeling. Feminist theorists have pointed out that the thought-feeling hierarchy is one of the structures historically used by men to oppress women. In heterosexual relationships, these theorists assert, if a man is able to represent the woman's position as an emotional perspective, then he has won the argument — his is the voice worth hearing (Belenky, Clinchy, Goldberger, & Tarule, 1986; Reinharz, 1979).

The way of knowing ascribed to "rational man" defines logical abstraction as the highest level of thought — symbolic logic, mathematics, signifiers far removed from their organic function. Piaget's delineation of formality fails to appreciate these androcentric forces of decontextualization. Unlike Piaget's objective cognition, women's ways of knowing are grounded on an identification with organic life and its preservation. Rational man contends that emotions are dangerous because they exert a disorganizing effect on the progress of science. Informed by feminist perspectives and critical constructivist epistemology, post-formal teachers admit that, indeed, emotions do exert a disorganizing effect on traditional logocentric ways of knowing and rationalistic cognitive theory. But, they argue, such disorganization is a positive step in the attempt to critically accommodate our perceptions of ourselves and the world around us. Emotions thus become powerful thinking mechanisms that, when combined with logic, create a cognitive process that extends our ability to make sense of the universe (Fee, 1982; Mahoney & Lyddon, 1988; Reinharz, 1979).

Non-Linear Holism — Transcending Simplistic Notions of the Cause-Effect Process
Post-formality challenges the **hegemony**[o] of Cartesian-Newtonian logocentric formality, as it reverses the hierarchy of cause-effect, the temporality of modernist cause-effect rationality. In formalist thinking, cause has always been considered the origin, logically and temporally prior to effect. Post-formality upsets the certainty of this easy process by asserting that effect is what causes the cause to become a cause. Such a displacement requires a significant re-evaluation of common sense in the mundane, in everyday language. In this context, we begin to understand that while the formal operational orientation functions on the basis of the Cartesian assumption of linear causality, the post-formal perspective assumes reciprocity and holism (Kramer, 1983; Van Hesteran, 1986). Holism implies that a phenomenon can't be understood by reducing it to smaller units; it can be appreciated only by viewing it as a non-linear process, an integrated whole. It is the opposite of reductionism. For example, in a film the value and significance of a particular image is lost when considered in isolation. When perceived in relationship to the rest of the film's images, it is understood as part of an organic whole. The film is the process, the totality — not a succession of discrete images (Bohm & Peat, 1987; Talbot, 1986).

This returns us again to David Bohm's conception of the implicate order. The implicate order of a film, or a piece of music, or a painting is constantly unfolding from an original perception in the mind of the artist. More tradi-

---

[o] **Hegemony**, as derived from the work of Italian theorist Antonio Gramsci, is used to express how certain groups manage to dominate others. An analysis of hegemony is especially concerned with how the imposition of particular ideologies and forms of authority results in the reproduction of social and institutional practices through which dominant groups maintain not only their positions of privilege and control, but also the consensual support of other members of society.

tional conceptions of the creative process use a machine model, implying that the whole emerges out of an accumulation of detail — the whole is built out of a set of pieces. Thus, we see an important distinction between formal and post-formal thinking: creative unfolding representing a post-formal act and the sequential accumulation of detail representing a formal act. In any creative act there is an implicate order that emerges as an expression of the creator's whole life. The formal attempt to separate this holism into parts misses the essence of the creative process. Indeed, the attempt to teach based on this formalist, linear assumption will contribute little to the cultivation of creativity (Bohm & Peat, 1987).

Thus, creative thinking originates in the holistic depths of an implicate order. Such an order does not operate in a Newtonian universe of absolute, linear time. Events happen simultaneously rather than in a particular order of succession. When Einstein or Mozart or Da Vinci saw whole structures of physics, music, or art in a single flash of insight, they grasped the implicate order, the overall structure of a set of relationships all at once. Cognitive theorists have spoken of simultaneity for years, but they have rarely dealt with how to accomplish it. Post-formality can be more specific as it reconceptualizes the process of analysis. The flash of insight where all things are considered at once involves connecting to the current of the implicate order. It is not easy to teach products of Cartesian-Newtonian consciousness construction to think in terms of this simultaneous cognitive process and the holism it implies. Modernist thinkers have become accustomed to thinking that formal cognition with its scientific method is the zenith of human consciousness. We learn in the formal milieu to direct our attention to partial aspects of reality and to focus on a linearity consistent with our metaphors for time. In this formalist partiality we leave the whole stream of continuity, as we separate the humanities from the sciences, work from play, love from philosophy, reading from painting, the private from the public, and the political from the cognitive. The cognitive process as conceptualized by post-formalism invokes deconstruction to undermine the simple literalism of intended meanings. At the same time, this process embraces a holism that subverts formal thinking's notion of cause-effect linearity. Teachers who employ this post-formal cognitive process will be far better equipped to "read" their classrooms and the requirements of educational bureaucracies. Such teachers will be prepared to articulate the contradictions between society's educational and social goals and the realities of school practice.

CONTEXTUALIZATION

Attending to the Setting The development of a context in which an observation can assume its full meaning is a key element in the construction of a post-formal mode of thinking. The literal meaning of context is "that which is braided together." Awareness of this braiding induces post-formal thinkers to examine the ecology of everything, as they realize that facts derive meaning only in the context created by other facts. For instance, only in recent years has the medical profession begun to examine the context of disease — some physicians even argue that we should study the milieu and not simply the symptoms (Ferguson, 1980). In the same way, post-formal educators have begun to acknowledge that the contextualization of what we know is more important than content. In response to technicist educators who argue the importance of content, the need to "master" the basics as an initial step of learning, post-formal teachers maintain that once a fabric of relevance has been constructed, content learning naturally follows (Ferguson, 1980).

An example of the way meaning is dependent on context might involve a listener who lacks adequate context to understand the "order" of a musical form. In many cases, such a listener will judge an avant-garde composition as meaningless. Europeans, upon hearing African music, for instance, attempted to assess it in the terms of another musical form. Unable to appreciate the context that gave meaning to the African music, the Europeans did not hear the intentions of the composers and performers with their subtle rhythms and haunting melodies. They heard primitive noise (Bohm & Peat, 1987).

Cartesian-Newtonian thinking fails to convey a valuable perspective on cognition and teaching, as it fails in its reductionism to account for context. In modern empirical research, so-called scientific controls contribute to a more perfect isolation of the context being investigated. Attention to circumstances surrounding the object of inquiry must be temporarily suspended. This suspension of attention is based on the assumption that these extraneous circumstances will remain static long enough to allow the study to be validated. Of course, these extraneous circumstances never remain static. They are constantly interacting and shaping. To exclude them is to distort reality (Longstreet, 1982). In settings such as schools, student and teacher behavior cannot be understood without careful attention to the setting and the individuals' relationships to the traditions, norms, roles, and values that are inseparable from the lived world of the institutions. The inability of Cartesian-Newtonian researchers to say very much that is meaningful about school life is due in part to their lack of regard for the context — the often invisible, but foundational aspects of organizational life (Eisner, 1984; Wilson, 1977). John Dewey (1916) reflected this idea long ago when he argued that many thinkers regard knowledge as self-contained, as complete in itself. Knowledge, Dewey contended, could never be viewed outside the context of its relationship to other information. We only have to call to mind, Dewey wrote, what passes in our schools as acquisition of knowledge to understand how it is decontextualized and lacks any meaningful connection to the experience of students. Anticipating our notion of post-formality, Dewey concluded that an individual is a sophisticated thinker in the degree to which he or she sees an event not as something isolated, "but in its connection with the common experience of mankind" (Dewey, 1916).

Understanding the Subtle Interaction of Particularity and Generalization
Grounded in the Cartesian-Newtonian universe, formal thinking often emphasizes the production of generalizations. The post-formal teacher's concern with the particular, the unique experience of each learner, seems rather unscientific to the modernist educational scientist. To the post-formal teacher, the scientism, the obsession with generalization of the formal thinker are not especially helpful in the everyday world of the classroom. Formal generalization is out of sync with the rhythm of everyday life with its constant encounters with the novel and the unexpected — the particular.

When thinking is captured by Cartesian-Newtonian generalization, the nature of the particular is missed when it is treated as a sample of a species or a type — it is not itself, it is a representative. Viewed in this way, the particularistic, the individualistic has no proper name; it is alienated and anonymous. Children are interesting to the empirical researcher only as they represent something other than themselves. Joe Kincheloe and William Pinar's (1991) theory of place, which grounds post-formality's transcendence of mere generalization or mere particularity, fights formality's reductionist tendency. Place, as social theory, brings the particular into focus, but in a way that grounds it contextually in a larger understanding of the social forces that shape it. Place is the entity that brings the particularistic into focus; a sense of place sharpens our understanding of the individual and the psychological and social forces that direct her or him. Place, in other words, grounds our ways of seeing by providing the contextualization of the particular — a perspective often erased in formal forms of abstract thinking. Such contextualization connects post-formal thinkers with the insight of the visceral — its lust, fear, joy, love, and hate.

Post-formal thinking returns the particular to the educational conversation. Existing educational research focuses, for example, on public activities. Questions of social justice are public questions, often uninterested in the particularity of individual or family experience. As we are acculturated by the school, such tendencies induce us to repudiate the intimacy of our own autobiographies. Concepts as personal as epistemology are transformed into the height of abstraction, as our way of knowing becomes a public word connected with abstract theory. Indeed, the mere implication that epistemology is personal raises collegial eyebrows. In such a context, concern with the general and the abstract turns us away from place. The particularity, for example, of our home lives marked by thrilling, frightening, shameful, and proud moments is out-of-bounds in the public discourse of generalization. Such notions are translated into the everyday practice of schooling. As our children progress to the upper grades, too often they are taught to leave their particular autobiographies behind; these narratives have no place in the "real work" of school. Teachers who let themselves be known too well by students are immediately under suspicion. The curriculum is a public domain, as education leads us out of our intimate place to a world of public anonymity. Post-formal teachers fight such tendencies by drawing on student autobiography, theater, and literature to connect public knowledge to our private lives, to the formation of our subjectivities (Grumet, 1988).

Uncovering the Role of Power in Shaping the Way the World Is Represented   The way we make sense of the world around us is not as much a product of our own ability to assimilate information as it is the result of **dominant ideologies**P or forces of power in the larger society. This dominant power insidiously blocks our ability to critically accommodate. As it blocks our recognition of exceptions, it undermines our attempt to modify our assimilated understandings of ourselves and the world. When educational leaders use particular words, metaphors, and models to design programs and policies, they reflect the effects of the influence of power. When teachers unquestioningly accept these models and metaphors and employ them to ground their instructional practices, they unwittingly allow power to shape their professional lives. Power, as Foucault (1980, 1984) argued, has served to censor and repress like a great superego; but, he continues, it also serves to produce knowledge, creating effects at the level of the formation of consciousness. As a censor in our thinking as practitioners, power serves to reward particular ways of seeing and acting. For example, teachers who desire to be recognized as successful learn to follow particular norms and conventions that may have little to do with teaching and learning per se. When teachers internalize these norms and conventions, they allow power to create a context that dictates their views of appropriate "ways of being" (Cherryholmes, 1988; Giroux, 1992; McLaren, 1989).

Post-formal thinkers, operating at a meta-cognitive level, are able to understand the way power shapes their own lives. Post-formal teachers realize that in school, power often silences the very people that education purports to empower. This is the great paradox of contemporary schooling and teacher education: educators speak of empowerment as a central goal, but often ignore the way power operates to subvert the empowerment of teachers and students. Failing to ask how curricular knowledge is produced, educational analysts infrequently address which social voices are represented in the curriculum and which voices are excluded. When such questions are not asked, the attempt to move to a higher order of cognition is undermined as both teachers and students fail to explore the ways that social forces have contributed to the production of their identities, their ability to function in the world (Giroux & McLaren, 1988). Does it matter that we come from rich or poor homes, White or non-White families? These questions are not recognized as cognitive questions or questions of power — indeed, they are often not recognized at all. In the post-formal attempt to contextualize cognition, such questions of power must be seriously considered.

P **Dominant ideologies** are bodies of ideas held by cultural groups that are politically, socially, and economically in positions of power and are therefore able to impose on the greater society, through various social institutions and practices, particular traditions, bodies of knowledge, discourse styles, language uses, values, norms, and beliefs, usually at the expense of others.

CONCLUSION

If knowledge and consciousness are social constructions, then so is post-formal thinking — for it also emerges from a particular historical and social location. Recognizing post-formal thinking as historically situated, we in no way intend for it to be portrayed as an essential list of what constitutes higher order thinking. We offer it simply as a heuristic, an aid to further one's thinking about cognition. Post-formal thinking always includes an elastic clause — a rider that denies any claim of the objective existence of a post-formal way of thinking. It is one perspective from a particular point in the web of reality; a mere starting point in our search for what constitutes a higher level of understanding.

REFERENCES

Aronowitz, S. (1992). *The politics of identity: Class, culture, and social movements.* New York: Routledge.

Belenky, M., Clinchy, B., Goldberger, N., & Tarule, J. (1986). *Women's ways of knowing: The development of self, voice, and mind.* New York: Basic Books.

Bohm, D., & Edwards, M. (1991). *Changing consciousness.* San Francisco: Harper.

Bohm, D., & Peat, F. (1987). *Science, order, and creativity.* New York: Bantam Books.

Bourdieu, P., & Passeron, J. (1977). *Reproduction: In education, society, and culture.* Beverly Hills, CA: Sage.

Bozik, M. (1987, November). *Critical thinking through creative thinking.* Paper presented to the Speech Communication Association, Boston.

Briggs, J. (1990). *Fire in the crucible.* Los Angeles: Jeremy Tarcher.

Capra, F. (1982). *The turning point: Science, society, and the rising culture.* New York: Simon & Schuster.

Case, R. (1985). *Intellectual development: Birth to adulthood.* New York: Academic Press.

Cherryholmes, C. (1988). *Power and criticism: Poststructural investigations in education.* New York: Teachers College Press.

Codd, J. (1984). Introduction. In J. Codd (Ed.), *Philosophy, common sense, and action in educational administration* (pp. 8–28). Victoria, Australia: Deakin University Press.

Combs, A., & Holland, M. (1990). *Synchronicity: Science, myth, and the trickster.* New York: Paragon House.

Courtney, R. (1988). *No one way of being: A study of the practical knowledge of elementary arts teachers.* Toronto: MGS.

Culler, J. (1981). *The pursuit of signs: Semiotics, literature, deconstruction.* Ithaca, NY: Cornell University Press.

Culler, J. (1982). *On deconstruction: Theory and criticism after structuralism.* Ithaca, NY: Cornell University Press.

Daines, J. (1987). Can higher order thinking skills be taught? By what strategies? In R. Thomas (Ed.), *Higher order thinking: Definition, meaning and instructional approaches* (pp. 3–6). Washington, DC: Home Economics Education Association.

de Lauretis, T. (1986). Feminist studies/critical studies: Issues, terms, and contexts. In T. de Lauretis (Ed.), *Feminist studies/Critical studies* (pp. 1–19). Bloomington: Indiana University Press.

Derrida, J. (1976). *Of grammatology.* Baltimore: Johns Hopkins University Press.

Dewey, J. (1916). *Democracy and education.* New York: Free Press.

Eisner, E. (1984). Can educational research inform educational practice? *Phi Delta Kappan,* 65, 447–452.

Fee, E. (1982). Is feminism a threat to scientific objectivity? *International Journal of Women's Studies, 4,* 378–392.

Ferguson, M. (1980). *The Aquarian conspiracy: Personal and social transformation in our time.* Los Angeles: J. P. Tarcher.

Fiske, D. (1986). Specificity of method and knowledge in social science. In D. Fiske & R. Shweder (Ed.), *Metatheory in social science: Pluralisms and subjectivities* (pp. 61–82). Chicago: University of Chicago Press.

Fosnot, C. (1988, January). *The dance of education.* Paper presented to the Annual Conference of the Association for Educational Communication and Technology, New Orleans.

Foucault, M. (1980). *Power/knowledge: Selected interviews and other writings, 1972–1977* (Ed. Colin Gordon). New York: Pantheon.

Foucault, M. (1984). *The Foucault reader* (Ed. P. Rabinow). New York: Pantheon.

Gardner, H. (1983). *Frames of mind: The theory of multiple intelligences.* New York: Basic Books.

Gardner, H. (1989). *To open minds.* New York: Basic Books.

Gardner, H. (1991). *The unschooled mind: How children think and how schools should teach.* New York: Basic Books.

Giroux, H. (1992). *Border crossings: Cultural workers and the politics of education.* New York: Routledge.

Giroux, H., & McLaren, P. (1988). Teacher education and the politics of democratic reform. In H. Giroux (Ed.), *Teachers as intellectuals: Toward a critical pedagogy of learning.* Granby, MA: Bergin & Garvey.

Gordon, E., Miller, F., & Rollock, D. (1990). Coping with communicentric bias in knowledge production in the social sciences. *Educational Researcher, 19*(3), 14–19.

Gramsci, A. (1988). *An Antonio Gramsci reader* (Ed. David Forgacs). New York: Schocken Books.

Greene, M. (1988). *The dialectic of freedom.* New York: Teachers College Press.

Grumet, M. (1988). *Bitter milk: Women and teaching.* Amherst: University of Massachusetts Press.

Grumet, M. (1992). The curriculum: What are the basics and are we teaching them? In J. Kincheloe & S. Steinberg (Eds.), *Thirteen questions: Reframing education's conversation.* New York: Peter Lang.

Hutcheon, L. (1988). *A poetics of postmodernism.* New York: Routledge.

Jensen, K. (1984). Civilization and assimilation in the colonized schooling of Native Americans. In P. Altbach & G. Kelly (Eds.), *Education and the colonial experience* (pp. 155–179). New Brunswick: Transaction Books.

Kanpol, B. (1992). *Towards a theory and practice of teacher cultural politics: Continuing the postmodern debate.* Norwood, NJ: Ablex.

Kegan, R. (1982). *The evolving self: Problem and process in human development.* Cambridge, MA: Harvard University Press.

Kincheloe, J. (1991). *Teachers as researchers: Qualitative paths to empowerment.* New York: Falmer Press.

Kincheloe, J., & Pinar, W. (1991). Introduction. In J. Kincheloe & W. Pinar (Eds.), *Curriculum as social psychoanalysis: Essays on the significance of place* (pp. 1–23). Albany: State University of New York Press.

Klahr, D., & Wallace, J. (1976). *Cognitive development: An information processing view.* Hillsdale, NJ: Erlbaum.

Kramer, D. (1983). Post-formal operations? A need for further conceptualization. *Human Development, 26,* 91–105.

Kristeva, J. (1980). *Desire in language: A semiotic approach to literature and art* (Ed. Leon S. Roudiez). New York: Columbia University Press.

Lave, J. (1988). *Cognition in practice.* Cambridge, Eng.: Cambridge University Press.

Lawler, J. (1975). Dialectical philosophy and developmental psychology: Hegel and Piaget on contradiction. *Human Development, 18,* 1–17.

Leshan, L., & Margenau, H. (1982). *Einstein's space and Van Gogh's sky: Physical reality and beyond.* New York: Macmillan.
Longstreet, W. (1982). Action research: A paradigm. *The Educational Forum, 46*(2), 136–149.
Maher, F., & Rathbone, C. (1986). Teacher education and feminist theory: Some implications for practice. *American Journal of Education, 94*(2), 214–235.
Mahoney, M., & Lyddon, W. (1988). Recent developments in cognitive approaches to counseling and psychotherapy. *The Counseling Psychologist, 16*(2), 190–234.
McLaren, P. (1986). *Schooling as ritual performance: Towards a political economy of educational symbols and gestures.* London: Routledge.
McLaren, P. (1989). *Life in schools.* New York: Longman.
McLaren, P. (forthcoming). Postmodernism/post-colonialism/pedagogy. *Education and Society.*
McLeod, J. (1987). *Ain't no makin' it.* Boulder, CO: Westview Press.
Miller, J. (1990). *Creating spaces and finding voices: Teachers collaborating for empowerment.* Albany: State University of New York Press.
Munby, H., & Russell, T. (1989). Educating the reflective teacher: An essay review of two books by Donald Schön. *Journal of Curriculum Studies, 21,* 71–80.
Myers, L. (1987). The deep structures of culture: Relevance of traditional African culture in contemporary life. *Journal of Black Studies, 18*(1), 72–85.
Nixon, J. (1981). Postscript. In J. Nixon (Ed.), *A teachers' guide to action research.* London: Grant McIntyre.
Nyang, S., & Vandi, A. (1980). Pan Africanism in world history. In M. Asante & A. Vandi (Eds.), *Contemporary black thought: Alternative analyses in social and behavioral science.* Beverly Hills: Sage.
O'Loughlin, M. (1992, September). *Appropriate for whom? A critique of the culture and class bias underlying developmentally appropriate practice in early childhood education.* Paper presented to Conference on Reconceptualizing Early Childhood Education: Research, Theory, and Practice, Chicago.
Pagano, J. (1990). *Exiles and communities: Teaching in the patriarchal wilderness.* Albany: State University of New York Press.
Piaget, J. (1970). Piaget's theory. In P. Mussen (Ed.), *Manual of child psychology, vol. 1* (pp. 703–732). New York: Wiley.
Piaget, J. (1977). *The essential Piaget* (Eds. H. Gruber & J. Voneche). New York: Basic Books.
Piaget, J., & Garcia, R. (1989). *Psychogenesis and the history of science* (Trans. H. Feider). New York: Columbia University Press.
Piaget, J., & Inhelder, B. (1968). *The psychology of the child.* New York: Basic Books.
Pinar, W. (1975). The analysis of educational experience. In W. Pinar (Ed.), *Curriculum theorizing: The reconceptualists.* Berkeley: McCutchan.
Ponzio, R. (1985). Can we change content without changing context? *Teacher Education Quarterly, 12*(3), 39–43.
Reinharz, S. (1979). *On becoming a social scientist.* San Francisco: Jossey-Bass.
Reinharz, S. (1982). Experiential analysis: A contribution to feminist research. In G. Bowles & R. Klein (Eds.), *Theories of woman's studies* (pp. 162–191). Boston: Routledge & Kegan Paul.
Reynolds, R. (1987). Einstein and psychology: The genetic epistemology of relativistic physics. In D. Ryan (Ed.), *Einstein and the humanities* (pp. 169–176). New York: Greenwood Press.
Riegel, K. (1973). Dialectic operations: The final period of cognitive development. *Human Development, 16,* 346–370.
Rifkin, J. (1989). *Entropy: Into the greenhouse world.* New York: Bantam Books.
Scholes, R. (1982). *Semiotics and interpretation.* New Haven: Yale University Press.
Schön, D. (1983). *The reflective practitioner: How professionals think in action.* New York: Basic Books.

Schön, D. (1987). *Educating the reflective practitioner.* San Francisco: Jossey-Bass.
Talbot, M. (1986). *Beyond the quantum.* New York: Bantam Books.
Walkerdine, V. (1984). Developmental psychology and the child-centered pedagogy: The insertion of Piaget into early education. In J. Henriques, W. Hollway, C. Urwin, C. Venn, & V. Walkerdine (Eds.), *Changing the subject* (pp. 153–202). New York: Methuen.
Walkerdine, V. (1988). *The mastery of reason: Cognitive development and the production of rationality.* London: Routledge.
Walkerdine, V. (1992, April). *Redefining the subject in situated cognition theory.* Paper presented to the American Educational Research Association, San Francisco.
Welch, S. (1991). An ethic of solidarity and difference. In H. Giroux (Ed.), *Postmodernism, feminism, and cultural politics: Redrawing educational boundaries* (pp. 83–99). Albany: State University of New York Press.
Whitson, J. (1991). *Constitution and curriculum.* New York: Falmer.
Wilson, S. (1977). The use of ethnographic techniques in educational research. *Review of Educational Research, 47,* 245–265.
Van Hesteran, F. (1986). Counselling research in a different key: The promise of human science perspective. *Canadian Journal of Counselling, 20*(4), 200–234.

Part Two:
The Process of Learning and Teaching

INTRODUCTION:
A CALL FOR CRITICAL EDUCATORS

As illustrated by the authors in Part One of *Breaking Free,* critical pedagogy asserts both that educators work and speak from within historically and socially determined relations of power, and that educational research, practices, and curricula are forms of ideological and cultural production deeply implicated in the construction of knowledge and social relations. Teachers who work within the traditional paradigm, with its model of teacher as knower/lecturer and student as passive recipient of information, inevitably reproduce and maintain particular forms of identity, meaning, authority, and interaction, whether they are aware of it or not. At the same time, teachers themselves speak from various positions of privilege that are determined by their race, ethnicity, class, and gender. While this can serve to legitimate the voices of some teachers and students, it can also work to silence others. In the same way, curricula can serve either to affirm, produce, or exclude certain voices and lifestyles. What's worse, it can also work to demean, deny, or disfigure the lived experience of a great many people who are not part of the dominant group. As Cameron McCarthy contends in chapter 8, "Rethinking Liberal and Radical Perspectives on Racial Inequality in Schooling: Making the Case for Nonsynchrony," "American schools are principal sites for the production and naturalization of myths and ideologies that systematically disorganize and neutralize minority cultural identities" (p. 163). Pedagogy and curricula are thus not only composed of particular experiences and interests, but also represent a site of struggle over whose values and versions of authority and history will be central to the educational process.

In order to affirm and engage the complexity of diverse human histories and perceptions, and cross the socially and economically constructed borders of race, gender, ethnicity, class, sexual orientation, etc., a fundamental tenet of critical pedagogy, as exemplified by the following authors, is the need to include both teachers' and students' voices in the learning process. This move away from traditional relational restraints works to make the teachers' and students' location, experiences, and perceptions in their private and public lives the point of departure for dialogue and text for debate. In examining the social construction of knowledge, values, and interaction across "difference," the idea is not for teachers to be abusive by silencing students or placing their identities on trial. Instead, the process is to be unsettling only to the degree that it forces all of those involved to recognize their role in accepting and perpetuating oppression of any kind. Critically examining their own perspectives enables everyone to avoid the debilitating ramifications of relativism in which any and all positions and practices are equally acceptable, that is, *they are simply different*. The critical reflection, debate, and negotiation in such dialogue affords the necessary conditions for all classroom participants to act as knower, learner, and teacher, and to reach beyond their own boundaries. This in turn creates space for a more critical and democratic exchange of ideas.

However, as Paulo Freire is quick to point out in the following dialogue with Donaldo Macedo, teachers who make the conscious effort "to divest of authoritarianism" should never completely surrender their authority as teacher. Elaborating on how education is always directive and rigorous, Freire contends,

> I consider myself a teacher and always a teacher. I have never pretended to be a facilitator. I always teach to facilitate. . . . Teachers maintain a certain level of authority through the depth and breadth of knowledge of the subject matter that they teach. The teacher who claims to be a facilitator and not a teacher is renouncing, for reasons unbeknownst to us, the task of teaching and, hence, the task of dialogue. (pp. 200–201)

The initial step towards eradicating authoritarian practices and creating necessary self-empowering and inclusive conditions is the development of an awareness of one's own location in history, society, and privilege. This ongoing political reflection would require theorizing in order to help make sense of the everyday world so as to inform our practices. Unfortunately, theory is shunned in public education, making *praxis* — the integration of theoretical understanding and critique of society (that is, its historical, ideological, sociopolitical, and economic influences and structures) and action that endeavors to transform both the individual and their environment — an impossibility. As educators, we need to participate in the creation of new theories and languages of critique and possibility capable of engaging standard academic boundaries, such as epistemological restraints, that have limited the potential of public education.

All of the authors in Part Two, instead of blaming educators, support the power and possibility of teachers as transformative intellectuals who can serve in the pivotal role of opening up cracks of social agency through inclusive, meaningful, and liberatory practices.

10

A Dialogue:
Culture, Language, and Race

PAULO FREIRE and DONALDO P. MACEDO

Brazilian educator Paulo Freire has been the most widely recognized and influential theorist and educator of critical pedagogy. Perhaps best known for his literacy work in the decolonization process of Latin America and Africa, and for his first book, *Pedagogy of the Oppressed*, his insights have also been circulated among a number of educators in the United States. While the theoretical grounding and implications of Freire's practices are profound, at the foundation of such work is the conviction that a critical, multicultural democracy should be the driving force of the struggle for freedom. For Freire, the notion of conscientization, history, praxis, and dialogue are central to such a struggle.

Conscientization (i.e., critical consciousness) is the ability to analyze, problematize (pose questions), and affect the sociopolitical, economic, and cultural realities that shape our lives. Such a level of consciousness, according to Freire, requires that people place themselves in history, the assumption being that we are never independent of the social and historical forces that surround us. That is, we all inherit beliefs, values, and ideologies that need to be critically understood and transformed if necessary. For Freire, this process of transformation requires praxis and dialogue. "Praxis" refers to the relationship between theoretical understanding and critique of society (that is, its historical, ideological, sociopolitical, and economic influences and structures) and action that seeks to transform individuals and their environments. Arguing that people cannot transform a given situation simply through awareness or the best of intentions, nor through unguided action, Freire contends that we as active subjects must move from action to reflection and from reflection upon action to a new action.

The process of learning and knowing requires dialogue in which the sharing of experiences with others should not be understood in psychological terms alone, but needs to be infused with an ideological analysis and a political project capable of eradicating oppressive practices and institutions both in education and society. Unfortunately, Freire's notion of dialogue has been widely misinterpreted and misappropriated by educators and used as an uncritical method.

The following is part of an ongoing dialogue that Paulo Freire and Cape Verdean educator Donaldo Macedo have been having since 1983. It not only challenges the frequent misinterpretations of Freire's leading philosophical ideas by conservative and some liberal educators (especially around the notion of dialogic teaching, and the role of the teacher as opposed to facilitator in the classroom), but also addresses current criticisms of Freire's work along the lines of gender and race. The dialogue also embraces other contemporary educational issues, as the two critical educators discuss what it means for teachers to educate for a critical citizenry in the increasingly multiracial and multicultural world of the twenty-first century.

MACEDO: In their attempt to cut the chains of oppressive educational practices, many North American educators blindly advocate the dialogical model, creating, in turn, a new form of methodological rigidity laced with benevolent oppression — all done under the guise of democracy with the sole excuse that it is for the students' own good. As educators, many of us have witnessed pedagogical contexts in which we are implicitly or explicitly required to speak, to talk about our experiences, as an act of liberation. We all have been at conferences where speakers have been chastised because they failed to locate themselves in history. In other words, the speakers failed to give primacy to their experiences in addressing issues of critical democracy. It does not matter that the speakers had important and insightful things to say. This is tantamount to dismissing Marx because he did not entrance us with his personal, lived experiences. Another form of rigidity manifested in these educational practices modeled on your leading ideas is the process in which teachers relinquish their authority to become what is called a facilitator. Becoming a facilitator signals, in the view of many educators, a democratization of power in the classroom. Can you speak about these issues and perhaps clarify them?

FREIRE: Donaldo, let me begin responding by categorically saying that I consider myself a teacher and always a teacher. I have never pretended to be a facilitator. What I want to make clear also is in being a teacher, I always teach to facilitate. I cannot accept the notion of a facilitator who facilitates so as not to teach.

The true comprehension of dialogue must differentiate the role that only facilitates from the role that teaches. When teachers call themselves facilitators and not teachers, they become involved in a distortion of reality. To begin with, in de-emphasizing the teacher's power by claiming to be a facilitator, one is being less than truthful to the extent that the teacher turned facilitator maintains the power institutionally created in the position. That is, while facilitators may veil their power, at any moment they can exercise power as they wish. The facilitator still grades, still has certain control over the curriculum, and to deny these facts is to be disingenuous. I think what creates this need to be a facilitator is the confusion between authoritarianism and authority. What one cannot do in trying to divest of authoritarianism is relinquish one's authority as teacher. In fact, this does not really happen. Teachers maintain a certain level of authority through the depth and breadth of knowledge of the subject matter that they teach. The teacher who claims to be a facilitator and not a teacher is renouncing, for reasons unbeknownst to us, the task of teaching and, hence, the task of dialogue.

Another point worth making is the risk of perceiving facilitators as nondirective. I find this to be a deceitful **discourse**;[a] that is, a discourse from the perspective of the dominant class.

Only in this deceitful discourse can educators talk about a lack of direction in teaching. I do not think that there is real education without direction. To the extent that all educational practice brings with it its own transcendence, it presupposes an objective to be reached. Therefore, practice cannot be nondirective. There is no educational practice that does not point to an objective; this proves that the nature of educational practice has direction. The facilitator who claims that "since I respect students I cannot be directive, and since they are individuals deserving respect, they should determine their own direction," does not deny the directive nature of education that is independent of his own subjectivity. Rather, this facilitator denies himself or herself the pedagogical, political, and epistemological task of assuming the role of a subject of that directive practice. This facilitator refuses to convince his or her learners of what he or she thinks is just. This educator, then, ends up helping the power structure. To avoid reproducing the values of the power structure, the educator must always combat a laissez-faire pedagogy, no matter how progressive it may appear to be.

Authoritarian educators are correct, even though they are not always theoretically explicit, when they say that there is no education that is non-directive. I would not disagree with these educators; but, I would say that to claim to be a facilitator is authoritarian to the extent that the facilitators make their own objectives and dreams the directives that they give to learners in

---

[a] A **discourse** represents the ways in which reality is perceived through and shaped by historically and socially constructed ways of making sense, that is, language, complex signs, and practices that order and sustain particular forms of social existence. These systems of communication, which are constructions informed by particular ideologies, play a significant role in shaping human subjectivities and social reality, and can work to either confirm or deny the life histories and experiences of the people who use them. If the rules that govern what is acceptable in a particular society are exclusive, discourse can be a major site of contention in which different groups struggle over meaning and ideology.

their educational practice. Facilitators are authoritarian because, as subjects of the educational practice, they reduce learners to objects of the directives they impose.

While educators divest of an authoritarian educational practice, they should avoid falling prey to a laissez-faire practice under the pretext of facilitating. On the contrary, a better way to proceed is to assume the authority as a teacher whose direction of education includes helping learners get involved in planning education, helping them create the critical capacity to consider and participate in the direction and dreams of education, rather than merely following blindly. The role of an educator who is pedagogically and critically radical is to avoid being indifferent, a characteristic of the facilitator who promotes a laissez-faire education. The radical educator has to be an active presence in educational practice. But, educators should never allow their active and curious presence to transform the learners' presence into a shadow of the educator's presence. Nor can educators be a shadow of their learners. The educator who dares to teach has to stimulate learners to live a critically conscious presence in the pedagogical and historical process.

MACEDO: I believe that to renounce the task of teaching under the guise of facilitating is part and parcel of a paternalistic ideology.

FREIRE: Exactly. The true issue behind the act of facilitating remains veiled because of its ideological nature. In the end, the facilitator is renouncing his or her duty to teach — which is a dialogical duty. In truth, the teacher turned facilitator rejects the fantastic work of placing an object as a mediator between him or her and the students. That is, the facilitator fails to assume his or her role as a dialogical educator who can illustrate the object of study. As a teacher, I have the responsibility to teach, and in order to teach, I always try to facilitate. In the first place, I am convinced that when we speak of dialogue and education, we are speaking, above all, about practices that enable us to approach the object of knowledge. In order to begin to understand the meaning of a dialogical practice, we have to put aside the simplistic understanding of dialogue as a mere technique. Dialogue does not represent a somewhat false path that I attempt to elaborate on and realize in the sense of involving the ingenuity of the other. On the contrary, dialogue characterizes an epistemological relationship. Thus, in this sense, dialogue is a way of knowing and should never be viewed as a mere tactic to involve students in a particular task. We have to make this point very clear. I engage in dialogue not necessarily because I like the other person. I engage in dialogue because I recognize the social and not merely the individualistic character of the process of knowing. In this sense, dialogue presents itself as an indispensable component of the process of both learning and knowing.

MACEDO: I could not agree with you more. I am reminded of how educators who embrace your notion of dialogue mechanistically reduce the epistemological relationship of dialogue to a vacuous, feel-good comfort zone. For instance, in a graduate class I taught last semester in which we discussed extensively an anti-racist pedagogy, many White teachers felt uncomfortable when the non-White students made connections between the assigned theoretical readings and their own lived experience with racism. In discussing her feelings of discomfort, a White teacher remarked that "we should spend at least three weeks getting to know each other so as to become friends before taking on sensitive issues such as racism." In other words, this White teacher failed to recognize her privileged position that enabled her to assume she can negotiate the terms under which classmates from oppressed groups can state their grievances. It is as if in order to be able to speak the truth about racism or to denounce racist structures, non-Whites must first befriend their White classmates. The inability of this White teacher to acknowledge her privileged position in demanding to negotiate her comfort zone before grievances against racism are made makes her unable to realize that, in most instances, certain groups such as African Americans are born and live always without any comfort zone, much less the privilege to assume they can negotiate the appropriate comfort zone within a graduate course.

FREIRE: All of this leads us to consider another dimension that is implicit, but not always clear, in relation to the concept of dialogue. That is to say, the dialogue about which we are now speaking, the dialogue that educators speak about, is not the same as the dialogue about a walk up the street, for example, which becomes no more than the object of mere conversation with friends in a bar. In this case, people are not necessarily engaged in a search for the delimitation of a knowable object. Here I am speaking with respect to dialogue in a strictly epistemological perspective. What then does dialogue require as a sine qua non condition?

MACEDO: If in this sense the object of knowledge is the fundamental goal, the dialogue as conversation about individuals' lived experiences does not truly constitute dialogue. In other words, the appropriation of the notion of dialogical teaching as a process of sharing experiences creates a situation in which teaching is reduced to a form of group therapy that focuses on the psychology of the individual. Although some educators may claim that this process creates a pedagogical comfort zone, in my view it does little beyond making the oppressed feel good about their own sense of victimization. Simply put, I do not think that the sharing of experiences should be understood in psychological terms only. It invariably requires a political and ideological analysis as well. That is, the sharing of experiences must always be understood within a social praxis that entails both reflection and political action. In short, dialogue as a process of learning and knowing must always involve a political project with the objective of dismantling oppressive structures and mechanisms prevalent both in education and society.

Part of the reason why many teachers who claim to be Freire-inspired end up promoting a laissez-faire, feel-good pedagogy is because many are only exposed to, or interpret, your leading ideas at the level of cliché. By this I mean that many professors who claim to be Freire-inspired present to their students a watered-down translation of your philosophical positions in the form of a lock-step methodology. Seldom do these professors require their students to read your work as a primary source and, in cases where they do read, let's say, *Pedagogy of the Oppressed,* they often have very little knowledge of other books that you have published. For example, I have been in many educational contexts throughout the country where students ask me, "Why is it that my professors are always talking about Freire and the dialogical method and yet they never ask us to read Freire?" This point was made poignant some time ago in a workshop when a teacher began the presentation of her project by saying, "My project is Freirean inspired. I'll be talking about Freire even though I haven't read his books yet." Assigning students secondary or tertiary sources is very common within education programs in the United States. The end result is that professors become translators of the primary source's leading ideas. In so doing, they elevate their status by introducing translated materials that students almost blindly consume as innovative and progressive and, in some instances, also begin to identify these translated ideas with the professor-translator and not with the original author. This occurs because students have been cut off from the primary source. On the other hand, the professor-translator assumes falsely that the primary source is too difficult for students, which points to the paternalistic notion that future teachers are not capable of engaging with complex, theoretical readings. This false assumption leads, unfortunately, to the total deskilling of teachers in that it kills epistemological curiosity.

FREIRE: You are absolutely correct. I think that your posture indicates clearly that you understand very well the difference between dialogue as a process of learning and knowing and dialogue as conversation that mechanically focuses on the individual's lived experience, which remains strictly within the psychological sphere.

MACEDO: In the United States, even many educators who like your work mistakenly transform your notion of dialogue into a method, thus losing sight of the fact that the fundamental goal of dialogical teaching is to create a process of learning and knowing that invariably involves theorizing about the experiences shared in the dialogue process. Unfortunately, some strands of critical pedagogy engage in an overdose of experiential celebration that offers a **reductionist**[b] view of identity, leading Henry Giroux to point out that such pedagogy leaves identity and experience removed from the problematics of power, agency, and history. By overindulging in the legacy and importance of their respective voices and experiences, these educators often fail to move beyond a notion of difference structured in polarizing binarisms

---

[b] To be **reductionistic** is to simplify a particular phenomenon so as to mask its complexity. For example, arguing that social reality is shaped solely by socioeconomic status and class conflict obscures the multiple and interconnecting relationships of other significant human experiences (such as race, gender, and sexual orientation) and their effects on perception and struggle.

and uncritical appeals to the discourse of experience. I believe that it is for this reason that some of these educators invoke a romantic pedagogical mode that exoticizes discussing lived experiences as a process of coming to voice. At the same time, educators who misinterpret your notion of dialogical teaching also refuse to link experiences to the **politics of culture**[c] and critical democracy, thus reducing their pedagogy to a form of middle-class narcissism. This creates, on the one hand, the transformation of dialogical teaching into a method invoking conversation that provides participants with a group therapy space for stating their grievances. On the other hand, it offers the teacher as facilitator a safe pedagogical zone to deal with his or her class guilt. It is a process that bell hooks characterizes as nauseating in that it brooks no dissent.

FREIRE: Yes, yes. In the end, what these educators are calling dialogical is a process that hides the true nature of dialogue as a process of learning and knowing. What you have described can provide certain dialogical moments, but, in general, it is a mere conversation overly focused on the individual and removed from the object of knowledge. Understanding dialogue as a process of learning and knowing establishes a previous requirement that always involves an epistemological curiosity about the very elements of the dialogue.

MACEDO: I agree; there has to be a curiosity about the object of knowledge. Otherwise, you end up with dialogue as conversation, where individual lived experiences are given primacy. I have been in many contexts where the over-celebration of one's own **location**[d] and history often eclipses the possibility of engaging the object of knowledge by refusing to struggle directly, for instance, with the readings, particularly if these readings involve theory.

FREIRE: Yes. Curiosity about the object of knowledge and the willingness and openness to engage theoretical readings and discussions is fundamental. However, I am not suggesting an over-celebration of theory. We must not negate practice for the sake of theory. To do so would reduce theory to pure

---

[c] **Culture** in this sense is a terrain of lived experiences and institutional forms organized around diverse elements of struggle and domination. In other words, culture embodies the lived experiences and behaviors that are the result of the unequal distribution of power along such lines as race, gender, class, ethnicity, age, and sexual orientation. As people interact with existing institutions and social practices in which the values, beliefs, bodies of knowledge, styles of communication, and biases of the dominant culture are imposed, they are often stripped of their power to articulate and realize their own goals. For example, the efforts in the United States to enforce a "common culture" (an unnegotiated foundation of values, ethics, meaning, histories, and representations — "*our* cultural heritage") or a "common sense" (a selective view of social reality in which difference is viewed as deviant or a deficit), is in fact the imposition of a homogenizing social paradigm (known as ideological domination or *hegemony*) that severely limits the possibility for a critical multicultural democracy.

[d] Coming out of feminist scholarship, **location**, or "positionality," refers to the place that a person occupies within a set of social relationships. This position is often determined by such categories as gender, class, race, language, ethnicity, sexual orientation, age, and physical ability.

verbalism or intellectualism. By the same token, to negate theory for the sake of practice, as in the use of dialogue as conversation, is to run the risk of losing oneself in the disconnectedness of practice. It is for this reason that I never advocate either a theoretic elitism or a practice ungrounded in theory, but the unity between theory and practice. In order to achieve this unity, one must have an epistemological curiosity — a curiosity that is often missing in dialogue as conversation.

Returning to my original point, I would like to reiterate that human beings are, by nature, curious beings. They are ontologically curious. In order to be more rigorous, I would venture to say that curiosity is not a phenomenon exclusively human, but exclusively vital. That is, life is curious, without which life cannot survive. Curiosity is as fundamental to our survival as is pain. Without the ability to feel pain, and I am here referring to physical pain and not moral pain, we could possibly jump from a fourth-floor apartment without anticipating the consequences. The same would be true if we put our hands in fire. Pain represents one of the physical limitations on our practices. Thus, dialogue, as a process of learning and knowing, presupposes curiosity. It implies curiosity.

Teachers who engage in an educational practice without curiosity, allowing their students to avoid engagement with critical readings, are not involved in dialogue as a process of learning and knowing. They are involved, instead, in a conversation without the ability to turn the shared experiences and stories into knowledge. What I call epistemological curiosity is the readiness and eagerness of a conscious body that is open to the task of engaging an object of knowledge.

The other curiosity without which we could not live is what I call spontaneous curiosity. That is, along the lines of aesthetics, I may find myself before a beautiful tall building and I spontaneously exclaim its beauty. This curiosity does not have as its fundamental objective the apprehension and the understanding of the raison d'etre of this beauty. In this case, I am gratuitously curious.

As you pointed out earlier, Donaldo, one of the difficulties often confronted by an educator in assuming an epistemologically curious posture is that, at certain moments, the educator falls prey to the bureaucratization of the mind, becoming a pure methodologist. The bureaucratized educator is the one who assigns time slots for students to take turns speaking in a bureaucratized, if not vulgarized, democracy without any connection with the object of knowledge. In this case, the educator turned facilitator becomes mechanical, mechanizing the entire dialogue as a process of learning and knowing so as to make it a mechanical dialogue as conversation. In a bureaucratized dialogue as conversation, both students and teacher speak and speak, all convinced that they are engaged in a substantive educational practice just because they are all participating in an unknown bureaucratized discourse that is not connected to an object of knowledge. This pattern is not dialogical because you cannot have dialogue without a posture that is epistemologically curious. The educator who wants to be dialogical cannot relinquish his or her authority as a teacher, which requires epistemological curiosity, to become a facilitator who merely orchestrates the participation of students in pure verbalism.

MACEDO: This bureaucratized dialogical process orchestrated by the facilitator who falsely relinquishes his or her authority as teacher ends up being a process that gives rise to politics without content.

FREIRE: In my view, each class is a class through which both students and teachers engage in a search for the knowledge already obtained so they can adopt a dialogical posture as a response to their epistemological inquietude that forces the revision of what is already known so they can know it better. At the same time, it is not easy to be a dialogical teacher because it entails a lot of work. What is easy is to be a pure descriptivist.

MACEDO: You can also have the other extreme: A descriptive dialogue.

FREIRE: Of course you can.

MACEDO: This is what happens a lot with those teachers who relinquish their authority in order to become facilitators and, in the process, impose their bureaucratized dialogical method in a rigid manner that may require, for example, that all students must speak even if they choose not to do so. This rigidity transforms dialogical teaching, not into a search for the object of knowledge, but into a superficial form of democracy in which all students must forcefully participate in a turn-taking task of "blah-blah-blah." I have had the experience of students suggesting to me that I should monitor the length of time students talk in class in order to ensure equal participation for all students. In most instances, these suggestions are raised without any concern that the turn-at-talk be related to the assigned readings. In fact, in many cases, students go through great lengths to over-emphasize the process of turn-taking while de-emphasizing the critical apprehension of the object of knowledge. In the end, their concerns attempt to reduce dialogue to a pure technique. I want to make it clear that in criticizing the mechanization of turn-at-talk I do not intend to ignore the voices that have been silenced by the inflexible, traditional method of lecturing. What is important to keep in mind is not to develop a context whereby the assignment of turn-taking to give voice to students results in a new form of rigid imposition. Instead, it is important to create pedagogical structures that foster critical engagement as the only way for the students to come to voice. The uncritical license to take equal turns speaking in a rigid fashion gives rise to a "blah-blah-blah" dialogue resulting in a form of silencing while speaking. Critical educators should avoid at all costs the blind embracing of approaches that pay lip-service to democracy and should always be open to multiple and varied approaches that will enhance the possibility for epistemological curiosity with the object of knowledge. The facile and uncritical acceptance of any methodology regardless of its progressive promise can easily be transformed into a new form of methodological rigidity that constitutes, in my view, a form of methodological terrorism. A vacuous dialogue for conversation only is pernicious to the extent that it deskills students by not creating pedagogical spaces for epistemological curiosity, critical consciousness, and agency, which is the only way through which one can transcend valorized experience to embrace new knowledge in order to universalize one's own experience.

FREIRE: Exactly. This is where dialogical teaching ceases to be a true process of learning and knowing to become, instead, pure formalism; everything but dialogue. It represents a process to bureaucratize the mind. The educator who is really dialogical has a tiring task to the extent that he or she has to 1) remain epistemologically curious, and 2) practice in a way that involves epistemological curiosity that facilitates his or her process of learning and knowing. The problem lies in the fact that students often have not sufficiently developed such habits. It is for this reason that many students end up reading only mechanically and can easily spend an entire semester doing so because they were not able to transcend the spontaneity of curiosity you spoke of earlier so as to engage the epistemological curiosity that involves methodological rigor. Students today find it difficult to engage in this type of educational rigor precisely because they are often not challenged to engage in a rigorous process of learning and knowing. The end result is that they often remain at the periphery of the object of knowledge. Their curiosity has not yet been awakened in the epistemological sense. It is for this reason that we now witness more and more a disequilibrium between chronological age and epistemological curiosity. In many cases, epistemological curiosity remains truncated, giving rise to students who are intellectually immature.

What dialogical educators must do is to maintain, on the one hand, their epistemological curiosity and, on the other hand, always attempt to increase their critical reflection in the process of creating pedagogical spaces where students become apprentices in the rigors of exploration. Without an increased level of epistemological curiosity and the necessary apprenticeship in a new body of knowledge, students cannot truly be engaged in a dialogue.

MACEDO: I think this is a very important point that needs to be highlighted. That is, when students lack both the necessary epistemological curiosity and a certain conviviality with the object of knowledge under study, it is difficult to create conditions that increase their epistemological curiosity so as to develop the necessary intellectual tools that will enable them to apprehend and comprehend the object of knowledge. If students are not able to transform their lived experiences into knowledge and to use the already acquired knowledge as a process to unveil new knowledge, they will never be able to participate rigorously in a dialogue as a process of learning and knowing. In truth, how can you dialogue without any prior apprenticeship with the object of knowledge and without any epistemological curiosity? For example, how can you dialogue about linguistics if the teacher refuses to create the pedagogical conditions that will apprentice students into the new body of knowledge? By this I do not mean that the apprenticeship process should be reduced to the authoritarian tradition of lecturing without student input and discussion.

FREIRE: As you can see, Donaldo, my pedagogical posture always implies rigor, and never a laissez-faire dialogue as conversation orchestrated by facilitators. A mere appearance does not transform itself into the concreteness and substanticity of the actual object. Then, you cannot realistically have a dialogue by simply thinking that dialogue is a kind of verbal ping-pong about one's historical location and lived experiences.

MACEDO: Unfortunately, that is what happens too frequently.

FREIRE: The problem that is posed concerning the question of location is important. I do not think that anyone can seriously engage in a search for new knowledge without using his or her point of view and historical location as a point of departure. This does not mean, however, that I should remain frozen in that location, but, rather, that I should seek to universalize it. The task of epistemological curiosity is to help students gain a rigorous understanding of their historical location so they can turn this understanding into knowledge, thus transcending and universalizing it. If one remains stuck in his or her historical location, he or she runs the risk of fossilizing his or her world disconnected from other realities.

MACEDO: I agree. We need to avoid making our historical, locational experience into barriers that impede the universalization of the object of knowledge. This object of knowledge needs to be generalizable.

Paulo, let me turn to criticism of your pedagogical proposals. You are criticized not only by conservative educators for what they characterize as your "radical ties," but some liberals also feel uncomfortable with your critical perspectives. For example, Gregory Jay and Gerald Graff have argued that your proposal, in *Pedagogy of the Oppressed,* to move students toward "a critical perception of the world" — which "implies a correct method of approaching reality" so they can get "a comprehension of total reality" — assumes that you already know the identity of the oppressed. As Jay and Graff point out, "Freire assumes that we know from the outset the identity of the 'oppressed' and their 'oppressors.' Who the oppressors and the oppressed are is conceived not as an open question that teachers and students might disagree about, but as a given of Freirean pedagogy."[1] Can you address these criticisms?

FREIRE: Over the years I have been the object of much criticism concerning my pedagogical proposals. The criticism that you just mentioned was made more frequently during the seventies than today. However, as you have attested, the same criticism appears and reappears every so often. In my recent book, *Pedagogy of Hope*, published in 1994, I address these criticisms by making my pedagogical position very clear so as to leave less room for individuals like Gerald Graff not only to misread and misinterpret my philosophical ideas concerning a pedagogy of the oppressed, but also to reflect critically on some of the concrete pedagogical proposals I have been making over the years. The problem with some of these individuals is that they have read my work fragmentally. That is, they continually refer to my book, *Pedagogy of the Oppressed*, which I published over twenty years ago, without making any reference to my later works, including *Reading the Word and the World*, which I coauthored with you, *The Politics of Education*, and *Pedagogy of Hope*, among others. Critics often treat my work as if I had only published *Pedagogy of the Oppressed* and that I have not done anything for the past twenty years.

MACEDO: I agree with you. Even many progressive educators who have embraced and been inspired by your work have only read it fragmentally. Thus, they also, sometimes, fall prey to misinterpretations of your ideas.

FREIRE: But, Donaldo, I am surprised that someone like Gerald Graff, who I think considers himself an honest intellectual, would have difficulty identifying oppressive conditions and fall prey to a form of misguided **relativism**.[e] I do not think it is difficult to identify the thirty-three million people in my country who are in constant danger of dying of hunger as belonging to the oppressed group. Even in the very rich United States, as my good friend Jonathan Kozol so succinctly shows in his book *Savage Inequalities*, it is not very difficult to identify oppressed people. For example, would Graff have difficulty identifying the oppressive conditions in East St. Louis, as documented by my friend Kozol?

> East St. Louis . . . has some of the sickest children in America. Of 66 cities in Illinois, East St. Louis ranks first in fetal death, first in premature birth, and third in infant death. Among negative factors listed by the city's health directory are the sewage running in the streets, air that has been fouled by the local plants, the high lead levels noted in the soil, poverty, lack of education, crime, dilapidated housing, insufficient health care, unemployment.[2]

If Graff has difficulty identifying the oppressive conditions described above, he fits very well within the framework presented in your new book, *Literacies of Power: What Americans Are Not Allowed to Know*, which characterizes intellectuals who engage in the social construction of not seeing. As you point out, if you cannot see it, you cannot name it, which results in what you

---

[e] This is a caveat about the dangers of **relativism** in which efforts to eliminate oppression and eradicate the marginalization of difference are paralyzed by such questions as, "What is difference?" or "What is oppression?"

have categorized as a "discourse of not naming it," proving the old proverb, "The eyes do not see; they only record while the mind sees."

MACEDO: This is the real issue. To the extent that the mind can be ideologically controlled, it filters in order to transform what the eyes record, as is perhaps the case with Gerald Graff's reluctance to identify the oppressed and their oppressors. Graff's relativistic posture concerning the identity of the oppressed versus the oppressor eclipses the possibility for students to critically understand "the multiple experiences of identity by both historicizing it and revealing its partiality and incompleteness [and that] its limits are realized in the material nature of experience as it marks the body through the specificity of place, space and history."[3] This is very much in line with John Fiske's notion that "there is a material experience of homelessness that is of a different order from the cultural meanings of homelessness . . . but the boundary between the two cannot be drawn sharply. Material conditions are inescapably saturated with culture and, equally, cultural conditions are inescapably experienced as material."[4] As suggested by Fiske, the ideological and material conditions that produce oppression cannot be hidden blindly by the refusal to name the oppressor. The existence of oppression does not depend on the refusal or willingness to simply name it. Such oppression instead must be seen as part of the politics of representation that engages a particular project, and for you, Paulo, is defined by the ongoing struggle to promote and expand democratic social relations. The virtue of a radical democratic project is that it provides an ethical referent both for engaging in a critique of its own authority and as part of a wider expression of authority. In my view, what needs to be pedagogically engaged is not merely who is really oppressed, but the social, economic, and cultural conditions that lead to the creation of savage inequalities in East St. Louis and in the human misery of ghetto life, where African Americans and other oppressed groups materially experience the loss of their dignity, the denial of human citizenship, and, in many cases, outright violent and criminal acts committed by those institutions responsible for implementing the law, as we vividly witnessed in the beating of Rodney King by members of the Los Angeles police force. Those who materially experience oppression have little difficulty identifying their oppressors. The adoption of a relativistic posture concerning the oppressed and the oppressor not only points to Graff's privileged position that enables him to intellectualize oppression so as to make it abstract, but is also not unlike those individuals who attempt to rewrite the history of oppression as mere narratives. I believe that to be suspicious of one's own politics should not be an excuse to attempt to understand and address how power can work to oppress and exploit.

FREIRE: The issues that you just raised, Donaldo, are at the heart of the critical posture I call for in my educational proposals. As you can see, the criticism that my work proposes to know a priori what the oppressed peasants should know and what is best for them indicates that the individuals who critique me were, at best, able to read *Pedagogy of the Oppressed* mechanistically, thus superficially, and, at worst, they misread my book. Let me try to address some of the issues that they have raised, even though I may repeat what I clearly discussed in the *Pedagogy of Hope*.

As usual, I never deal with themes directly. I always do what I have been referring to as an epistemological approximation to the object of knowledge. I sometimes leave the linearity of my inquiry, so as to develop a global grasp of the object of knowledge in order to apprehend the total essence before I can learn it. Now, for example, in attempting to put myself critically in front of Graff's critique of my work, I would begin by saying that as men and women we are cultural beings endowed with the option to choose. We are also cultural beings who can make our own decisions and, for this reason, we are cultural beings endowed with the ability to rupture. It is impossible to decide without rupturing. It is not possible to opt without choosing one over the other. Then, we can conclude that we are innately programmed to choose, to make decisions, and to take positions in the world. We are born programmed to learn. Thus, we are programmed to learn, to teach, and, in doing so, our human agency cannot be reduced to any form of determinism. Because we are programmed to learn, to know, and to teach, we are born also with an undefined curiosity. It is for this reason that I consider the death of curiosity that sometimes happens in schools, a form of ontological violence, because curiosity is part of human **ontology**.[f]

If what I have just said is true, why should the educator hide his or her option, including his or her political position? On the other hand, it is not the role of the educator to impose his or her position. This is what has been said of my work. I have never advanced any pedagogical proposal that called for teachers to impose their political perspective. On the contrary, I have always fought against any form of imposition, any form of anti-democratic practice, and any form of social injustice. However, in doing so, I have never had the need to hide or the fear of hiding my political beliefs. Making my beliefs bare does not constitute, in my view, a form of imposition.

MACEDO: I agree. I think the courage to make your beliefs known, particularly your political ideals, does not point to any form of imposition. In my view, it is plain honesty. Unfortunately, we are living in a culture, particularly an academic culture, that requires courage in order to speak the truth. Our conviviality with the lie is not only rewarded, but is astutely veiled under the guise of objectivity, a form of lie in itself. What we need to understand is that the very claim of objectivity necessarily involves a dimension of subjectivity. Thus, it is **dialectical**.[g]

---

[f] Concerned with the nature of reality, **ontology** is the study of being, or the meaning of existence.

[g] While there are a number of definitions and interpretations of **dialectics**, for the general purposes of critical pedagogy, this concept refers to the interconnecting and contradicting relationships that constitute a particular phenomenon, for example, among the economic, political, social, and cultural dimensions of society. A dialectical analysis is also often used to show

FREIRE: Certainly. I think what constitutes an imposition is to engage with the oppressed educationally without providing them with the critical tools to understand their world, the tools that they were denied by not giving them access to education, to literacy, so they can read the word as well as the world. The educator who pretends to be objective and, in doing so, denies the oppressed the pedagogical space to develop a critical posture towards the world, particularly the world that has reduced them to a half-human object, exploited and dehumanized, is an educator who is complicit with the ideology of the oppressor. If objectivity means omission of historical truths that may prevent the oppressed from critically exercising their innate ability to opt, to decide, then objectivity and non-directivity in education is, in some real sense, a form of imposition. In other words, by not engaging the oppressed critically so they can understand the veiled ideology that continually dehumanizes them, the educator is in complicity with the oppressor. To do so is to be indifferent towards the plight of the oppressed who have been violated in terms of their capacity to opt and to decide. In the face of the denial to educate the oppressed and the ever-present violence perpetrated against their humanity, to not create pedagogical structures where the educator can make it feasible for the oppressed to retake what has been denied them, including the ability to think critically and the option to act on their world as **subjects of history and not objects,**[h] constitutes a veiled imposition of the oppressive conditions that have been responsible for their subordinated status to begin with. For example, illiteracy is not something that the peasants in Brazil created for themselves. It was imposed on them so as to deny them the ability to understand their historical conditions. This imposed illiteracy is, in my view, a violence against the peasants' human rights. To work with peasants in order to put an end to this violence and crime against humanity is not an imposition, but an act of courage that should lead to liberation.

If we are cultural beings with the capacity to learn and to opt, to discover knowledge, then we create because we discover, since, for human beings, to discover is to create. If all of this is true, the education of human beings should never be restricted to a true intellectual training that limits itself to merely exposing students to what Graff calls a pedagogy of conflict — as if all existed on an equal basis — without creating conditions that will enable

---

how every idea or force has its opposite/contradiction. For example, the dialectic of "oppressor" is the reality of the "oppressed." Such an analysis holds both "opposing" concepts together at once to see how they interconnect and play off each other.

[h] A **subject** is an active participant and not simply an entity that is acted upon, manipulated, and controlled as an object of history. A basic tenet of critical pedagogy is that only as active, critical subjects are we able to make substantive change. In the literature the term *objectification* is used to refer to people being seen/acted upon as objects. This is the process through which one becomes the object of learning strategies (e.g., this is designed for African Americans, you're Black, therefore . . .), rather than a knowledgeable participant in the construction of deep and meaningful learning experiences.

students to understand the nature of the ideologies that created the conflicts in the first place. But, even if education were merely an intellectual training, it would have to exert itself so as to enable people to become conscious beings, conscious of their world and, for this reason, it could never remain at a pure technical posture. Even if education were purely technical intellectual training it would eventually transcend the pure training and respond to our innate programming to learn and to know and to be curious. What technical training sometimes does, and with some success, is to constrain our human nature as knowing beings. Thus, education involves a globalizing practice. It is a practice that does not only involve technical knowledge, but also world knowledge. Therefore, the oppressed need to develop the necessary critical tools that will enable them to read their world so they can apprehend the globality of their reality and choose what world they want for themselves.

MACEDO: This is precisely what some of your critics claim, that you propose to know what world the oppressed want to be in. What if the oppressed do not want the world that you may have in mind for them?

FREIRE: I think that those who say this about me and my pedagogical proposals have totally misunderstood my work. In the first place, I cannot propose to the oppressed the world that I believe would be best for them. Obviously I can't. On the other hand, I cannot hide from the oppressed what I think about their situation as oppressed people nor refuse to talk with them about ways in which their lives could be improved. I have, as an educator, the right to think and dream about a world that is less oppressive and more humane toward the oppressed, just as the poet has the right to write and to dream about a utopian world. This does not mean that I am going to incarnate Picasso's art, but he had all the right to see the world the way he saw it. I would be imposing if I had the power to tell the oppressed the following: you either opt for liberation or be killed. What I do in my pedagogical proposal is to present them with possibilities to opt for an alternative. Should they reject the choice to opt for an alternative, then there is little that I can do as an educator. Imposition is when one willfully refuses to present alternatives and multiple points of reference.

MACEDO: That is what the conservative right does, in fact, by denying students opportunities to juxtapose historical events and facts so as to relate these events in order to have a global reading of reality.

FREIRE: Exactly. Conservative educators have the right to propose their view of the world. And as a student, I also have the right to reject this conservative position. What educators cannot do is to impose their view. What educators must do is to never fail to debate various positions without imposing any. Then, any pedagogical proposal is to challenge students around various hypotheses. However, these proposals must be dealt with from a concrete reality. Without anchoring these hypotheses in a concrete reality, the educator runs the risk of erasing the framework within which the tools for critical understanding of reality can be developed. For example, how can I teach peasants in Brazil without helping them understand the reasons why thirty-three million of them are dying of hunger? What I would have to tell these thirty-three million peasants is that to die from hunger is not a predetermined destiny. I would have to share with them that to die from hunger is a social anomaly. It is not a biological issue. It is a crime that is practiced by the capitalist economy of Brazil against thirty-three million peasants. I need to also share with them that the Brazilian economy is not an autonomous entity. It is a social production, a social production that is amoral and diabolical and should be considered a crime against humanity. What I cannot do as a teacher is to tell them not to discuss hunger but to think of it only as a phenomenon. I think teaching peasants how to read the word hunger and to look it up in the dictionary is not sufficient. They also need to know the reasons behind their experience of hunger. It is not sufficient only to discuss hunger. The peasants need also to understand those ideological elements that generate and maintain the hunger that is killing them and their children daily. As they study and discuss the raison d'etre of hunger, they will begin to see the asymmetrical social and economic distribution of wealth that contributes to their misery.

MACEDO: If you don't mind, let me interrupt you. What if these peasants do not want to know the reasons behind hunger and the asymmetrical distribution of wealth? Your insistence on this form of analysis may be viewed as an imposition.

FREIRE: I think that the issue is not purely pedagogical. It requires an ethical posture. I would ask the educator who criticizes my pedagogy as a form of imposition the following: If one day after class a student waits and, after all the other students leave, approaches the teacher and says, "I am thinking of committing suicide right here in front of you. I think I am going to kill myself now," does the teacher allow the student to kill himself because it is his wish to do so, or does he try to intervene ethically to try to prevent a tragedy? As you see, Donaldo, by not intervening so as not to impose, the teacher commits an ethical error. I think it is an ethical duty for educators to intervene in challenging students to critically engage with their world so they can act upon it and on it. I do not accept the present philosophical posture in which truth is relative and lies and truths are merely narratives. They have the right to say so. They also have the right to say, as some thinkers have been saying, that with the fall of communism we have reached the end of history. They have all the right to propose what they want to propose, as I also have the right to reject their proposals. I would have to point out that history continues, and I cannot remain silent before an error. By the same token, if a student wants to kill himself in front of me in my class, I cannot remain neutral. I must intervene, as I must intervene in teaching the peasants that their hunger is socially constructed and work with them to help identify those responsible for this social construction, which is, in my view, a crime against humanity.

MACEDO: I agree with the need to intervene, not only pedagogically but also ethically. However, before any intervention, an educator must have **political clarity**[i] — a posture that makes many liberals like Graff very uncomfortable to the degree that he considers "Radical educational theorists like [you], Henry Giroux, and Stanley Aronowitz . . . [as having a] tunnel-vision style of . . . writing . . . which speaks of but never to those who oppose its premises."[5] The assumption that you, Giroux, and Aronowitz engage in a "tunnel-vision style of . . . writing" is not only false, but also points to a distorted notion that there is an a priori agreed-upon style of writing that is monolithic, available to all, and "free of jargon." This blind and facile call for writing clarity represents a pernicious mechanism used by academic liberals who suffocate discourses different from their own. Such a call often ignores how language is being used to make social inequality invisible. It also assumes that the only way to **deconstruct**[j] ideologies of oppression is through a discourse that involves what these academics characterize as a language of clarity.

When I was working with you on the book *Literacy: Reading the Word and the World,* I asked a colleague whom I considered to be politically progressive and to have a keen understanding of your work to read the manuscript. Yet, during a discussion we had of our book, she asked me, a bit irritably, "Why do you and Paulo insist on using this Marxist jargon? Many readers who may enjoy reading Paulo may be put off by the jargon." I was at first taken aback, but proceeded to explain calmly to her that the equation of Marxism with jargon did not fully capture the richness of your analysis. In fact, I reminded her that your language was the only means through which you could have done justice to the complexity of the various concepts dealing with oppression. For one thing, I reminded her, "Imagine that instead of writing the *Pedagogy of the Oppressed* you had written the *Pedagogy of the Disenfranchised.*" The first title utilized a discourse that names the oppressor, whereas the second fails to do so. If you have "oppressed," you must have "oppressor." What would be the counterpart of disenfranchised? The *Pedagogy of the Disenfranchised* dislodges the agent of the action while leaving in doubt who bears the responsibility for such action. This leaves the ground wide open

---

[i] Not to be confused with "political correctness," **political clarity** (which Paulo Freire refers to as "conscientization") is the awareness of the historical, sociopolitical, economic, cultural, and subjective reality that shapes our lives, and our ability to transform that reality. Lilia Bartolomé further explains that "political awareness/clarity" is "the process through which individuals come to better understand possible linkages between macro-level political, economic, and social variables and subordinated groups' academic performance at the micro-level classroom" (p. 235).

[j] Generally associated with the work of French theorist Jacques Derrida, **deconstruction** is an analytic process through which the deep, unconscious meaning of texts is examined. Within a critical pedagogical framework, deconstruction often refers to the analytic process of taking apart (i.e., dissecting, critically inquiring, problematizing) a phenomenon in order to understand its construction.

for blaming the victim of disenfranchisement for his or her own disenfranchisement. This example is a clear case in which the object of oppression can also be understood as the subject of oppression. Language such as this distorts reality.

And yet, mainstream academics like Graff seldom object to these linguistic distortions that disfigure reality. I seldom hear academics on a crusade for "language clarity" equate mainstream terms such as "disenfranchised" or "ethnic cleansing," for example, to jargon status. On the one hand, they readily accept "ethnic cleansing," a euphemism for genocide, while, on the other hand, they will, with certain automatism, point to the jargon quality of terms such as "oppression," "subordination," and "praxis." If we were to deconstruct the term "ethnic cleansing" we would see that it prevents us from becoming horrified by Serbian brutality and horrendous crimes against Bosnian Muslims. The mass killing of women, children, and the elderly and the rape of women and girls as young as five years old take on the positive attribute of "cleansing," which leads us to conjure a reality of "purification" of the ethnic "filth" ascribed to Bosnian Muslims, in particular, and to Muslims the world over, in general.

I also seldom heard any real protest from these same academics who want "language clarity" when, during the Gulf War, the horrific blood bath of the battlefield became a "theater of operation," and the violent killing of over one hundred thousand Iraqis, including innocent women, children, and the elderly by our "smart bombs," was sanitized into a technical term, "collateral damage." I can go on and on giving such examples to point out how academics who argue for language clarity not only seldom object to language that obfuscates reality, but often use the same language as part of the general acceptance that the "standard" discourse is a given and should remain unproblematic. Although these academics accept the dominant standard discourse, they aggressively object to any discourse that both fractures the dominant language and bares the veiled reality in order to name it. Thus, a discourse that names it becomes, in their view, imprecise and unclear, and wholesale euphemisms such as "disadvantaged," "disenfranchised," "educational mortality," "theater of operation," "collateral damage," and "ethnic cleansing" remain unchallenged since they are part of the dominant social construction of images that are treated as unproblematic and clear.

I am often amazed to hear academics complain about the complexity of a particular discourse because of its alleged lack of clarity. It is as if they have assumed that there is a monodiscourse that is characterized by its clarity and is also equally available to all. If one begins to probe the issue of clarity, we soon realize that it is class specific, thus favoring those of that class in the meaning-making process.

The following two examples will bring the point home: Henry Giroux and I gave a speech at Massassoit Community College in Massachusetts to approximately three hundred unwed mothers who were part of a GED program. The director of this program later informed us that most of the students were considered functionally illiterate. After Henry's speech, during the question and answer period, a woman got up and eloquently said, "Professor Giroux, all my life I have felt the things you talked about. I just didn't have a language to express what I have felt. Today I have come to realize that I do have a language. Thank you." And you, Paulo, told me this story of what happened to you at the time you were preparing the English translation of *Pedagogy of the Oppressed.* Remember, you gave an African American student at Harvard a chapter of the book to read to see how she would receive it. A few days later, when you asked the woman if she had read it, she enthusiastically responded, "Yes. Not only did I read it, but I gave it to my sixteen-year-old son to read. He read the whole chapter that night and in the morning said, 'I want to meet the man who wrote this. He is talking about me.'" The question that I have for all those "highly literate" academics who find Giroux's and your discourse so difficult to understand is, Why is it that a sixteen-year-old boy and a poor, "semiliterate" woman could so easily understand and connect with the complexity of both Giroux's and your language and ideas, and the academics, who are the most literate, find the language incomprehensible?

I believe that the answer has little to do with language and everything to do with ideology. That is, people often identify with representations that they are either comfortable with or that help deepen their understanding of themselves. The call for language clarity is an ideological issue, not merely a linguistic one. The sixteen-year-old and the semiliterate poor woman could readily connect with your ideology, whereas the highly literate academics are "put off" by some dimensions of the same ideology. It is, perhaps, for this reason that a university professor I know failed to include your work in a graduate course on literacy she taught. When I raised the issue with her, she explained that students often find your writing too difficult and cumbersome. It could also be the reason why although the Divinity School at Harvard University offers a course entitled "Education for Liberation," where students study you and James Cone extensively, no such opportunities are available at Harvard's School of Education.

For me, the mundane call for language simplicity and clarity represents yet another mechanism to dismiss the complexity of theoretical issues, particularly if these theoretical constructs interrogate the prevailing dominant ideology. It is for this very reason that Gayatri Spivak correctly pointed out that the call for "plain prose cheats." I would go a step further and say, "The call for plain prose not only cheats, it also bleaches."

For me, it is not only plain prose that bleaches. Graff's pedagogy of "teaching the conflict" also bleaches to the extent that it robs students of the opportunity to access the critical discourses that will enable them not only to deconstruct the colonial and **hegemonic**[k] paradigms, but will also help

---

[k] **Hegemony**, as derived from the work of Italian theorist Antonio Gramsci, is used to express how certain groups manage to dominate others. An analysis of hegemony is especially concerned

them realize that one cannot teach the conflict as if, all of a sudden, it fell from the sky. The conflict must be anchored in those competing histories and ideologies that generated the conflict in the first place. David Goldberg captures this problem when he argues that Graff's suggestion

> presupposes that educators — even the humanists of Graff's address — occupy a neutral position, or at least can suspend their prejudices, in presenting the conflicts, and that the conflicts are fixed and immobile. One cannot teach the conflicts (or anything else, for that matter) by assuming this neutral "view from nowhere," for it is no view at all. In other words, the Assumption of a View from Nowhere is the projection of local values as neutrally universal ones, the globalizing of ethnocentric values, as Stam and Shohat put it.[6]

The problem with the teaching of the conflict is that the only referent for engaging authority is a methodological one. As a result, Graff demeans the ability of oppressed people to name their oppression as a pedagogical necessity and, at the same time, he dismisses the politics of pedagogy that "could empower 'minorities' and build on privileged students' minimal experience of otherization to help them imagine alternative subject positions and divergent social designs."[7]

FREIRE: As you can see, Donaldo, in criticizing my educational proposal as being too directive, these educators are also directive. There is no neutral education. All education is directive.

MACEDO: Paulo, if you don't mind, I would like to turn at this point to what I believe to be one of the most pressing educational challenges we face as we approach the end of this century. I would like to turn to the issue of multiculturalism. You mentioned to me a talk you gave in Jamaica where you stressed the need to find unity in diversity. How do you propose to achieve this noble goal when multicultural conflicts are intensifying everywhere?

FREIRE: A very first step is to understand the nature of multicultural coexistence so as to minimize the glaring ignorance of the cultural other. Part of this understanding implies a thorough understanding of the history that engenders these cultural differences. We need to understand that: a) there are intercultural differences that exist due to the presence of such factors as class, race, and gender and, as an extension of these, you have national differences; and b) these differences generate ideologies that, on the one hand, support discriminatory practices and, on the other hand, create **resistance.**[1]

---

with how the imposition of particular ideologies and forms of authority results in the reproduction of social and institutional practices through which dominant groups maintain not only their positions of privilege and control, but also the consensual support of other members of society.

[1] **Resistance** (oppositional identity) has traditionally been attributed to deviant behavior, individual pathology, learned helplessness, cultural deprivation, and genetic flaws. Critical ped-

The culture that is discriminated against does not generate the discriminatory ideology. Discrimination is generally generated by the hegemonic culture. The discriminated culture may give rise to an ideology of resistance that, as a function of its experience with struggle, adopts cultural behavior patterns that are more or less pacifist. In other instances, resistance is manifested in rebellious forms that are more or less indiscriminately violent. However, sometimes resistance emerges as a critical reflection leading toward the re-creation of the world. There is an important point that needs to be underlined: to the extent that these relations between these ideologies are dialectical, they interpenetrate each other. These relations do not take place in pure form and they can change from person to person. For example, I can be a man as I am and not necessarily be a *machista*. I can be Black, but in defending my economic interests, I might become complicit with White discrimination.

MACEDO: This is absolutely correct: Clarence Thomas, President Bush's Supreme Court appointee, represents an example of the interface between class and race ideologies par excellence. In his case, race is not a guarantee that the interests of millions of oppressed African Americans who have not yet broken loose from the yoke of White racism will be protected. Clarence Thomas's class interests override his race position. Thus, we cannot lump the many factors that cut across cultural difference into one monolithic cultural entity.

FREIRE: It is impossible to understand these differences without an analysis of ideologies and their relations between power and lack of power. These ideologies, whether discriminatory or resistant, embody themselves in special forms of social or individual behavior that vary from context to context. These ideologies express themselves in language — in the syntax and the semantics — and also in concrete forms of acting, of choosing, of valuing, of dressing, and even in the way one says hello on the street. These relations are dialectical. The level of these relations, their contents, their maximum dose of power revealed in the superior air one demonstrates, the distance, the coldness with which those in power treat those without power, the greater or lesser degree of accommodation or rebellion with which the dominated people respond to oppression — all of these are fundamental in the sense of overcoming the discriminatory ideologies so we can live in utopia; no more discrimination, no more rebelliousness or accommodation, but Unity in Diversity.

It is impossible to think, however, of overcoming oppression, discrimination, passivity, or pure rebellion without first acquiring a critical comprehension of history in which these intercultural relations take place in a dialecti-

---

agogy, on the other hand, sees resistance as a legitimate response to domination, used to help individuals or groups deal with oppression. From this perspective, resistance in any form should be part of a larger political project that is working towards change.

cal form. Thus, they are contradictory and part of a historical process. Second, we cannot think of overcoming oppression without political pedagogical projects that point to the transformation or the reinvention of the world.

Let's speak a little about the first question, the comprehension of the history that we have. As historical beings, our actions are not merely historical, but also are historically conditioned. Sometimes, without wanting to, in acting we are consciously clear with respect to the conception of history that defines us. Hence, I recognize the importance of discussions in courses of teacher preparation concerning the different ways we comprehend history that make us as we make it.

Let's talk succinctly of some different ways we reflect on our presence in the world and in which we find ourselves. One way of seeing ourselves is as spiritual beings, endowed with reason and the ability to make judgements, capable of distinguishing between good and bad, marked by original sin, thus needing to avoid at all costs falling into sin. From this perspective, falling into sin is viewed as always being preceded by strong temptations and the search for the road to salvation. Here sin and its negation become such that the former signals absolute weakness and the latter a facile cry of victory, in which human existence, reduced to this struggle, ends up almost losing itself in the fear of freedom or in the Puritanical hypocrisy that is a form of staying with the ugliness and rejecting the beauty of purity. History, in truth, is the history of the search for the beauty of purity, the salvation of the soul through the escape from sin. The prayers, the penitences, and promises are the principal arms and fundamental methods of action for those who idealistically experiment with this conception of history. Liberation theology signifies a radical rupture with this magical-mystical religiosity discussed above and, by putting its roots in the concrete context of experiences of women and men, God's people, it speaks of another comprehension of history that is, in reality, made by us. According to this interpretation of history, God is a presence. However, his presence does not prevent people from making their own history. On the contrary, God pushes people not only to make history, but to do so without negating the rights of others just because they are different from us.

With relation to the future, I would like to highlight two other comprehensions of history. Both are immobilizing and deterministic. The first has in the future a mere repetition of the present. In general, this is how the dominant class thinks. The tomorrow for them is always their present, as dominance is reproduced only with adverbial alterations. There is no place in this historical conception for a substantive overcoming of racial, sexual, linguistic, and cultural discrimination.

Blacks continue to be considered inferior, but now they can sit anywhere on the bus. . . . Latin Americans are good people, but they are not practical. . . . Maria is an excellent young woman; she is Black *but* she is intelligent. . . . In the three examples, the adversative co-function *but* is impregnated with ideology that is authoritarianly racist and discriminatory.

Another conception of history is, just as much as the others, at very least conditioned by practices regardless of the area. The cultural, educational, and economic relations among nations, and the environmental, scientific, technological, artistic, and communication areas reduce the tomorrow to a given fact. The future is predetermined, a type of fate, of destiny. The future is not problematic. On the contrary, it is unyielding. The dialectic that this vision of history reclaims, and has its origin in a certain Marxist dogmatism, is the domesticated dialectics. We know synthesis before we experience the dialectical collision between thesis and antithesis.

Another way of understanding history is to submit it to the caprice of individual will. The individual, from whom the social is dependent, is the subject of history. His or her conscience is the arbitrary maker of history. For this reason, the better education shapes individuals, that much better are their hearts, that much more will they who are full of beauty make the ugly world become beautiful. According to this vision of history, the role of women and men in the world is to take care of their hearts, leaving out, untouched, the social structures.

I see history exactly as do the liberation theologians, among whom I feel very good, and am in total disagreement with the other comprehensions of history I have discussed. For me, history represents a time of possibilities and not determinism. And if it is a time of possibilities, the first consequence that comes to the fore is that history does not only exist, but also requires freedom. To struggle for freedom is possible when we insert ourselves in history so as to make ourselves equally possible. Instead of being the constant persecutor of sin in order to be saved, we need to view history as possibility so we can both liberate and save ourselves. This is possible only through a historical perspective in which men and women are capable of assuming themselves, as both objects and subjects of history, capable of reinventing the world in an ethical and aesthetic mold beyond the cultural patterns that exist. This makes sense when we discuss communication as a new phase of continuous change and innovation. This, then, necessitates the recognition of the political nature of this struggle.

To think of history as possibility is to recognize education as possibility. It is to recognize that if education cannot do everything, it can achieve some things. Its strength, as I usually say, resides in its weakness. One of our challenges as educators is to discover what historically is possible in the sense of contributing toward the transformation of the world, giving rise to a world that is rounder, less angular, more humane, and in which one prepares the materialization of the great Utopia: Unity in Diversity.

MACEDO: After your public lecture at Harvard University in November of 1994, an African American woman talked impatiently to me inquiring why it is that your work on liberation struggles does not ever address the race issue in general, and the African American plight in particular. Can you address this criticism and attempt to clarify how your pedagogy takes on the role of race in liberation struggles?

FREIRE: In the first place, when I wrote the *Pedagogy of the Oppressed,* I tried to understand and analyze the phenomenon of oppression with respect to its social, existential, and individual tendencies. In doing so, I did not focus specifically on oppression marked by specificities such as color, gender, race, and so forth. I was extremely more preoccupied with the oppressed as a social class. But this, in my view, does not at all mean that I was ignoring the racial oppression that I have denounced always and struggled against even as a child. My mother used to tell me that when I was a child, I used to react aggressively, not physically, but linguistically, against any manifestation of racial discrimination. Throughout my life, I have worked against all forms of racial oppression, which is in keeping with my desire and need to maintain coherence with my political posture. I could not write on the defense of the oppressed while being a racist, just as I could not be a *machista* either.

In the second place, I would like to point out that today I have spoken and written a great deal about the question of race in my deep quest to fight against any form of discrimination. You need to keep in mind that my work is not limited to the *Pedagogy of the Oppressed,* and that all my writings are not available in English. It is exactly because of my growing awareness over the years concerning the specificities of oppression along the lines of language, race, gender, and ethnicity that I have been defending the fundamental thesis of Unity in Diversity, so that the various oppressed groups can become more effective in their collective struggle against all forms of oppression. To the extent that each specificity of oppression contains itself within its historical location and accepts the profile that was created by the oppressor, it becomes that much more difficult to launch an effective fight that will lead to victory. For example, when the oppressors speak of the minorities, in this process they hide the basic element of oppression. The label "minority" distorts and falsifies the reality if we keep in mind that the so-called minorities actually constitute the majority, while the oppressors generally represent the dominant ideology of a minority.

MACEDO: This is how language is used to distort reality so as to make social discrimination invisible. The same ideological mechanisms operate with the label *people of color,* which has even been embraced by many racial and ethnic groups to designate themselves. By calling non-White racial and ethnic groups "people of color," one is proposing that white is not a color, even though colorless white as a proposition is a semantic impossibility. Ideologically, "people of color" functions as a mechanism to make "White" as an ideological category invisible. However, it is precisely through this invisibility that the dominant White supremacy makes the ideological distinction against which all non-White groups are measured so as to be devalued and denigrated. This process facilitates the continued dance with bigotry without having to take responsibility for the poisonous effects of racism.

FREIRE: You are absolutely right. That is why I argue that the oppressed groups cannot and should not accept the dominant class's categorization of them as "minority" and, in the process, remain divided along race, class, gender, language, and ethnicity lines. Such divisions may lead not only to a form of **essentialism**,[m] but also make it more difficult for these groups to dismantle the oppressive structures that rob them of their humanity. By noting this, I do not want to minimize the specific historical location of oppression. In fact, it is only through one's historical location that one is able to develop the critical tools to understand the globality of oppression. What I want to make very clear to all oppressed groups, including racial, gender, linguistic, and ethnic groups, is that I maintain a great solidarity with their struggles against their oppressive conditions and that I have been expressing this more and more explicitly in my work.

MACEDO: You and I have talked extensively about the racial issue in other discussions we have had. Without wanting to press you on this question, I think it is important to address each aspect of the criticism leveled against your work concerning race. Therefore, I think it is important to clarify your position even if you have to repeat yourself.

Some educators in North America also point out that your theory of oppression does not speak directly to the issue of race. They argue that you have failed to assign the appropriate weight to race as a fundamental factor of oppression. In their view, your class analysis oversimplifies the role of race and its historical location of oppression. Can you discuss your views on this issue?

FREIRE: I became keenly aware during the decade of the twenties of the cruel symbolic and material violence perpetrated against Blacks in my country, even though some Brazilians like to think that there is no racism in Brazil. Even our own language contradicts this ignorant but never innocent position, given the verbal violence that Blacks endure in their day-to-day struggle for survival. Like the issue of gender, race as an ideological category did not feature predominantly, as I mentioned before in this discussion, in my early work, particularly in *Pedagogy of the Oppressed*. However, once again as mentioned earlier, my critics should not use *Pedagogy of the Oppressed* as the only measure to evaluate my solidarity with subordinate racial groups, particularly Africans and African Americans.

My involvement with literacy campaigns in various African countries, particularly Guinea-Bissau and São Tomé and Principe, speak of my commitment and my fight against all racial oppression and my admiration for the

---

[m] **Essentialism** ascribes a fundamental nature or a biological determinism to humans (i.e., men are naturally aggressive, and women are naturally nurturing) through attitudes about identity, experience, knowledge, and cognitive development. Within this monolithic and homogenizing view, categories such as race and gender become gross generalizations and single-cause explanations about individual character. However, critical Feminists have argued that gender is not the only determinant of a woman's identity, and that one must also look at the multiple and interconnecting relationships such as race, class, and sexual orientation in order to understand experience.

courage of Black people in Africa in throwing out the colonizers. Obviously, the race situation in Africa is somewhat different than that of the United States and we should — and I am becoming more and more aware of this — always take into consideration both the historical specificity and the different forms of oppression. In other words, in Africa, the vast majority of the population is Black, while the White colonizers represented only a small minority. The challenge for me in Africa, as I pointed out in *Letters to Guinea-Bissau: Pedagogy in Process*, was to be cautious always and aware of my role as an outsider who had been invited to provide some help with the transformation of the inherited colonial educational structure. In many discussions, as well as in many letters I wrote to my colleagues in Guinea-Bissau, I always stressed the importance of a thorough analysis of culture in the development of a liberatory educational plan. In fact, the importance of culture was not my idea, since their leader Amilcar Cabral understood extremely well the role of culture in the struggle for liberation. As I have said to you in our many discussions, Donaldo, I learned immense amounts from Cabral's insights, particularly from his analysis of culture.

The issue of race in Guinea-Bissau, as well as in other African countries where I worked, is different, in my view, from that of the United States. The challenge for the liberators and educators was to understand how race as an ideological category served to legitimize the colonizers' exploitation and domination. When colonizers used the pretext of racial inferiority to dehumanize Africans, relegating them to subhuman status, as I said before, almost animal-like creatures, the anti-colonialist struggle had to take race as a determinant factor in their condemnation of colonialism. At least, in my denunciation of colonialism, I always felt revolted by the raw racism of the colonialist ideology. My collaboration in the fight against colonialism invariably involved a fight against racism. All anti-colonialist leaders and intellectuals fighting to break their countries from the yoke of colonialism were very clear about the colonizers' violent racism. From Amilcar Cabral to Franz Fanon you find brilliant analyses of the cruel and tragic history of racist imperialism.

MACEDO: Albert Memmi's work is a prime example of a penetrating analysis of racism as the mainstay of colonialism. For Memmi, "it is significant that racism is part of colonialism throughout the world: and it is not coincidence. Racism sums up and symbolizes the fundamental relation which unites colonialists and colonized."[8] Paulo, we need however, to understand what has happened to the role of race once the colonialists were defeated and expelled from the colonized countries.

FREIRE: Yes. Here is where we need to understand how culture is cut across by race, gender, class, ethnicity, and languages. In the post-independence reconstruction of these African nations, where the population is all Black, other factors may play a more significant role. For example, take Guinea-Bissau with its multiple cultural, linguistic, and ethnic groups. The challenge during post-independence is to understand how to reconcile the historical specificities of these differences and successfully achieve national unity. In this complex analysis, we cannot underestimate the role of class.

MACEDO: This is an important factor. The understanding of class as an ideological category becomes important so as to prevent the generalization that reduces all analysis to race. For instance, the petit bourgeois class of African functionaries who assimilated to the colonial cultural values is part of the same racial entity, but has a very different ideological orientation and aspiration for the new nation. I think what we need to avoid is a framework of analysis that collapses all of these factors into one monolithic entity of race. The same is true, to a degree, of African Americans in the United States. It would be a big mistake to view all African Americans as one monolithic cultural group without marked differences. Although U.S. Supreme Court Justice Clarence Thomas is Black, there is a tremendous gulf between him and, let us say, our friend bell hooks, even though they share the same race and class positions. They differ, however, significantly in their ideological orientations and on gender issues. Similar gulfs exist between the vast mass of African Americans who remain subordinated and reduced to ghettoes and middle-class African Americans who, in some sense, have also partly abandoned the subordinated mass of African Americans. I am reminded of a discussion I had with a personal friend of Martin Luther King Jr., who had joined him in the important struggle to end Black segregation and oppression during the sixties. During our discussion, King's friend remarked, "Donaldo, you are right. We are using unreflexively the dominant discourse based on euphemisms such as 'economically marginal' and avoid more pointed terms such as 'oppression.' I confess that I often feel uneasy when I am invited to discuss at institutions issues pertaining to the community. In reality, I haven't been there in over twenty years." Having achieved great personal success and having moved to a middle-class reality, this African American gentleman began to experience a distance from other African Americans who remain abandoned in ghettos.

In a recent discussion with a group of students, a young African American man who attends an Ivy League university told me that his parents usually vote with the White middle-class, even if, in the long run, their vote is detrimental to Black people. Thus we see again that race, itself, is not necessarily a unifying force.

FREIRE: You see, Donaldo, things have not changed much with respect to those who work for anti-racist and anti-sexist movements, but oppose the presence of class in a comprehensive social analysis. You remember the discussion we had in Boston with my wife Nita and an African American friend who is a college professor who refused to accept class as a significant factor in social analysis of the African American reality. You remember that we tried to point out to her that while one cannot reduce the analysis of racism to social class, we cannot understand racism fully without a class analysis, for to do one at the expense of the other is to fall into a sectarianist position, which is as despicable as the racism that we need to reject.

MACEDO: Paulo, we also need to keep in mind that the level of violent racism in the United States gives primacy to race in most contexts. For instance, a recent discussion I had with a taxi driver in Washington, DC, highlights this point. During our conversation, the taxi driver told me that he was from Ghana and he showed me pictures of his wife and his son who were still there. I asked him if they were going to join him in the United States, and he quickly responded, "Oh, no! I don't want to expose my son to the racism I have to deal with. You see, I got a master's degree in business administration five years ago and the only job I was able to get is driving this taxi. Back home, I am somebody; here, I'm just a nigger."

I think what is important is to approach race analysis through a convergent framework where race is cut across by such factors as class, gender, culture, language, and ethnicity. The brilliant work of bell hooks that unmasks African American male sexist orientation brings home the point that these historical specificities, even within the same race, give rise to multiple identities that should never be collapsed into one monolithic entity. However, it would also be a major mistake to give class primacy so as to diminish the urgency of analyses concerning racism. This would be a mechanism that would play to the White supremacists, who prefer to keep the ideological structure of racism unexamined. We have to always bear in mind that in a society that is so violently racist, a movement into a middle-class reality does little for African Americans when they are outside their professional contexts. They are still followed in stores, not because they are being rendered great service, but because they are Black. Being a renowned intellectual did little for Cornel West, who watched nine taxis go by, all refusing to pick him up as a passenger in the streets of New York just because of the color of his skin. Henry Louis Gates Jr.'s prominence as a scholar did not lessen the racism he had to face at Duke University. bell hooks's eminence as a major feminist scholar does not lessen the pain of racism coupled with sexism that she endures. Having written eight highly acclaimed feminist books still does not provide her access to the media and magazines, as enjoyed by many White feminists such as Naomi Wolf. bell hooks recently noted:

> I have written eight feminist books. None of the magazines that have talked about your book, Naomi, have ever talked about my books at all. Now, that's not because there aren't ideas in my books that have universal appeal. It's because the issue that you raised in *The Beauty Myth* is still about beauty. We have to acknowledge that all of us do not have equal access.[9]

For me, the real issue is never to fall into a false dichotomy between race and class. The fundamental challenge is to accept Derrick Bell's "continuing quest for new directions in our struggle for racial justice, a struggle we must continue even if . . . racism is an integral, permanent, and indestructible component of this society."[10]

FREIRE: Absolutely. It is the work of African Americans, such as our friends bell hooks, Toni Morrison, Cornel West, Manning Marable, and Derrick Bell, among many others, that will help point us to a pedagogy of hope, born from the painful experiences of dehumanizing racism.

NOTES

1. Gregory Jay and Gerald Graff, "A Critique of Critical Pedagogy," in *Higher Education Under Fire*, ed. Michael Berube and Gary Nelson (New York: Routledge, 1995), p. 203.
2. Jonathan Kozol, *Savage Inequalities: Children in America's Schools* (New York: Crown, 1991), p. 20.
3. Henry Giroux, "Transgression of Difference," Series introduction to *Culture and Difference: Critical Perspectives on Bicultural Experience* (Westport, CT: Bergin & Garvey, in press).
4. John Fiske, *Power Plays, Power Works* (London: Verso Press, 1994), p. 13.
5. Gerald Graff, "Academic Writing and the Uses of Bad Publicity," in *Eloquent Obsessions*, ed. Mariana Torgornick (Durham, NC: Duke University Press, 1994), p. 215.
6. David Theo Goldberg, "Introduction," in *Multiculturalism: A Critical Reader*, ed. David Theo Goldberg (Oxford, Eng.: Blackwell, 1994), p. 19.
7. Robert Stam and Ella Shohat, "Contested Histories: Eurocentrism, Multiculturalism, and the Media," in *Multiculturalism: A Critical Reader*, ed. David Theo Goldberg (Oxford, Eng.: Blackwell, 1994), p. 320.
8. Albert Menni, *The Colonizer and the Colonized* (Boston: Beacon Press, 1991), pp. 69–70.
9. bell hooks, Gloria Steinem, Uruashi Vaid, and Naomi Wolf, "Get Real about Feminism: The Myths, the Backlash, the Movement," *Ms. Magazine*, September/October 1993, p. 41.
10. Derrick Bell, *Faces at the Bottom of the Well: The Permanance of Racism* (New York: Basic Books, 1992), p. xiii.

11

Beyond the Methods Fetish: Toward a Humanizing Pedagogy

LILIA I. BARTOLOME

In the preceding chapter, Paulo Freire and Donaldo Macedo discussed the way in which educators in the United States reduce Freire's notion of dialogue to a method, losing sight of the need to link teachers' and students' experiences to the politics of culture and critical democracy. In this chapter, Lilia Bartolomé argues that the current focus on finding the right "methods" to improve the academic achievement of students who have historically been oppressed hides the less visible but more important reasons for their performance: the asymmetrical power relations of society that are maintained in the schools, and the deficit view of minority students (seeing students as culturally in need of "fixing") that school personnel uncritically, and often unknowingly, hold. Bartolomé argues instead for the infusion of a humanizing pedagogy that respects and uses the multiple perspectives, histories, and intelligences of students as an integral part of pedagogical practice.

Discussing two approaches in particular that show promise when implemented within a humanizing pedagogical framework — "culturally responsive education" and "strategic teaching" — Bartolomé emphasizes the need for teachers to become politically aware of their own location, as well as their relationship with students, and to treat them as knowers and active participants in their own learning.

Much of the current debate regarding the improvement of minority student academic achievement occurs at a level that treats education as a primarily

technical[a] issue (Giroux, 1992). For example, the historical and present day academic underachievement of certain culturally and linguistically **subordinated**[b] student populations in the United States (e.g., Mexican Americans, Native Americans, Puerto Ricans) is often explained as resulting from the lack of cognitively, culturally, and/or linguistically appropriate teaching methods and educational programs. As such, the solution to the problem of academic underachievement tends to be constructed in primarily methodological and mechanistic terms dislodged from the sociocultural reality that shapes it. That is, the solution to the current underachievement of students from subordinated cultures is often reduced to finding the "right" teaching methods, strategies, or prepackaged curricula that will work with students who do not respond to so-called "regular" or "normal" instruction.

Recent research studies have begun to identify educational programs found to be successful in working with culturally and linguistically subordinated minority student populations (Carter & Chatfield, 1986; Lucas, Henze, & Donato, 1990; Tikunoff, 1985; Webb, 1987). In addition, there has been specific interest in identifying teaching strategies that more effectively teach culturally and linguistically "different" students and other "disadvantaged" and "at-risk" students (Knapp & Shields, 1990; McLeod, in press; Means & Knapp, 1991; Tinajero & Ada, 1993). Although it is important to identify useful and promising instructional programs and strategies, it is erroneous to assume that blind replication of instructional programs or teacher mastery of particular teaching methods, in and of themselves, will guarantee successful student learning, especially when we are discussing populations that historically have been mistreated and miseducated by the schools.

This focus on methods as solutions in the current literature coincides with many of my graduate students' beliefs regarding linguistic minority education improvement. As a Chicana professor who has taught anti-racist multicultural education courses at various institutions, I am consistently confronted at the beginning of each semester by students who are anxious to learn the latest teaching methods — methods that they hope will somehow magically work on minority students.[1] Although my students are well-intentioned individuals who sincerely wish to create positive learning environ-

---

[a] As defined by Bartolomé in footnote 1 of her original article, "the term **technical** refers to the positivist tradition in education that presents teaching as a precise and scientific undertaking and teachers as technicians responsible for carrying out (preselected) instructional programs and strategies."

[b] As defined by Bartolomé in footnote 2 of her original article, "**subordinated** refers to cultural groups that are politically, socially, and economically subordinate in the greater society. While individual members of these groups may not consider themselves subordinate in any manner to the White 'mainstream,' they nevertheless are members of a greater collective that historically has been perceived and treated as subordinate and inferior by the dominant society. Thus it is not entirely accurate to describe these students as minority students, since the term connotes numerical 'minority' rather than the general low status (economic, political, and social) these groups have held and that I think is important to recognize when discussing their historical academic underachievement."

ments for culturally and linguistically subordinated students, they arrive with the expectation that I will provide them with easy answers in the form of specific instructional methods. That is, since they (implicitly) perceive the academic underachievement of subordinated students as a technical issue, the solutions they require are also expected to be technical in nature (e.g., specific teaching methods, instructional curricula and materials). They usually assume that: 1) they, as teachers, are fine and do not need to identify, interrogate, and change their biased beliefs and fragmented views about subordinated students; 2) schools, as institutions, are basically fair and democratic sites where all students are provided with similar, if not equal, treatment and learning conditions; and 3) children who experience academic difficulties (especially those from culturally and linguistically low-status groups) require some form of "special" instruction since they obviously have not been able to succeed under "regular" or "normal" instructional conditions. Consequently, if nothing is basically wrong with teachers and schools, they often conclude, then linguistic minority academic underachievement is best dealt with by providing teachers with specific teaching methods that promise to be effective with culturally and linguistically subordinated students. To further complicate matters, many of my students seek *generic* teaching methods that will work with a variety of minority student populations, and they grow anxious and impatient when reminded that instruction for any group of students needs to be tailored or individualized to some extent. Some of my students appear to be seeking what María de la Luz Reyes (1992) defines as a "one size fits all" instructional recipe. Reyes explains that the term refers to the assumption that instructional methods that are deemed effective for **mainstream**[c] populations will benefit *all* students, no matter what their backgrounds may be. She explains that the assumption is

> similar to the "one size fits all" marketing concept that would have buyers believe that there is an average or ideal size among men and women.... Those who market "one size fits all" products suggest that if the article of clothing is not a good fit, the fault is not with the design of the garment, but those who are too fat, too skinny, too tall, too short, or too high-waisted. (p. 435)

I have found that many of my students similarly believe that teaching approaches that work with one minority population should also fit another (see Vogt, Jordan, & Tharp, 1987, for an example of this tendency). Reyes argues that educators often make this "one size fits all" assumption when

---

[c] As defined by Bartolomé in footnote 4 of her original article, "**mainstream** refers to the U.S. macroculture that has its roots in Western European traditions. More specifically, the major influence on the United States, particularly on its institutions, has been the culture and traditions of White, Anglo-Saxon Protestants (WASP) (Golnick & Chinn, 1986). Although the mainstream group is no longer composed solely of WASPs, members of the middle class have adopted traditionally WASP bodies of knowledge, language use, values, norms, and beliefs."

discussing instructional approaches, such as process writing. For example, as Lisa Delpit (1988) has convincingly argued, the process writing approach that has been blindly embraced by mostly White liberal teachers often produces a negative result with African American students. Delpit cites one Black student:

> I didn't feel she was teaching us anything. She wanted us to correct each other's papers and we were there to learn from her. She didn't teach anything, absolutely nothing.
>
> Maybe they're trying to learn what Black folks knew all the time. We understand how to improvise, how to express ourselves creatively. When I'm in a classroom, I'm not looking for that, I'm looking for structure, the more formal language.
>
> Now my buddy was in a Black teacher's class. And that lady was very good. She went through and explained and defined each part of the structure. This [White] teacher didn't get along with that Black teacher. She said she didn't agree with her methods. But *I* don't think that White teacher *had* any methods. (1988, p. 287)

The above quote is a glaring testimony that a "one size fits all" approach often does not work with the same level of effectiveness with all students across the board. Such assumptions reinforce a disarticulation between the embraced method and the sociocultural realities within which each method is implemented. I find that this "one size fits all" assumption is also held by many of my students about a number of teaching methods currently in vogue, such as cooperative learning and whole language instruction. The students imbue the "new" methods with almost magical properties that render them, in and of themselves, capable of improving students' academic standing.

One of my greatest challenges throughout the years has been to help students to understand that a myopic focus on methodology often serves to obfuscate the real question — which is why in our society, subordinated students do not generally succeed academically in schools. In fact, schools often **reproduce**[d] the existing **asymmetrical power relations**[e] among cultural groups (Anyon, 1988; Gibson & Ogbu, 1991; Giroux, 1992; Freire, 1985). I believe that by taking a **sociohistorical**[f] view of present-day conditions and concerns that inform the lived experiences of socially perceived minority

---

[d] Within theories of **cultural reproduction**, schools, educators, and curricula are generally viewed as mechanisms of ideological control that work to reproduce and maintain dominant beliefs, values, norms, and oppressive practices. This reproductive process is mediated, in part, through the "hidden curriculum" — the hidden agenda of maintaining the status quo through specific schooling practices.

[e] **Asymmetrical power relations** refers to unequal access to power in society.

[f] A **sociohistorical** lens works from the assumption that we are never independent of the social and historical forces that surround us. That is, we all inherit beliefs, values, and ideologies that need to be critically understood and transformed where necessary. Arguing that history is not

students, prospective teachers are better able to comprehend the **quasi-colonial**[g] nature of minority education. By engaging in this critical sociohistorical analysis of subordinated students' academic performance, most of my graduate students (teachers and prospective teachers) are better situated to reinterpret and reframe current educational concerns so as to develop pedagogical structures that speak to the day-to-day reality, struggles, concerns, and dreams of these students. By understanding the historical specificities of marginalized students, these teachers and prospective teachers come to realize that an uncritical focus on methods makes invisible the historical role that schools and their personnel have played (and continue to play), not only in discriminating against many culturally different groups, but also in denying their humanity. By robbing students of their culture, language, history, and values, schools often reduce these students to the status of subhumans who need to be rescued from their "savage" selves. The end result of this cultural and linguistic eradication represents, in my view, a form of dehumanization. Therefore, any discussion having to do with the improvement of subordinated students' academic standing is incomplete if it does not address those discriminatory school practices that lead to dehumanization.

In this article, I argue that a necessary first step in reevaluating the failure or success of particular instructional methods used with subordinated students calls for a shift in perspective — a shift from a narrow and mechanistic view of instruction to one that is broader in scope and takes into consideration the sociohistorical and political dimensions of education. I discuss why effective methods are needed for these students, and why certain strategies are deemed effective or ineffective in a given sociocultural context. My discussion will include a section that addresses the significance of teachers' understanding of the political nature of education, the reproductive nature of schools, and the schools' continued (yet unspoken) deficit views of subordinated students. By conducting a critical analysis of the sociocultural realities in which subordinated students find themselves at school, the implicit and explicit antagonistic relations between students and teachers (and other school representatives) take on focal importance.

As a Chicana and a former classroom elementary and middle school teacher who encountered negative race relations that ranged from teachers' outright rejection of subordinated students to their condescending pity, fear, indifference, and apathy when confronted by the challenges of minority student education, I find it surprising that little minority education literature

---

predetermined, critical pedagogy contends that we should be active subjects of history (shapers of history), rather than objects that are acted upon, manipulated, and controlled.

[g] This reference to **colonialism** emanates from a postcolonial theoretical framework. "Postcolonialism" confronts the ideologies, authority, discourses, and social relations that have driven the West's oppressive legacy of colonialism and imperialism, and that structure Western institutions, social practices, knowledge, and texts.

deals explicitly with the very real issue of antagonistic race relations between subordinated students and White school personnel (see Ogbu, 1987, and Giroux, 1992, for an in-depth discussion of this phenomenon).

For this reason, I also include in this article a section that discusses two instructional methods and approaches identified as effective in current education literature: culturally responsive education and strategic teaching. I examine the methods for pedagogical underpinnings that — under the critical use of politically clear teachers — have the potential to challenge students academically and intellectually while treating them with dignity and respect. More importantly, I examine the pedagogical foundations that serve to humanize the educational process and enable both students and teachers to work toward breaking away from their unspoken antagonism and negative beliefs about each other and get on with the business of sharing and creating knowledge. I argue that the informed way in which a teacher implements a method can serve to offset potentially unequal relations and discriminatory structures and practices in the classroom and, in doing so, improve the quality of the instructional process for both student and teacher. In other words, politically informed teacher use of methods can create conditions that enable subordinated students to move from their usual passive position to one of active and critical engagement. I am convinced that creating pedagogical spaces that enable students to move **from object to subject position**[h] produces more far-reaching, positive effects than the implementation of a particular teaching methodology, regardless of how technically advanced and promising it may be.

The final section of this article will explore and suggest the implementation of what Donaldo Macedo (1994) designates as an

> anti-methods pedagogy that refuses to be enslaved by the rigidity of models and methodological paradigms. An anti-methods pedagogy should be informed by a critical understanding of the sociocultural context that guides our practices so as to free us from the beaten path of methodological certainties and specialisms. (p. 8)

Simply put, it is important that educators not blindly reject teaching methods across the board, but that they reject uncritical appropriation of methods, materials, curricula, etc. Educators need to reject the present methods fetish so as to create learning environments informed by both action and reflection. In freeing themselves from the blind adoption of so-called effective (and sometimes "teacher-proof") strategies, teachers can begin the reflective process, which allows them to recreate and reinvent teaching methods and materials by always taking into consideration the sociocultural realities that can either limit or expand the possibilities to humanize education. It is

---

[h] Critical pedagogy calls for a person to be an active participant (shaper) and not simply an entity to be acted upon, manipulated, and controlled. It is believed that only as active, critical subjects are we able to make substantive change.

important that teachers keep in mind that methods are social constructions that grow out of and reflect ideologies that often prevent teachers from understanding the pedagogical implications of asymmetrical power relations among different cultural groups.

THE SIGNIFICANCE OF TEACHER POLITICAL CLARITY

In his letter to North American educators, Paulo Freire (1987) argues that technical expertise and mastery of content area and methodology are insufficient to ensure effective instruction of students from subordinated cultures. Freire contends that, in addition to possessing content area knowledge, teachers must possess **political clarity**[i] so as to be able to effectively create, adopt, and modify teaching strategies that simultaneously respect and challenge learners from diverse cultural groups in a variety of learning environments.

Teachers working on improving their political clarity recognize that teaching is not a politically neutral undertaking. They understand that educational institutions are socializing institutions that mirror the greater society's culture, values, and norms. Schools reflect both the positive and negative aspects of a society. Thus, the unequal power relations among various social and cultural groups at the societal level are usually reproduced at the school and classroom level, unless concerted efforts are made to prevent their reproduction. Teachers working toward political clarity understand that they can either maintain the status quo, or they can work to transform the sociocultural reality at the classroom and school level so that the culture at this micro-level does not reflect macro-level inequalities, such as asymmetrical power relations that relegate certain cultural groups to a subordinate status.

Teachers can support positive social change in the classroom in a variety of ways. One possible intervention can consist of the creation of heterogeneous learning groups for the purpose of modifying low-status roles of individuals or groups of children.[2] Elizabeth Cohen (1986) demonstrates that when teachers create learning conditions where students, especially those perceived as low status (e.g., limited English speakers in a classroom where English is the dominant language, students with academic difficulties, or those perceived by their peers for a variety of reasons as less able), can demonstrate their possession of knowledge and expertise, they are then able to see themselves, and be seen by others, as capable and competent. As a result, contexts are created in which peers can learn from each other as well.

---

[i] As defined by Bartolomé in footnote 5 of her original article, "**political clarity** refers to the process by which individuals achieve a deepening awareness of the sociopolitical and economic realities that shape their lives and their capacity to recreate them. In addition, it refers to the process by which individuals come to better understand possible linkages between macro-level political, economic, and social variables and subordinated groups' academic performance at the micro-level classroom. Thus, it invariably requires linkages between sociocultural structures and schooling."

A teacher's political clarity will not necessarily compensate for structural inequalities that students face outside the classroom; however, teachers can, to the best of their ability, help their students deal with injustices encountered inside and outside the classroom. A number of possibilities exist for preparing students to deal with the greater society's unfairness and inequality that range from engaging in explicit discussions with students about their experiences, to more indirect ways (that nevertheless require a teacher who is politically clear), such as creating democratic learning environments where students become accustomed to being treated as competent and able individuals. I believe that the students, once accustomed to the rights and responsibilities of full citizenship in the classroom, will come to expect respectful treatment and authentic estimation in other contexts. Again, it is important to point out that it is not the particular lesson or set of activities that prepares the student; rather, it is the teacher's politically clear educational philosophy that underlies the varied methods and lessons/activities she or he employs that make the difference.

Under ideal conditions, competent educators simultaneously translate theory into practice *and* consider the population being served and the sociocultural reality in which learning is expected to take place. Let me reiterate that command of a content area or specialization is necessary, but it is not sufficient for effectively working with students. Just as critical is that teachers comprehend that their role as educators is a political act that is never neutral (Freire, 1985, 1987, 1993; Freire & Macedo, 1987). In ignoring or negating the political nature of their work with these students, teachers not only reproduce the status quo and their students' low status, but they also inevitably legitimize schools' discriminatory practices. For example, teachers who uncritically follow school practices that unintentionally or intentionally serve to promote tracking and segregation within school and classroom contexts continue to reproduce the status quo. Conversely, teachers can become conscious of, and subsequently challenge, the role of educational institutions and their own roles as educators in maintaining a system that often serves to silence students from subordinated groups.

Teachers must also remember that schools, similar to other institutions in society, are influenced by perceptions of socioeconomic status (SES), race/ethnicity, language, and gender (Anyon, 1988; Bloom, 1991; Cummins, 1989; Ogbu, 1987). They must begin to question how these perceptions influence classroom dynamics. An important step in increasing teacher political clarity is recognizing that, despite current liberal rhetoric regarding the equal value of all cultures, low SES and ethnic minority students have historically (and currently) been perceived as deficient. I believe that the present methods-restricted discussion must be broadened to reveal the deeply entrenched deficit orientation toward "difference" (i.e., non-Western European race/ethnicity, non-English language use, working-class status, femaleness) that prevails in the schools in a deeply "cultural" ideology of White supremacy. As educators, we must constantly be vigilant and ask how the deficit orientation has affected our perceptions concerning students from subordinated populations and created rigid and mechanistic teacher-student relations (Cummins, 1989; Flores, Cousin, & Diaz, 1991; Giroux & McLaren, 1986). Such a model often serves to create classroom conditions in which there is very little opportunity for teachers and students to interact in meaningful ways, establish positive and trusting working relations, and share knowledge.

OUR LEGACY:
A DEFICIT VIEW OF SUBORDINATED STUDENTS

As discussed earlier, teaching strategies are neither designed nor implemented in a vacuum. Design, selection, and use of particular teaching approaches and strategies arise from perceptions about learning and learners. I contend that the most pedagogically advanced strategies are sure to be ineffective in the hands of educators who implicitly or explicitly subscribe to a belief system that renders ethnic, racial, and linguistic minority students at best culturally disadvantaged and in need of fixing (if we could only identify the right recipe!), or, at worst, culturally or genetically deficient and beyond fixing.[3] Despite the fact that various models have been proposed to explain the academic failure of certain subordinated groups — academic failure described as *historical, pervasive,* and *disproportionate* — the fact remains that these views of difference are deficit-based and deeply imprinted in our individual and collective psyches (Flores, 1982, 1993; Menchaca & Valencia, 1990; Valencia, 1986, 1991).

The deficit model has the longest history of any model discussed in the education literature. Richard Valencia (1986) traces its evolution over three centuries:

> Also known in the literature as the "social pathology" model or the "cultural deprivation" model, the deficit approach explains disproportionate academic problems among low status students as largely being due to pathologies or deficits in their sociocultural background (e.g., cognitive and linguistic deficiencies, low self-esteem, poor motivation). . . . To improve the educability of such students, programs such as compensatory education and parent-child intervention have been proposed. (p. 3)

Barbara Flores (1982, 1993) documents the effect this deficit model has had on the schools' past and current perceptions of Latino students. Her historical overview chronicles descriptions used to refer to Latino students over the last century. The terms range from "mentally retarded," "linguistically handicapped," "culturally and linguistically deprived," and "semilingual," to the current euphemism for Latino and other subordinated students: the "at-risk" student.

Similarly, recent research continues to lay bare our deficit orientation and its links to discriminatory school practices aimed at students from groups perceived as low status (Anyon, 1988; Bloom, 1991; Diaz, Moll, & Mehan, 1986; Oaks, 1986). Findings range from teacher preference for Anglo students, to bilingual teachers' preference for lighter skinned Latino students (Bloom, 1991), to teachers' negative perceptions of working-class parents as compared to middle-class parents (Lareau, 1990), and, finally, to unequal teaching and testing practices in schools serving working-class and ethnic minority students (Anyon, 1988; Diaz et al., 1986; Oaks, 1986; U.S. Commission on Civil Rights, 1973). Especially indicative of our inability to consciously acknowledge the deficit orientation is the fact that the teachers in these studies — teachers from all ethnic groups — were themselves unaware of the active role they played in the differential and unequal treatment of their students.

The deficit view of subordinated students has been critiqued by numerous researchers as ethnocentric and invalid (Boykin, 1983; Diaz et al., 1986; Flores, 1982; Flores et al., 1991; Sue & Padilla, 1986; Trueba, 1989; Walker, 1987). More recent research offers alternative models that shift the source of school failure away from the characteristics of the individual child, their families, and their cultures, and toward the schooling process (Au & Mason, 1983; Heath, 1983; Mehan, 1992; Philips, 1972). Unfortunately, I believe that many of these alternative models often unwittingly give rise to a kinder and more liberal, yet more concealed version of the deficit model that views subordinated students as being in need of "specialized" modes of instruction — a type of instructional "coddling" that mainstream students do not require in order to achieve in school. Despite the use of less overtly ethnocentric models to explain the academic standing of subordinated students, I believe that the deficit orientation toward difference, especially as it relates to low socioeconomic and ethnic minority groups, is very deeply ingrained in the ethos of our most prominent institutions, especially schools, and in the various educational programs in place at these sites.

It is against this sociocultural backdrop that teachers can begin to seriously question the unspoken but prevalent deficit orientation used to hide SES, racial/ethnic, linguistic, and gender inequities present in U.S. classrooms. And it is against this sociocultural backdrop that I critically examine two teaching approaches identified by the educational literature as effective with subordinated student populations.

POTENTIALLY HUMANIZING PEDAGOGY: TWO PROMISING TEACHING APPROACHES

Well-known approaches and strategies such as cooperative learning, language experience, process writing, reciprocal teaching, and whole language activities can be used to create humanizing learning environments where students cease to be treated as objects and yet receive academically rigorous instruction (Cohen, 1986; Edelsky, Altwerger, & Flores, 1991; Palinscar & Brown, 1984; Pérez & Torres-Guzmán, 1992; Zamel, 1982). However, when these approaches are implemented uncritically, they often produce negative results, as indicated by Lisa Delpit (1986, 1988). Critical teacher applications of these approaches and strategies can contribute to discarding deficit views of students from subordinated groups, so that they are treated with respect and viewed as active and capable subjects in their own learning.

Academically rigorous, student-centered teaching strategies can take many forms. One may well ask, is it not merely common sense to promote approaches and strategies that respect, recognize, utilize, and build on students' existing knowledge bases? The answer would be, of course, yes, it is. However, it is important to recognize, as part of our effort to increase our political clarity, that these practices have *not* typified classroom instruction for students from marginalized populations. The practice of learning from and valuing student language and life experiences *often* occurs in classrooms where students speak a language and possess **cultural capital**[j] that more closely matches that of the mainstream (Anyon, 1988; Lareau, 1990; Winfield, 1986).

Jean Anyon's (1988) classic research suggests that teachers of affluent students are more likely than teachers of working-class students to utilize and incorporate student life experiences and knowledge into the curriculum. For example, in Anyon's study, teachers of affluent students often designed creative and innovative lessons that tapped students' existing knowledge bases; one math lesson, designed to teach students to find averages, asked them to fill out a possession survey inquiring about the number of cars, television sets, refrigerators, and games owned at home so as to teach students to average. Unfortunately, this practice of tapping students' already existing knowledge and language bases is not commonly utilized with student populations traditionally perceived as deficient. Anyon reports that teachers of working-class students viewed them as lacking the necessary cultural capital, and therefore imposed content and behavioral standards with little consideration and respect for student input. Although Anyon did not generalize beyond her sample, other studies suggest the validity of her findings for ethnic minority student populations (Diaz et al., 1986; Moll, 1986; Oaks, 1986).

The creation of learning environments for low SES and ethnic minority students, similar to those for more affluent and White populations, requires that teachers discard deficit notions and genuinely value and utilize students' existing knowledge bases in their teaching. In order to do so, teachers must confront and challenge their own social biases so as to honestly begin to perceive their students as capable learners. Furthermore, they must remain

---

[j] As defined by Bartolomé in footnote 8 of her original article, "**cultural capital** refers to Pierre Bourdieu's concept that certain forms of cultural knowledge are the equivalent of symbolic wealth in that these forms of "high" culture are socially designated as worthy of being sought and possessed. These cultural (and linguistic) knowledge bases and skills are socially inherited and are believed to facilitate academic achievement. See Lamont and Lareau, 1988, for a more in-depth discussion regarding the multiple meanings of cultural capital in the literature."

open to the fact that they will also learn from their students. Learning is not a one-way undertaking.

It is important for educators to recognize that no language or set of life experiences is inherently superior, yet our social values reflect our preferences for certain language and life experiences over others. Student-centered teaching strategies such as cooperative learning, language experience, process writing, reciprocal teaching, and whole language activities (if practiced consciously and critically) can help to offset or neutralize our deficit-based failure and recognize subordinated student strengths. Our tendency to discount these strengths occurs whenever we forget that learning only occurs when prior knowledge is accessed and linked to new information.

Beau Jones, Annemarie Palinscar, Donna Ogle, and Eileen Carr (1987) explain that learning *is* the act of linking new information to prior knowledge. According to their framework, prior knowledge is stored in memory in the form of knowledge frameworks. New information is understood and stored by calling up the appropriate knowledge framework and then integrating the new information. Acknowledging and using existing student language and knowledge makes good pedagogical sense, and it also constitutes a humanizing experience for students traditionally *de*humanized and disempowered in the schools. I believe that strategies identified as effective in the literature have the potential to offset reductive education in which "the educator as *the one who knows* transfers existing knowledge to the learner as *the one who does not know*" (Freire, 1985, p. 114, emphasis added). It is important to repeat that mere implementation of a particular strategy or approach identified as effective does not guarantee success, as the current debate in process writing attests (Delpit, 1986, 1988; Reyes, 1991, 1992).

Creating learning environments that incorporate student language and life experiences in no way negates teachers' responsibility for providing students with particular academic content knowledge and skills. It is important not to link teacher respect and use of student knowledge and language bases with a laissez-faire attitude toward teaching. It is equally necessary not to confuse academic rigor with rigidity that stifles and silences students. The teacher is the authority, with all the resulting responsibilities that entails; however, it is not necessary for the teacher to become authoritarian in order to challenge students intellectually. Education can be a process in which teacher and students mutually participate in the intellectually exciting undertaking we call learning. Students *can* become active subjects in their own learning, instead of passive objects waiting to be filled with facts and figures by the teacher.

I would like to emphasize that teachers who work with subordinated populations have the responsibility to assist them in appropriating knowledge bases and **discourse**[k] styles deemed desirable by the greater society. However,

---

[k] A **discourse** represents the ways in which reality is perceived through and shaped by historically and socially constructed ways of making sense, that is, language, complex signs, and practices

this process of appropriation must be additive, that is, the new concepts and new discourse skills must be added to, not subtracted from, the students' existing background knowledge. In order to assume this additive stance, teachers must discard deficit views so they can use and build on life experiences and language styles too often viewed and labeled as "low class" and undesirable. Again, there are numerous teaching strategies and methods that can be employed in this additive manner. For the purposes of illustration, I will briefly discuss two approaches currently identified as promising for students from subordinated populations. The selected approaches are referred to in the literature as culturally responsive instructional approaches and strategic teaching.

CULTURALLY RESPONSIVE INSTRUCTION: THE POTENTIAL TO EQUALIZE POWER RELATIONS

Culturally responsive instruction grows out of cultural difference theory, which attributes the academic difficulties of students from subordinated groups to cultural incongruence or discontinuities between the learning, language use, and behavioral practices found in the home and those expected by the schools. Ana María Villegas (1988, 1991) defines culturally responsive instruction as attempts to create instructional situations where teachers use teaching approaches and strategies that recognize and build on culturally different ways of learning, behaving, and using language in the classroom.

A number of classic ethnographic studies document culturally incongruent communication practices in classrooms where students and teachers may speak the same language but use it in different ways. This type of incongruence is cited as a major source of academic difficulties for subordinated students and their teachers (see Au, 1980; Au & Mason, 1983; Cazden, 1988; Erickson & Mohatt, 1982; Heath, 1983; Philips, 1972). For the purposes of this analysis, one form of culturally responsive instruction, the Kamehameha Education Project reading program, will be discussed.

The Kamehameha Education Project is a reading program developed as a response to the traditionally low academic achievement of native Hawaiian students in Western schools. The reading program was a result of several years of research that examined the language practices of native Hawaiian children in home and school settings. Observations of native Hawaiian children showed them to be bright and capable learners; however, their behavior

---

that order and sustain particular forms of social existence. These systems of communication, which are constructions informed by particular ideologies, play a significant role in shaping human subjectivities and social reality, and can work to either confirm or deny the life histories and experiences of the people who use them. If the rules that govern what is acceptable in a particular society are exclusive, discourse can be a major site of contention in which different groups struggle over meaning and ideology.

in the classroom signaled communication difficulties between them and their non-Hawaiian teachers. For example, Kathryn Hu-Pei Au (1979, 1980) reports that native Hawaiian children's language behavior in the classroom was often misinterpreted by teachers as being unruly and without educational value. She found that the children's preferred language style in the classroom was linked to a practice used by adults in their homes and community called "talk story." She discusses the talk story phenomenon and describes it as a major speech event in the Hawaiian community, where individuals speak almost simultaneously and where little attention is given to turn taking. Au explains that this practice may inhibit students from speaking out as individuals because of their familiarity with and preference for simultaneous group discussion.

Because the non-Hawaiian teachers were unfamiliar with talk story and failed to recognize its value, much class time was spent either silencing the children or prodding unwilling individuals to speak. Needless to say, very little class time was dedicated to other instruction. More important, the children were constrained and not allowed to demonstrate their abilities as speakers and possessors of knowledge. Because the students did not exhibit their skills in mainstream accepted ways (e.g., competing as individuals for the floor), they were prevented from exhibiting knowledge via their culturally preferred style. However, once the children's interaction style was incorporated into classroom lessons, time on task increased and, subsequently, students' performance on standardized reading tests improved. This study's findings conclude that educators can successfully employ the students' culturally valued language practices while introducing the student to more conventional and academically acceptable ways of using language.

It is interesting to note that many of the research studies that examine culturally congruent and incongruent teaching approaches also inadvertently illustrate the equalization of previous asymmetrical power relations between teachers and students. These studies describe classrooms where teachers initially imposed participation structures upon students from subordinated linguistic minority groups and later learned to negotiate with them rules regarding acceptable classroom behavior and language use (Au & Mason, 1983; Erickson & Mohatt, 1982; Heath, 1983; Philips, 1972). Thus these studies, in essence, capture the successful negotiation of power relations, which resulted in higher student academic achievement and increased teacher effectiveness. Yet there is little explicit discussion in these studies of the greater sociocultural reality that renders it perfectly normal for teachers to automatically disregard and disrespect subordinated students' preferences and to allow antagonistic relations to foment until presented with empirical evidence that legitimizes the students' practices. Instead, the focus of most of these studies rests entirely on the cultural congruence of the instruction and not on the humanizing effects of a more democratic pedagogy. Villegas (1988) accurately critiques the cultural congruence literature when she states:

> It is simplistic to claim that differences in languages used at home and in school are the root of the widespread academic problems of minority children. Admittedly, differences do exist, and they can create communication difficulties in the classroom for both teachers and students. Even so, those differences in language must be viewed in the context of a broader struggle for power within a stratified society. (p. 260)

Despite the focus on the cultural versus the political dimensions of pedagogy, some effort is made to link culturally congruent teaching practices with equalization of classroom power relations. For example, Kathryn Au and Jana Mason (1983) explain that "one means of achieving cultural congruence in lessons may be to *seek a balance between the interactional rights of teachers and students,* so that the children can participate in ways comfortable to them" (p. 145, emphasis added). Their study compared two teachers and showed that the teacher who was willing to negotiate with students either the topic of discussion or the appropriate participation structure was better able to implement her lesson. Conversely, the teacher who attempted to impose both topic of discussion *and* appropriate interactional rules was frequently diverted because of conflicts with students over one or the other.

Unfortunately, as mentioned earlier, interpretations and practical applications of this body of research have focused on the *cultural* congruence of the approaches. I emphasize the term *cultural* because in these studies the term "culture" is used in a restricted sense devoid of its dynamic, ideological, and political dimensions. Instead, culture is treated as synonymous with ethnic culture, rather than as "the representation of lived experiences, material artifacts and practices *forged within the unequal and* **dialectical**[1] relations that different groups establish in a given society at a particular point in historical time" (Giroux, 1985, p. xxi, emphasis added). I use this definition of culture because, without identifying the political dimensions of culture and subsequent unequal status attributed to members of different ethnic groups, the reader may conclude that teaching methods simply need to be ethnically congruent to be effective — without recognizing that not all ethnic and linguistic cultural groups are viewed and treated as equally legitimate in classrooms. Interestingly enough, there is little discussion of the various socially perceived minority groups' subordinate status vis-à-vis White teachers and peers in these studies. All differences are treated as ethnic cultural differences and not as responses of subordinated students to teachers from dominant groups, and vice versa.

---

[1] While there are a number of definitions and interpretations of **dialectics**, for the general purposes of critical pedagogy, this concept refers to the interconnecting and contradicting relationships that constitute a particular phenomenon, for example, among the economic, political, social, and cultural dimensions of society. A dialectical analysis is also often used to show how every idea or force has its opposite/contradiction. For example, the dialectic of "oppressor" is the reality of the "oppressed." Such an analysis holds both "opposing" concepts together at once to see how they interconnect and play off each other.

Given the sociocultural realities in the above studies, the specific teaching strategies may not be what made the difference. Indeed, efforts to uncritically export the Kamehameha Education Project reading program to other student populations resulted in failure (Vogt et al., 1987). It could well be that the teachers' effort to negotiate and share power by treating students as equal participants in their own learning is what made the difference in Hawaii. Just as important is the teachers' willingness to critically interrogate their deficit views of subordinated students. By employing a variety of strategies and techniques, the Kamehameha students were allowed to interact with teachers in egalitarian and meaningful ways. More importantly, the teachers also learned to recognize, value, use, and build upon students' previously acquired knowledge and skills. In essence, these strategies succeeded in creating a comfort zone so students could exhibit their knowledge and skills and, ultimately, empower themselves to succeed in an academic setting. Teachers also benefitted from using a variety of student-centered teaching strategies that humanized their perceptions of treatment of students previously perceived as deficient. Ray McDermott's (1977) classic research reminds us that numerous teaching approaches and strategies can be effective, so long as trusting relations between teacher and students are established and power relations are mutually set and agreed upon.

STRATEGIC TEACHING: THE SIGNIFICANCE OF TEACHER-STUDENT INTERACTION AND NEGOTIATION

Strategic teaching refers to an instructional model that explicitly teaches students learning strategies that enable them consciously to monitor their own learning. This is accomplished through the development of reflective cognitive monitoring and metacognitive skills (Jones, Palinscar, Ogle, & Carr, 1987). The goal is to prepare independent and metacognitively aware students. This teaching strategy makes explicit for students the structures of various text types used in academic settings and assists students in identifying various strategies for effectively comprehending the various genres. Although text structures and strategies for dissecting the particular structures are presented by the teacher, a key component of these lessons is the elicitation of students' knowledge about text types and their own strategies for making meaning before presenting them with more conventional academic strategies.

Examples of learning strategies include teaching various text structures (i.e., stories and reports) through frames and graphic organizers. *Frames* are sets of questions that help students understand a given topic. Readers monitor their understanding of a text by asking questions, making predictions, and testing their predictions as they read. Before reading, frames serve as an advance organizer to activate prior knowledge and facilitate understanding. Frames can also be utilized during the reading process by the reader to monitor self-learning. Finally, frames can be used after a reading lesson to summarize and integrate newly acquired information.

Graphic organizers are visual maps that represent text structures and organizational patterns used in texts and in student writing. Ideally, graphic organizers reflect both the content and text structure. Graphic organizers include semantic maps, chains, and concept hierarchies, and assist the student in visualizing the rhetorical structure of the text. Beau Jones and colleagues (1987) explain that frames and graphic organizers can be "powerful tools to help the student locate, select, sequence, integrate and restructure information — both from the perspective of understanding and from the perspective of producing information in written responses" (p. 38).

Although much of the research on strategic teaching focuses on English monolingual mainstream students, recent efforts to study linguistic minority students' use of these strategies show similar success. This literature shows that strategic teaching improved the students' reading comprehension, as well as their conscious use of effective learning strategies in their native language (Avelar La Salle, 1991; Chamot, 1983; Hernandez, 1991; O'Malley & Chamot, 1990; Reyes, 1987). Furthermore, these studies show that students, despite limited English proficiency, were able to transfer or apply their knowledge of specific learning strategies and text structure to English reading texts. For example, Jose Hernandez (1991) reports that sixth-grade limited English proficient students learned, in the native language (Spanish), to generate hypotheses, summarize, and make predictions about readings. He reports:

> Students were able to demonstrate use of comprehension strategies even when they could not decode the English text aloud. When asked in Spanish about English texts the students were able to generate questions, summarize stories, and predict future events in Spanish. (p. 101)

Robin Avelar La Salle's (1991) study of third- and fourth-grade bilingual students shows that strategic teaching in the native language of three expository text structures commonly found in elementary social studies and science texts (topical net, matrix, and hierarchy) improved comprehension of these types of texts in both Spanish and English.

Such explicit and strategic teaching is most important in the upper elementary grades, where students are expected to focus on the development of more advanced English literacy skills. Beginning at about third grade, students face literacy demands distinct from those encountered in earlier grades. Jeanne Chall (1983) describes the change in literacy demands in terms of stages of readings. She explains that at a stage three of reading, students cease to "learn to read" and begin "reading to learn." Students in third and fourth grade are introduced to content area subjects such as social studies, science, and health. In addition, students are introduced to expository texts (reports). This change in texts, text structures, and in the functions of reading (reading for information) calls for teaching strategies that will prepare students to comprehend various expository texts (e.g., cause/effect, compare/contrast) used across the curriculum.

Strategic teaching holds great promise for preparing linguistic minority students to face the new literacy challenges in the upper grades. As discussed before, the primary goal of strategic instruction is to foster learner independence. This goal in and of itself is laudable. However, the characteristics of strategic instruction that I find most promising grow out of the premise that teachers and students must interact and negotiate meaning as equals in order to reach a goal.

Teachers, by permitting learners to speak from their own vantage points, create learning contexts in which students are able to empower themselves throughout the strategic learning process. Before teachers attempt to instruct students in new content or learning strategies, efforts are made by the teacher to access student prior knowledge so as to link it with new information. In allowing students to present and discuss their prior knowledge and experiences, the teacher legitimizes and treats as valuable student language and cultural experiences usually ignored in classrooms. If students are encouraged to speak on what they know best, then they are, in a sense, treated as experts — experts who are expected to refine their knowledge bases with the additional new content and strategy information presented by the teacher.

Teachers play a significant role in creating learning contexts in which students are able to empower themselves. Teachers act as cultural mentors of sorts when they introduce students not only to the culture of the classroom, but to particular subjects and discourse styles as well. In the process, teachers assist the students in appropriating the skills (in an additive fashion) for themselves so as to enable them to behave as "insiders" in the particular subject or discipline. Jim Gee (1989) reminds us that the social nature of teaching and learning must involve apprenticeship into the subject's or discipline's discourse in order for students to do well in school. This apprenticeship includes acquisition of particular content matter, ways of organizing content, and ways of using language (oral and written). Gee adds that these discourses are not mastered solely through teacher-centered and directed instruction, but also by "apprenticeship into social practices through scaffolded and supported interaction with people who have already mastered the discourse" (p. 7). The apprenticeship notion can be immensely useful with subordinated students if it facilitates the acceptance and valorization of students' prior knowledge through a mentoring process.

Models of instruction, such as strategic teaching, can promote such an apprenticeship. In the process of apprenticing linguistic minority students, teachers must interact in meaningful ways with them. This human interaction not only assists students in acquiring new knowledge and skills, but it also often familiarizes individuals from different SES and racial/ethnic groups, and creates mutual respect instead of the antagonism that so frequently occurs between teachers and their students from subordinated groups. In this learning environment, teachers and students learn from each other. The strategies serve, then, not to "fix" the student, but to equalize power relations and to humanize the teacher-student relationship. Ideally, teachers are forced to challenge implicitly or explicitly held deficit attitudes and beliefs about their students and the cultural groups to which they belong.

BEYOND TEACHING STRATEGIES: TOWARDS A HUMANIZING PEDAGOGY

When I recall a special education teacher's experience related in a bilingualism and literacy course that I taught, I am reminded of the humanizing effects of teaching strategies that, similar to culturally responsive instruction and strategic teaching, allow teachers to listen, learn from, and mentor their students. This teacher, for most of her career, had been required to assess her students through a variety of closed-ended instruments, and then to remediate their diagnosed "weaknesses" with discrete skills instruction. The assessment instruments provided little information to explain why the student answered a question either correctly or incorrectly, and they often confirmed perceived student academic, linguistic, and cognitive weaknesses. This fragmented discrete skills approach to instruction restricts the teacher's access to existing student knowledge and experiences not specifically elicited by the academic tasks. Needless to say, this teacher knew very little about her students other than her deficit descriptions of them.

As part of the requirements for my course, she was asked to focus on one Spanish-speaking, limited English proficient special education student over the semester. She observed the student in a number of formal and informal contexts, and she engaged him in a number of open-ended tasks. These tasks included allowing him to write entire texts, such as stories and poems (despite diagnosed limited English proficiency), and to engage in "think-alouds" during reading.[4] Through these open-ended activities, the teacher learned about her student's English writing ability (both strengths and weaknesses), his life experiences and world views, and his meaning-making strategies for reading. Consequently, the teacher constructed an instructional plan much better suited to her student's academic needs and interests. And even more important, she underwent a humanizing process that allowed her to recognize the varied and valuable life experiences and knowledge her student brought into the classroom.

This teacher was admirably candid when she shared her initial negative and stereotypic views of the student and her radical transformation. Despite this teacher's mastery of content area, her lack of political clarity blinded her to the oppressive and dehumanizing nature of instruction offered to linguistic minority students. Initially, she had formed an erroneous notion of her student's personality, worldview, academic ability, motivation, and academic potential on the basis of his Puerto Rican ethnicity, low SES background, limited English proficiency, and moderately learning-disabled label. Because of the restricted and closed nature of earlier assessment and instruction, the teacher had never received information about her student that challenged her negative perceptions. Listening to her student and reading his poetry and stories, she discovered his loving and sunny personality, learned his personal history, and identified academic strengths and weaknesses. In the process, she discovered and challenged her deficit orientation. The following excerpt from this student's writing exemplifies the power of the student voice for humanizing teachers:

> My Father
>
> I love my father very much. I will never forget what my father has done for me and my brothers and sisters. When we first came from Puerto Rico we didn't have food to eat and we were very poor. My father had to work three jobs to put food and milk on the table. Those were hard times and my father worked so hard that we hardly saw him. But even when I didn't see him, I always knew he loved me very much. I will always be grateful to my father. We are not so poor now and so he works only one job. But I will never forget what my father did for me. I will also work to help my father have a better life when I grow up. I love my father very much.

The process of learning about her student's rich and multifaceted background enabled this teacher to move beyond the rigid methodology that had required her to distance herself from the student and to confirm the deficit model to which she unconsciously adhered. In this case, the meaningful teacher-student interaction served to equalize the teacher-student power relations and to humanize instruction by expanding the horizons through which the student demonstrated human qualities, dreams, desires, and capacities that closed-ended tests and instruction never captured.

I believe that the specific teaching methods implemented by the teacher, in and of themselves, were not the significant factors. The actual strengths of methods depend, first and foremost, on the degree to which they embrace a humanizing pedagogy that values the students' background knowledge, culture, and life experiences, and creates learning contexts where power is shared by students and teachers. Teaching methods are a means to an end — humanizing education to promote academic success for students historically under-served by the schools. A teaching strategy is a vehicle to a greater goal. A number of vehicles exist that may or may not lead to a humanizing pedagogy, depending on the sociocultural reality in which teachers and students operate.

The critical issue is the degree to which we hold the moral conviction that we must humanize the educational experience of students from subordinated populations by eliminating the hostility that often confronts these students. This process would require that we cease to be overly dependent on methods as technical instruments and adopt a pedagogy that seeks to forge a cultural democracy where all students are treated with respect and dignity. A true cultural democracy forces teachers to recognize that students' lack of familiarity with the dominant values of the curriculum "does not mean . . . that the lack of these experiences develop in these children a different 'nature' that determines their absolute incompetence" (Freire, 1993, p. 17).

Unless educational methods are situated in the students' cultural experiences, students will continue to show difficulty in mastering content area that is not only alien to their reality, but is often antagonistic toward their culture and lived experiences. Further, not only will these methods continue to fail students, particularly those from subordinated groups, but they will never lead to the creation of schools as true cultural democratic sites. For this reason, it is imperative that teachers problematize the prevalent notion of "magical" methods and incorporate what Macedo (1993) calls an anti-methods pedagogy, a process through which teachers 1) critically deconstruct the ideology that informs the methods fetish prevalent in education, 2) understand the intimate relationships between methods and the theoretical underpinnings that inform these methods, and 3) evaluate the pedagogical consequences of blindly and uncritically replicating methods without regard to students' subordinate status in terms of cultural, class, gender, and linguistic difference. In short, we need

> an anti-methods pedagogy that would reject the mechanization of intellectualism . . . [and] challenge teachers to work toward reappropriation of endangered dignity and toward reclaiming our humanity. The anti-methods pedagogy adheres to the eloquence of Antonio Machado's poem, "Caminante, no hay camino, se hace camino al andar." (Traveler, there are no roads. The road is created as we walk it [together])." (Macedo, 1993, p. 8)

REFERENCES

Anyon, J. (1988). Social class and the hidden curriculum of work. In J. R. Gress (Ed.), *Curriculum: An introduction to the field* (pp. 366–389). Berkeley, CA: McCutchan.

Au, K. H. (1979). Using the experience text relationship method with minority children. *The Reading Teacher, 32,* 677–679.

Au, K. H. (1980). Participant structures in a reading lesson with Hawaiian children: Analysis of a culturally appropriate instructional event. *Anthropology and Educational Quarterly, 11,* 91–115.

Au, K. H., & Mason, J. M. (1983). Cultural congruence in classroom participation structures: Achieving a balance of rights. *Discourse Processes, 6,* 145–168.

Avelar La Salle, R. (1991). *The effect of metacognitive instruction on the transfer of expository comprehension skills: The interlingual and cross-lingual cases.* Unpublished doctoral dissertation, Stanford University.

Bloom, G. M. (1991). *The effects of speech style and skin color on bilingual teaching candidates' and bilingual teachers' attitudes toward Mexican American pupils.* Unpublished doctoral dissertation, Stanford University.

Boykin, A. W. (1983). The academic performance of Afro-American children. In J. T. Spence (Ed.), *Achievement and achievement motives: Psychological and sociological approaches* (pp. 322–369). San Francisco: W. H. Freeman.

Carter, T. P., & Chatfield, M. L. (1986) Effective bilingual schools: Implications for policy and practice. *American Journal of Education, 95,* 200–232.

Cazden, C. (1988). *Classroom discourse: The language of teaching and learning.* Portsmouth, NH: Heinemann.

Chall, J. (1983). *Stages of reading development.* New York: McGraw-Hill.

Chamot, A. U. (1983). How to plan to transfer curriculum from bilingual to mainstream instruction. *Focus, 12.* (A newsletter avialable from The George Washington University National Clearinghouse for Bilingual Education, 1118 22nd St. NW, Washington, DC 20037)

Cohen, E. G. (1986). *Designing groupwork: Strategies for the heterogeneous classroom.* New York: Teachers College Press.

Cummins, J. (1989). *Empowering minority students.* Sacramento: California Association of Bilingual Education.

Delpit, L. (1986). Skills and other dilemmas of a progressive black educator. *Harvard Educational Review, 56,* 379–385.

Delpit, L. (1988). The silenced dialogue: Power and pedagogy in educating other people's children. *Harvard Educational Review, 58,* 280-298.

Diaz, S., Moll, L. C., & Mehan, H. (1986). Sociocultural resources in instruction: A context-specific approach. In *Beyond language: Social and cultural factors in schooling language minority students* (pp. 187–230). Los Angeles: California State University, Evaluation, Dissemination and Assessment Center.

Edelsky, C., Altwerger, B., & Flores, B. (1991). *Whole language: What's the difference?* Portsmouth, NH: Heinemann.

Erickson, F., & Mohatt, G. (1982). Cultural organization of participation structures in two classrooms of Indian students. In G. Spindler (Ed.), *Doing the ethnography of schooling: Educational anthropology in action* (pp. 133–174). New York: Holt, Rinehart and Winston.

Flores, B. M. (1982). *Language interference or influence: Toward a theory for Hispanic bilingualism.* Unpublished doctoral dissertation, University of Arizona at Tucson.

Flores, B. M. (1993, April). *Interrogating the genesis of the deficit view of Latino children in the educational literature during the 20th century.* Paper presented at the American Educational Research Association Conference, Atlanta.

Flores, B., Cousin, P. T., & Diaz, E. (1991). Critiquing and transforming the deficit myths about learning, language and culture. *Language Arts, 68,* 369-379.

Freire, P. (1985). *The politics of education: Culture, power and liberation.* South Hadley, MA: Bergin & Garvey.

Freire, P. (1987). Letter to North-American teachers. In I. Shor (Ed.), *Freire for the classroom* (pp. 211–214). Portsmouth, NJ: Boynton/Cook.

Freire, P. (1993). *A pedagogy of the city.* New York: Continuum Press.

Freire, P., & Macedo, D. (1987). *Literacy: Reading the word and the world.* South Hadley, MA: Bergin & Garvey.

Gee, J. P. (1989). Literacy, discourse, and linguistics: Introduction. *Journal of Education, 171,* 5–17.

Gibson, M. A., & Ogbu, J. U. (1991). *Minority status and schooling: A comparative study of immigrant and involuntary minorities.* New York: Garland.

Giroux, H. (1985). Introduction. In P. Freire, *The politics of education: Culture, power and liberation* (pp. xi-xxv). South Hadley, MA.: Bergin & Garvey.

Giroux, H. (1992). *Border crossing: Cultural workers and the politics of education.* New York: Routledge.

Giroux, H., & McLaren, P. (1986). Teacher education and the politics of engagement: The case for democratic schooling. *Harvard Educational Review, 56,* 213–238.

Golnick, D. M., & Chinn, P. C. (1986). *Multicultural education in a pluralistic society.* Columbus, OH: Merrill.

Heath, S. B. (1983). *Ways with words.* New York: Cambridge University Press.

Hernandez, J. S. (1991). Assisted performance in reading comprehension strategies with non-English proficient students. *Journal of Educational Issues of Language Minority Students, 8,* 91–112.

Jones, B. F., Palinscar, A. S., Ogle, D. S., & Carr, E. G. (1987). *Strategic teaching and learning: Cognitive instruction in the content areas.* Alexandria, VA: Association for Supervision and Curriculum Development.

Knapp, M. S., & Shields, P. M. (1990). *Better schooling for the children of poverty: Alternatives to conventional wisdom: Vol. 2. Commissioned papers and literature review.* Washington, DC: U.S. Department of Education.

Lamont, M., & Lareau, A. (1988). Cultural capital-allusions, gaps and glissandos in recent theoretical developments. *Sociological Theory, 6,* 153–168.

Langer, J. A. (1986). *Children reading and writing: Structures and strategies.* Norwood, New Jersey: Ablex.

Lareau, A. (1990). *Home advantage: Social class and parental intervention in elementary education.* New York: Falmer Press.

Lucas, T., Henze, R., & Donato, R. (1990). Promoting the success of Latino language-minority students: An exploratory study of six high schools. *Harvard Educational Review, 60,* 315–340.

Macedo, D. (1994). Preface. In P. McLaren & C. Lankshear (Eds.), *Conscientization and resistance* (pp. 1–8). New York: Routledge.

McDermott, R. P. (1977). Social relations as contexts for learning in school. *Harvard Educational Review, 47,* 198–213.

McLeod, B. (Ed.). (in press). *Cultural diversity and second language learning.* Albany: State University of New York Press.

Means, B., & Knapp, M. S. (1991). *Teaching advanced skills to educationally disadvantaged students.* Washington, DC: U.S. Department of Education.

Mehan, H. (1992). Understanding inequality in schools: The contribution of interpretive studies. *Sociology of Education, 65*(1), 1-20.

Menchaca, M., & Valencia, R. (1990). Anglo-Saxon ideologies in the 1920s–1930s: Their impact on the segregation of Mexican students in California. *Anthropology and Education Quarterly, 21,* 222–245.

Moll, L. C. (1986). Writing as communication: Creating learning environments for students. *Theory Into Practice, 25,* 102–110.

Oaks, J. (1986). Tracking, inequality, and the rhetoric of school reform: Why schools don't change. *Journal of Education, 168,* 61–80.

Ogbu, J. (1987). Variability in minority responses to schooling: Nonimmigrants vs. immigrants. In G. Spindler & L. Spindler (Eds.), *Interpretive ethnography of education* (pp. 255–280). Hillsdale, NJ: Lawrence Erlbaum Associates.

O'Malley, J., & Chamot, A. U. (1990). *Learning strategies in second language acquisition.* New York: Cambridge University Press.

Palinscar, A. S., & Brown, A. L. (1984). Reciprocal teaching of comprehension fostering and comprehension-monitoring activities. *Cognition and Instruction, 1*(23), 117–175.

Pérez, B., & Torres-Guzmán, M. E. (1992). *Learning in two worlds: An integrated Spanish/English biliteracy approach.* New York: Longman.

Philips, S. U. (1972). Participant structures and communication competence: Warm Springs children in community and classroom. In C. B. Cazden, V. P. John, & D. Hymes (Eds.), *Functions of language in the classroom* (pp. 370–394). New York: Teachers College Press.

Reyes, M. de la Luz. (1987). Comprehension of content area passages: A study of Spanish/English readers in the third and fourth grade. In S. R. Goldman & H. T. Trueba (Eds.), *Becoming literate in English as a second language* (pp. 107–126). Norwood, NJ: Ablex.

Reyes, M. de la Luz. (1991). A process approach to literacy during dialogue journals and literature logs with second language learners. *Research in the Teaching of English, 25,* 291–313.

Reyes, M. de la Luz. (1992). Challenging venerable assumptions: Literacy instruction for linguistically different students. *Harvard Educational Review, 62,* 427–446.

Sue, S., & Padilla, A. (1986). Ethnic minority issues in the U.S.: Challenges for the educational system. In *Beyond language: Social and cultural factors in schooling language minority students* (pp. 35–72). Los Angeles: California State University, Evaluation, Dissemination and Assessment Center.

Tikunoff, W. (1985). *Applying significant bilingual instructional features in the classroom.* Rosslyn, VA: National Clearinghouse for Bilingual Education.

Tinajero, J. V., & Ada, A. F. (1993). *The power of two languages: Literacy and biliteracy for Spanish-speaking students.* New York: Macmillan/McGraw-Hill.

Trueba, H. T. (1989). Sociocultural integration of minorities and minority school achievement. In *Raising silent voices: Educating the linguistic minorities for the 21st century* (pp. 1–27). New York: Newbury House.

U. S. Commission on Civil Rights. (1973). *Teachers and students: Report V. Mexican-American study: Differences in teacher interaction with Mexican-American and Anglo students.* Washington, DC: Government Printing Office.

Valencia, R. (1986, November 25). *Minority academic underachievement: Conceptual and theoretical considerations for understanding the achievement problems of Chicano students.* Paper presented to the Chicano Faculty Seminar, Stanford University.

Valencia, R. (1991). *Chicano school failure and success: Research and policy agendas for the 1990s.* New York: Falmer Press.

Villegas, A. M. (1988). School failure and cultural mismatch: Another view. *Urban Review, 20,* 253–265.

Villegas, A. M. (1991). *Culturally responsive pedagogy for the 1990s and beyond.* Paper prepared for the Educational Testing Service, Princeton, NJ.

Vogt, L. A., Jordan, C., & Tharp, R. G. (1987). Explaining school failure, producing school success: Two cases. *Anthropology & Education Quarterly, 18,* 276–286.

Walker, C. L. (1987). Hispanic achievement: Old views and new perspectives. In H. T. Trueba (Ed.), *Success or failure: Learning and the language minority student* (pp. 15–32). New York: Newbury House.

Webb, L. C. (1987). *Raising achievement among minority students.* Arlington, VA: American Associates of School Administrators.

Winfield, L. F. (1986). Teachers beliefs toward academically at risk students in inner urban schools. *Urban Review, 18,* 253–267.

Zamel, V. (1982). Writing: The process of discovering meaning. *TESOL Quarterly, 16,* 195–209.

NOTES

1. "Chicana" refers to a woman of Mexican ancestry who was born and/or reared in the United States.
2. Elizabeth Cohen (1986) explains that in the society at large there are status distinctions made on the basis of social class, ethnic group, and gender. These status distinctions are often reproduced at the classroom level, unless teachers make conscious efforts to prevent this reproduction.
3. For detailed discussions regarding various deficit views of subordinated students over time, see Flores, Cousin, and Diaz, 1991; also see Sue and Padilla, 1986.
4. "Think-alouds" refers to an informal assessment procedure where readers verbalize all their thoughts during reading and writing tasks. See J. A. Langer, 1986, for a more in-depth discussion of think-aloud procedures.

12

A Discourse Not Intended for Her: Learning and Teaching within Patriarchy

MAGDA LEWIS and ROGER I. SIMON

Feminists have had an enormous impact on the experiential and theoretical insights around the politics of identity and difference, and in the development of critical pedagogies.

By interrogating the politics of everyday life as a force of social change, feminists have shown that women are silenced in a variety of settings, including the classroom. Illustrating a specific way in which modes of interaction can exclude, Magda Lewis and Roger Simon examine the dominant (humanist) discourse, which supports male domination through socially constructed male traits and activities that are represented as being essentially human. Lewis and Simon, one as a female student and the other as a male teacher, describe and analyze the process of silencing as it occurred in a graduate seminar designed to explore the relationship between language and power. They call for the development of a multiplicity of critical discourses that do not suffocate differences and that work toward liberatory practices.

We recommend that readers unfamiliar with the work of "poststructuralists" see the explanation of it in the glossary.

> Listen to the voices of the women and the voices of the men; observe the space men allow themselves, physically and verbally, the male assumption that people will listen, even when the majority of the group is female. Look at the faces of the silent, and of those who speak. Listen to a woman groping

for language in which to express what is on her mind, sensing that the terms of academic discourse are not her language, trying to cut down her thought to the dimension of a discourse not intended for her. (Rich, 1979, pp. 243–244)

In the spring of 1985, the two of us participated in a graduate seminar, one as faculty/teacher, the other as a student; one of us is a man, the other a woman. Our common interest in this seminar was in exploring questions concerning the relation between **text** and **discourse**[a] seen in light of a consideration of the relation between language and power. Although our interests were common, our experience of the class was very different. This article tells of this difference as it emerged and as it continues to be understood by us. We struggled over finding a common voice in this shared — yet different — experience. But the results of our search for a single voice were never satisfactory, as one or the other of us was unintentionally but inevitably silenced. As our dialogue continued, it became clear to us that the difficulty we were having in our attempt to speak with a single voice had not so much to do with us as individuals but rather more powerfully with our different relations to those social, political, and economic practices that make possible the privilege of men over women: *patriarchy*.

In her now classic article, Hartmann (1984) defines patriarchy as a social system characterized by "the systematic dominance of men over women" (p. 194). It emerges as a "set of social relations between men, which have a material base, and which, though hierarchical, establish or create interdependence and solidarity among men that enable them to dominate women. Though patriarchy is hierarchical, and men of different classes, races, or ethnic groups have different places in the patriarchy, they also are united in their shared relationship of dominance over their women: they are dependent on each other to maintain that domination" (p. 197). Hartmann goes on to say that "*patriarchy is not simply hierarchical organization* but hierarchy in which *particular* people fill particular places. It is in studying patriarchy that we learn why it is women who are dominated and how" (p. 199).

Patriarchy so defined has the potential to obliterate the will, desire, and capacity of particular individuals, be they women or men, to form personal

---

[a] As defined by Lewis and Simon in footnote 1 of their original article, "**discourse** refers to particular ways of organizing meaning-making practices. Discourse as a mode of governance delimits the range of possible practices under its authority and organizes the articulation of these practices within time and space although differently and often unequally for different people. Such governance delimits fields of relevance and definitions of legitimate perspectives and fixes norms for concept elaboration and the expression of experience. **Text** refers to a particular concrete manifestation of practices organized within a particular discourse. In everyday life, meaning-making does not exist in isolation, but forms complexes that are organized contingently through time and space. Examples of text include written passages, oral communication, nonverbal communication accomplished through body movement and expression, and visual forms of representation such as paintings, photographs, and sculpture. For further elaboration of these concepts, see Terdiman (1985)."

and collective relationships that are not based on an acceptance of male prerogative. We do not minimize the importance of such struggles. Nonetheless, what we sometimes think of as our private lives are not separable from the social forms within which they are constituted. Patriarchy is a social form that continues to play on and through our subjectivities, affecting conceptually organized knowledge as well as elements that move us, without being consciously expressed. It continues to provide us with different vantage points, and positions us differently within relations of power. For this reason we have decided to keep our voices separate, not in order to provide a dialogue but to juxtapose our differences as the ground on which we could formulate a reconstructed practice that would counter patriarchy.

We realize that women constitute only one of many disadvantaged social groups that include people of color, people of racial and ethnic minorities, people in countries dominated politically and economically by imperialist powers, and people who must work in exploitative relations of wage labor or commodity exchange, all of whom suffer disempowerment and silencing. Within this article we do not discuss race and class dynamics, not because we think such concerns less important than gender or that gender relations can be understood outside the context of other social relations, but because the specific events we speak about in this essay occurred among a homogenous group of people with respect to race and class. Our discussion of patriarchy, however, is clearly linked to other forms of domination and we would argue that counter-patriarchic practices have a strong relevance to other struggles against unjust social relations.

Magda Lewis

The overwhelming experience of women in a society dominated by men is that of being silenced.[1] This has not only been shown over and over again by a growing number of feminist writers, but can be graphically documented in the daily lives of all women. The search for examples does not have to be long or intensive. A woman I sat next to on a recent train trip summed it up exquisitely. After the conductor, the steward, and the railroad's public relations representative overlooked her in their various dealings with the passengers, she turned to me and said, "Sometimes I think I must be invisible. People don't see me. They don't hear me. Sometimes I wonder if I am really here." This was a woman, a grandmother, a secretary, who had never read Spender's (1982) *Invisible Women*. I passed on that reference along with a couple of others and she promised to read at least one of them. But she admitted feeling reluctant to buy books with titles like *Sex, Gender and Society* (Oakley, 1972), or *Women's Oppression Today* (Barrett, 1980). *Invisible Women*, she thought, sounded sufficiently like the title of a science fiction novel that she could smuggle it into the house without arousing her husband's suspicion. She implied that if her husband were aware of its subject, the book would surely be banned from the house and her reading even more closely monitored.

Is this an extreme example? I don't think so. It is simply a particular manifestation of a general social condition that is played out among men and women on a daily basis in a variety of forms and places.[2] The example is instructive, however, in that it uncovers the power relations within which men's lives and interests circumscribe those of women. I equivocate deliberately on the word "interest" for I do indeed intend both meanings of the word — what interests men as well as what is in their interest.

As we parted company, my seatmate said, "You younger women have it made. You know what you want and you are so outspoken, people listen to you. Women my age never had a chance." Had there been time I could have explained; I could have told her what I am about to say here, that she and I inhabit the same world, that we are both engaged in the collective struggle to claim our **voice**,[b] to be heard, to become visible.

Roger Simon

The department we are in consists largely of male faculty members. While this department is not the most extreme example of the male character of academic institutions, it is important to make this point simply to highlight the fact that women graduate students are familiar with the negotiations and accommodations that are required of them in order to survive in the world of male academia.[3] Shaped by the political/theoretical discourse of socialist feminine and critical pedagogy, my daily experiences in this context have fed my interest in the project of feminist pedagogy.[4] What has made me most uneasy is the growing realization of my complicity in the practice of gender domination, which is constructed on the one hand through the relationship between language use and nonverbal practices, and on the other, through the moral regulation of people that results from the limitation of what are considered appropriate forms of thought, expression, and behavior.

In the spring of 1985 I developed and taught a new graduate course entitled "Discourse, Text, and Subjectivity." This course was designed to explore questions concerning the relation between language and power. I intended that the participating students would develop with me a way of framing questions that explore the relation between language and the enhancement of human possibility; for example, how language enters into such questions as who we are and what we are able to be and do. It is an issue that begins to crystallize when we ask how language can be not only a vehicle for learning but, in Foucault's terms, a form of "government" as well.[5] Foucault allows this word the broad meaning it had in the sixteenth century. "Government" referred then not only to political structures or to the man-

---

[b] **Voice** simply refers to people's authentic self-expression, with an understanding that people are situated in personal histories of engagement with their surroundings/communities through which voice is shaped by class, cultural, racial, and gender identities. Finding one's/using one's voice refers to a quality of authenticity, that one is speaking with integrity and from a position of self-empowerment, or even liberation.

agement of states, but also to the way in which the conduct of individuals or groups might be directed: the government of children, of souls, of communities, of families, of the sick. To govern, in this sense, is to structure the possible field of human action. To think in these terms is to ask how language is linked to the freedom of women and men, a question that points to a concern with discourse as the concrete process of morally regulated expression and the central component of the production of subjectivity.

Magda Lewis
While all of us — students and teacher, women and men — came to this new course for a variety of personal and professional reasons, we also came with an intact social repertoire. We came carrying the baggage of our governed selves. For the women this meant that we already knew that what we said and how we said it was not quite as important to our male colleagues as the fact that we spoke at all. In a set of social relations where women's ideal discursive state within patriarchy has been defined as silence, a woman speaking is itself a political act (Spender, 1980). Under these conditions, the very act or intention of speaking becomes an intrusion and a potential basis for a violent reaction on the part of those who have decreed our silence. Ultimately, for individuals who transgress the limits of patriarchy, the forces of regulation are without a doubt swift, sure, and relentless.

As we began to take up the first of the assigned readings, the interesting and significant work by Dorfman, *The Empire's Old Clothes* (1983), the social dynamics in the class were aggravating but not unusual: the men monopolized not only the speaking time but the theoretical and social agenda as well. They sparred, dueled, and charged at each other like gladiators in a Roman arena. Yet their camaraderie intensified with each encounter. Throughout this exchange, the women were relegated to the position of spectators. When a woman speaks, it means that a man cannot speak, and when a man cannot speak it means that the social relations among the men are disrupted. Women, therefore, have no place on this playing field. Independently, we felt our exclusion more and more intensely the more we struggled to find room for our voices and to locate ourselves in the discourse.

Roger Simon
For several weeks I held discussions after class with a few students on how to break the discursive monopoly. I felt I had to do something to alter the situation, and so I became more and more of a "gatekeeper," trying to make room in the discussion for people who were not speaking. At one point we thought that introducing literature on men's dominance of conversation in mixed gender groups might help, but I resisted this, as I thought it too much of a "diversion" from my planned agenda. I held to the steady but not very successful path of "space-making": asking for comments from those women who had not yet spoken, repositioning myself at the table so that I could see most of the women and perhaps through eye contact and body language

encourage their entry into the conversation, noticing when a woman did try to speak, and cutting off those men who had been speaking most often.

Of course, these tactics did nothing to alter the deeply sedimented forms of inequality at work in the class. These tactics simply shifted the focus from a masculine discursive monopoly to women's silence. What I missed here was the fact that the women knew (despite my efforts) that it was not a safe place to speak. Women know that being allowed to speak can be a form of tyranny.[6] I was and still am unsure of why I backed away from confronting this fact — and my complicity in the situation. Knowing, however, that one cannot donate freedom, I deliberately imposed one limit on myself. I knew that as a male teacher I could not, from my position of authority (a position established by my being a man and a professor), overtly name and make topical the oppressive relations in the class. Perhaps this was partly the reason for my reluctance to introduce special readings in the course as a vehicle for raising the issue of the gender relations of the class. Retrospectively, what was needed was not a pedagogy that itself structured not "women as the question," but rather a practice wherein women could "enunciate the question" (Felman, 1981).

Magda Lewis

The feeling of being in a space that is not one's own is familiar to women in a society marked fundamentally by patriarchy.[7] It is not that there were not ideological differences among the men in how they took up the agenda of the class or in how they envisioned its pedagogical implications. In many instances, there was more in common both pedagogically and ideologically between groups of men and women than between people of the same gender. But since the overriding issue in this class was not the politics of curriculum but rather the politics of gender, ideological differences among the men were obliterated by the desire to structure gender solidarity.

Because patriarchy organizes the political and economic forms within which we must survive, regardless of our gender, class, or racial and ethnic identification, all men can benefit in some way from belonging to the dominant group. At the most mundane level, this means that, for men, the boundaries of social relations are so extended that a whole range of social behaviors that is seen to be acceptable for them is deemed to be inappropriate for women, irrespective of their social class or ethnic and racial origin.

In the context of our course, this meant that the men were allowed to speak at length — and did. Their speaking was seldom if ever interrupted. When a woman and a man began speaking at the same time, the woman always deferred to the man. Women's speaking was often reinterpreted by the men through phrases such as "what she *really* means. . . ." More than just a few times the actual talk of women was attributed in a later discussion by a man to a man. Women's ideas — sometimes reworded, sometimes not — were appropriated by men and then passed off as their own. Whenever a woman was able to cut through the oppressive discourse, the final attempt at silencing took the form of aggressive yelling. It became clear to us that the reversal of this dynamic would have been totally unacceptable to those who held the power of legitimation.

Gender solidarity is not rooted first and foremost in some vague notions about sociality but rather in the politics and economics of patriarchy. This is not to say, however, that "homosociality" is not an important strategic position from which to maintain and reinforce male dominance, or that such homosociality does not have extremely effective and deeply felt results.[8] Rather, men's political and economic advantage continues to be confirmed, supported, and legitimized through a social discourse that arises from their particular relations to one another.

Women have found legitimation only to the extent that we have been able or willing to appropriate the male agenda, a particularly self-violating form of escape from domination that in the end turns out to be no escape at all. The price we pay for this appropriation is the disclaiming of our collective experience of oppression, an act that forfeits our voice and gives overt support to the dominant social, political, and economic forms. We, as women, have appropriated to a large extent the terms of our own subjection. This is not a case of **false consciousness.**[c] Rather, we have accepted the powerlessness of these terms to define a discourse within which we can speak partly because we are powerless to do otherwise. While many feminists are clear about the need for women to legitimate each other and thereby begin to break away from the patriarchic stranglehold, it is also clear that intellectual assault is just one of many forms of violation that act in concert to disempower women. Given the complexity of the relationships between physical, emotional, psychological, and intellectual abuse, it is clearly not easy for women to subvert this assault.

Roger Simon

From the beginning I had planned to use Radway's *Reading the Romance* (1984) as a key text in the course. At the time I had no idea how pivotal a text it would be. In this book, Radway examines extensively both the production and consumption of mass-marketed popular romance novels. Radway's work is unique in that she not only develops an ideological critique of the novels she examines, but she also analyzes empirically and theoretically the reading of these books as part of the discursive practices of a particular group of women. She not only identifies the way they use and read romance novels, but also gives us an understanding of how packaged forms of romance are integrated into daily lives that are historically and structurally

[c] Linked to the notion that social institutions like schools are agents of ideological control that work to reproduce dominant beliefs, values, norms, and forms of oppression, **false consciousness** is the point at which members of society buy into their own exploitation and subordination, and become uncritical tools of production and consumption. More contemporary concepts referring to a similar phenomena are: *domestication, mystification of reality, dysconsciousness, anesthetized, the social construction of not seeing, manufactured consent,* and *colonization of the mind.*

constituted within patriarchic social practices of courtship, sexuality, and marriage. Radway questions how, why, by whom, and with what purposes and meanings such books are read. In examining the readings produced by the women she studies, Radway reveals contradictory constructions of **resistance**[d] and regulation. Hence, she shows how we can investigate the reading of a text as a form of social practice that can be examined for the work it does in organizing subjectivity. What provoked me to rethink my pedagogy was not our examination of women reading romance, but the experience of the women students' reading Radway's text under the determinant conditions of our graduate seminar.

Magda Lewis
Despite conversations and discussions that took place between small groups of women as the course proceeded, by the time we came to Radway's book the women in the class had been all but muted. Either because we had been oppressed into silence or because we had made a conscious decision to refrain from the discussion as a form of resistance to being silenced — how ironic that the result in both cases should be the same — we had become prisoners or exiles within a wall of silence. The reason the text of the book enraged us was, in part, the context within which we read it and our realization that what was going on with the women in Radway's study was precisely what was going on with us in the classroom. Her study demanded a response. As the male-defined resistance to the formulation of our response intensified, it became clearer to us (the women) that what we were engaged in in this class was a struggle not just for ourselves but for all women — including those women who are reading the romance.

Had we not been required to read Radway's study in this context we might never have been pushed to the outer limits of our **marginality.**[e] While we could doubt ourselves, our capabilities, our understanding, and even our experiences within the context of most male-defined academic discourse, in this instance the disjunction between content and process became obvious. We knew we had not only an experiential base from which to take up Radway's agenda, but a lived theoretical framework from which to understand it as well.

---

[d] **Resistance** (oppositional identity) has traditionally been attributed to deviant behavior, individual pathology, learned helplessness, cultural deprivation, and genetic flaws. Critical pedagogy, on the other hand, sees resistance as a legitimate response to domination, used to help individuals or groups deal with oppression. From this perspective, resistance in any form should be part of a larger political project that is working towards change.

[e] To **marginalize** is to force an individual or group out of mainstream society, limiting their access to political and economic power, or to push ideas and concepts that conflict with dominant ideologies to the fringes of academic debate, labelling them as important only to special interest groups. While critical pedagogy is certainly concerned with understanding the lives of those on the margins (and creating self-empowering conditions to escape such oppression), one of its central purposes is to deconstruct the ideologies and practices of the existing dominant center that in fact creates such segregation.

Women are politically disempowered, economically disadvantaged, and socially delegitimated, not as individuals (although it is as individuals that the effects are felt most often and most brutally) but as a group. We occupy particular positions in our homes, in our employment, and in the street that lead to experiences different from those of groups who are more advantageously positioned. The material basis of women's and men's lives, therefore, plays a major role not only in how they are positioned but also in how their particular social perspective arises. What is often forgotten by both women and men but is important to remember is that this process is man-made — although not without a struggle — and therefore neither natural nor neutral.

We needed to understand that what we were experiencing was indeed a collective experience, and we needed to know what this collective experience was about. Our reading of Radway's *Reading the Romance* was the catalyst that enabled us to understand the divisive and **individualizing**[f] process embedded in the taken-for-granted prerogative of male discourse. As a collective we could more easily challenge the oppressive boundaries and limited interpretations imposed through such discourse.

It is important to understand that the disjunction between male and female discourse does not arise out of the distinction between objective knowledge on the one hand and subjective knowledge on the other. Rather, it is reflective of the disparity in the relations of power between men and women. This implies that women's experience and discursive forms are defined by men as illegitimate *within the terms of men's experience and men's discursive forms.* The assertion that women's knowledge is based on personal experience while men's knowledge is based on objective grounds obliterates, first and foremost, the relationship between education, personal experience, and politics. The only education that can have meaning is education that is personal and therefore political. The ingenuousness of an educational process that attempts to obliterate the personal and political is profoundly silencing.

Roger Simon
With the introduction of *Reading the Romance* into the course, more was at stake than just the struggle for "air-time." I did not realize at the time that Radway's book, as a text dealing with how particular women named their own experience within patriarchy, would have the capacity to crystallize a perception of past events in the class in a way that made the present visible as a "revolutionary moment" (Buck-Morss, 1981).

What was about to happen has subsequently become a significant episode in my attempt to clarify the basis of a counter-patriarchic pedagogy. Being clear about the concrete conditions that prefigure this episode seems to

---

[f] As defined by Lewis and Simon in footnote 10 of their original article, "**individualizing** refers to a process of constructing the 'self' so that a person views herself or himself as the unique proprietor of one's thoughts, capacities, and feelings. It is a construction basic to the historically constituted political formation which has arisen in Canada and the United States since 1850. For an extensive discussion, see MacPherson (1962)."

require an elaboration of what it means to be "muted." Being muted is not just a matter of being unable to claim a space and time within which to enter a conversation. Being muted also occurs when one cannot discover forms of speech within conversation to express meanings and to find validation from others.

As we begin the discussion of *Reading the Romance,* the majority of male students in the class and I defined the issues raised within the text in an abstract and distanced language. In my authoritative position as instructor I validated and legitimated this "preferred" theoretical discourse insofar as I encouraged it and — more important — participated in it. Through this very particular and academic form of homosociality, we simultaneously excluded and silenced the women sitting among us. This is not at all to say that the women in the class were incapable of full participation in our theoretical mode of conversation. It is, rather, to acknowledge that women experiencing patriarchy not only in our class but also at home, at work, and in the streets would have something different to say about Radway's text from that which is abstractly constructed by men.

Within the frame of patriarchy, the men in the class could not speak any other way about the substance of this text. While our own lives do not preclude our considering female oppression, for us it can only be the experience and situation of an **Other**.[g] We can discuss this experience and situation, we can analyze it, and it can become a provocation for our moral anger. But if we alone take up women's experience of patriarchy, it will be within a discourse that is distanced and abstract. The double problem in this case was that my own objective for the course included the development of a "theoretical fluency," which meant, in part, legitimating and *encouraging* the meaningful use of what for many of the students were new terminology and concepts. I had wanted to use "Reading the Romance" as an example of how we could understand the relation between language, power, and subjectivity. It was to this end that I was encouraging a discussion of Radway in abstract terms, appropriating her text to my agenda of introducing students to a new theoretical position. But at this moment the women did not wish to engage in these abstractions. Thus the lived relations of patriarchic power that specified who controlled how we would study mediated our "difference" into inequality. Worse, with the women silenced, we were doing what I said earlier should never be done, enunciating women's problems.

Magda Lewis
Silence can turn into rage when we realize that who "speaks" and whose authority governs that speaking cannot be disassociated from those relations

---

[g] In a society in which the dominant referent for defining "difference" is based on White, middle-class, heterosexual male characteristics, **Other** refers to anybody that is considered outside of, or at odds with, this prevailing paradigm. In the literature, one often finds the use of the term "decentering." This refers to an attempt to rupture the undemocratic hierarchy (or centrality) of the dominant beliefs, values, and practices.

of power that mark the structures within which individuals live their daily lives. How we knew that the occasion we chose to cast aside our silence was the right one demands an articulation of "soft" data about body language and a profound sensibility to nonverbal discourse that at times becomes the only means of communication between and among members of oppressed groups. As women in the class, we knew we had to confront our silencing concretely.

It is important to signal that what happened to the women in this class was not just consciousness-raising — as important as that is — but, more important, it was a moment of politicization. This always implies collective action and, to the extent that it challenges the status quo, such action is always revolutionary and difficult. Suddenly and forcefully the revolutionary moment became concrete. While we were waiting for the elevator during one of our breaks, a moment of solidarity was precipitated by what may have seemed an offhand comment made to me by one of the other women: "I can't go back into that room."

I responded with an invitation to talk. The usual practice during breaks had been for the men and women students to sit together — a time of informal discussion during which the same dominant discourse prevailed. The two of us took our coffee and tea and moved to a private space. Other women noticed and joined us. Some went to get the rest of the women until all but one of us were gathered. The possibility of this action was facilitated by the deliberate practice of the instructor to absent himself during our breaks. Our gathering was not unnoticed by the male students, whose body language and joking demands to know "what's going on" punctuated our construction as the Other. Only one of the men asked if he could join us, in a show of solidarity. While his gesture was appreciated, his presence, however unobtrusive, would have been silencing. We said no. Our meeting was seen to be and was an overtly political act. As we talked, the anger came in floods.

Without jeopardizing personal confidences, I want to relate some of the discussion that took place during our break:

> "I don't understand what they [the men] are talking about. I feel like I'm not as well educated as them. I haven't done too much reading in this area. They know so much more than I. I just feel that if I said anything they'd say, what is she doing in this class, she doesn't know anything, so I keep my mouth shut."

> "I haven't got the right language so I always feel like such a dummy. I don't really want to talk because if I do they [the men] will realize how stupid I am."

> "I feel very angry and uncomfortable in that room. They have no right to talk about us like that. I feel so embarrassed. It's like men passing around pornographic pictures. I don't think it's appropriate."

"I've talked a few times, but nothing I say seems to make a difference. What I say never gets taken up. It's like I hadn't said anything. So I've given up. Why bother?"

"They talk about those women [in Radway's study] as if they were me. I don't sit at home reading junk like that. I've worked all over the world and have done many interesting things. In this class it's like none of that counts. You're a woman so you must sit at home reading cheap romance novels. That life isn't my life, and I resent being compared to them. But then I get angry at myself for saying that. Why do I want to distance myself from those women? We are no different, they and I."

"I always have the feeling you get when people are talking about you as if you don't exist but in fact you're sitting right there. It's the way people talk about children or mental incompetents."

"You know, they are just like little boys, always demanding attention and monopolizing all the time. I just sit back and think, let them have their say. Sometimes I think it's quite funny."

It was now not as individuals but as a group that we uncovered the perspective from which the men in the class discussed Radway's work, drawing as they did on their own version of what women were supposed to be like. Thus we were able to discern the subtleties of how they twisted the analysis until the subjects of Radway's study fit the image that was required to sustain the notion of male superiority. We came to understand the oppressive relation within which women become the subjects of male discourse. It became clear that the only difference between us and the women in Radway's study was that as graduate students we lived out and contested the patriarchic social relations under different circumstances. The oppression was no less felt, and the struggle was no less difficult. We were the women in Radway's study. The women in Radway's study were us. In a moment of collective insight we understood that we are our history, and our history is laid within patriarchy. To deny that we are a collective body is to deny not only our history, but also the possibilities for healing and recovery. Realizing our identity with the women in Radway's study was the first step in releasing us from the bonds of patriarchy.

When we connected with, talked, and listened to each other we became a viable political force in this context. We reappropriated our voice, found support in each other, and were able (for a short time and certainly not completely) to lift the oppression. Our act of refusing silence produced a moment of speaking. After our extended break we returned to the class, each of us prepared to make a statement. What we could never have accomplished individually became possible for us as a group. We disrupted the male agenda and appropriated our space.

But this is not altogether a happy story. On the one hand it was clear that, as the term continued, a true sense of equality and understanding was achieved on occasion between some of the women and some of the men. On the other hand this was not a miraculous transformation of patriarchy. The men became conscious of their own speaking and began to monitor themselves and each other. Moreover, being "given" time and space had its own oppressive moments in that the power of control over such time and space had not changed. Nonetheless, the power dynamics were made explicit.

I suspect that all women, like those of us in this class, have lived this struggle, have felt anguish in response to the strength-sapping power of the oppressor pushing us to the edge and demanding us to conform, and felt terror and rage welling up from the depths of our being when sometimes in hopelessness we think that conforming would be so much easier. Most of the time the strength is there to keep up the struggle. But when it seeps away, it is these golden touchstones, the reference points signifying a collective struggle, that enable us to say we are not alone.

Roger Simon

It is ironic to realize in retrospect that we were producing concretely a "textbook" example of how the privileged use of language can be an act of domination and an occasion for resistance, while I strove to show the class that same point through reading Radway's book. This course met for two-and-one-half hours a week for thirteen weeks. Within this constraint I had an agenda that I thought gave form and justification to naming our collective weekly meetings as a credit course in a graduate department of education. My agenda is most simply described as the systematic discussion of an assigned set of readings (supplemented by lectures and assignments) examining various aspects of the relation between language and power. I have long felt that an important purpose of graduate teaching is to empower students through the development of the practical competence that is inherent in theorizing. Theorizing has meant to me exploring ways of comprehending and thinking about situations. What I had to offer was the possibility of a discourse that might clarify and critique existing educational practices and create new possibilities.

How this agenda is to be accomplished so that it might work to empower all our students remains a central teaching problem. Barthes (1982) has emphasized that "what is oppressive in our teaching is not, finally, the knowledge or the culture it conveys, but the discursive forms through which we propose them. Since our teaching has as its object taken in the inevitability of power, *method* can really bear only on the means of loosening, baffling or, at the very least, lightening this power." Corrigan (1984) agrees with this point and emphasizes that "we face a plenitude of naming claims which erase, by mentalizing, our very bodies. Language embodies power never more strongly as where it renders bodies powerless. We have been colonized (and subsequently have become the colonizer) through the enforced modalities of a required, encouraged, rewarded discursivity" (p. 8). We must beware of discursive forms that colonize and silence bodies — all bodies.[9] Forms of discourse that do not allow an answer to the question, "Where is *my body* in that text?" silence us.

I am trying to understand how particular discursive forms — those social, political, and economic relations extended over space and time in concrete practices — subjugate the experiences of some people. This happens when a particular text is taken to be *the* text and therefore the locus of silence and terror. Discourse becomes the assertion of certainty when it naturalizes a specific regime of truth manifested in patriarchy as the Law of the Father, God, Nature, or any other form of rule.

We must ask ourselves: Does our teaching, our use of particular sets of practices and forms of discussion, subjugate? It is clear to me that mine sometimes does. As an example, read the words of one of my doctoral students. I had suggested that she read some of Foucault's work in light of the problems she had in analyzing her thesis data. After reading the text she wrote me a short note:

> To sort out the content from how Foucault projects it is impossible for me. He is disembodied, disassociated, beyond knowledge, beyond human frailty, a single phallus waving in the breeze, frightened of the breeze and certainly wretchedly ambivalent about the need for communication imposed by writing. To read Foucault means entering that space, becoming part of it (because of the inseparability of content/context of utterance) which is very destructive for me, despite the possibilities Foucault holds out for what I am trying to study.

Now I do not read Foucault that way. I cannot dismiss the type of discourse associated with Foucault. It always seems so rich to me and teaches me so much about the very issues we have been writing about here. Within the political/ethical project out of which I teach, I identify it as a discourse that can make an important difference in how we understand our world and our lives so as to make possible practices of justice, caring, and solidarity. This is a crucial paradox for any male teacher within patriarchy. What can we offer that will not become a form of malefic generosity?

TOWARDS COUNTER-PATRIARCHIC PRACTICE

Aided by our juxtaposed reflections, what can we say together about teaching and learning within patriarchy that encourages a collective educative practice bound by a politics of solidarity rather than opposition? We pose this question in particular reference to mixed-gender education. This is not to deny the importance of recent feminist reconsiderations of the value of all-female learning situations,[10] but rather to pose the possibility of a counter-patriarchic pedagogy in the mixed gender institutions within which we work and study.

We begin by suggesting several qualities required by a counter-patriarchic form of teaching and learning, qualities for which both students and teachers must take responsibility. The first is the embodied quality of discourse: the fact that oppression is enacted not by theoretical concepts but by real people in concrete situations. Put most simply, this means that theories don't oppress, people do. In that people are differentially placed socially, politically, and economically, there can be no text that one can claim as displaying a rational, neutral, androgynous form. To the extent that academic discourse appears objective and distanced (and is understood and privileged in this way) it becomes a vehicle for domination. It devalues alternative perspectives, understanding, and articulation of experience. It denies the lived reality of difference as the ground on which to pose questions of theory and practice. It favors one set of values over others as they are generated by the multiplicity of human experiences.

It is the experience of the reality of lived difference that critical pedagogic practice must claim as the agenda for discussion. This means that both students and teacher must find space within which the experience of their daily lives can be articulated in its multiplicity. In practice this always implies a struggle — a struggle over assigned meaning, a struggle over discourse as the expression of both form and content, a struggle over interpretation of experience, and a struggle over **"self."**[h] But it is this very struggle that forms the basis of a pedagogy that liberates knowledge and practice. It is a struggle that makes possible new knowledge that expands beyond individual experience and hence redefines our identities and the real possibilities we see in the daily conditions of our lives. The struggle is itself a condition basic to the realization of a process of pedagogy: it is a struggle that can never be won — or pedagogy stops. It is the struggle through which new knowledge, identities, and possibilities are introduced that may lead to the alteration simultaneously of circumstances and selves.

We emphasize that our position does not require teachers either to suppress or abandon what and how they know — essential aspects of what they bring to teaching. Indeed, the struggle over meaning-making is lessened without such resources. However, teachers and students must find forms within which a single discourse does not become the locus of certainty and certification. In particular, teachers must ask how they can help create a space for the mutual engagement of lived difference that is not framed in

---

[h] As Lewis and Simon explain in footnote 13 of their original article, "We take the notion of **self** to be non-unitary and multiple. A struggle over self refers to the situation where one is confronted with multiple, often contradictory, discursive possibilities for naming and claiming one's identities."

oppositional terms requiring the silencing of a multiplicity of voices by a single dominant discourse.

It is clear from the separate accounts of the episode we have written about that such a meeting must rest on a politics of solidarity which requires the contestation of patriarchic relations. What does this mean? If social relations are to change, it is not enough for women to be explicit about their experience of oppression. It is necessary for those men who believe that liberating politics and practices can truly humanize our world to question the privileged status of their own practices. Men have to resist using male prerogative to shape social relations and set the historical agenda. Women's struggles are not just against the silence imposed from within and without: they are also against the silence created by our failure to make explicit men's experience of the practice of domination. We need to understand the meaning of this powerful form of male silence. An emancipatory pedagogy requires that explicitness be taken up as a political position by men as well as women. This questioning of one's privileged practices is not a call for declarations of guilt but rather for the unequivocal acknowledgment that one's embodiment as "man" accrues privileges and prerogatives that are not equally available to all and which therefore must be refused. It requires that we understand that emancipation is not just freedom from power over us but also freedom from our power over others. Hence, men need to be located differently not just in relation to women but in relation to themselves.

Irigaray (1985) has suggested that "the first question to ask is . . . how can women analyze their own exploitation, inscribe their own demands, within an order prescribed by the masculine? Is a woman's politics possible within that order?" (p. 81). This is neither the first nor the only question to ask. As our colleague Ann-Louise Brookes has suggested, we must simultaneously ask the following: "In an order prescribed by the masculine, how might men analyze the methods of exploitation that they use to inscribe and make legitimate their claims about human freedom? How might men move from a voice of authority to a voice of questioning in their attempt to freely speak about exploitation?"

In the context of our seminar, what could men have done differently that would have rejected the assumption of male privilege? First of all, it would have been necessary for them not to see the women's developing political protest as individual moments of hysteria, for which the cure was the calming hand of the Father. Second, it would have been necessary for them to take equal responsibility for naming patriarchy as an immorally oppressive social form that denies freedom and human possibility. There is no easy answer to how this could have been done. If men are to participate in the emancipatory project, they can neither assume the burden of providing women's freedom and legitimacy nor enjoy the luxury of remaining silent in the face of oppression. To declare solidarity with women under either of these conditions can be rightly challenged as insincere. Learning how to listen, how to hear, how to see, and how to watch is a precondition to becoming fully aware. But this is insufficient. The men needed to risk more than a comfortable indignation that declares solidarity with women without requiring action on their conviction. Men need to embody forms that do not express and construct masculinity as defined within patriarchy. One cannot simply donate freedom from a position that does not challenge privilege. As is the case for any oppressor group, for men to ally themselves with the oppressed, they must understand the power of their privilege and the privilege of their power, and self-consciously divest themselves of both. It is important to note that emancipatory practices are only truly emancipatory when they challenge our own privilege, whether we accrue such privilege by the color of our skin, our class position, our age, or our gender.

In the context of our seminar, what was required was a position from which a man could say, "While I have had complicity with and benefit from what is happening here, it has become offensive and is no longer acceptable to me." The precondition is that men accept that no single voice can speak for our multiple experiences; that no simple understanding of how things are and how they ought to be can derive from a limited perspective; and that ultimately, in the push and pull of social and political relations, they might have to yield.

We are arguing here for a pedagogical project that allows a polyphony of voices, a form that legitimates the expression of difference differently. To struggle for a practice supportive of the equality of possibility we need to speak on our own terms, ones framed by *our desire for solidarity and freedom*. But such desire cannot be taken for granted. We must ask and ask again, who needs to listen?

REFERENCES

Barrett, M. (1980). *Women's oppression today*. London: Verso Editions.
Barthes, R. (1982). Inaugural lecture, Collège de France. In S. Sontag (Ed.) *A Barthes reader* (pp. 457–478). New York: Hill & Wang.
Buck-Morss, S. (1981, July–August). Walter Benjamin — Revolutionary writer. *New Left Review, 128,* 50–75.
Bunch, C., & Pollack, S. (Eds.). (1983). *Learning our way: Essays in feminist education*. Trumansburg, NY: Crossing Press.
Corrigan, P. (1984). *The body of intellectuals/the intellectual's body*. Unpublished manuscript.
Dorfman, A. (1983). *The empire's old clothes: What the Lone Ranger, Babar, and other innocent heroes do to our minds*. New York: Pantheon Books.
Fanon, F. (1967). *Black skins, white masks*. New York: Grove Press.
Felman, S. (1981). Re-reading femininity. In *Feminist readings: French texts/American contexts* (pp. 19–44). (From *Yale French Studies, 62*).
Finn, G. (1982). On the oppression of women in philosophy, or whatever happened to objectivity? In A. Miles & G. Finn, *Feminism in Canada: From pressure to politics* (pp. 145–173). Montreal: Black Rose Books.
Foucault, M. (1982). The subject and power. *Critical Inquiry, 8,* 777–789.

Fox-Genovese, E. (1982, May–June). Placing women's history in history. *New Left Review 133,* 5–29.

Hartmann, H. (1984). The unhappy marriage of Marxism and feminism: Towards a more progressive union. In R. Dale, G. Esland, R. Ferguson, & M. McDonald (Eds.), *Education and the state: Politics, patriarchy, and practice* (Vol. 2, pp. 191–210). Sussex: Falmer Press.

Howe, F. (1984). *Myths of co-education.* Bloomington: Indiana University Press.

Imray, L., & Middleton, A. (1983). Public and private: Marking the boundaries. In E. Gamarnikow, D. Morgan, J. Purvis, & D. Taylorson (Eds.), *The public and the private* (pp. 12–27). London: Heinemann.

Irigaray, L. (1985). *This sex which is not one.* Ithaca, NY: Cornell University Press.

MacPherson, C. B. (1962). *The political theory of possessive individualism.* Oxford: Clarendon Press.

McVicker, C., Belenky, M., Goldberger, N., & Tarule, J. (1985). Connected education for women. *Journal of Education, 167,* 28–45.

Morgan, D. (1981). Man, masculinity, and the process of sociological inquiry. In H. Roberts (Ed.), *Doing feminist research* (pp. 83–113). London: Routledge & Kegan Paul.

Oakley, A. (1972). *Sex, gender, and society.* London: Temple Smith.

Radway, J. (1984). *Reading the romance: Women, patriarchy, and popular literature.* Chapel Hill: University of North Carolina Press.

Rich, A. (1979). *On lies, secrets, and silence: Selected prose, 1966–1978.* New York: Norton.

Shaw, J. (1980). Education and the individual: Schooling for girls, or mixed schooling — A mixed blessing? In R. Deem (Ed.), *Schooling for women's work* (pp. 66–75). London: Routledge & Kegan Paul.

Smith, D. (1978). A peculiar eclipsing: Women's exclusion from man's culture. *Women's Studies International Quarterly, 1,* 281–295.

Spender, D. (1980). *Man made language.* London: Routledge & Kegan Paul.

Spender, D. (Ed.). (1981). *Men's studies modified: The impact of feminism on the academic disciplines.* Toronto: Pergamon Press.

Spender, D. (1982). *Invisible women: The schooling scandal.* London: Writers & Readers Publishers.

Terdiman, R. (1985). *Discourse/counter-discourse: The theory and practice of symbolic resistance in 19th century France.* Ithaca: Cornell University Press.

Thompson, J. (1983). *Learning liberation: Women's response to men's education.* London: Croom Helm.

NOTES

1. For discussions of various forms of such silencing, see Rich (1979), Smith (1978), and Spender (1980, 1981).
2. Radway (1984) documents the extent to which men are not tolerant of women's reading, particularly if it can be construed as a challenge to the balance of power in a marriage.
3. For a detailed first person analysis of such negotiations, see Finn (1982).
4. No single perspective defines the notion of feminist pedagogy. For a variety of discussions see, for example, Bunch and Pollock (1983), McVicker, Belenky, Goldberger, and Tarule (1985), and Thompson (1983).
5. Corrigan (1984) points out that the English translation of the concept to which Foucault (1982) refers is better expressed as *governance* not government. For explicit discussion of how governance works within patriarchic social forms, see Fox-Genovese (1982).
6. My thanks to Ann-Louise Brookes for pointing this out to me.

7. For an excellent discussion of this issue, see Imray and Middleton (1983).
8. The concept of homosociality is introduced and discussed in Morgan (1981).
9. There is an extensive body of literature about the issue of language colonizing bodies in the context of discussions of racism and colonialism. See, for example, Fanon (1967).
10. See, for example, the discussion of feminist proposals for sex-segregated schools and classes in Shaw (1980) and Howe (1984).

We acknowledge Ann-Louise Brooks and Phillip Corrigan for their insightful comments during the completion of this article and thank them for their courageous participation in emancipatory pedagogy.

13

Teachers as Political Actors: From Reproductive Theory to the Crisis of Schooling

DENNIS CARLSON

An important demand of critical pedagogy is that one constantly question the plethora of theories, including our own, to ensure that they do not become new totalizing narratives — that is, theories that suppress difference into unifying schemes that attempt to explain every aspect of social reality. Critical theories of education, in focusing on the *social reproductive* function of school systems (i.e., systems of ideological control that work to maintain dominant beliefs, values, norms, and oppressive practices), often fail to emphasize the potential of teachers as agents of educational and social change. Illustrating how theories evolve, Dennis Carlson takes a critical look at theories of reproduction and argues that teachers can be important agents for transformative change in schools. As such, he reviews the historical development of teachers' professional and trade union movements, contending that they too remain a powerful force for social agency. Carlson contends that since teachers are victims of the current system of public education, their collective interests as workers are more compatible with transformative than mere reformist change.

Critical theorists of "schooling" — that state-sponsored institutional process by which the young are inducted into adult work and citizenship roles — have tended to view teachers rather simplistically as the witting or unwitting servants of power and direct agents of the state. Teachers are viewed as heavily implicated in the reproduction of oppressive worldviews, modes of work behavior, and social and technical relations of production. We may refer to this as the reproductive theory of teaching, with the role of the teacher subsumed under the various schooling processes (sorting, selecting, transmitting, disciplining) through which the **dominant culture**[a] is reproduced in schools and classrooms. In comparison to an earlier, overly romanticized view of teaching, which placed the teacher on a pedestal as the keeper of knowledge, seeker of truth, and guide for curious young minds, this reproductive theory has been refreshingly less naive. It has been suggested, for example, that given existing socioeconomically structured inequalities, schooling must be heavily impositional, especially for those who are most disadvantaged through the schooling process. By this I mean that it must be imposed, in an authoritarian manner and against some resistance, upon students whose schooling prepares them for the lower rungs of a highly inequitable social and labor hierarchy, and who consequently do not believe that the system is designed to meet their "needs." Furthermore, within the context of advanced capitalist formations, reproductive theory has made it clear that the schools are not, and cannot be, fully autonomous. Schooling cannot be significantly humanized, and the schools cannot be made sites for the liberation of each student's human potential, unless that is a more general democratization of society and of institutional and political control. That is, to transform schooling, we need to transcend advanced capitalist ideologies and organizational forms.

Unfortunately, a theory of how the dominant culture is reproduced through the schooling process leads to an excessively one-sided and politically pessimistic appraisal of what goes on in schools and of the role teachers play in support of the status quo. The schools are, after all, sites of deep-rooted conflicts and contradictions; and teachers are among the most vocal in their opposition to "the way things are," for their work is made more difficult by the reproductive role of the schools and the animosities and motivation problems it generates among many of their students. Also, because teachers tend to resist taking on the dehumanizing "dirty work" of social class reproduction, they cannot be trusted to make curricular and instructional decisions which support this reproductive role. They have therefore been bureaucratically subordinated, rigidly boxed in by a predetermined curriculum, and held accountable for attaining instructional "productivity" goals. The domination and exploitation of teachers as workers is thus coextensive with a system of schooling which is highly impositional vis-à-vis students. For all the recent talk about treating teachers more like

[a] **Dominant culture** refers to the existing institutions and social practices in which the values, beliefs, bodies of knowledge, styles of communication, and biases of the dominant group not only prevail in society, but are also imposed on others. For example, the efforts in the United States to enforce a "common culture" (an unnegotiated foundation of values, ethics, meaning, histories and representations — "*our* cultural heritage") or a "common sense" (a selective view of social reality in which difference is viewed as deviant or a deficit), is in fact the imposition of a homogenizing social paradigm (also known as ideological domination, or *hegemony*) that severely limits the possibility for a critical multicultural democracy.

professionals, there is no reason to believe that significant teacher empowerment can occur under the current system of bureaucratic state schooling and within the context of a highly inequitable socioeconomic system. As long as schooling remains partly a mechanism for reproducing an inequitable system, reforms designed to make the system operate more efficiently are likely to heighten the contradictions and exploitation experienced by teachers — a situation which may encourage them to push for alternative models of teaching and schooling.

In the following pages I develop a framework for better understanding teachers as they present a challenge to schooling in capitalist America. In particular I argue that teachers' collective occupational culture — as represented by their professional and trade-union movements — incorporates conceptions of teachers' interests in the schools that are potentially transformative. So far, little critical attention has been focused on teachers' collective occupational culture. It would seem that a contestational theory of teaching needs to be grounded in collective rather than merely individual analyses of teachers, since teachers' power is amplified when it is collectivized. It is understandable that a theory which emphasizes the reproductive aspects of schooling would focus on individual classroom practitioners, for it is at the classroom level that the teacher most clearly participates in processes that reproduce the dominant culture and generate inequalities among students (although even here teacher resistance may be significant). When the focus shifts to the collective organization and presentation of teachers' interests as workers in the schools, however, the oppositional aspects of teaching stand out.

To develop these various arguments, I divide my comments into several major sections. In the first, I indicate how teachers have typically been portrayed in various critical theories of schooling that have been influential over the past several decades. These include a revisionist theory of de-schooling and the corporate state, a structural-functional theory of schooling in the advanced capitalist state, and a cultural theory of class cultural production and reproduction. I point to some of the important insights as well as the conceptual limitations of each of these critical theories. In a second major section, I present a critical analysis of teachers' collective occupational culture and locate this analysis within a discussion of working-class culture in America more generally. For example, I indicate how teachers' own brand of professional unionism has been influenced by notions of craft unionism and professional job control rights, "company unionism" and the professional educational "family," and industrial unionism and the militant professional. In a brief concluding section, I take up the issues of crisis tendencies and dilemmas of reform under the current system of schooling. I suggest that while some recent reform commissions have accurately appraised the importance of changing the role of the teacher in order to achieve "excellence" in education, severe limits exist on the extent to which change is possible within the parameters of corporate state schooling.

CRITICAL THEORIES OF SCHOOLING AND THE ROLE OF THE TEACHER

Although there is no *one* coherent critical theory of schooling, certain general agreements tend to exist among those who write from a leftist perspective on the reproductive role of the schools. Since the mid-1960s three distinct but related critical theories have been popularized in education. The first of these is associated with a critique of schooling in the corporate state and with proposals for "de-schooling";[1] the second is associated with a structural-functional theory in which the teacher is understood in terms of "objective" location within the class structure and within processes of social and economic reproduction;[2] and the third is associated with a class cultural theory that focuses attention on the everyday resistances and accommodations of teachers as they actively participate in and partially shape their working environment.[3] While each of these traditions of critical theoretical research on the schools provides important insights into the role of teachers as political actors within the schooling process, each is also limited in some important ways.

Revisionism, De-Schooling, and Teaching

Beginning in the late 1960s, a group of revisionist historians began to challenge the conventional wisdom of the liberal-pluralistic model of schooling: that the public schools are an expression of democratic principles and have served the common good by providing individuals with the knowledge, skills, and equality of opportunity they need to achieve their potentials and actively participate in democratic self-government.[4] In arguing against this popular image of the schools the revisionists painted a picture of elite control of public education. The schools were seen to have been imposed upon the working classes by elite socioeconomic groups in order to socialize the young to be good workers. The revisionists depicted a system of schooling that was, by the early twentieth century, increasingly under top corporate and state control and increasingly implicated in the efficient sorting of students for the differential demands of the labor market.

The revisionists' treatment of schooling in the corporate state, and their romanticization of a pre-industrial American past with minimal state regulation and maximum individual freedom, aligned their work with that of Ivan Illich and his more theoretical argument for de-schooling. In *De-Schooling Society* Illich argued that "by monopolizing schooling, the state vastly extends its control over all aspects of life, including work, leisure, politics, and even family." Consequently, increased spending on state schools only "escalates their destructiveness" (pp. 8–9). Illich also denied that public school teachers served any true pedagogic service of imparting useful knowledge and skills to the young. "Teaching, it is true, may contribute to certain kinds of learning of subject matters as goes on in school" (p. 29). Schools may thus be viewed as institutions that "create jobs for schoolteachers, no matter what their pupils learn from them" (p. 30). Illich's political proposal to liberate education from these conditions was to break up the public school monopoly through a voucher plan, which would provide state grants directly to parents, to be used in the education of their children in the school or skill center of their choice. He envisioned, ultimately, a de-schooled society where state educational credentials would be replaced by institutions that enabled people to be "spontaneous, independent, yet related to each other" (p. 52).[5]

Although this political response of abandoning public schools in favor of teaching in "free schools" in the supposedly less-colonized private sphere is less popular today than it was in the early 1970s, it has continued to influence serious leftist scholarship on the schools. It has even led some critics to endorse the voucher system for "privatizing" state schooling.[6] According to this proposal, parents would receive lump-sum allotments to be spent on the education of their children, in the private schools of their choice. Robert Everhart has recently called on leftists to support a voucher plan based on the presumption that the public schools, since they cannot be reformed sufficiently from within, must be circumvented.[7] He dismissed public school teachers as possible allies in fighting corporate state interests in the schools, since it seems "unreasonable to expect most teachers in the public school system, as it is presently constituted, to defy vested interests and favor a liberatory education which, in the end, might seriously challenge their own role as members of the state bureaucracy" (p. 51). As for the teachers' collective associations and unions, Everhart concludes that "most educators in these associations possess a minimal sense of class consciousness and see themselves more as educational **technicians**[b] than as sharing major class or cultural interests with their students" (p. 51).

I do not mean to imply that building counterinstitutions within capitalist society is totally without merit; but de-schooling is not the most effective strategy to overcome the problems that confront public education. In fact, taken as a primary strategy, de-schooling may actually play into the hands of conservative more than democratic Left political interests. After all, the voucher plan itself is a legislative proposal sponsored by the political Right in America and endorsed by the Reagan administration. Business interests see it as a means of turning over control of the schooling process to the supposedly more efficient and more cost-effective business sector. For-profit schools would also, one presumes, be run in a more economically functional manner (thereby increasing the reproductive role of the schools) and thus be organized to keep teachers under tight managerial control and to reduce the cost of their labor.

[b] Emanating from the positivist tradition, technocratic models, which conceptualize teaching and learning as a discrete and scientific undertaking, embrace depersonalized methods for educating students that often translate into the regulation and standardization of teacher practices and curricula, and rote memorization of selected "facts" that can easily be measured through standardized testing. As such, the role of the teacher is reduced to that of a **technician** — an uncritical, "objective," and "efficient" distributor of information.

This political shortsightedness of the revisionist theory of schooling, despite its generally accurate description of the historical shift of power to the corporate state and the loss of community control, is related to several important conceptual problems. First, there is no clear distinction made between the state as it currently exists and as it might exist in a democratic Left alternative. Not capitalist domination of the state and capitalist modes of bureaucratic organization, but the state and bureaucracy per se tend to become defined by revisionists as the evils. Public schools would surely play an important, perhaps more important, role under some form of democratic socialism. Contrary to the de-schooling model, schools would be needed to instill democratic and egalitarian values and to impart useful knowledge and skills to the young — all of the things dominant groups have *claimed* the schools currently provide, and which the revisionists have shown they do not. Finally, all this is related to a larger problem. There is no clear or coherent conception of class, or of the contradictions and struggles of class society, in the revisionist theory. To overcome some of these problems, I now turn to the second critical theory of schooling, grounded in a Marxist class analysis.

Structural-Functionalism and Teaching

The dominant theory of schooling that has influenced critically minded educators' view of teachers and teaching is grounded in a neo-Marxian structural-functionalism. It is associated in Europe with the work of the French structuralists, most notably Louis Althusser and Nicos Poulantzas, and in the United States with the work of Samuel Bowles and Herbert Gintis and that of Harry Braverman (although Braverman's work does not directly address schooling).[8] These various theorists of advanced capitalism differ in a number of ways. For our purposes, however, I will focus on their similarities. The structural-functionalists share an understanding of the special role of the state in social and economic reproduction, a functional view of the schools as an apparatus of the state, and a **reductionist**[c] treatment of teachers as the agents or functionaries of schooling. According to Althusser, the school is the single most important institution of the "Ideological State Apparatuses." As a direct consequence of their differentiated as well as common experiences in state schools, students are socialized to assume appropriate personality traits, work norms, and worldviews "needed" in the economy. Bowles and Gintis refer to the "correspondence" or the "congruence" between "the personality traits conducive to proper work performance on the job and those which are rewarded with high grades in the classroom."[9]

To appreciate more specifically how teachers are treated within this theory of schooling, we must understand a bit more about the structural-functionalists' view of teachers' "objective" location within the process of the appro-

---

[c] To be **reductionistic** is to simplify a particular phenomenon so as to mask its complexity. For example, arguing that social reality is shaped solely by socioeconomic status and class conflict obscures the multiple and interconnecting relationships of other significant human experiences (such as race, gender, and sexual orientation) and their effects on perception and struggle.

priation of surplus value, which determines their class position. Structural-functionalism is associated with the notion that a "new" class (or subclass) was organized in late or monopoly capitalism, concurrent with the last great consolidation of industry and the growth of the state as a central legitimating agency, which began near the turn of the twentieth century. This class is variously called the "new petit bourgeois," the "professional-managerial class," and the "new middle class."[10] It is defined as an intermediary class between the two great camps in capitalist society: labor and capital. Its collective political function is to supervise the capitalists' appropriation of surplus value (profit) in the production process, help extract more surplus value from labor, and indoctrinate workers (or future workers) with the values of discipline, respect for authority, and so forth, that are essential to the appropriation process. Included in this class, among others, are shop-floor supervisors and managers, efficiency experts and accountants, clerical workers, engineers, bureaucratic planners and technicians, *and* teachers. Teachers supervise, discipline, and indoctrinate future workers in the service of capital. Structural-functionalists generally argue that because members of this class serve as agents of capitalist interests and do not directly add anything of value to what is produced by human labor, their work cannot be considered "productive." Instead, along with management and capital, they live off the surplus value created by labor. Supposedly, there would be no need for this "unproductive" labor under socialism, for the domination and indoctrination of labor and of future labor would no longer be necessary. Some "unproductive" jobs would disappear; others, including teaching, would serve new, productive roles. Teachers' work would become productive to the extent that teachers provided the young with important skills and knowledge that contributed to their capacity for socially beneficial and personally enhancing work in the community.

While structural-functionalist analysis therefore recognizes that teaching *could* be productive labor in another social context, it is clearly viewed as unproductive labor under advanced capitalism. Kevin Harris remarks in this regard: "Teachers are the effective agents in schools. . . . Their political function *qua* teachers, then, parallels the political function of schooling. . . . Just as schooling is a direct form of political control over children, teaching is a direct political struggle with children, especially working-class children."[11] Similarly, Paul Walker notes that "the fact that a person is fulfilling the teaching function puts them in a relationship which perpetuates the elitism, the paternalism, the control of knowledge and the corresponding passivity and resentment which constitute significant class barriers between the two groups [teachers and working-class children]."[12] Bowles and Gintis devote little attention to teachers or teaching per se, since their concern is with the overall process of schooling, but they do quote from Paulo Freire's account of the "banking" concept of education, in which the teacher is viewed as the "depositor." According to Freire, "instead of communicating, the teacher issues communiqués and makes deposits which the students patiently receive, memorize, and repeat. This is the 'banking' concept of education.... The teacher teaches and the students are taught.... The teacher chooses and enforces his choice and the students comply.... The teacher acts and the students have the illusion of acting through the action of the teacher."[13]

Even though teachers are understood as agents of capital and the state within structural-functional theory, they are also recognized more sympathetically as victims of exploitation and oppression themselves within the hierarchical, bureaucratically-organized school system. This other side of the structural-functional argument is expressed through the notion of the proletarianization of the new middle class. Proletarianization as a system imperative is thought to be related to two aims of capital. The first is to gain ever more complete control of the labor process at the "point" of production.

In the twentieth century, this has been achieved primarily through the rationalization and standardization of work tasks which allow management to dictate each step in the work process, along with new bureaucratic rules and procedures to which workers are held accountable. As Braverman argues, these new forms of scientific management and bureaucratic control have had the effect of deskilling workers in complex craft knowledge and reskilling them as followers of a routine work format.[14] Deskilled workers consequently suffer from job routinization and close supervision, and they lack avenues for advancement within the job hierarchy. A second aim of capital in proletarianizing middle-class workers is decreasing the cost of their labor. By lowering the skill requirements necessary for work, management is able to buy labor more cheaply on the labor market by drawing from among the large pool of semiskilled workers. Because members of the new middle class are paid employees, along with actual productive workers, they are susceptible to this same logic of proletarianization. This trend is evident even as the new middle class continues to serve the ideological and political functions of capital, a situation which places this class in an objectively contradictory position, torn between identification with capital and identification with labor.

When we examine trends in teaching, we indeed find evidence to support Bowles and Gintis's contention that the concentration of decisionmaking power in education along with the quest for economic rationalization "had the same disastrous consequences for teachers that bureaucracy and rationalization of production had on most other workers."[15] Let me point to three current aspects of the proletarianization of teaching. First, new instructional technologies and programmed instructional materials may be having the effect of deskilling teachers in the traditional craft skills of teaching: that is, subject matter knowledge and pedagogic knowledge (knowledge of the learning process and human motivation).[16] Teachers are reskilled by these new instructional technologies and methods more as "classroom managers," supervisors of a predetermined classroom production process. Their job becomes one of keeping students "on task," disciplining those who disrupt the production process, and keeping track of production records — primarily through administering and recording standardized test data. Harris concludes that if present trends continue, "the proletarianized teacher will control children more and instruct them less."[17] A second aspect of teachers' proletarianization is the intensification of their labor. The demands of the prespecified curriculum, frequent testing, and classroom supervisory duties have all made the school day more hurried, less relaxed, and less satisfying for both teachers and students. Michael Apple describes this continuing intensification of teachers' labor, along with that of other works in the economy, as having "many symptoms from the trivial to the more complex — from no time at all to even go to the bathroom, have a cup of coffee, or relax, to having a total absence of time to keep up with one's field."[18] The results of this intensification, according to Apple, may be a reduction of the *quality* of school services. "While traditionally, 'human service professionals' have equated doing good work with the interests of their clients or students, intensification tends to contradict the traditional interest in work well done."[19] Finally, the proletarianization of teaching promotes the continuing cheapening and increased substitutability of teachers' labor. For all the talk of raising teachers' salaries, their real wages continue to decline relative to other similarly educated workers.[20] Furthermore, as the curriculum becomes more technologically predetermined and individualized into skill kits that are designed to be teacher-proof, more and more actual classroom instruction can be delegated to less qualified, lower paid, inexperienced, and even unlicensed teachers. According to a recent report by the Council for Basic Education, the use of underqualified and inexperienced "permanent substitutes" is one of the "dirty little secrets" of public education, particularly in urban areas.[21] These factors relate to another underlying problem of schooling in advanced capitalism: the tendency for the state, and by implication state schools, to exist in a more or less permanent state of fiscal crisis. Teachers, like other groups of state workers, have been the victims of this crisis, as school management has constantly sought ways of lowering the labor costs of schooling.

Having described the structural-functional theory of teaching and teachers, with its emphasis upon both the reproductive role of teaching and the proletarianization of teachers, I will now examine each of these notions in a more critical vein, indicating some of the benefits as well as limitations inherent in this perspective. With regard to the view of teachers as agents of an oppressive schooling process, structural-functionalism has revealed the inadequacies of the old liberal-pluralist model of schools and teachers as agents of social progress and equality of opportunity by indicating how the schools function to uphold the existing, highly inequitable social and economic order. Of course, the state and state schools are not mere "puppets" of elite interests; their relative autonomy is enhanced by the fact that they are outside of the direct production and profit sphere and thus one step removed from direct economic determination. Nevertheless, while the schools are not mere puppets of elite interests, there is general agreement on the Left that the state *is* decisively constrained by external forces originating in the economic sphere.[22] Any political movement that hopes to challenge the present organization and functioning of the schools must begin with a recognition that the state, and state schools, *are* strongly, of not directly, determined by the reproductive needs of capital, and cannot be made to serve fundamentally differing purposes short of a socialist reorganization of society. This means that teachers are in a very constrained position in schools. Their efforts to develop cooperative relations with students, based on mutual respect and trust, take place within the socially structured objective conflict between teachers and students, particularly between teachers and working-class students.

But the functional description of teaching, taken alone, is not only inaccurate in its overdeterminism and its conflation of teaching and schooling; it is also politically disempowering, for it promotes a pessimism about teachers' potential contribution to social transformation that the Left should do its utmost to fight rather than encourage. Indeed, Philip Wexler has argued that terms such as "reproduction," "socialization," and **"hegemony"**[d] may actually contribute in a paradoxical way to reproductive forces by enhancing political apathy.[23] For critically minded teachers currently working, or planning to work, in public school systems, such notions can be devastating because they simply reinforce the dominant ideological picture of workers as isolated cogs in an all-encompassing system. In criticizing structural-functional accounts of teaching, Madan Sarup comments: "If all that they [teachers] are doing is directly reproducing pupils as units to be slotted into the labor market their job hardly seems worth doing."[24]

The structural-functional reproductive theory of teaching, then, engenders a cynicism about "working in the system" while encouraging an effort to build counterinstitutions, which seems shortsighted as a political strategy. But what of the political implications of the proletarianization of teachers? Here, I think, structural-functionalism is more helpful politically, although this image of teachers also has limitations. Proletarianization suggests that teachers increasingly identify with working-class discontents and political interests. Not only does proletarianization link teachers' occupational interests with a broad working-class movement for change; it more directly links their interests to certain fundamental changes in the schools. For example, opposition to proletarianization also implies opposition to the further bureaucratization and centralization of decisionmaking in the schools, to dominant management ideologies and production metaphors, to an objectified cur-

---

[d] **Hegemony**, as derived from the work of Italian theorist Antonio Gramsci, is used to express how certain groups manage to dominate others. An analysis of hegemony is especially concerned with how the imposition of particular ideologies and forms of authority results in the reproduction of social and institutional practices through which dominant groups maintain not only their positions of privilege and control, but also the consensual support of other members of society.

riculum with more standardized testing, and to the general predetermination of learning "inputs" and "outputs" that all act in one way or another to deskill and subordinate teachers.

Unfortunately, the structural-functional model will take us no further in exploring these issues, since it is basically a theory of how the system *functions* to maintain the status quo. As Robert William Connell comments in this regard, "It is difficult for discussions of the reproduction needs of an *a priori*-defined structure to come up with explanations that are anything other than functional. This is a chronic problem in structuralist Marxism's accounts of class, ideology, and the state."[25] Functional explanations are of some heuristic value in describing how a particular institution reproduces class relations, and in depicting the objective relations that individuals enter into within institutional settings over which they experience no direct control.[26] But functionalist explanations are never sufficient in themselves. They need to be integrated with a less deterministic and reified theory of social processes and actors. Classes, occupational groups, and individuals are not merely analytic abstractions; they are historically embedded agents of action, and their actions and beliefs have real consequences that cannot be totally determined.

Class Culture, Resistances and Accommodations, and Teaching

Marx spoke of class as an objective category in some of his more economic writings. He referred, for example, to the working class "in itself," the objective social reality created by capital as part of the appropriation of surplus value and defined by its technical relation to the production process. But elsewhere, Marx clearly uses class in a cultural and historical sense, the working class "for itself," a subjective agent, as it makes itself, even if this making of a class is not always an entirely self-aware of politicized process that directly challenges the hegemony of capital. Both an objective *and* a cultural conception of class are essential to our understanding of teachers. Unfortunately, the structural-functional theory of schooling helps us understand only the former. Since the mid-1970s, and particularly with the publication of Paul Willis's *Learning to Labour* in England, some critical theorists of schooling have begun to emphasize the active production of class culture — including culturally specific resistances — within the overall dynamic of social and economic production.[27] Willis was particularly interested in the class culture of working-class students; and he shows us how a group of rather delinquent adolescent boys, "the lads," as they call themselves, actively construct a counterschool culture that gains them some measure of autonomy and that helps them cope with some of the more debilitating aspects of the classroom work routine. Willis also shows, however, how "the lads," in a paradoxical manner, also contribute to their own domination in the schooling process. For example, the rejection of school credentials and knowledge, along with the refusal to compete for grades, involves elements of an active resistance to domination within the system and an insightful appraisal of some of the worst aspects of the ideology of competition and self-advancement. But these beliefs and practices also lock "the lads" into a pattern of school failure that ensures their future status as members of the manual working-class.

The class cultural theory, which Willis applies to working-class students, may be applied as well to teachers. Its relevance is in understanding the everyday practices and beliefs of teachers as they "make" their roles in schools and classrooms, both as they resist their treatment as proletarianized functionaries of the state and also as they participate in, or acquiesce to, existing relations and ideologies in schooling. In proposing the basis for a class-cultural theory of teaching, I will refer to two sets of concepts that have been widely used in cultural studies, and are central to the class-cultural argument. One set of concepts includes *penetrations* and *limitations,* and the other set includes *resistance* and *accommodations.* The first set of terms is used by Willis. The second set of terms has been used by Eugene Genovese, in *Roll, Jordan, Roll: The World the Slaves Made,* to describe the response of Black Americans to their enslavement; and by Jean Anyon in "Intersections of Gender and Class: Accommodation and Resistance by Working-Class and Affluent Females to Contradictory Sex-Role Ideologies," in *Gender, Class, and Education.*[28] Both penetration and resistance designate a rejection of domination. We may think of penetrations as ideological and resistances as behavioral. Willis uses the term penetration "to designate impulses within a cultural form towards the penetration of the conditions of existence of its members and their position within the social whole."[29] Resistances are corresponding behavioral responses that challenge, in some way, the given "definition of the situation." For example, in the industrial sphere, "goldbricking," "soldiering" (pressuring new workers to slow down to the pace established by the work group), production-line stoppages, and other forms of worker resistance represent attempts to sabotage and subvert the official production goals, or to make the work situation more tolerable, or to gain some formal control of work. The notions of penetration and resistance imply a strength and resiliency among oppressed groups as they daily engage in a form of guerrilla warfare against the institutional authority and work processes that most visibly oppress them. The other side of the picture is that ideological penetrations are typically limited in important ways that stop short of seriously challenging the status quo. Willis uses the term limitation to designate those "blocks, diversions, and ideological effects which confuse and impede the full development and expression of working class discontents."[30] They thus promote an accommodation to the system, in which resistance is kept largely circumscribed and defensive, aimed at gaining a measure of protection and freedom *within* dominant structures.

One interesting case study of teachers along these lines is provided by Harry Wolcott in *Teachers versus Technocrats,* an ethnographic account of teachers in one school district and their reactions to an "innovation" — in this case, a planning-programming budgeting system, designed at a nearby university-based research and development center and mandated by the central school administration.[31] The system called for more quantification of learning outputs, more testing, and more recordkeeping among teachers. Wolcott identified a spectrum of responses to the new system, ranging from resistance to compliance, with active and passive forms of each. Some of these responses were: *routine acceptance* — "I don't like it, but I use it" (p. 197) or "I'm going through the motions" (p. 199); *antagonistic acceptance* — complaining loudly but in the end swallowing the "bitter medicine" (p. 199); *Innovative acceptance* — modifying the form or intent of the innovation so that "we're still doing what we've always done" (p. 200); a *wait-and-see attitude* — which allows the teacher to either go along or resist at a later date; *dropping out* — leaving the system or quietly doing the minimum; *heel dragging* — "Just drag your heels a little bit and wait. It will all pass" (p. 202); *dialogue management* with the system coordinators — involving "playing dumb" or "playing silent"; *consciously subverting the program* — by, for example, reporting false data. According to one teacher: "I cheated. I put what I thought would look good. I think 75 percent looks good. I put in 80 percent" (p. 206). Wolcott projects an overall image of fragile compliance by teachers, with a good deal of ongoing resistance on a number of levels. These resistances do not seriously challenge the prerogative of school management in imposing the new system on teachers; but they do impede the system's effectiveness once it is adopted, and they represent at least a partial penetration of the managerial ideology that lies behind changes.

The final picture that emerges from a class-cultural analysis of teachers' everyday working lives is one of great specificity and detail. Through ethnographic studies of teachers' actual work experiences, such as Wolcott's, we can see that the processes of social and economic reproduction operate in an often paradoxical rather than deterministic manner, with room for reappropriations and resistances by teachers within the schools. However, the focus upon individual resistances — which are not typically politicized in an overt fashion and which remain largely individualized expressions of discontent — means that the class-cultural theory of schooling has also, and somewhat ironically, tended to perpetuate a pessimistic view of teachers' power to rethink radically their position and mount a serious challenge to the status quo. Teachers' everyday resistances are important, but so long as they remain depoliticized and "kept in the closet" of the self-contained classroom, it is difficult to see how they represent a serious threat to system stability. As Jean Anyon remarks: "While accommodation and resistance as modes of daily activity provide . . . ways of negotiating individually felt social conflict or oppression, this individual activity of everyday life remains just that: individual, fragmented, and isolated from group effort. It is thus politically weakened."[32]

TRADE UNIONISM, PROFESSIONALISM, AND TEACHERS' WORK CULTURE

Teachers, I have suggested, need to be understood both as individual occupiers and as makers of a role within the schooling process. As such, teachers are far from the passive role players implied in structural-functional analyses, and they show signs of active resistance to their disempowerment in the state bureaucracy. But the futility of individual resistance highlights the fact that, as workers, teachers' interests are also collective in nature, and their collective occupational culture is a powerful force in the schools. My concern is with how and to what extent teachers' collective occupational movement has served to accommodate teachers' interests to existing corporate state forms of schooling and, conversely, how that movement has linked teachers' interests with a countervailing conception of schooling that challenges the existing system. In analyzing teachers' collective occupational culture as it has developed in this century, I will also establish some links between the way teachers have understood their interests and the way other groups of workers within U.S. working-class culture have understood their interests, both in the workplace and in society. The contemporary American labor movement contains within it a number of strands of historical development. We may speak of three dominant strands or forms of trade union ideology and practice: craft unionism, company unionism, and industrial unionism — understanding that these forms are not totally separable.[33] Each of these forms of trade unionism has influenced teachers and each relates to teachers' professional occupational culture.

Craft Unionism and Teacher Professionalism

In the late nineteenth century in America, factories rapidly replaced cottage industry forms of semiautonomous production by skilled craftpersons, and out of this transformation the first form of American trade unionism emerged: craft unionism.[34] The early craft unions, organized first as the Knights of Labor and later as the American Federation of Labor (AFL), exercised significant control over the point of production in many factories through an elaborate system of negotiated contractual "rights." The first of these was that new members would enter the trade only after an extended apprenticeship period, during which they would be closely trained and supervised by "master" craftpersons. New workers, through apprenticeship, were thus initiated into the "secrets" of the craft, secrets already known by management or non-union workers. A second right won by the early craft-union movement was that of establishing the guidelines for performing work: the work ethics, performance standards, and even pay scales. Finally, union stewards in each factory had the right to enforce work rules and production standards. All of this meant a good deal of everyday job control by individual practitioners, groups of workers, and the trade as a whole. This early form of job control, however, was increasingly and successfully challenged by new "scientific management" principles and techniques described in the previous section. Through task specification and job regimentation, management set out to wrest control of the "point of production" from workers and break the grip of craft unions in industry. The traditional rights of the craft unions were systematically eroded through the deskilling and substitutability of labor associated with scientific management. Nevertheless, vestiges of a craft-union orientation continue to be evident in sectors of the labor force, especially in those fields where the work, by its nature, is difficult or impossible to totally predetermine, and where some degree of worker discretion is required. This includes the now relatively few members of the skilled trades in industry and in the public sphere (police, fire fighters, and teachers). To some degree, workers in each of these fields have opposed the further erosion of job-control rights by the bureaucratic institutions within which they work, and have instead upheld the ideal of craft control.

A number of links exist between conceptions of craft unionism and job-control rights among practitioners of the skilled trades and conceptions of the professional rights of teachers. Of course, the professional conception of workers' interests has its historical roots in the development of the new middle class rather than the manual working class; but as indicated earlier, pressures toward the proletarianization of the professional class of workers exist, which have served to draw their interests closer to those of the skilled trades. When teachers argue that they should be treated more as professionals, they imply that they, as individual practitioners and as an occupational group, should be granted more job-control rights, including greater control over the organization of classroom activities, curriculum selection, teacher evaluation, teacher licensing, teacher preparation through apprenticeship with "master" teachers, occupational-ethics performance standards, and so forth. Teacher unions and professional associations have sought to use the collective bargaining process along with legislative lobbying to press for these rights and they have met with some limited but nevertheless important success. For example, at the local level, teacher contracts often include language pertaining to teacher-union membership on various policy advisory committees, involvement in establishing textbook-selection guidelines, participation in planning and conducting in-service training programs, input into teacher evaluation procedures, and participation in planning and implementing new programs. Teachers have also won the right not to participate in noninstructional and nonprofessional activities such as monitoring halls, lunchrooms, and buses.[35]

A professional or craft orientation to understanding workers' interests, I have suggested, implies a concern with broadening the job-control rights of individual practitioners and the occupational group as a whole. As such, it may be considered countervailing to the status quo, for it advances workers' demands for more direct control over work processes than is allowable within the existing corporate and bureaucratic state structures. A high level of job control is more consistent with democratic Left approaches to work organization, in which there is a strong emphasis upon worker involvement in "shop-floor" level decisions, both in planning and implementing production processes, with individual workers and worker teams given more discretion in carrying out their everyday work tasks. Teachers' concern with gaining greater job control through collective bargaining and through political lobbying thus fundamentally challenges the top-down model of bureaucratic control that is characteristic of schooling under corporate and state domination. This also means that there are clear limits to the extent that school management can safely concede to teachers' demands without significantly obstructing the schools' reproductive role. Teachers may find that the harder they push the school administration, the more intransigence and resistance they face. To the extent, however, that teachers begin to demand and expect job-control and professional rights that the institution cannot readily deliver, they reveal the institution's limit and present dominant interests in the schools with a serious problem of control and legitimization.

The limitations of a strict job-control orientation to workers' interests derive from the fact that within the current labor hierarchy, skilled trade and professional workers represent a "labor aristocracy" of sorts, who may perceive their rights in an exclusionary fashion. That is, they may seek to exclude other groups who have an investment in work processes, including the community and, ultimately, the broader society, by seeking exclusive rights to evaluate work. Teachers who follow this logic often argue that community groups and parents should have little or no say over how their children are educated, since only teachers, as professionals, can adequately decide what is needed for each child. As practitioners of a craft, teachers should have special rights associated with expertise, but it is more important to expand their own power by supporting proposals of other largely disenfranchised groups, including parents, the community, and even students, if they are to mobilize broad support for a fundamental democratic restructuring of control in the schools. Job control and professionalism for teachers are worth supporting. But they are only part of what is needed, and therefore insufficient on their own.

Company Unionism and the "Family" of Professional Educators

Company unionism was the second major form of trade unionism to develop out of working-class culture in America.[36] In the progressive era, spanning roughly the first three decades of this century, both labor and business leaders gave at least formal support to the notion that the company is or should be a "family," with management and various types and levels of workers cooperating by performing their specialized roles to insure high levels of productivity and product quality. Labor, in this view, was the associate rather than the critic or natural adversary of capital and business interests, and labor unions were expected to devote themselves to improving productivity and product quality so that workers might share in the financial rewards of an efficiently run business. Groups such as the powerful National Civic Federation promoted company unionism as a solution to industrial relations in the new industrial state. It brought business and labor leaders together in support of one overarching principle: "The only solidarity natural in industry is the solidarity which unites all those in the same business establishment, whether employer or employed."[37] A new partnership between business and labor was heralded as the "American answer" to industrial conflict. Like good parents or guardians, business leaders were expected to look after the interests of their workers and listen to their grievances before making decisions. In return, labor was expected to abandon the use of militant strike tactics and radical politics.

On the shop floor, however, the partnership between business and labor was never strong, since cooperation and trust were not consistent with the continuation of top-down control and with the further disempowerment and deskilling of workers through new forms of bureaucratic and technical control. One of the dilemmas of advanced capitalism is that business needs the more or less willing cooperation of labor to achieve its goals effectively, yet is driven by opposing pressure further to exploit and dominate labor as a form of human capital in the production process. Since labor resists its further exploitation, the very structuring of the relations of production generates an underlying conflict. The ideology of the "company family" becomes difficult to sustain for extended periods. In the end, the dysfunctions that are generated by current corporate and bureaucratic state modes of organization and control — including high levels of conflict, worker apathy, absenteeism, and declining quality standards — may threaten capitalism less than real worker participation in decisionmaking would. If this is indeed the case, then belief in the "company family" ideology perpetuates a false sense of optimism about the potential for business and labor to cooperate within the context of corporate capitalism.

The ideology of the company family and the company union had a major impact on public education during the progressive era. The various rungs of professional educators that were represented in the hierarchy of state-directed public schools made up the members of the professional-educational family, all supposedly working together — each performing his or her specialized role, based on technical expertise. The dominant force for the promotion of a company family ideology in the schools in the first half of this century was the National Education Association (NEA). Each professional educators' group was organized as a division within the "united" NEA, and all were, in theory, equal. In fact, the NEA reflected in its organizational structure and in its power distribution the inequalities between teachers, administrators, and superintendents. The latter group clearly controlled key leadership positions. As Anthony Cresswell and Michael Murphy report, "the NEA was an integral part of the control mechanism of American public education. . . . It urged school boards and citizens to trust in their professional superintendent and his staff."[38] As late as 1964, on the eve of the collective bargaining era in education, the NEA excluded teachers from positions of influence, even though teachers represented 85 percent of NEA membership. In that year its executive committee of eleven members included only two teachers; its board of trustees of six members had only one teacher; and its 75-member board of directors included only 22 teachers.[39]

Teachers were organized as the single largest division in NEA locals. The locals were, in effect, their company unions. Teachers had no right to bargain with school-district administrators or the school boards. Instead, the NEA supported a system whereby teachers were limited to making requests and pleas. Like children within the educational family, teachers were expected to subordinate their own interests to the larger purposes and interests that educational administrators, state planners, and policymakers supposedly represented. When teachers complained that their concerns were ignored by their bureaucratic superiors, that their grievances were not seriously listened to, or that their salaries were too low, they were accused of being unprofessional, and of placing their own self-interest before the interests of children. Stephen Cole notes in this regard: "For the NEA, professions differed from other occupations in one major respect: the primary goal of professionals was to provide service to clients and the community.... If the members of an occupational group showed too great a concern with financial rewards, their status as professionals would be weakened; hence, early in its history, the NEA claimed that discussions of teacher salaries were 'unprofessional.'"[40] For these and other reasons I will examine shortly, the grand alliance between teachers and administrators began to fail by the early 1960s, with teachers' recognition that they could not trust the bureaucratic school management to look out for teachers' interests. As in industry, state bureaucratic control in public education proved incompatible with notions of cooperation, trust, and partnership between teachers and administrators, and the 1960s witnessed the transformation and rebirth of the NEA as a teachers' union, along the lines of industrial unionism.

Industrial Unionism and the "Great Bargain" in the Schools

While craft and company unionism, as historical and cultural phenomena, are expressions of the interests and beliefs of skilled craft workers and "semi-professionals" or bureaucratized professionals (the situation of teachers), the third form of trade unionism to emerge from American work culture developed first among the ranks of semiskilled assembly line workers, that expanding stratum of the labor force that was virtually created by the technological transformation of production in industry. The prominence, since the 1960s, of industrial-union forms of organization, ideology, and practice among teachers reflects the degree to which teachers have been bureaucratically subordinated and their work deskilled under contemporary forms of schooling. Industrial unionism has its roots in the 1920s, when workers in the new mass-production industries began to organize; but it was not until the 1930s that industrial unionism became a powerful and unpredictable force to be reckoned with by business and the state. This came as a result of the formation of the Congress of Industrial Workers (CIO), under the impact of the period's deteriorating economic conditions.[41] The industrial unions had recognized one fundamental fact of industrial life: while workers, as individuals, exercised less and less control over their work, they exercised considerable collective power to "shut down the line," which they could use to press for certain demands. This is precisely what they did with some success through the tactic of the sit-down strike. In the deteriorating social and economic conditions of the depression, business and labor were caught in an intense struggle, the resolution of which was unclear. The response of the Roosevelt administration, which proved successful in defusing the situation, was to forge a "great bargain" between the two warring camps. Corporate liberals agreed "to accept an enlarged role for the government and to share power with other organized interest groups as a way of ensuring economic stability and the long-term political hegemony of business."[42] Labor was to be formally recognized by business as possessing certain rights, including the rights to organize and to be represented by unions in collective negotiations with management. In return, labor leaders agreed to limit the scope of bargaining to wages and working conditions and not to engage in militant actions like sit-down strikes. While strikes were still technically legal, they were increasingly restricted by state-imposed "cooling off" periods with arbitration or through direct political pressure. The state thus came to play a much more direct role in stabilizing the conflicts of the workplace. In 1936 Congress passed the Wagner Act to formalize the "great bargain" and established the National Labor Relations Board to oversee its terms.

Industrial unionism as we know it today is a direct outgrowth of this great bargain forged in the 1930s, the latest American answer to the "labor problem." The Wagner Act gave labor the legitimacy and formal power that it had long sought. Collective bargaining was thus heralded by most observers as a major victory for labor. It did prove to be moderately successful as a means of pressing labor's economic interests, but only under conditions of an expanding economy. Collective bargaining has not been able to prevent wage rollbacks and worker layoffs in times of recession. Perhaps most significant, industrial unionism — which reached the height of its power in the late 1950s with the merger of the CIO and the older AFL — never really challenged the continuing efforts at deskilling labor through new mass-production technologies or challenged the rights or prerogatives of management to plan, supervise, and evaluate production without input from workers. The industrial-union movement in America has focused much of its energy on realizing for workers a very consumer-oriented conception of the "good life": work itself was not to be overly debilitating and the working environment was to be safe; workers' interests were perceived to lie in maximizing their economic remuneration and (while holding wages constant) minimizing the time and effort expended at work. The "payoff" of the industrial system for workers was to be the promised ever-expanding standard of living, based on an ever-expanding economy. Such a rendering of workers' interests was also in keeping with business interests and business conceptions of labor. It was therefore a very accommodating ideology. It ceases to be accommodating, however, as soon as the system cannot deliver on its promise of an expanding standard of living. Furthermore, while under this system of accommodation bargaining may be formally limited to wages and working conditions, the conflict that lies behind bargaining often spills over into petty disputes and confrontations between management representatives and union representatives that absorb a good deal of time and energy for both parties and that threaten the system's stability.

While the collective bargaining approach to industrial relations has come under increasing pressure in the 1980s, it appeared to be working well in the early 1960s. It is not surprising, therefore, to find that the collective bargaining and industrial-union models were promoted by state leadership as well as by organized labor to formalize relations between public employees and the management of state bureaucratic agencies, including the public schools. The "great bargain" between public employees and the state was also forged by a Democratic president, John Kennedy, who extended collective bargaining rights to federal employees through executive order. With federal backing, the Kennedy executive order was used as a model for similar state- and local-level legislation and executive orders. By the end of the 1960s, most teachers in America had become unionized.

Much of the direct impetus for these changes in the schools and among teachers must be attributed to the efforts of the AFL-CIO. Organized labor was perhaps the most interested of all parties in extending collective bargaining to the public schools, since union membership had begun to decline in the 1950s, with a change in the labor force. Between 1950 and 1960, factory labor had declined from 13 million to 11.5 million workers. Simultaneously, the number of white-collar and professional workers had jumped dramatically from 29 million to 37 million.[43] Although this latter group comprised a full 43 percent of the labor force by 1960, only three percent were unionized.[44] If these trends continued, as they were expected to, organized labor would have to be content to represent a shrinking power base. Consequently, teachers were identified by labor leadership as a "target group" of public employees who could make the most difference in reversing these trend, should they be successfully organized. Walter Reuther, president of the United Auto Workers, declared that "the importance of a growing, active teachers' union to all of organized labor cannot be too greatly stressed";[45] and another union official asked, "How long will a file clerk go on thinking a union is below her dignity, when the teacher next door belongs?"[46] Reuther, and the Industrial Union Department (IUD) he headed within the CIO, were assigned the task of organizing teachers, starting with New York City. With IUD financial and staff support, the United Federation of Teachers (UFT) was organized in New York City and quickly moved to stage a one-day walkout by teachers in 1960 to win the rights to unionize, which they subsequently did. The UFT easily won a follow-up election to decide who would be the sole representative of the city's teachers in collective negotiations with the school board.

Although the efforts of the AFL-CIO were intended to organize teachers under the American Federation of Teachers' banner and gain bargaining rights for AFT affiliates, the effect was to draw the much larger NEA into the battle to represent the nation's teachers in collective bargaining. The NEA leadership was initially confused and hesitant in the face of these rapid developments because it was still officially committed to the idea of a professional association that represented all educators and that presented a united front to the public, even though, as I indicated earlier, the NEA operated, in fact, to contain teachers' grievances within "company union" structures. By the early 1960s, however, there were stirrings within the NEA classroom-teachers division, particularly among urban teachers, who became enthusiastic and encouraged by the militant stance of the UFT in demanding that teachers' rights be recognized. With the backing of these teachers, the secretary treasurer of the IUD, James Carey, was invited to participate as a representative of organized labor in a 1962 convention symposium on "Public Education Tomorrow." He minced few words in challenging teachers to abandon the pursuit of the Holy Grail of professional statutes and to accept trade union perspectives. "One of the prime troubles — if not the chief curse of the teaching *industry* [emphasis mine] is precisely that word 'profession.' That term, as it is used so frequently here, implies that your craft is somewhat above this world of ours; it implies a detachment, a remoteness from the daily battle of the streets, in the neighborhoods and cities."[47] Carey concluded with this comparison: "If the charwomen of the schools have sense enough to band together and organize and negotiate contracts, and the teachers do not, I wonder sometimes who should have the degrees."[48]

By the mid-1960s, the NEA was an association undergoing rapid transformation, with teachers pushing for more control, and with the traditional nonteacher leadership struggling to contain the rising tide of discontent, fearful that teachers might desert the NEA for the pro-collective-bargaining AFT. In an effort to appease teachers, the NEA leadership voted to allow local affiliates to represent teachers as collective bargaining agents, but this only fueled the fires of change, since administrators, superintendents, and supervisory personnel were now placed in the ethically and legally confusing position of bargaining against fellow association members. This led these groups to sever their formal ties to the NEA, a process completed by 1972.[49] Teachers now had their own national, well-organized association for the first time.

The adoption of collective bargaining procedures in education as in industry was viewed initially by many as a victory for organized labor, and teachers in particular. It *was* a victory to the extent that it mobilized teachers around a cause, and it demonstrated that teachers could use their collective power to make the system respond to their interests. In the first several years of collective bargaining in New York City, for example, the UFT was able to increase the average pay of the city teacher by over $1,000.[50] Unfortunately, these initial gains have not continued, and the sense of teacher empowerment fostered in the 1960s has given way to a mood of frustration. In the fiscal crisis of the mid-1970s, which hit local government hardest, teacher associations and unions had to negotiate wage rollbacks and staff cutbacks, which in most cases have not yet been fully overcome.[51] The courts and state legislatures have also moved to restrict strike actions by teachers through binding arbitration requirements and through stiff fines and jail sentences for teachers who participate in strike activity. Finally, the local school budget has lost much of its flexibility in recent years as the funding burden has increasingly shifted to the state level, beyond the direct realm of local collective bargaining. With more and more of the school budget predetermined and regulated by the state, administrators and teachers bargain within a box of fiscal constraints.

Industrial unionism in the schools, then, has not continued to benefit teachers, and it tends to trap teachers in a pattern of narrowly economic demands. Nevertheless, there exist, within industrial unionism, a number of elements representing a potential challenge to the social and political system. First, even a "wage package" orientation towards workers' interests is not to be completely disparaged, because the fight to prevent the permanent depression of teachers' wages below the value of their labor is inextricably linked to other aspects of their proletarianization. As "cheap labor," teachers fall victim to commonsense assumptions about how such cheap labor can or should be treated. Furthermore, teacher unions, like other trade unions, have focused heavily on economic demands primarily because they are limited to such a sphere of bargaining by law. There is little reason to presume that they have voluntarily narrowed their concerns to economic remuneration, even if they have often acquiesced to bargaining on this level. In fact, as I indicated earlier, there is evidence that teachers have sought, with limited success, to expand the scope of bargaining beyond the wage package into the realm of job-control and professional rights.

Another, more important influence of industrial unionism in bringing teachers into confrontation with the capitalist state is that it draws them closer to an identification with the political interests of a broad working-class movement in the United States. Teacher unions have become very active in partisan politics, particularly since the early 1970s, when legislation was passed allowing for the organization of so-called political action committees (PACs) by various interest groups that engage in political lobbying and make campaign contributions.[52] Generally, teacher union PACs, most notably NEA-PAC, have followed the political lead of organized labor. While the objectives of this political agenda do not presently extend beyond support of corporate state welfarism, which is designed to compensate somewhat for the highly inequitable effects of the socioeconomic system, they may become radicalized in times of economic crisis. This is the threat of industrial unionism, and one not taken lightly by corporate and state leaders. Teachers have resorted to militancy in the past to back up their demands, and even in the relatively calm 1980s, there is evidence among teachers of deep discontent, frustration, and anger that threaten to lead to militant job actions.

CONCLUSION:
TEACHERS' WORK AND THE DILEMMA OF SCHOOL REFORM

I have moved in this essay from a discussion of teachers as agents of an oppressive schooling process to an examination of teachers as oppressed workers within the bureaucratic organization of the schools, and I have suggested that these two phenomena — the oppressive role of teaching in advanced capitalist society and the fact that teachers are bureaucratically oppressed — are linked in complex ways. Most basically, if reproductive work in the schools entails a good deal of "dirty work," such as disciplining, disempowering, and sorting students, then the social and political system must carefully circumscribe the role of the teacher in an attempt to ensure that teachers do not resist or alter their role in the reproductive processes. I have also suggested that teachers, both individually and, more significantly, as an occupational group, have not been passive automatons in the face of the changes that have transformed public education in this century; they have resisted in various ways that are at least potentially consistent with democratic Left political principles. In their collectivity and in their solidarity with other groups of workers and oppressed peoples, teachers potentially represent a serious challenge to the dominant reproductive goals of schooling in advanced capitalism. Teachers' collective occupational culture therefore presents itself as an important research concern in the critical theory of schooling. Teachers have too often been treated in a deterministic and functional manner by critical theorists, and this has led to an over-pessimistic appraisal of their real or potential role in social and political conflicts and movements. In order to overcome these problems in the critical theory of schooling, we need to direct much more of our attention to specific areas of potential conflict between labor and capital in the schools, and we need to document the simultaneous influence of both accommodative and countervailing ideologies and practices among teachers as they have historically developed.

In this brief concluding section, let me attempt to locate teachers as political actors within the most recent round of reform proposals in education, sparked by various corporate and state-sponsored commission reports over the past several years. Beginning with *A Nation at Risk,* all of these reports focus, in one way or another, on the "crisis of excellence" in public education.[52] From a critical perspective, the reports indicate that elite social, political, and economic groups are concerned that the schools are not adequately serving a reproductive function. The present system of bureaucratized control has been associated with a culture of mediocrity among both teachers and students, a high school dropout rate of nearly 50 percent for minority and economically disadvantaged students, an inability to attract and hold "the best and the brightest" in teaching, and a continuing conflict between teachers and administrators that undermines the smooth operation of the system. Obviously, then, reproductive processes are not carried out in a smooth, uncontested manner in the schools, and they are accomplished only at a substantial price. The state system of bureaucratic schooling is crippled, but it limps along, attempting to ward off each new crisis.

Two basic lines of reform are open to elite corporate and state groups to help deal with endemic system dysfunctions. The first of these is repressive: with regard to teachers, it implies, following *A Nation at Risk,* more top-down accountability and more use of "output" standards of student achievement to evaluate and differentially reward teachers. One problem with more top-down accountability, and consequently more subordination of teachers and students to the managerial work plan, is that it generates more discontent and further alienates teachers and students from managerial goals.

The other option for reform open to elite groups is based on a recognition that the "human factor" remains essential to effective education, and that in order to attract, hold, and encourage excellent teachers, we will need to improve dramatically the conditions of their work. Generally, this line of reform is associated with moves to treat teachers more "professionally." On the surface it seems to be based on sound reasoning. A good example of this liberal line of reasoning is provided by the recent Carnegie Forum report entitled, *A Nation Prepared: Teachers for the Twenty-First Century.*[54] The report proclaims: "Teachers must think for themselves if they are to help others think for themselves, be able to act independently and collaborate with others, and render critical judgment. They must be people whose knowledge is wide-ranging and whose understanding runs deep" (p. 44). The report recognizes that without fundamental changes in teachers' working conditions, tensions and conflicts and teacher "burnout" will prove to be persistent phenomena: "Many of the best people now staffing our schools . . . are immensely frustrated — to the point of cynicism. . . . They see the bureaucratic structure within which they work becoming even more limited. . . . Their work roles and the conditions under which many of them work more nearly resemble those of semi-skilled workers on the assembly line rather than those of professionals" (p. 46). The report concludes, however, on a note of optimism. Surely, it implies, now that everyone can see what should be done — that teachers should be treated more as professionals — fundamental change is at hand. Although "far-reaching changes in our schools and in educational policy" will be needed, "there is every reason to be optimistic about the country meeting the challenge" (p. 46).

The optimism of the Carnegie Forum report and of this general line of reform is, I think, ill-founded, for it lacks an analysis of the impediments that stand in the way of the humanistic and teacher-empowering types of reform they propose. It implies that given enough political leadership and popular support, nothing stands in the way of reorganizing the schools along radically new lines. Yet, as I have suggested throughout this essay, the organization of schools is powerfully constrained by the role they serve in reproducing the structured inequalities and **ideologies of domination**[e] typical of advanced capitalist society. Reproductive work necessitates a great deal of top-down control, including the bureaucratic subordination of teachers. The paradox of reform under existing conditions is that the system cannot create the conditions most suitable to the pursuit of excellence by teachers and students without giving teachers and students much more control over the schooling process; and there is no assurance that teachers and students will then use their newfound power, or define excellence, in ways that are consistent with corporate and state interests. Neither can the system afford the economic concessions needed to maintain a more fully professional work force. A democratic Left perspective must insist that while the system may be humanized somewhat under existing political and economic conditions, strong pressures will exist to reassert top-down bureaucratic control and disempower teachers (along with students) within the schooling process. We will need to move beyond the priorities and social organizational forms of U.S. industrial capitalism in order to implement more basic changes. A single institution like the schools cannot be restructured at will independent of a restructuring of other important institutions — including the economic and political.

I have indicated that there is some reason to believe that teachers might participate in the articulation of an alternative voice for change in the schools and the broader society that goes beyond the limits of current corporate and state models. At present, the elements of teachers' occupational interests that are potentially countervailing to the capitalist state remain largely depoliticized and poorly linked. However, there is no reason to expect that they will remain so indefinitely. Teacher trade unionism, for all of its limitations, remains a powerful force for the development of a radical ideology and practice among teachers, especially if the fiscal crisis of the state deepens in the years ahead. In the meantime, progressive-minded teachers can work on the individual level to test the limits of classroom organization and curriculum control, and consciously strive to lessen the reproductive role they assume with the schooling process by encouraging critical, creative work among their students. On the collective occupational level, teachers can build on **countervailing ideologies**[f] and practices that already exist within teacher unionism and professionalism as forms of work

---

[e] **Dominant ideologies** are bodies of ideas held by cultural groups that are politically, socially, and economically in positions of power and are therefore able to impose on the greater society, through various social institutions and practices, particular traditions, bodies of knowledge, discourse styles, language uses, values, norms, and beliefs, usually at the expense of others.

[f] **Countervailing ideologies (also referred to as "counter-discourses") are** languages of critique, demystification, and agency capable of contesting dominant oppressive beliefs and practices.

culture and attempt better to link and politicize issues related to teachers' work and the structuring and direction of public education. Only by critically reflecting on their own roles in the schooling process, theorizing about what could be, and working to promote specific changes consistent with a broad vision of a just society, can teachers expand and realize their capacity to challenge the status quo in ways that are transformative rather than merely reformist.

NOTES

1. Ivan Illich, *De-Schooling Society* (New York: Harper & Row, 1970).
2. Louis Althusser, "Ideology and Ideological State Apparatuses," in his *Lenin and Philosophy and Other Essays* (London: New Left Books, 1971).
3. Paul Willis, *Learning to Labour: How Working Class Kids Get Working Class Jobs* (Westmead, Eng.: Saxon House, 1977).
4. Revisionist histories include, for example, Michael Katz, *Class, Bureaucracy and Education* (Cambridge: Harvard University Press, 1968) and Joel Spring, *Education and the Rise of the Corporate State* (Boston: Beacon Press, 1972) and *The Sorting Machine: National Educational Policy Since 1945* (New York: McKay, 1976). A concise statement of the revisionist perspective on schooling is provided by Clarence Karier in his foreword to Robert Everhart, ed., *The Public School Monopoly: A Critical Analysis of Education and the State in American Society* (Cambridge: Ballinger Books, 1981).
5. Illich, *De-Schooling Society.*
6. Everhart, *Public School Monopoly.*
7. Everhart, "Leftist Agendas, Educational Vouchers: Toward a Critical Appraisal," *Interchange,* 14(3) (1983), 46–64.
8. Althusser, "Ideology and Ideological State Apparatuses"; Poulantzas, *Classes in Contemporary Capitalism* (London: New Left Books, 1975); Bowles and Gintis, *Schooling in Capitalist American* (New York: Basic Books, 1976); and Braverman, *Labour and Monopoly Capital* (London: Monthly Review Press, 1974).
9. Bowles and Gintis, *Schooling in Capitalist America,* p. 9.
10. Poulantzas uses the term "new petit bourgeoisie." See also Guglielmo Carchedi, *On the Economic Identification of Social Classes* (New York: Routledge & Kegan Paul, 1977) and Barbara Ehrenreich, "The Professional-Managerial Class," in *Between Labor and Capital,* ed. Paul Walker (Montreal: Black Rose, 1978), pp. 5–48.
11. Harris, *Teachers and Classes: A Marxist Analysis* (New York: Routledge & Kegan Paul, 1982), p. 90.
12. Walker, "Introduction," *Between Labor and Capital,* p. xix.
13. Cited by Bowles and Gintis in *Schooling in Capitalist America,* p. 40.
14. Braverman, *Labour and Monopoly Capital.*
15. Bowles and Gintis, *Schooling in Capitalist America,* p. 204.
16. For a discussion of the deskilling of teaching through new curricular technologies, see Michael Apple, "Curricular Form and the Logic of Technical Control," in *Ideology and the Practice in Schooling,* ed. Apple and Lois Weis (Philadelphia: Temple University Press, 1983), pp. 143–166, and Dennis Carlson, "'Updating' Individualism and the Work Ethic: Corporate Logic in the Classroom," *Curriculum Inquiry,* 12 (1982), 125–160.
17. Harris, *Teachers and Classes,* p. 73.
18. Apple, "Work, Gender and Teaching," *Teachers College Record,* 84, 1982 p. 618.
19. Apple, "Work, Gender and Teaching," p. 618.

20. According to Linda Darling-Hammond, (*Beyond the Commission Reports: The Coming Crisis in Education*, Santa Monica, CA: Rand Corporation, 1984), teacher salaries are well below those for most other occupations requiring a college degree, and have declined 15 percent in real dollar terms over the past decade.
21. Council for Basic Education, *Making Do in the Classroom: A Report on the Misassignment of Teachers* (Washington, DC, 1985) and Fred Hechinger, "'Dirty Little Secret' of Unlicensed Teachers," *New York Times*, 8 Oct. 1985, p. C-8.
22. The issue as to how much relative autonomy the state has in carrying out its role within advanced capitalist society is one of considerable dispute among neo-Marxists. For a discussion of this, see Ralph Miliband, "State Power and Class Interests," *New Left Review, 138* (March-April 1983), 57–68.
23. Wexler, "Ideology and Education: From Critique to Class Action," *Interchange, 13*(3) (1982), 53–68.
24. Sarup, *Education, State, and Crisis: A Marxist Perspective* (New York: Routledge & Kegan Paul, 1982), p. 49.
25. Connell, *Which Way Is Up? Essays on Sex, Class, and Culture*, in chap. 3, "Crisis Tendencies in Patriarchy and Capitalism" (London: Allen & Unwin, 1983), p. 36.
26. See Erik O. Wright, "Giddens' Critique of Marxism," *New Left Review, 138* (March-April 1983), 11–35.
27. Willis, *Learning to Labour;* see also Michael Apple, ed., *Cultural and Economic Reproduction in Education: Essays on Class, Ideology, and the State* (New York: Routledge & Kegan Paul, 1982).
28. Genovese, *Roll, Jordan, Roll: The World the Slaves Made* (New York: Vintage, 1972); Anyon, "Intersections of Gender and Class: Accommodation and Resistance by Working-Class and Affluent Females to Contradictory Sex-Role Ideologies," in *Gender, Class, and Education*, ed. Sandra Walker and Len Barton (Barcombe, Eng.: Falmer Press, 1983), pp. 19–38.
29. Willis, *Learning to Labour*, p. 119.
30. Willis, *Learning to Labour*, p. 119.
31. Wolcott, *Teachers versus Technocrats: An Educational Innovation in Anthropological Perspective* (Eugene: University of Oregon Press, 1977).
32. Anyon, "Intersections of Gender and Class," p. 34.
33. Marx laid the foundation for both "pessimistic" and "optimistic" appraisals of the trade union movement. He observed: "Trade Unions work well as centers of resistance against the encroachments of capital"; however, "they fail generally from limiting themselves to a guerrilla war against the effects of the existing system, instead of simultaneously trying to change it" (cited in Joseph A. Banks, *Marxist Sociology in Action: A Sociological Critique of the Marxist Approach to Industrial Relations* [London: Faber & Faber, 1970], p. 48). In traditional U.S. labor history, as exemplified by John Commons, "American Shoemaker, 1648 to 1895" in *Labor and Administration* (New York: Kelley, 1913/1964), pp. 219–266 and Selig Perlman, *A Theory of the Labor Movement* (New York: Macmillan, 1928), trade unions are treated simply as self-interested economic organizations for workers, with little potential for socialist political action. More recently in America, scholarship on the labor movement has been strongly influenced by C. Wright Mills's *The New Men of Power: America's Labor Leaders* (New York: Harcourt Brace, 1948) and "The Labor Leaders and the Power Elite," in *Industrial Conflict*, ed. Arthur Kornhauser et al. (New York: McGraw-Hill, 1954). Mills argued that rather than form a power block independent of corporate and state interests, labor leaders have been coopted into the "power elite" and have served as "managers of discontent." Finally, some recent labor historians have begun to reassert a more optimistic view of the labor movement in America, including David Milton's *The Politics of U.S. Labor: From the Great Depression to the New Deal* (New York: Monthly

Review Press, 1982) and David Montgomery's *Workers' Control in America: Studies in the History of Work, Technology, and Labor Struggles* (New York: Cambridge University Press, 1979). Milton writes: "The potential always exists that trade unions might become political. The present rulers of Poland understand precisely the significance of this truth" (p. 14).

34. For a discussion of craft unionism in America, see Banks, *Marxist Sociology in Action*, pp. 250–266; Susan Hirsch, *Roots of the American Working Class: The Industrialization of Crafts in Newark, 1800–1860* (Philadelphia: University of Pennsylvania Press, 1978); Montgomery, *Workers' Control in America*, pp. 8–90; and Perlman, *Theory of the Labor Movement*, pp. 155–236.
35. See Walter Bailey and David Neale, "Teachers and School Improvement," *Educational Forum*, 45 (Nov. 1980), 69–76, and Joan Retsinas, "Teachers: Bargaining for Control," *American Educational Research Journal*, 19 (1982), 353–372.
36. Company unionism is the term used by Perlman (p. 21) and by Richard Henry Tawney in *The American Labour Movement and Other Essays* (New York: St. Martin's Press, 1979), p. 59.
37. Perlman, *Theory of the Labor Movement*, p. 211.
38. Cresswell and Murphy, *Teachers, Unions, and Collective Bargaining in Public Education* (Berkeley: McCutchan, 1980), p. 97.
39. Michael Moskow, "Teacher Organizations: An Analysis of Issues," in *Readings on Collective Negotiations in Education*, ed. Myron Lieberman and Michael Moskow (Chicago: Rand McNally, 1967), p. 243.
40. Cole, *The Unionization of Teachers: A Case Study of the UFT* (New York: Praeger, 1969), p. 4.
41. Tawney, *American Labour Movement*, pp. 46–47.
42. Steve Fraser, "From the 'New Unionism' to the New Deal," *Labor History*, 25 (1984), 407.
43. Cole, *Unionization of Teachers*, p. 165.
44. Allan West, *The National Education Association: The Power Base for Education* (New York: Free Press, 1980), p. 54.
45. West, *National Education Association*, p. 55.
46. West, *National Education Association*, p. 55.
47. National Education Association, *Addresses and Proceedings of the Representative Assembly* (Washington, DC, 1962), p. 52.
48. NEA, *Address and Proceedings*, p. 52.
49. West, *National Education Association*, pp. 74, 84.
50. Cole, *Unionization of Teachers*, p. 21.
51. For a study of the effects of fiscal crisis in New York City, see Joan Weitzman, *City Workers and Fiscal Crisis: Cutbacks, Givebacks, and Survival* (New Brunswick: Rutgers University Press, 1979).
52. David Stephens, "President Carter, the Congress, and the NEA: Creating the Department of Education," *Political Science Quarterly*, 98 (1983–84), p. 644.
53. The National Commission on Excellence, *A Nation at Risk: The Imperative for Educational Reform* (Washington, DC: U.S. Government Printing Office, 1983).
54. Excerpts from the report by the Carnegie Forum's Task Force on Teaching as a Profession, *A Nation Prepared: Teachers for the Twenty-First Century*, in *Chronicles of Higher Education*, 21 May 1986, pp. 43–51.

14

Teacher Education and the Politics of Engagement: The Case for Democratic Schooling

HENRY A. GIROUX and PETER McLAREN

Although many of the authors in this volume have pointed to the dire need for teacher education programs to foster the development of critical and socially responsible educators, Henry Giroux and Peter McLaren argue that many of the recently recommended public school reforms either sidestep or abandon the principles underlying education for a democratic citizenry. Yet, these authors contend that the historical precedent, set by John Dewey and others in the early part of this century, suggests ways of reconceptualizing teaching and public schooling that revive the values of democracy, citizenship, and social justice. They demonstrate that teachers, as "transformative intellectuals," can reclaim space in schools for the exercise of critical citizenship via ethical and political discourses that recast, in liberatory terms, the relationships among authority and teacher work, and schooling and the social order. Moreover, the authors outline a teacher education curriculum that links the critical study of power, language, culture, and history to the practice of a critical pedagogy, one that values student experience and student voice.

As far back as 1890, a teacher from New England named Horace Willard cogently argued that in contrast to members of other professions, teachers lived "lives of mechanical routine, and were subjected to a machine of supervision, organization, classification, grading, percentages, uniformity, promotions, tests, examination."[1] Nowhere, Willard decried, was there room in the school culture for "Individuality, ideas, independence, originality, study, investigation."[2] Forty years later Henry W. Holmes, dean of Harvard University's new Graduate School of Education, echoed these sentiments in his criticism of the National Survey of the Education of Teachers in 1930. According to Holmes, the survey failed to support teachers as independent critical thinkers. Instead, it endorsed a view of the teacher as a "routine worker under the expert direction of principals, supervisors, and superintendents."[3] Holmes was convinced that if teachers' work continued to be defined in such a narrow fashion, schools of education would eventually respond by limiting themselves to forms of training that virtually undermined the development of teachers as critically-minded intellectuals.

At different times both of these noteworthy critics of American education recognized that any viable attempt at educational reform must address the issue of teacher education. Most important was their conviction that teachers should function professionally as intellectuals, and that teacher education should be inextricably linked to critically transforming the school setting and, by extension, the wider social setting.

In the early part of the century, a number of experimental teacher education programs managed to shift the terrain of struggle for democratic schooling from a largely rhetorical platform to the program site itself. One such program was organized around New College, an experimental teacher training venture affiliated with Columbia University, Teachers College between 1927 and 1953. Spokespersons from New College proclaimed "that a sound teacher education program must lie in a proper integration of rich scholarship, educational theory, and professional practice."[4] Furthermore, New College embarked on a training program based on the principle that "it is the peculiar privilege of the teacher to play a large part in the development of the social order of the next generation."[5] The College's first announcement claimed that if teachers were to escape from the usual "academic lock step . . . [they] required contact with life in its various phases and understanding of it — an understanding of the intellectual, moral, social, and economic life of the people."[6]

The idea that teacher education programs should center their academic and moral objectives on the education of teachers as critical intellectuals, while simultaneously advancing democratic interests, has invariably influenced the debates revolving around the various "crises" in education over the last fifty years.[7] Moreover, it has been precisely because of the presence of such an idea that a rationale eventually could be constructed which linked schooling to the imperatives of democracy and classroom pedagogy to the dynamics of citizenship. This is not to suggest, however, that either public education or teacher training programs were overburdened by a concern for democracy and citizenship.[8] Nevertheless, the historical precedent for educating teachers as intellectuals and developing schools as democratic sites for social transformation might begin to define the way in which public education and the education of teachers *could* be appropriately perceived today. We wish, in other words, to build upon this precedent in order to argue for the education of teachers as transformative intellectuals. We use the term "intellectual" in the manner described by Frank Lentricchia:

> By "intellectual" I do not mean what traditional Marxism has generally meant — a bearer of the universal, the political conscience of us all. Nor do I mean "a radical intellectual" in the narrowest of understandings of Antonio Gramsci — an intellectual whose practice is overtly, daily aligned with and empirically involved in the working class. By intellectual I refer to the *specific intellectual* described by Foucault — one whose radical work of transformation, whose fight against repression is carried on at the specific institutional site where he finds himself and on the terms of his own expertise, on the terms inherent to his own functioning as an intellectual.[9]

By the term "transformative intellectual," we refer to one who exercises forms of intellectual and pedagogical practice which attempt to insert teaching and learning directly into the political sphere by arguing that schooling represents both a struggle for meaning and a struggle over power relations. We are also referring to one whose intellectual practices are necessarily grounded in forms of moral and ethical discourse exhibiting a preferential concern for the suffering and struggles of the disadvantaged and oppressed. Here we extend the traditional view of the intellectual as someone who is able to analyze various interests and contradictions within society to someone capable of articulating emancipatory possibilities and working towards their realization. Teachers who assume the role of transformative intellectuals treat students as critical agents, question how knowledge is produced and distributed, utilize **dialogue,**[a] and make knowledge meaningful, critical, and ultimately emancipatory.[10]

We argue in this paper that within the current discourse on educational reform[11] there exists, with few exceptions,[12] an ominous silence regarding the role that both teacher education and public schooling should play in advancing democratic practices, critical citizenship, and the role of the teacher as intellectual. Given the legacy of democracy and social reform bequeathed to us by our educational forebears, such as John Dewey and George Counts, this silence not only suggests that some of the current reformers are suffering from political and **historical amnesia;**[b] it also points to the ideological interests that underlie their proposals. Regrettably, such in-

---

[a] As defined by Donaldo Macedo and Paulo Freire, **dialogue** "as a process of learning and knowing must always involve a political project with the objective of dismantling oppressive structures and mechanisms prevalent both in education and society" (p. 203). Thus, the sharing of experiences with others should not be understood in psychological terms alone, but needs to be infused with an ideological analysis and a political project capable of eradicating oppressive practices and institutions both in education and society.

[b] This term implies that people develop a limited and limiting sense of history through the socialization process in which selective historical memories are imposed. **Historical amnesia** is used to explain how negative and or dangerous memories that threaten or question the status

terests tell us less about the ills of schooling than they do about the nature of the real crisis facing this nation — a crisis which, in our view, not only augurs poorly for the future of American education, but underscores the need to reclaim a democratic tradition presently in retreat. Bluntly stated, much of the current literature on educational reform points to a crisis in American democracy itself.

The discourse of recent educational reform characteristically excludes certain proposals from consideration. For instance, missing from the various privileged discourses that have fashioned the recent reform movement, and absent among the practices of public school teachers whose participation in the current debate on education has been less than vigorous, are concerted attempts at democratizing schools and empowering students to become critical, active citizens. This reluctance on the part of teachers has had a particularly deleterious effect, since the absence of proposals for rethinking the purpose of schools of education around democratic concerns has further strengthened the ideological and political pressures that define teachers as **technicians**[c] and structure teacher work in a demeaning and overburdening manner. Kenneth Zeichner underscores this concern when he writes:

> It is hoped that future debate in teacher education will be more concerned with the question of which educational, moral and political commitments ought to guide our work in the field rather than with the practice of merely dwelling on which procedures and organizational arrangements will most effectively help us realize tacit and often unexamined ends. Only after we have begun to resolve some of these necessarily prior questions related to ends should we concentrate on the resolution of more instrumental issues related to effectively accomplishing our goals.[13]

The current debate provides an opportunity to critically analyze the ideological and material conditions — both in and out of schools — that contribute to teacher passivity and powerlessness. We also believe that recognition of the failure to link the purposes of public schooling to the imperatives of economic and social reform provides a starting point both for examining the ideological shift in education that has taken place in the 1980s and for developing a new language of democracy, empowerment, and possibility in which teacher education programs and classroom practices can be defined.

---

quo are excluded from public consciousness and classroom inquiry. How, for example, do the histories of women, Blacks, Native Americans, working-class groups, and others whose past experiences contradict the "moral foundation" of the existing dominant structures of society get eliminated or simply rewritten? Critical pedagogy calls for the resurrection of such memories and buried knowledge for the purpose of creating more critically democratic societies.

[c] Emanating from the positivist tradition, technocratic models, which conceptualize teaching and learning as a discrete and scientific undertaking, embrace depersonalized methods for educating students that often translate into the regulation and standardization of teacher practices and curricula, and rote memorization of selected "facts" that can easily be measured through standardized testing. As such, the role of the teacher is reduced to that of a **technician** — an uncritical, "objective," and "efficient" distributor of information.

Our central concern is in developing a view of teacher education that defines teachers as transformative intellectuals and schooling as part of an ongoing struggle for democracy. In developing our argument, we will focus on four considerations. First, we will analyze the dominant new conservative positions that have generated current educational reforms in terms of the implications these viewpoints hold for the reorganization of teacher education programs. Second, we will develop a rationale for organizing teacher education programs around a critical view of teacher work and authority, one that we believe is consistent with the principles and practices of democracy. Third, we will present some programmatic suggestions for analyzing teacher education as a form of cultural politics. Finally, we will argue for a critical pedagogy that draws upon the many-sided conversations and voices that make up community life.

EDUCATION REFORM AND THE RETREAT FROM DEMOCRACY

Underlying the educational reforms proposed by the recent coalition of conservatives and liberals, conveniently labeled "the new conservatives," is a discourse that both edifies and mystifies their proposals. Capitalizing upon the waning confidence of the general public and a growing number of teachers in the effectiveness of public schools, the new conservatives argue for educational reform by faulting schools for a series of crises that include everything from a growing trade deficit to the breakdown of family morality.[14] As is the case with many public issues in the age of Ronald Reagan, the new conservatives have seized the initiative by framing their arguments in a terse rhetoric that resonates with a growing public concern about downward mobility in hard economic times, that appeals to a resurgence of chauvinistic patriotism, and that points toward a reformulation of educational goals along elitist lines. Such a discourse is dangerous not only because it misconstrues the responsibility schools have for wider economic and social problems — a position that has been convincingly refuted and need not be argued against here[15] — but also because it reflects an alarming ideological shift regarding the role schools should play in relation to society. The effect of this shift, launched by the new right's full-fledged attack on the educational and social reforms of the 1960s, has been to redefine the purpose of education so as to eliminate its citizenship function in favor of a narrowly defined labor market perspective. The essence and implications of this position have been well-documented by Barbara Finkelstein.

> Contemporary reformers seem to be recalling public education from its traditional utopian mission — to nurture a critical and committed citizenry that would stimulate the processes of political and cultural transformation and refine and extend the workings of political democracy.... Reformers seem to imagine public schools as economic rather than political instrumentalities. They forge no new visions of political and social possibilities.

> Instead, they call public schools to industrial and cultural service exclusively.... Reformers have disjoined their calls for educational reform from calls for a redistribution of power and authority, and the cultivation of cultural forms celebrating pluralism and diversity. As if they have had enough of political democracy, Americans, for the first time in a one hundred and fifty-year history, seem ready to do ideological surgery on their public schools — cutting them away from the fate of social justice and political democracy completely and grafting them onto elite corporate, industrial, military, and cultural interests.[16]

It is important to recognize that the new conservative attack on the reforms of the last decade has resulted in a shift away from defining schools as agencies of equity and justice. There is little concern with how public education could better serve the interests of diverse groups of students by enabling them to understand and gain some control over the sociopolitical forces that influence their destinies. Rather, via this new discourse, and its preoccupation with accountability schemes, testing, accreditation, and credentializing, educational reform has become synonymous with turning schools into "company stores." It now defines school life primarily by measuring its utility against its contribution to economic growth and cultural uniformity. Similarly, at the heart of the present ideological shift is an attempt to reformulate the purpose of public education around a set of interests and social relations that define academic success almost exclusively in terms of the accumulation of capital and the logic of the marketplace. This represents a shift away from teacher control of the curriculum and toward a fundamentally technicist form of education that is more directly tied to economic modes of production. Moreover, the new conservatives provide a view of society in which authority derives from technical expertise and culture embodies an idealized tradition that glorifies hard work, industrial discipline, **domesticated**[d] desire, and cheerful obedience. Edward Berman has deftly captured the political nature of this ideological shift.

> Architects of the current reform have, to their credit, dropped the rhetoric about the school as a vehicle for personal betterment. There is little pretense in today's reports or the resultant programs that individual improvement and social mobility are important concerns of a reconstituted school system. The former rhetoric about individual mobility has given way to exhortations to build educational structures that will allow individual students to make a greater contribution to the economic output of the corporate state. There are few rhetorical flourishes to obfuscate this overriding objective.[17]

---

[d] The term **domesticate** refers to the process by which people learn to internalize the dominant values and behaviors that render individuals and groups unable, or unwilling, to recognize oppressive practices. Similar concepts: *manufacture consent, anesthetize, colonize the mind.*

The ideological shift that characterizes the current reform period is also evident in the ways in which teacher preparation and classroom pedagogy are currently being defined. The rash of reform proposals for reorganizing schools points to a definition of teacher work that seriously exacerbates conditions which are presently eroding the authority and intellectual integrity of teachers. In fact, the most compelling aspect of the influential reports, especially the widely publicized *A Nation at Risk, Action for Excellence,* and *A Nation Prepared: Teachers for the 21st Century,* is their studious refusal to address the ideological, social, and economic conditions underlying poor teacher and student performance.[18] For example, as Frankenstein and Louis Kampf point out, public school teachers constantly confront conditions "such as the overwhelming emphasis on quantification (both in scoring children and keeping records), the growing lack of control over curriculum (separating conception from execution) and over other aspects of their work, the isolation from their peers, the condescending treatment by administrators, and the massive lay-offs of veteran teachers."[19]

Instead of addressing these issues, many of the reforms taking place at the state level further consolidate administrative structures and prevent teachers from collectively and creatively shaping the conditions under which they work. For instance, at both the local and federal levels, the new educational discourse has influenced a number of policy recommendations, such as competency-based testing for teachers, a lockstep sequencing of materials, mastery learning techniques, systematized evaluation schemes, standardized curricula, and the implementation of mandated "basics."[20] The consequences are evident not only in the substantively narrow view of the purposes of education, but also in the definitions of teaching, learning, and literacy that are championed by the new management-oriented experience, and fostering active and critical citizenship, schools are redefined through a language that emphasizes standardization, competency, and narrowly-defined performance skills.

Within this paradigm, the development of curricula is increasingly left to administrative experts or simply adopted from publishers, with few, if any, contributions from teachers who are expected to implement the new programs. In its most ideologically offensive form, this type of prepackaged curriculum is rationalized as teacher-proof and is designed to be applied to any classroom context regardless of the historical, cultural, and socioeconomic differences that characterize various schools and students.[21] What is important to note is that the deskilling of teachers appears to go hand-in-hand with the increasing adoption of management-type pedagogies.

> Viewing teachers as semiskilled, low-paid workers in the mass production of education, policymakers have sought to change education, to improve it, by "teacher-proofing" it. Over the past decade we have seen the proliferation of elaborate accountability schemes that go by acronyms like MBO (management by objectives), PBBS (performance-based budgeting sys-

tems), CBE (competency-based education), CBTE (competency-based teacher education), and MCT (minimum competency testing).[22]

The growing removal of curriculum development and analysis from the hands of teachers is related to the ways technocratic rationality is used to redefine teacher work. This type of rationality increasingly takes place within a social division of labor in which thinking is removed from implementation and the model of the teacher becomes that of the technician or white-collar clerk. Likewise, learning is reduced to the memorization of narrowly defined facts and isolated pieces of information that can easily be measured and evaluated. The significance of the overall effects of this type of rationalization and bureaucratic control on teacher work and morale has been forcefully articulated by Linda Darling-Hammond. She writes:

> In a Rand study of teachers' views of the effect of educational policies on their classroom practices, we learned from teachers that in response to policies that prescribe teaching practices and outcomes, they spend less time on untested subjects, such as science and social studies; they use less writing in their classrooms in order to gear assignments to the format of standardized tests; they resort to lectures rather than classroom discussions in order to cover the prescribed behavioral objectives without getting "off the track"; they are precluded from using teaching materials that are not on prescribed textbook lists, even when they think these materials are essential to meet the needs of some of their students; and they feel constrained from following up on expressed student interests that lie outside of the bounds of mandated curricula. . . . And 45 percent of the teachers in this study told us that the single thing that would make them leave teaching was the increased prescriptiveness of teaching content and methods — in short, the continuing deprofessionalization of teaching.[23]

The ideological interests that inform the new conservative proposals are based on a view of morality and politics that is legitimated through an appeal to custom, national unity, and tradition. Within this discourse, democracy loses its dynamic character and is reduced to a set of inherited principles and institutional arrangements that teach students how to adapt rather than to question the basic precepts of society. What is left in the new reform proposals is a view of authority constructed around a mandate to follow and implement predetermined rules, to transmit an unquestioned cultural tradition, and to sanctify industrial discipline. Couple these problems with large classes, excessive paperwork, fragmented work periods, and low salaries, and it comes as no surprise that teachers are increasingly leaving the field.[24]

In effect, the ideological shift at work here points to a restricted definition of schooling, one that almost completely strips public education of a democratic vision where citizenship and the politics of possibility are given serious consideration. When we argue that the recent conservative or "blue-ribbon" reform recommendations lack a politics of possibility and citizenship, we mean that primacy is given to education as economic investment, that is, to pedagogical practices designed to create a school-business partnership and make the American economic system more competitive in world markets. A politics of possibility and citizenship, by contrast, refers to a conception of schooling in which classrooms are seen as active sites of public intervention and social struggle. Moreover, this view maintains that possibilities exist for teachers and students to redefine the nature of critical learning and practice outside of the imperatives of the corporate marketplace. The idea of a politics and project of possibility is grounded in Ernst Bloch's idea of "natural law" wherein "the standpoint of the victims of any society ought to always provide the starting point for the critique of that society."[25] Such a politics defines schools as sites around which struggles should be waged in the name of developing a more just, humane, and equitable social order both within and outside of schools.

We have spent some time analyzing the new conservative discourse and the ideological shift it represents because in our view the current reforms, with few exceptions, pose a grave threat to both public schooling and the nature of democracy itself. The definition of teaching and learning provided by this discourse ignores, as we have pointed out, the imperative of viewing schools as sites of social transformation where students are educated to become informed, active, and critical citizens. The gravity of this ideological shift is hardly ameliorated by the fact that even public schooling's more liberal spokespersons have failed to develop a critical discourse that challenges the **hegemony**[e] of **dominant ideologies.**[f] For example, the highly publicized reports by John Goodlad, Theodore Sizer, Ernest Boyer, and others neither acknowledge nor utilize the radical tradition of educational scholarship.[26] While the liberal position does take the concepts of equality of opportunity and citizenship seriously, we are, nevertheless, left with analyses of schooling that lack a sufficiently critical understanding of the ways in which power has been used to favor select groups of students over others. In addition, we are given only a cursory treatment of the political economy of schooling, with its scattered history of dishonorable linkages to corporate interests and ideology. Furthermore, we are provided with little understanding of how the **hidden curriculum**[g] in schools works in a subtly discrimi-

---

[e] **Hegemony**, as derived from the work of Italian theorist Antonio Gramsci, is used to express how certain groups manage to dominate others. An analysis of hegemony is especially concerned with how the imposition of particular ideologies and forms of authority results in the reproduction of social and institutional practices through which dominant groups maintain not only their positions of privilege and control, but also the consensual support of other members of society.

[f] **Dominant ideologies** are bodies of ideas held by cultural groups that are politically, socially, and economically in positions of power and are therefore able to impose on the greater society, through various social institutions and practices, particular traditions, bodies of knowledge, discourse styles, language uses, values, norms, and beliefs, usually at the expense of others.

[g] This refers to the unspoken agenda in schools that socializes students into the dominant ideology and discourse in which they become uncritical tools of the work force. The **hidden**

nating way to discredit the dreams, experiences, and knowledges associated with students from specific class, racial, and gender groupings.[27]

In the absence of any competing critical agenda for reform, the new conservative discourse encourages teacher education institutions to define themselves primarily as training sites that provide students with the technical expertise required to find a place within the corporate hierarchy. Thomas Popkewitz and Allan Pitman have characterized the ideology underlying the current reform proposals, moreover, as betraying a fundamental elitism since it basically adopts a perspective of society that is undifferentiated by class, race, or gender. The logic endemic to these reports, the authors argue, demonstrates an attachment to possessive individualism and instrumental rationality. In other words: "Quantity is seen as quality. Procedural concerns are made objects of value and moral domains. The teacher is a facilitator . . . or a counselor. . . . Individualization is pacing through a common curriculum. . . . Flexibility in instruction is to begin 'where the student is ready to begin'. . . . There is no discussion of what is to be facilitated or the conceptions of curriculum to guide procedures."[28]

Furthermore, Popkewitz and Pitman see a distinctive shift from a concern with equity to a slavish regard for a restricted notion of excellence. That is, the concept of excellence that informs these new reports "ignores the social differentiations while providing political symbols to give credibility to education which only a few can appreciate."[29] What is rightly being stressed is that the concept of excellence fashioned in the reports is designed to benefit "those who have already access to positions of status and privilege through accidents of birth."[30]

Given the context in which teaching and learning are currently being defined, it becomes all the more necessary to insist on an alternative view of teacher education, one which, in refusing to passively serve the existing ideological and institutional arrangements of the public schools, is aimed at challenging and reforming them.

TEACHER EDUCATION:
DEMOCRACY AND THE IMPERATIVE OF SOCIAL REFORM

We want to return to the idea that the fundamental concerns of democracy and critical citizenship should be central to any discussion of the purpose of teacher education. In doing so, we will organize our discussion around two arguments. The first represents an initial effort to develop a critical language with which to reconstruct the relationship between teacher education programs and the public schools, on the one hand, and public education and

---

curriculum functions to erase or distort the experiences and perceptions of individuals and groups from specific backgrounds, such as class, race, gender, and sexual orientation.

society on the other. The second, and more detailed, argument presents a view of authority and teacher work that attempts to define the political project we believe should underlie the purpose and nature of teacher education programs.

If teacher education programs are to provide the basis for democratic struggle and renewal in our schools, they will have to redefine their current relationship to such institutions. As it presently stands, schools of education rarely encourage their students to take seriously the imperatives of social critique and social change as part of a wider emancipatory vision. If and when education students begin to grapple with these concerns at the classroom level, it is invariably years after graduation. Our own experiences in teacher education institutions — both as students and as instructors — have confirmed for us what is generally agreed to be commonplace in most schools and colleges of education throughout the United States: that these institutions continue to define themselves essentially as service institutions which are generally mandated to provide the requisite technical expertise to carry out whatever pedagogical functions are deemed necessary by the various school communities in which students undertake their practicum experiences.[31] In order to escape this political posture, teacher education programs need to reorient their focus to the critical transformation of public schools rather than to the simple reproduction of existing institutions and ideologies.[32]

One starting point would be to recognize the importance of educating students in the languages of critique and possibility; that is, providing teachers with the critical terminology and conceptual apparatus that will allow them not only to critically analyze the democratic and political shortcomings of schools, but also to develop the knowledge and skills that will advance the possibilities for generating and cultivating a deep respect for a democratic and ethically-based community. In effect, this means that the relationship of teacher education programs to public schooling would be self-consciously guided by political and moral considerations. Dewey expressed well the need for educators to make political and moral considerations a central aspect of their education and work when he distinguished between "education as a function of society" and "society as a function of education."[33] In simple terms, Dewey's distinction reminds us that education can function either to create passive, risk-free citizens or to create a politicized citizenry educated to fight for various forms of public life informed by a concern for justice, happiness, and equality. At issue here is whether schools of education are to serve and reproduce the existing society or to adopt the more critical role of challenging the social order so as to develop and advance its democratic imperatives. Also at issue is developing a rationale for defining teacher education programs in political terms that make explicit a particular view of the relationship between public schools and the social order, a view based on defending the imperatives of a democratic society.

Public Schools as Democratic Public Spheres

Our second concern is directed to the broader question of how educators should view the purpose of public schooling. Our position echoes Dewey in that we believe public schools need to be defined as democratic **public spheres.**[h] This means regarding schools as democratic sites dedicated to self- and social empowerment. Understood in these terms, schools can be public places where students learn the knowledge and skills necessary to live in a critical democracy. Contrary to the view that schools are extensions of the workplace or front-line institutions in the corporate battle for international markets, schools viewed as democratic public spheres center their activities around critical inquiry and meaningful dialogue. In this case, students are given the opportunity to learn the discourse of public association and civic responsibility. Such a discourse seeks to recapture the idea of a critical democracy that commands respect for individual freedom and social justice. Moreover, viewing schools as democratic public spheres provides a rationale for defending them, along with progressive forms of pedagogy and teacher work, as agencies of social reform. When defined in these terms, schools can be defended as institutions that provide the knowledge, skills, social relations, and vision necessary to educate a citizenry capable of building a critical democracy. That is, school practice can be rationalized in a political language that recovers and emphasizes the transformative role that schools can play in advancing the democratic possibilities inherent in the existing society.[34]

Authority and Intellectuals:
Rethinking the Nature and Purpose of Teacher Work

Redefining the notion of authority in emancipatory terms is central to understanding and legitimating teacher work as a critical practice. The importance of such a task can be made clearer by highlighting the significance of authority as part of the fundamental discourse of schooling.

First, as a form of legitimation, authority is inescapably related to a particular vision of what schools should be as part of a wider community and society. Thus, questions about school and teacher authority help to make both visible and problematic the presuppositions of the officially sanctioned discourses and values that legitimate the institutional and social arrangements constituting everyday life in schools. For example, questions might be raised about the nature and source of the authority which legitimates a particular type of curriculum, the way school time is organized, the political

---

[h] **Public spheres** in the critical sense are public arenas for citizens in which political participation, outside of direct government and economic influence and intervention, is enacted through dialogue and debate. Schools are envisioned by critical pedagogues as "public spheres," wherein classrooms are active sites of public intervention and social struggle, rather than mere adjuncts of corporate and partisan interests. Because mainstream society is constituted by particular oppressive ideologies, these critical spheres are also referred to as "counterpublics."

consequences of tracking students, the social division of labor among teachers, and the patriarchal basis of authority. In this way, the concept of authority raises issues about the ethical and political basis of schooling. That is, it calls into serious question the role that school administrators and teachers play as intellectuals in both articulating and implementing their particular views or ideologies. In short, the category of authority reinserts the primacy of the political into the language of schooling by highlighting the social and ideological function that educators serve in elaborating, enforcing, and legitimating schooling as a particular form of social life, that is, as a particular set of ideas and practices that occur within historically defined contexts.

Second, if the concept of authority is to provide a legitimating basis for rethinking the purpose of meaning of teacher education, it must be reconstituted around a view of community life in which morality in everyday existence is fundamental to the meaning of democracy.[35] A form of *emancipatory* authority needs to be developed, one that can illuminate the connection and importance of two questions that teacher education programs should take as a central point of inquiry in structuring the form and content of their curricula. These are: What kind of society do educators want to live in? What kind of teaching and pedagogy can be developed and legitimated by a view of authority that takes democracy and critical citizenship seriously? Authority, in this view, rests on the assumption that public schooling should promote forms of morality and sociality in which students learn to encounter and engage social differences and diverse points of view. In addition, schools should prepare students for making choices regarding forms of life that have morally different consequences. This means that educators must replace pedagogical practices which emphasize disciplinary control and one-sided character formation with practices that are based on an emancipatory authority, ones which enable students to engage in critical analysis and to make choices regarding what interests and knowledge claims are most desirable and morally appropriate for living in a just and democratic state. Equally important is the need for students to engage in civic-minded action in order to remove the social and political constraints that restrict the victims of this society from leading decent and humane lives.

A reconstituted notion of emancipatory authority suggests, in this case, that teachers are bearers of critical knowledge, rules, and values through which they consciously articulate and **problematize**[i] their relationship to each other, to students, to subject matter, and to the wider community. This view of authority exposes and challenges the dominant view of teachers as primarily technicians or public servants whose role is to implement rather

---

[i]Associated with critical thinking/inquiry (that is, being able to understand, analyze, and affect the sociohistorical, economic, cultural, and political realities that shape our lives), **problematizing** is the process of posing questions in order to deconstruct a particular phenomenon so as to understand its construct.

than to conceptualize pedagogical practice. Moreover, the category of emancipatory authority dignifies teacher work by viewing it as an intellectual practice with respect to both its formal characteristics and the nature of the content discussed. Teacher work becomes a form of intellectual labor opposed to the pedagogical divisions between conception and practice, and production and implementation, that are currently celebrated in a number of educational reforms. The concept of teacher as intellectual carries with it the political and ethical imperative to judge, critique, and reject those approaches to authority that reinforce a technical and social division of labor that silences and disempowers both teachers and students. In other words, emancipatory authority is a concept which demands that teachers and others critically confront the ideological and practical conditions which enable or constrain them in their capacity as transformative intellectuals.

It is important to stress that the concept of emancipatory authority provides the theoretical basis for defining teachers not merely as intellectuals but, more specifically, as transformative intellectuals. The distinction is important because transformative intellectuals are not merely concerned with empowerment in the conventional sense, that is, with giving students the knowledge and skills they will need to gain access to some traditional measure of economic and social mobility in the capitalist marketplace. Rather, for transformative intellectuals, the issue of teaching and learning is linked to the more political goal of educating students to take risks and to struggle within ongoing relations of power in order to alter the oppressive conditions in which life is lived. To facilitate this goal, transformative intellectuals need to make clear the nature of the appeals to authority they are using to legitimate their pedagogical practices. In other words, educators need to specify the political and moral referents for the authority they assume in teaching particular forms of knowledge, in taking stands against forms of oppression, and in treating students as if they ought also to be concerned about social justice and political action.

In short, this reconstituted version of authority is important because it contains elements of a language of both criticism and possibility. As part of the language of critique, the notion of emancipatory authority provides a discourse through which educators can critically examine views of authority often used by conservatives and others to link the purpose of schooling to a **reductionist**[j] view of patriotism and patriarchy. As part of the language of possibility, authority as an emancipatory practice provides the scaffolding with which one can connect the purpose of schooling to the imperatives of what Benjamin Barber calls a "strong democracy," a democracy characterized

---

[j] To be **reductionistic** is to simplify a particular phenomenon so as to mask its complexity. For example, arguing that social reality is shaped solely by socioeconomic status and class conflict obscures the multiple and interconnecting relationships of other significant human experiences (such as race, gender, and sexual orientation) and their effects on perception and struggle.

by citizens capable of seriously confronting public issues through ongoing forms of public debate and social action.[36]

In our view, the most important referent for this particular view of authority rests in a commitment to address the many instances of suffering that characterize the present society. This suggests a recognition and identification with "the perspective of those people and groups who are marginal and exploited."[37] In its practical dimension, such a commitment represents a break from the bonds of isolated liberal individuality and a desire to engage with others in political struggles that challenge the existing order of society as being institutionally repressive and unjust. It is important to note that transformative intellectuals can serve to act, as Welch points out, as bearers of dangerous memory.[38] This means that such intellectuals can link knowledge to power by bringing to light and teaching the **subjugated histories,**[k] experiences, stories, and accounts of those who suffer and struggle within conditions that are rarely made public or analyzed through the official discourses of public schooling. Thus, we can point to the histories of women, blacks, working-class groups, and others whose histories challenge the moral legitimacy of the structures of society and therefore contain knowledge too "dangerous" to make visible. Of course, teachers of "dangerous memory" must do more than excavate historical reason and subjugated knowledge; they must also make clear that people are called to struggle, that political alternatives do in fact exist, and that such buried knowledge needs to be appropriated in the interest of creating more critically democratic societies.

RETHINKING THE NATURE OF TEACHER EDUCATION

We would like to bring the foregoing discussion to bear on the more practical mission of reconstructing teacher education programs around a new vision of democratic schooling and teaching for critical citizenship. Consequently, we shall devote the remainder of our discussion to outlining, in more detailed and programmatic terms, what we feel are some essential components and categories for a teacher education curriculum and a critical pedagogy for the schools.

As we have argued, most teacher education programs have been, and continue to be, entirely removed from a vision and a set of practices dedicated to the fostering of critical democracy and social justice. A repeated criticism made by educators working within the radical tradition has been that, as it currently exists, teacher education rarely addresses either the moral implications of societal inequalities within our present form of indus-

---

[k] **Subjugated histories** are the excluded, silenced, or marginalized memories and experiences of subordinated populations. Critical pedagogy calls for learners to become active participants in the reconstruction and transformation of their own identities and histories.

trial capitalism or the ways in which schools function to reproduce and legitimate these inequalities.[39]

Usually when classroom life is discussed in teacher education programs, it is presented fundamentally as a one-dimensional set of rules and regulative practices, rather than as a cultural terrain where a variety of interests and practices collide in a constant and often chaotic struggle for dominance. Thus, prospective teachers frequently receive the impression that classroom culture is essentially free from ambiguity and contradiction. According to this view, schools are supposedly devoid of all vestiges of contestation, struggle, and cultural politics.[40] Furthermore, classroom reality is rarely presented as if it were socially constructed, historically determined, and reproduced through institutionalized relationships of class, gender, race, and power. Unfortunately, this dominant conception of schooling vastly contradicts what the student teacher often experiences during his or her practicum or fieldsite work, especially if the student is placed in a school largely populated by economically disadvantaged and disenfranchised students. Yet, student teachers are nevertheless instructed to view schooling as a neutral terrain devoid of power and politics. It is against this transparent depiction of schooling that prospective teachers, more often than not, view their own ideologies and experiences through a dominant theoretical and cultural perspective that remains largely unquestioned. Most important, teachers in this situation have no grounds upon which to question the dominant cultural assumptions that shape and structure the ways in which they respond to and influence student behavior.

Consequently, many student teachers who find themselves teaching working-class or minority students lack a well-articulated framework for understanding the class, cultural, ideological, and gender dimensions that inform classroom life. As a result, cultural differences among students often are viewed uncritically as deficiencies rather than as strengths, and what passes for teaching is in actuality an assault on the specific histories, experiences, and knowledges that such students use both to define their own identities and to make sense of their larger world. We use the term "assault" not because such knowledge is openly attacked — but because it is devalued through a process that is at once subtle and debilitating. What happens is that within the dominant school culture, subordinate knowledge is generally ignored, marginalized, or treated in a disorganized fashion. Such knowledge is often treated as if it did not exist, or treated in ways that disconfirm it. Conversely, ideologies that do not aid subordinate groups in interpreting the reality they actually experience often pass for objective forms of knowledge. In this process prospective teachers lose an understanding of the relationship between culture and power as well as a sense of how to develop pedagogical possibilities for their students from the cultural differences that often characterize school and classroom life. In the section that follows, we will discuss the elements we feel should constitute a new model of teacher education, one that addresses the above issue more specifically.

TEACHER EDUCATION AS CULTURAL POLITICS

Our concern here is with reconstituting the grounds upon which teacher education programs are built. This means developing an alternative form of teacher education curriculum that supports what we call the construction of a cultural politics. In our view, such a programmatic approach to teacher education conceptualizes schooling as taking place within a political and cultural arena where forms of student experience and subjectivity are actively produced and mediated. In other words, we wish to stress the idea that schools do not merely teach academic subjects, but also, in part, produce student subjectivities or particular sets of experiences that are in themselves part of an ideological process. Conceptualizing schooling as the construction and transmission of subjectivities permits us to understand more clearly the idea that the curriculum is more than just an introduction of students to particular subject disciplines and teaching methodologies; it also serves as an introduction to a particular way of life.[41]

At this point, we must forgo a detailed specification of teaching practices and instead attempt to briefly sketch out particular areas of study crucial to the development of a reconceptualized teacher education curriculum. We assign the term "cultural politics" to our curriculum agenda because we feel that this term permits us to capture the significance of the sociocultural dimension of the schooling process. Furthermore, the term allows us to highlight the political consequences of interaction between teachers and students who come from dominant and **subordinate cultures.**[l] A teacher education curriculum as a form of cultural politics assumes that the social, cultural, political, and economic dimensions are the primary categories for understanding contemporary schooling.[42] Within this context, school life is conceptualized not as a unitary, monolithic, and ironclad system of rules and regulations, but as a cultural terrain characterized by varying degrees of accommodation, contestation, and **resistance.**[m] Furthermore, school life is understood as a plurality of conflicting languages and struggles, a place where classroom and street-corner cultures collide and where teachers, students, and school administrators often differ as to how school experiences and practices are to be defined and understood.

---

[l] **Subordinate cultures** refers to groups that are politically, socially, and economically disempowered in the greater society. As defined by Lilia Bartolomé, "While individual members of these groups may not consider themselves subordinate in any manner to the White 'mainstream,' they nevertheless are members of a greater collective that historically has been perceived and treated as subordinate and inferior by the dominant society. Thus it is not entirely accurate to describe these students as 'minority' students, since the term connotes numerical minority rather than the general low status (economic, political, and social) these groups have held" (p. 230).

[m] **Resistance** (oppositional identity) has traditionally been attributed to deviant behavior, individual pathology, learned helplessness, cultural deprivation, and genetic flaws. Critical pedagogy, on the other hand, sees resistance as a legitimate response to domination, used to help individuals or groups deal with oppression. From this perspective, resistance in any form should be part of a larger political project that is working towards change.

The imperative of this curriculum is to create conditions for student self-empowerment and self-constitution as an active political and moral subject. We are using the term "empowerment" to refer to the process whereby students acquire the means to critically appropriate knowledge existing outside of their immediate experience in order to broaden their understanding of themselves, the world, and the possibilities for transforming the taken-for-granted assumptions about the way we live. Stanley Aronowitz has described one aspect of empowerment as "the process of appreciating and loving oneself."[43] In this sense, empowerment is gained from knowledge and social relations that dignify one's own history, language, and cultural traditions. But empowerment means more than self-confirmation. It also refers to the process by which students are able to interrogate and selectively appropriate those aspects of the dominant culture that will provide them with the basis for defining and transforming, rather than merely serving, the wider social order.

The project of "doing" a teacher education curriculum based on cultural politics consists of linking critical social theory to a set of stipulated practices through which student teachers are able to dismantle and critically examine preferred educational and cultural traditions, many of which have fallen prey to an instrumental rationality that either limits or ignores democratic ideals and principles. One of our main concerns focuses on developing a language of critique and demystification that is capable of analyzing the latent interests and ideologies that work to socialize students in a manner compatible with the dominant culture. We are equally concerned, however, with creating alternative teaching practices capable of empowering students both inside and outside of schools. While it is impossible to provide a detailed outline of the courses of a curriculum for cultural politics, we want to comment on some important areas of analysis that should be central to such a program. These include the critical study of power, language, culture, and history.

Power

A pivotal concern of a teacher education curriculum that subscribes to a cultural politics approach is to assist student teachers in understanding the relationship between power and knowledge. Within the dominant curriculum, knowledge is often removed from the issue of power and is generally treated in a technical manner; that is, it is seen in instrumental terms as something to be mastered. That such knowledge is always an ideological construction linked to particular interests and social relations generally receives little consideration in teacher education programs. An understanding of the knowledge/power relationship raises important issues regarding what kinds of knowledge educators can provide to empower students, not only to understand and engage the world around them, but also to exercise the kind of courage needed to change the social order where necessary. Of considerable concern, then, is the need for student teachers to recognize that power relations correspond to forms of school knowledge that both distort the truth and produce it. That is, knowledge should be examined not only for the ways in which it might misrepresent or mediate social reality, but also for the ways in which it actually reflects peoples' experiences and, as such, influences their lives. Understood in this way, knowledge not only reproduces reality by distorting or illuminating the social world; it also has the more concrete function of shaping the day-to-day lives of people through their felt, relatively unmediated world of commonsense assumptions. This suggests that a curriculum for democratic empowerment must not only examine the conditions of school knowledge in terms of how it is produced and what particular interests it might represent, but should also scrutinize the effects of such knowledge as it is lived day-to-day. In short, prospective teachers need to understand that knowledge does more than distort, it also produces particular forms of life. Finally, in Michel Foucault's terms, knowledge contains hopes, desires, and wants that resonate positively with the subjective experience of a particular audience and such knowledge needs to be analyzed for the utopian promises often implicit in its claims.[44]

Language

In traditional and institutionally legitimated approaches to reading, writing, and second-language learning, language issues are primarily defined by technical and developmental concerns. While such concerns are indeed important, what is often ignored in mainstream language courses in teacher education programs is how language is actively implicated in power relations that generally support the dominant culture. An alternative starting point to the study of language recognizes the significance of Antonio Gramsci's notion that every language contains elements of a conception of the world. It is through language that we come to consciousness and negotiate a sense of identity, since language does not merely reflect reality, but plays an active role in constructing it. As language constructs meaning, it shapes our world, informs our identities, and provides the cultural codes for perceiving and classifying the world. This implies, of course, that within the available discourses of the school or the society, language plays a powerful role because it serves to "mark the boundaries of permissible discourse, discourage the clarification of social alternatives, and makes it difficult for the dispossessed to locate the source of their unease, let alone remedy it."[45] Through the study of language within the perspective of a cultural politics, prospective teachers can gain an understanding of how language functions to "position" people in the world, to shape the range of possible meanings surrounding an issue, and to actively construct reality rather than merely reflect it. As part of language studies, student teachers would become more knowledgeable about and sensitive to the omnipresence and power of language as constitutive of their own experiences and those of their potential students.[46] Student teachers would also benefit from an introductory understanding of European traditions of discourse theory and the textual strategies that characterize their methods of inquiry.[47] Furthermore, through an exposure to the semiotics of mass and popular cultures, students could at least learn the rudimentary methods of examining the various codes and meanings that are constitutive of both their own personal constructions of self and society and those of the students they work with during their practicum or on-site sessions.

History

The study of history should play a more expansive role in teacher education programs.[48] A critical approach to history would attempt to provide student teachers with an understanding of how cultural traditions are formed; it would also be designed to bring to light the various ways that curricula and discipline-based texts have been constructed and read throughout different historical periods. Furthermore, such an approach would be self-consciously critical of the problems surrounding the teaching of history as a school subject, since what is conventionally taught overwhelmingly reflects the perspectives and values of white, middle-class males. Too often excluded are the histories of women, minority groups, and indigenous peoples. This exclusion is not politically innocent when we consider how existing social arrangements are partly constitutive of and dependent upon the subjugation and elimination of the histories and voices of those groups marginalized and disempowered by the dominant culture. In addition, the concept of history can also help illuminate what kinds of knowledge are deemed legitimate and promulgated through the school curriculum. Conventional emphasis on chronological history "which traditionally saw its object as somehow unalterably 'there,' given, waiting only to be discovered"[49] would be supplanted by a focus on how specific educational practices can be understood as historical constructions related to the economic, social, and political events of a particular time and place. It is primarily through this form of historical analysis that students can recover what we referred to previously as "subjugated knowledges."[50] Our use of this term directs us to those aspects of history in which criticism and struggle have played a significant role in defining the nature and meaning of educational theory and practice. For example, students will have the opportunity to examine critically the historical contexts and interests at work in defining what forms of school knowledge become privileged over others, how specific forms of school authority are sustained, and how particular patterns of learning become institutionalized.

Within the format of a curriculum as a form of cultural politics, it is also necessary that the study of history be theoretically connected to both language and reading. In this context, language can be subsequently studied as "the bearer of history" and history can be analyzed as a social construction open to critical examination. The important linkage between reading and history can be made by emphasizing that "reading occurs within history and that the point of integration is always the reader."[51] In analyzing this relationship, teachers can focus on the cultural meanings that students use to understand a text. Such a focus will better equip student teachers to understand how the process of reading occurs within a particular student's cultural history and in the context of his or her own concerns and beliefs. This will also assist student teachers to become more critically aware of how students from subordinate cultures bring their own sets of experiences, as well as their own dreams, desires, and voices to the reading act.

Culture

The concept of culture, varied though it may be, is essential to any teacher education curriculum aspiring to be critical. We are using the term "culture" here to signify the particular ways in which a social group lives out and makes sense of its "given" circumstances and conditions of life.[52] In addition to defining culture as a set of practices and ideologies from which different groups draw to make sense of the world, we also want to refashion the ways in which cultural questions become the starting point for understanding the issue of who has power and how it is reproduced and manifested in the social relations that link schooling to the wider social order. The link between culture and power has been extensively analyzed in radical social theory over the past ten years. It is therefore possible to offer three insights from that literature that are particularly relevant for illuminating the political logic that underlies various cultural/power relations. First, the concept of culture has been intimately connected with the question of how *social relations are structured* within class, gender, and age formations that produce forms of oppression and dependency. Second, culture has been analyzed within the radical perspective not simply as a way of life, but as a *form of production* through which different groups in either their dominant or subordinate social relations define and realize their aspirations through asymmetrical relations of power. Third, culture has been viewed as a *field of struggle* in which the production, legitimation, circulation of particular forms of knowledge and experience are central areas of conflict. What is important here is that each of these insights raises fundamental questions about the ways in which inequalities are maintained and challenged in the sphere of culture.

The study of cultures — or, more specifically, what has come to be known as "cultural studies" — should become the touchstone of a teacher education curriculum. We feel this to be the case because cultural studies can provide student teachers with the critical categories necessary for examining school and classroom relations as social and political practices inextricably related to the construction and maintenance of specific relations of power. Moreover, by recognizing that school life is often mediated through the clash of dominant and subordinate cultures, prospective teachers can gain some insight into the ways in which classroom experiences are necessarily intertwined with their students' home life and street-corner culture. This point is meant to be more than a rallying cry for relevance; rather, it asserts the need for prospective teachers to understand the meaning systems that students employ in their encounters with forms of dominant school knowledge and social relations. It is important, therefore, that student teachers learn to analyze expressions of mass and popular culture, such as music videos, television, and film. In this way, a successful cultural studies approach would provide an important theoretical avenue for teachers to comprehend how ideologies become inscribed through representations of everyday life.

TOWARDS A CRITICAL PEDAGOGY FOR THE CLASSROOM

In the previous sections we have highlighted the importance of viewing schools as social and political sites involved in the struggle for democracy. In addition, we have reconsidered the relationship between authority and teacher work and have attempted to develop the theoretical rudiments of a program in which teacher education would be viewed as a form of cultural politics. In this final section, we shift the focus from questions of institutional purpose and teacher definition to the issues of critical pedagogy and student learning. In so doing, we point to some of the fundamental elements that we believe can be used to construct a critical pedagogy, one in which the issue of student interests or motivation is linked to the dynamics of self- and social empowerment. We wish to underscore here that the public schools shape and reinforce the attitudes that prospective teachers bring to their clinical experiences. By focusing on some of the theoretical elements that constitute a critical pedagogy, we attempt to clarify the link between our notion of a teacher education curriculum as a form of cultural politics and the actual dynamics of classroom pedagogy. With this in mind, we will now sketch out the rudiments of a critical discourse that defines classroom pedagogy within the parameters of a political project centering around the primacy of student experience, the concept of voice, and the importance of transforming schools and communities into democratic public spheres.

The Primacy of Student Experience

The type of critical pedagogy we are proposing is fundamentally concerned with student experience insofar as it takes the problems and needs of the students themselves as its starting point. On the one hand, a pedagogy of student experience encourages a critique of dominant forms of knowledge and cultural mediation that collectively shape student experiences; on the other hand, it attempts to provide students with the critical means to examine their own particular lived experiences and subordinate knowledge forms. This means assisting students in analyzing their own experiences so as to illuminate the processes by which they were produced, legitimized, or disconfirmed. R. W. Connell and his associates in Australia provide a cogent direction for this type of curricular approach in their formulation of the kinds of knowledge that should be taught to empower working-class students when they suggest:

> that working-class kids get access to formal knowledge via learning which begins with their own experience and the circumstances which shape it,

but does not stop there. This approach neither accepts the existing organization of academic knowledge nor simply inverts it. It draws on existing school knowledge and on what working-class people already know, and organizes this selection of information around problems such as economic survival and collective action, handling the disruption of households by unemployment, responding to the impact of new technology, managing problems of personal identity and association, understanding how schools work and why.[53]

Student experience is the stuff of culture, agency, and identity formation and must be given preeminence in an emancipatory curriculum. It is therefore imperative that critical educators learn how to understand, affirm, and analyze such experience. This means not only understanding the cultural and social forms through which students learn how to define themselves, but also learning how to engage student experience in a way that neither unqualifiedly endorses nor delegitimates such experience. This suggests that, first of all, knowledge has to be made meaningful to students before it can be made critical. School knowledge never speaks for itself; rather, it is constantly filtered through the ideological and cultural experiences that students bring to the classroom. To ignore the ideological dimensions of student experience is to deny the ground upon which students learn, speak, and imagine. Judith Williamson addresses this issue well.

> Walter Benjamin has said that the best ideas are no use if they do not make something useful of the person who holds them; on an even simpler level, I would add that the best ideas don't even exist if there isn't anyone to hold them. If we cannot get the "radical curriculum" across, or arouse the necessary interest in the "basic skills," there is no point to them. But in any case, which do we ultimately care more about: our ideas, or the child/student we are trying to teach them to?[54]

Students cannot learn "usefully" unless teachers develop an understanding of the various ways in which student perceptions and identities are constituted through different social domains. At stake is the need for student teachers to understand how experiences produced in the various domains and layers of everyday life give rise to the different voices students employ to give meaning to their worlds and, consequently, to their existence in the larger society. Of course, not all student experiences should be unqualifiedly affirmed or rendered legitimate since some of them undoubtedly will draw from an uncritical categorization and social construction of the world (as in racist and sexist stereotyping, for example). In this case, teachers must understand student experience as arising from multiple discourses and subjectivities, some of which must be interrogated more critically than others. It is crucial, therefore, that educators address the question of how aspects of the social world are experienced, mediated, and produced by students. Failure to do so will not only prevent teachers from tapping into the drives, emotions, and interests that give students their own unique voice, but will also make it equally difficult to provide the momentum for learning itself.

While the concept of student experience is being offered as central to a critical pedagogy, it should also be recognized as a central category of teacher education programs. This suggests that student practicums should be seen as sites where the question of how experience is produced, legitimized, and accomplished becomes an object of study for teachers and students alike. Unfortunately, most student practicums are viewed as either a rite of passage into the profession or merely a formal culminating experience in the teacher education program.

Student Voice and the Public Sphere
The concept of voice constitutes the focal point for a theory of teaching and learning that generates new forms of sociality as well as new and challenging ways of confronting and engaging everyday life. Voice, quite simply, refers to the various measures by which students and teachers actively participate in dialogue. It is related to the discursive means whereby teachers and students attempt to make themselves "heard" and to define themselves as active authors of their worlds. Displaying a voice means, to cite Mikhail Bakhtin, "retelling a story in one's own words."[55] More specifically, the term "voice" refers to the principles of dialogue as they are enunciated and enacted within particular social settings. The concept of voice represents the unique instances of self-expression through which students affirm their own class, cultural, racial, and gender identities. A student's voice is necessarily shaped by personal history and distinctive lived engagement with the surrounding culture. The category of voice, then, refers to the means at our disposal — the discourses available to us — to make ourselves understood and listened to, and to define ourselves as active participants in the world. However, as we have stressed previously, the dominant school culture generally represents and legitimates the voices of white males from the middle and upper classes to the exclusion of economically disadvantaged students, most especially females from minority backgrounds.[56] A critical pedagogy takes into account the various ways in which the voices that teachers use to communicate with students can either silence or legitimate them.

The concept of voice is crucial to the development of a critical classroom pedagogy because it provides an important basis for constructing and demonstrating the fundamental imperatives of a strong democracy. Such a pedagogy attempts to organize classroom relationships so that students can draw upon and confirm those dimensions of their own histories and experiences which are deeply rooted in the surrounding community. In addition, by creating active links with the community, teachers can open up their classrooms to its diverse resources and traditions. This presupposes that teachers familiarize themselves with the culture, economy, and historical traditions that belong to the surrounding community. In other words, teachers must assume a pedagogical responsibility for attempting to understand the relationships and forces that influence their students outside of the immediate context of the classroom. This responsibility requires teachers to develop their curricula and pedagogical practices around those community traditions, histories, and forms of knowledge that are often ignored within the dominant school culture. This can, of course, lead to a deeper understanding on the part of both teachers and students of how both "local" and **"official" knowledges**[n] get produced, sustained, and legitimated.

Teachers need to develop pedagogical practices that link student experiences with those aspects of community life that inform and sustain such experiences. For example, student teachers could compile oral histories of the communities in which they teach, which could then be used as a school and curricula resource — particularly in reading programs. In addition, they could work in and analyze how different community social agencies function so as to produce, distribute, and legitimate particular forms of knowledge and social relations. This would broaden their notion of pedagogical practices and help them to understand the relevance of their own work for institutions other than schools. Similarly, prospective teachers could develop organic links with active community agencies such as business, religious organizations, and other public spheres in an attempt to develop a more meaningful connection between the school curriculum and the experiences that define and characterize the local community. The concept of voice can thus provide a basic organizing principle for the development of a relationship between knowledge and student experiences and, at the same time, create a forum for examining broader school and community issues. In other words, teachers must become aware of both the transformative strengths and structures of oppression of the community-at-large and develop this awareness into curriculum strategies designed to empower students toward creating a more liberating and humane society. In short, teachers should be attentive to what it means to construct forms of learning in their classrooms that enable students to affirm their voices within areas of community life, that is, within democratic public spheres needing constant criticism, safeguarding, and renewal.

Steve Tozer is worth quoting at length on this issue:

> The process of fitting students for community life, then, is an effort to prepare students both for the existing community and to bring them to understand and to appreciate the historical values and ideas which point to a more ideal community than the one that exists . . . the teacher's duty is to recognize the historical ideals which make community life worth living, ideals upon which the larger society is founded: ideals of human dignity

---

[n] **Official knowledges** refer to the values, assumptions, and interpretations that reflect dominant ideologies and are at the core of mainstream public education. Such knowledge is abstracted from its sociohistorical and ideological construction, and is often misrepresented as being universal.

and equality, freedom, and mutual concern of one person for another. . . . This is not to say that teachers should prepare students for some nonexistent utopia. Rather, teachers must develop an understanding of the community as it exists *and* an understanding of what kind of people will be required to make it better. They can try to develop for themselves an ideal of the community their students should strive for, and they should help their students with the knowledge, the values and the skills they will need if they are to be resilient enough to maintain high standards of belief and conduct in an imperfect society.[57]

It is an unfortunate truism that when communities are ignored by teachers, students often find themselves trapped in institutions that not only deny them a voice, but also deprive them of a relational or contextual understanding of how the knowledge they acquire in the classroom can be used to influence and transform the public sphere. Implicit in the concept of linking classroom experiences to the wider community is the idea that the school is best understood as a polity, as a locus of citizenship. Within this locus, students and teachers can engage in a process of deliberation and discussion aimed at advancing the public welfare in accordance with fundamental moral judgments and principles. To bring schools closer to the concept of polity, it is necessary to define them as public spheres which seek to recapture the idea of critical democracy and community. In effect, we want to define teachers as active community participants whose function is to establish public spaces where students can debate, appropriate, and learn the knowledge and skills necessary to live in a critical democracy.

By pubic space we mean, as Hannah Arendt did, a concrete set of learning conditions where people come together to speak, to engage in dialogue, to share their stories, and to struggle together within social relations that strengthen rather than weaken possibilities for active citizenship.[58] School and classroom practices should, in some manner, be organized around forms of learning which serve to prepare students for responsible roles as transformative intellectuals, as community members, and as critically active citizens outside of schools.[59]

CONCLUSION

We began this essay by arguing that teacher education should be seriously rethought along the lines of the critical democratic tradition, a tradition which, regrettably, has been all but excluded from the current debates on American schooling. We have argued that this tradition provides the basis for rethinking the relationship of schooling to the social order and for restructuring the education of prospective teachers so as to prepare them for the role of transformative intellectual. Moreover, we have argued that teacher education programs must assume a central role in reforming public education and, in so doing, must assert the primacy of a democratic tradition in order to restructure school-community relations.

In our view, the search for a creative democracy undertaken at the beginning of the century by Dewey and others is presently in retreat, having been abandoned by liberals and radicals alike. This situation presents a dual challenge to critical educators: there is now an urgent need not only to resurrect the tradition of liberal democracy, but to develop a theoretical perspective that goes beyond it. In the current age of conservatism, public education must analyze its strengths and weaknesses against an ideal of critical democracy rather than the current corporate referent of the capitalist marketplace. Similarly, public education must fulfill the task of educating citizens to take risks, to struggle for institutional and social change, and to fight *for* democracy and *against* oppression both inside and outside of schools. Pedagogical empowerment necessarily goes hand-in-hand with social and political transformation.

Our position is indebted to Dewey but attempts to extend his democratic project. Dewey's struggle for democracy was primarily pedagogical and largely failed to develop an extended analysis of class relations and historically conditioned inequalities in society. Conversely, our position accentuates the idea that schools represent only one important site in the struggle for democracy. It is different from Dewey's view because it perceives the self- and social empowerment of students as involving not just the politics of classroom culture, but also political and social struggle outside of school sites. Such an approach acknowledges that critical pedagogy is but one intervention — albeit a crucial one — in the struggle to restructure the ideological and material conditions of everyday life. We are convinced that teacher education institutions and public schools can and should play an active and productive role in broadening the possibilities for the democratic promise of American schooling, politics, and society.

NOTES

1. Arthur G. Powell, "University Schools of Education in the Twentieth Century," *Peabody Journal of Education*, 54 (1976), 4.
2. Powell, "University Schools," p. 4.
3. George Counts, quoted in Powell, "University Schools," p. 4.
4. As quoted in Lawrence A. Cremin, David A. Shannon, and Mary Evelyn Townsend, *A History of Teachers College, Columbia University* (New York: Columbia University Press, 1954), p. 222.
5. Cremin, Shannon, and Townsend, *A History*, p. 222.
6. As quoted by George Counts in Cremin, Shannon, and Townsend, *A History*, p. 222.
7. For an interesting discussion of this issue, see Ira Katznelson and Margaret Weir, *Schooling for All: Class, Race, and the Decline of the Democratic Ideal* (New York: Basic Books, 1985).
8. See esp. the work of the revisionist historians of the 1960s. Among the representative works are Michael B. Katz, *The Irony of Early School Reform: Educational Innovation in Mid-Nineteenth Century Massachusetts* (Boston: Beacon Press, 1968); Colin Greer, *The Great School Legend* (New York: Basic Books, 1972); and Clarence J. Karier, Paul Violas, and Joel Spring, *Roots of Crisis: American Education in the Twentieth Century* (Chicago: Rand McNally, 1973).

9. Lentricchia, *Criticism and School Change* (Chicago: University of Chicago Press, 1983), pp. 6–7.
10. See Stanley Aronowitz and Henry A. Giroux, *Education under Siege: The Conservative, Liberal, & Radical Debate over Schooling* (South Hadley, MA: Bergin & Garvey, 1985).
11. We are using the term "discourse" to mean "a domain of language use subject to rules of formation and transformation," as quoted in Catherine Belsey, *Critical Practice* (London: Methuen, 1980, p. 160). Discourses may also be described as "the complexes of signs and practices which organize social existence and social reproduction. In their structured, material persistence, discourses are what give differential substance to membership of a social group or class or formation, which mediate an internal sense of belonging, and outward sense of otherness," as quoted in Richard Terdiman, *Discourse-Counter-Discourse* (New York: Cornell University Press, p. 54).
12. Aronowitz and Giroux, *Education under Siege;* and Ann Bastian, Colin Greer, Norm Fruchter, Marilyn Gittel, and Kenneth Haskins, *Choosing Equality: The Case for Democratic Schooling* (New York: New World Foundation, 1985).
13. Zeichner, "Alternative Paradigms of Teacher Education," *Journal of Teacher Education, 34* (1983), 8.
14. Some of the more representative writing on this issue can be found in Diane Ravitch, *The Troubled Crusade: American Education 1945–1980* (New York: Basic Books, 1983); John H. Bunzel, ed. *Challenge to American Schools: The Case for Standards and Values* (New York: Oxford University Press, 1985); Ravitch, *The Schools We Deserve: Reflections on the Educational Crises of Our Time.* (New York: Basic Books, 1985); and Edward Wynne, "The Great Tradition in Education: Transmitting Moral Values," *Educational Leadership, 43* (1985), 7.
15. Some of the best analyses are Lawrence C. Stedman and Marshall S. Smith, "Recent Reform Proposals for American Education," *Contemporary Education Review, 53* (1983), 85–104; Walter Feinberg, "Fixing the Schools: The Ideological Turn," *Issues in Education, 3* (1985), 113–138; Edward H. Berman, "The Improbability of Meaningful Educational Reform," *Issues in Education, 3* (1985), 99–112; Michael Apple, "National Reports and the Construction of Inequality," *British Journal of Sociology of Education* (1987); and Aronowitz and Giroux, *Education under Siege.*
16. Finkelstein, "Education and the Retreat from Democracy in the United States, 1979–198?," *Teachers College Record, 86* (1984), 280–281.
17. Berman, "Improbability," p. 103.
18. We are using the term "influential" to refer to those reports that have played a major role in shaping educational policy at both the national and local levels. These include The National Commission on Excellence in Education, *A Nation at Risk: The Imperative for Educational Reform* (Washington, DC: GPO, 1983); Task Force on Education for Economic Growth, Education Commission of the States, *Action for Excellence: A Comprehensive Plan to Improve Our Nation's Schools* (Denver: Education Commission of the States, 1983); The Twentieth Century Fund Task Force on Federal Elementary and Secondary Education Policy, *Making the Grade* (New York: The Twentieth Century Fund, 1983); Carnegie Corporation, *Education and Economic Progress: Toward a National Education Policy* (New York: Author, 1983); and Carnegie Forum on Education and the Economy, *A Nation Prepared: Teachers for the 21st Century* (Hyattsville, MD: Author, 1986).

Also considered are other recent reports on teacher education reform: The National Commission for Excellence in Teacher Education, *A Call for Change in Teacher Education* (Washington, DC: American Association of Colleges in Teacher Education, 1985); C. Emily Feistritzer, *The Making of a Teacher* (Washington, DC: National Center for Education Information, 1984); "Tomorrow's Teachers: A Report of the Holmes Group" (East Lansing, MI: Holmes Group, Inc., 1986); and Francis A. Maher and Charles H. Rathbone, "Teacher Education and Feminist Theory: Some Implications

for Practice," *American Journal of Education, 101* (1986), 214–235. For an analysis of many of these reports see Catherine Cornbleth, "Ritual and Rationality in Teacher Education Reform," *Educational Researcher, 15,* No. 4 (1986), 5–14.
19. Frankenstein and Kampf, "Preface," in Sara Freedman, Jane Jackson, and Katherine Boles, "The Other End of the Corridor: The Effect of Teaching on Teachers," *Radical Teacher, 23* (1983), 2–23. It is worth nothing that the Carnegie Forum's *A Nation Prepared* ends up defeating its strongest suggestions for reform by linking teacher empowerment to quantifying notions of excellence.
20. Stedman and Smith, "Recent Reform Proposals," pp. 85–104.
21. We are not automatically opposed to all forms of curricular software and technologies, such as interactive video disks and computers, as long as teachers become aware of the limited range of applications and contexts in which these technologies may be put to use. Certainly, we agree that some prepackaged curricula are more salient than others as instruments of learning. Too often, however, the use of such curricula ignores the contexts of the immediate classroom situation, the larger social milieu, and the historical juncture of the surrounding community. Furthermore, classroom materials designed to simplify the task of teaching and to make it more cost-efficient often separate planning or conception from execution. Many of the recent examples of predesigned commercial curricula are largely focused on competencies measured by standardized tests, precluding the possibility that teachers and students will be able to act as critical thinkers. See Michael W. Apple and Kenneth Teitelbaum, "Are Teachers Losing Control of Their Skills and Curriculum?" *Journal of Curriculum Studies, 18* (1986), 177–184.
22. Darling-Hammond, "Valuing Teachers: The Making of a Profession," *Teachers College Record, 87* (1985) 209–218.
23. Darling-Hammond, "Valuing Teachers," p. 209.
24. For an excellent theoretical analysis of this issue, see Freedman, Jackson, and Boles, "The Other End of the Corridor." For a more traditional statistical treatment, see Darling-Hammond, *Beyond the Commission Reports: The Coming Crisis in Teaching,* R-3177-RC (Santa Monica, CA: Rand Corporation, July 1984); National Education Association, *Nationwide Teacher Opinion Poll, 1983* (Washington, DC: Author, 1983); and American Federation of Teachers, *School As a Workplace: The Realities of Stress,* Vol. I (Washington, DC: Author, 1983).
25. Dennis J. Schmidt, "Translator's Introduction: In the Spirit of Bloch," in Ernst Bloch, *Natural Law and Human Dignity,* trans. Dennis J. Schmidt (Boston: MIT Press, 1986), p. xviii.
26. Goodlad, *A Place Called School: Prospects for the Future* (New York: McGraw-Hill, 1983); Sizer, *Horace's Compromise: The Dilemma of the American High School* (Boston: Houghton Mifflin, 1984); and Boyer, *High School: A Report on Secondary Education in America* (New York: Harper & Row, 1983).
27. For an overview and critical analysis of this literature, see Henry A. Giroux, "Theories of Reproduction and Resistance in the New Sociology of Education: A Critical Analysis," *Harvard Educational Review, 53* (1983), 257–293.
28. Popkewitz and Pitman, "The Idea of Progress and the Legitimation of State Agendas: American Proposals for School Reform," *Curriculum and Teaching, 1* (1986), p. 21.
29. Popkewitz and Pitman, "The Idea of Progress," p. 20.
30. Popkewitz and Pitman, "The Idea of Progress," p. 22.
31. Zeichner, "Alternative Paradigms"; and Jesse Goodman, "Reflections on Teacher Education: A Case Study and Theoretical Analysis," *Interchange, 15* (1984), 7–26. The fact that many teacher education programs have defined themselves as synonymous with instructional preparation has often given them a debilitating practical slant, leading to a limited conception of teaching as exercises in classroom management and control. Isolated courses on classroom management have had a tragic effect on how

teachers are able to critically interrogate the political implications of curricular decision-making and policy development. This predicament can be traced to a history of the academic politics that grew out of the separation of colleges of education from the liberal arts tradition and the arts and sciences faculty; see Donald Warren, "Learning from Experience: History and Teacher Education," *Educational Researcher*, 14, No. 10 (1985), 5–12.
32. For an excellent analysis of this issue, see National Coalition of Advocates for Students, *Barriers to Excellence: Our Children at Risk* (Boston: Author, 1985).
33. As quoted in Frank Lentricchia, *Criticism and Social Change* (Chicago: University of Chicago Press, 1985); see also Dewey, *Democracy and Education* (New York: Free Press, 1916) and *The Public and Its Problems* (New York: Holt, 1927).
34. Dewey, "Creative Democracy — The Task Before Us," in *Classic American Philosophers*, ed. Max Fisch (New York: Appleton-Century-Crofts, 1951), pp. 389–394; and Richard J. Bernstein, "Dewey and Democracy: The Task Ahead of Us," in *Post-Analytic Philosophy*, ed. John Rajchman and Cornell West (New York: Columbia University Press, 1985) pp. 48–62.
35. Henry A. Giroux, "Authority, Intellectuals and the Politics of Practical Learning," *Teachers College Record* (1986).
36. Barber, *Strong Democracy: Participating Politics for a New Age Theology of Liberation* (Berkeley: University of California Press, 1984).
37. Sharon Welch, *Communities of Resistance and Solidarity* (New York: Orbis Press, 1985), p. 31.
38. Welch, *Communities of Resistance*, p. 37.
39. Zeichner, "Alternative Paradigms"; Henry A. Giroux, *Ideology, Culture, and the Process of Schooling* (Philadelphia: Temple University Press, 1981); and John Sears, "Rethinking Teacher Education: Dare We Work Toward a New Social Order?" *Journal of Curriculum Theorizing*, 6 (1985), 24–79.
40. Of course, this is not true for all teacher education programs, but it does represent the dominant tradition characterizing them; see Zeichner, "Alternative Paradigms."
41. See John Ellis, "Ideology and Subjectivity," *in Culture, Media, Language*, ed. Stuart Hall, Dorothy Hobson, Andrew Lowe, and Paul Willis (Hawthorne, Australia: Hutchinson, 1980), pp. 186–194; see also Julian Henriques, Wendy Hollway, Cathy Urwin Couze Venn, and Valerie Walkerdine, *Changing the Subject* (New York: Methuen, 1984).
42. Henry A. Giroux and Roger Simon, "Curriculum Study and Cultural Politics," *Journal of Education*, 166 (1984), 226–238.
43. Stanley Aronowitz, "Schooling, Popular Culture, and Post-Industrial Society: Peter McLaren Interviews Aronowitz," *Orbit*, 17 (1986), 18.
44. Foucault, "The Subject of Power," in *Beyond Structuralism and Hermeneutics*, ed. Hubert Dreyfus and Paul Rabinow (Chicago: University of Chicago Press, 1982), p. 221.
45. T. J. Jackson Lears, "The Concept of Cultural Hegemony: Problems and Possibilities," *American Historical Review*, 90 (1985), 569–570.
46. Gary Waller, "Writing, Reading, Language, History, Culture: The Structure and Principles of the English Curriculum at Carnegie-Mellon University." Unpublished manuscript, Carnegie-Mellon University, 1985, p. 12.
47. We are primarily referring to the French school of discourse theory, as exemplified in the writings of Foucault; see his *The Archaeology of Knowledge*, trans. A. M. Sheridan Smith (London: Tavistock); see also the following works by Foucault: *Language, Counter-Memory, Practice: Selected Essays and Interviews*, Donald F. Bouchard, trans. Donald F. Bouchard and Sherry Simon (Ithaca, NY: Cornell University Press, 1979); and "Politics and the Study of Discourse," *Ideology and Consciousness*, 3 (1978), 7–26.
48. Waller, "Writing, Reading, Language," p. 12.
49. Waller, "Writing, Reading, Language," p. 14.

50. Foucault, "Two Lectures," in *Power/Knowledge*, ed. Colin Gordon (New York: Pantheon, 1980), pp. 78–108.
51. Waller, "Writing, Reading, Language," p. 14.
52. Henry A. Giroux, *Ideology, Culture, and the Process of Schooling* (Philadelphia: Temple University Press, 1981).
53. Robert W. Connell, Dean J. Ashenden, Sandra Kessler, Gary W. Dowsett, *Making the Difference: Schools, Families, and Social Division* (Winchester, MA: Allen & Unwin, 1982), p. 199; see also Peter McLaren, *Schooling as a Ritual Performance: Towards a Political Economy of Educational Symbols and Gestures* (London: Routledge & Kegan Paul, 1986).
54. Williamson, "Is There Anyone Here From a Classroom?," *Screen, 26* (Jan./Feb. 1984), 24; see also Henry A. Giroux, "Radical Pedagogy under the Politics of Student Voice," *Interchange, 17* (1986), 48–69.
55. As quoted in Harold Rosen, "The Importance of Story," *Language Arts, 63* (1986), 234.
56. For a thorough analysis of this, see Arthur Brittan and Mary Maynard, *Sexism, Racism and Oppression* (New York: Blackwell, 1984).
57. Tozer, "Dominant Ideology and the Teacher's Authority," *Contemporary Education, 56* (1985), 152–153.
58. Arendt, *The Human Condition* (Chicago: University of Chicago Press, 1958).
59. Attempts to link classroom instruction to community contexts are nowhere more important than during teachers' clinical experiences. On these occasions, prospective teachers should be assisted in making connections with progressive community organizations, especially those affiliated with local governmental council meetings, and should be encouraged to interview community leaders and workers in various community agencies linked to the school. This enhances the possibility that prospective teachers will make critically reflective links between classroom practices and the ethos and needs of the surrounding social and cultural milieu.

Glossary

Our objective in providing these heuristics should not be misinterpreted as an endorsement of fixed definitions and the mechanical process of rote memorization; we are simply attempting to provide readers unfamiliar with this work with the necessary signposts to enter the discussion. Reflective reading should always be a challenge to push us beyond our immediate ability and understanding. As these ideas vary from author to author, instead of being uncritically consumed, they should be understood, linked to one's own experience, and subsequently recreated to fit one's particular needs. The selected readings that accompany many of these terms and theories are also not meant to be prescriptions. Once again, they should provide the reader with a more profound understanding of various positions, and are intended to be critically appropriated and rewritten.

Americanization: *Americanization* is the socializing process through which individuals lose their cultural identity as the language, values, and beliefs of the dominant White majority are imposed. Schools, within such a process, are seen as an integral agent of assimilation.

banking notion of education: The *banking model of education* occurs when teachers perceive students as empty containers that need to be filled with preestablished bodies of knowledge. The narrowly defined "facts" and pieces of information that are transmitted are often disconnected from both teachers' and students' social realities. Students are thus treated as objects that are acted upon, rather than knowledgeable participants in the construction of deep and meaningful learning experiences. For a more in-depth discussion, see the following book in the annotated bibliography: Paulo Freire, *The Politics of Education: Culture, Power and Liberation*.

commodification: *Commodification* refers to the process by which culture is increasingly being held captive by the materialistic logic of capitalism in which everything/everybody is reduced to objects/commodities and thus to its/their market value. The consequence of this process is that people become uncritical tools of production and consumption — *commodified*. In this sense, schools function merely as adjuncts to corporations and the marketplace. For a more in-depth discussion, see Philip Wexler, *Social Analysis and Education* (New York: Routledge, 1988). See also the following books in the annotated bibliography: Michael W. Apple, *Ideology and Curriculum*; Peter McLaren, *Critical Pedagogy and Predatory Culture: Oppositional Politics in a Postmodern Era*.

counter-discourse (countervailing ideologies, counter-hegemonic practices): *Counter-discourses* are languages of critique, demystification, and agency capable of contesting dominant oppressive ideologies and practices.

critical thinking (critical consciousness/critical inquiry): Not to be confused with what's traditionally thought of as the higher order thinking skills (problem-solving skills), *critical* in this sense implies being able to understand, analyze, pose questions, and affect and effect the sociopolitical and economic realities that shape our lives. Throughout his work, Paulo Freire refers to this idea as "conscientization."

culture (cultural politics): Refuting the modernist notion of positivism, which, through claims to objectivity, truth, and certainty, defends a scientific basis for the study of culture, critical pedagogy focuses on the idea that *cultures* are always produced within particular social and historical conditions, and that any understanding of their production, reproduction, and representation is inherently subjective — that is, determined by one's own experiences, beliefs, values, and interests. Critical pedagogy views culture as a terrain of lived experiences and institutional forms organized around diverse elements of pleasure, struggle, and domination. In other words, culture embodies the lived experiences and behaviors that are the result of the unequal distribution of power along such lines as race, gender, class, ethnicity, age, and sexual orientation. As people interact with existing institutions and social practices in which the values, beliefs, bodies of knowledge, styles of communication, and biases of the dominant culture are imposed, they are often stripped of their power to articulate and realize their own goals. For example, the efforts in the United States to enforce a "common culture" (an unnegotiated foundation of values, ethics, meaning, histories, and representations — our "cultural heritage") or a "common sense" (a selective view of social reality in which difference is viewed as deviant or a deficit) is, in fact, the imposition of a homogenizing social paradigm (known as ideological domination or *hegemony*) that grossly limits the possibility for a critical multicultural democracy. As class and race are inextricably related to culture in the United States, middle-class realities are certainly different from those of the working class, as Black and Latino are to White; the critical question is, whose realities and interests are defining what it means to be an American? Focusing on the imposition of particular values in society, as well as the antagonistic relations and the resistance (opposition) that surfaces as a response to such domination, critical pedagogues view the contemporary cultural landscape as a terrain of conflict of differences. For a more in-depth discussion, see the following books in the annotated bibliography: Paulo Freire, *The Politics of Education: Culture, Power, and Liberation;* Henry Louis Gates Jr., *Loose Canons: Notes on the Culture Wars;* David Theo Goldberg, *Multiculturalism: A Critical Reader;* Simon During, *The Cultural Studies Reader;* Christine Sleeter and Peter McLaren, *Multicultural Education, Critical Pedagogy, and the Politics of Difference;* Gayatri Chakravorty Spivak, *Outside in the Teaching Machine.*

cultural capital: *Cultural capital* refers to Pierre Bourdieu's concept that different forms of cultural knowledge, such as language, modes of social interaction, and meaning, are valued hierarchically in society. Critical pedagogues argue that only those characteristics and practices (i.e., cultural wealth) of the dominant paradigm will facilitate academic achievement within mainstream schools that reflect that dominant and exclusionary ideology. For a more in-depth discussion of "cultural capital," as well as other insights of Bourdieu, see Richard Jenkins, *Key Sociologists: Pierre Bourdieu* (New York: Routledge, 1992). See also, in the annotated bibliography, Pierre Bourdieu and Jean-Claude Passeron, *Reproduction in Education, Society, and Culture; Offical Knowledge: Democratic Educaion in a Conservative Age.*

cultural reproduction: Critical social theorists argue that dominant ideologies and knowledge are built into social institutions that both privilege and exclude particular perspectives, voices, authorities, and representations. Within theories of *cultural reproduction,* schools, teachers, and curricula are viewed as mechanisms of ideological control that work to reproduce and maintain dominant beliefs, values, norms, and oppressive practices. This reproductive process is mediated, in part, through the "hidden curriculum" — the hidden agenda of maintaining the status quo through specific schooling practices. However, contemporary interpretations of reproduction theory do perceive culture as ever shifting and forming, and, as such, there is always room for teacher and student agency. For a more in-depth analysis of this process, see the Dennis Carlson essay in this collection. See also the following books in the annotated bibliography: Pierre Bourdieu and Jean-Claude Passeron, *Reproduction in Education, Society, and Culture;* Edward Said, *Culture and Imperialism;* Edward S. Herman and Noam Chomsky, *Manufacturing Consent: The Political Economy and Mass Media;* Henry Giroux, *Theory and Resistance in Education: A Pedagogy for the Opposition;* John Forester, *Critical Theory, Public Policy, and Planning Practice: Toward a Critical Pragmatism;* Samuel Bowles and Herbert Gintis, *Schooling in a Capitalist America: Educational Reform and the Contradictions of Economic Life;* Michelle Fine, *Framing Drop Outs: Notes on the Politics of an Urban High School.*

cultural worker: A *cultural worker* ("transformative intellectual" or "public intellectual"), in the best light, is an educator who critically engages learning (wherever it may take place) with the goal of working pedagogically and politically to ensure the development of a socially responsible citizenry and a critical, multicultural, democracy. However, in the negative sense, public figures, such as talk show hosts, are also cultural workers in that their interpretations can shape the ways in which different cultural groups interact by distorting the ways in which identities are depicted or "represented" in the mainstream.

deconstruction: Generally associated with the work of French theorist Jacques Derrida, *deconstruction* is an analytic process through which the deep, unconscious meaning of texts is examined. Within a critical pedagogical framework, deconstruction often refers to the analytic process of taking apart (i.e., dissecting, critically inquiring, problematizing) a phenomenon in order to understand its construction.

deficit model: The *deficit model* is used to explain the low academic achievement of students from oppressed groups as being due to individual or group pathology, cultural deprivation, or genetic limitations (e.g., cognitive and linguistic deficiencies, poor motivation). As Lilia Bartolomé describes in "Beyond the Methods Fetish," students perceived in this fashion are "in need of fixing (if we could only identify the right recipe!), or, at worst, culturally or genetically deficient and beyond fixing" (p. 180). For a more in-depth discussion, see B. M. Flores, P. T. Cousin, and E. Diaz, "Critiquing and Transforming the Deficit Myths about Learning, Language and Culture," *Language Arts,* 68 (1991), 369–379.

dialectics: While there are a number of definitions and interpretations of *dialectics,* for the general purposes of critical pedagogy, this concept refers to the interconnecting and contradicting relationships that constitute a particular phenomenon, for example, among the economic, political, social, and cultural dimensions of society. Steven Best and Douglas Kellner provide the following example of a dialectical analysis: "A dialectical analysis of advertising, for instance, would theorize its emergence in the capitalist economy and its economic functions and effects; it would also indicate how advertising appropriates certain cultural forms and in turn influences cultural production; and it would analyze the ways in which advertising techniques have been assimilated into and have transformed politics, thus analyzing the interconnections between advertising, the economy, politics, culture, and social life" (p. 264). A dialectical analysis is also often used to show how every idea, or force, has its opposite/contradiction. For example, the dialectic of "oppressor" is the reality of the "oppressed." Such an analysis holds both "opposing" concepts together at once to see how they interconnect and play off each other. For a more in-depth analysis, see the following books in the annotated bibliography: Steven Best and Douglas Kellner, *Postmodern Theory: Critical Interrogations;* Theodor W. Adorno, *Negative Dialectics;* Susan Buck-Morss, *The Origin of Negative Dialectics: Theodor W. Adorno, Walter Benjamin, and the Frankfurt Institute;* Paulo Freire, *The Politics of Education.*

dialogue: Rejecting the style of education in which students are passive recipients of preestablished knowledge, critical pedagogy, which calls for the use of *dialogue,* facilitates critical interaction between teachers and learners. Such dialogues need to be infused with ideological analysis and political action capable of eradicating oppressive practices and institutions both in education and society. For a more in-depth discussion, see the following books in the annotated bibliography: bell hooks, *Talking Back: Thinking Feminist, Thinking Black;* Paulo Freire and Donaldo Macedo, *Literacy: Reading the Word and the World;* bell hooks and Cornel West, *Breaking Bread: Insurgent Black Intellectual Life;* Michael Learner and Cornel West, *Jews and Blacks: Let the Healing Begin.*

discourse: A *discourse* represents the ways in which reality is perceived through and shaped by historically and socially constructed ways of making sense, that is, language, complex signs, and practices that order and sustain particular forms of social existence. These systems of communication, which are constructions informed by particular ideologies, play a significant role in shaping human subjectivities and social reality, and can work to either confirm or deny the life histories and experiences of the people who use them. If the rules that govern what is acceptable in a particular society are exclusive, discourse can be a major site of contention in which different groups struggle over meaning and ideology. For a more in-depth discussion, see Richard Terdiman, *Discourse-Counter Discourse* (New York: Cornell University Press, 1985). See also the following books in the annotated bibliography: James Paul Gee, *The Social Mind: Language, Ideology, and Social Practice;* Patricia Bizzell, *Academic Discourse and Critical Consciousness;* Norman Fairclough, *Critical Discourse Analysis: The Critical Study of Language.*

domesticate: The term *domesticate* refers to the process by which people learn to internalize the dominant values and behaviors that render individuals and groups unable, or unwilling, to recognize oppressive practices. Similar concepts: *manufacture consent, anesthetize, colonize the mind.* For a more in-depth discussion, see the following book in the annotated bibliography: Donaldo Macedo, *Literacies of Power: What Americans Are Not Allowed to Know.*

dominant ideologies: *Dominant ideologies* are bodies of ideas held by cultural groups that are politically, socially, and economically in positions of power and are therefore able to impose on the greater society, through various social institutions and practices, particular traditions, bodies of knowledge, discourse styles, language uses, values, norms, and beliefs, usually at the expense of others. For a more in-depth discussion, see the following books in the annotated bibliography: Russell Ferguson, Martha Gever, Trinh T. Minh-ha, Cornel West, *Out There: Marginalization and Contemporary Cultures;* Terry Eagleton, *Ideology: An Introduction;* Homi K. Bhabha, *Nation and Narration.*

essentialism: *Essentialism* ascribes a fundamental nature or a biological determinism to humans (i.e., men are naturally aggressive, and women are naturally nurturing) through attitudes about identity, experience, knowledge, and cognitive development. Within this monolithic and homogenizing view, categories such as race and gender become gross generalizations, and single-cause explanations about individual character. However, critical feminists have argued that gender is not the only determinant of a woman's identity, and that one must also look at the multiple and interconnecting relationships such as race, class, and sexual orientation in order to understand experience. William Tierney's use of "nonessentialist" points to the idea that universal knowledge does not exist, and that knowledge is instead a social construction (p. 144). Arguing against "cognitive essentialism," Joe Kincheloe and Shirley Steinberg point out that "cognitive development is not simply an innate dimension of human beings, but is rather motivated by sociohistorical, ideological, and other environmental influences (p. 300). For a more in-depth discussion, see the following books in the annotated bibliography: Naomi Schor and Elizabeth Weed, *The Essential Difference;* Judith Butler, *Gender Trouble: Feminism and the Subversion of Identity;* Michael Eric Dyson, *Reflecting Black: African-American Cultural Criticism.*

false consciousness: Linked to the notion that social institutions like schools are agents of ideological control that work to reproduce dominant beliefs, values, norms, and forms of oppression, *false consciousness* is the point at which members of society buy into their own exploitation and subordination, and become uncritical tools of production and consumption. The concept is no longer readily used because the dialectic/opposite of *false* implies that there is a *true* consciousness. In that emancipation is always uncertain and incomplete, this idea of universal truth is rejected by critical pedagogy. More contemporary concepts referring to a similar phenomenon are: *domesticated, mystification of reality, dysconscious, anesthetized, the social construction of not seeing, manufactured consent,* and *colonization of the mind.*

foundationalism: *Foundationalism* refers to the central core of knowledge, morals, and social standards (what's perceived as a set of absolute truths) that a modernist society is built upon. Critical social theories contest *foundationalism* and the myth of universality because they obfuscate the power relations that impose particular forms of authority, social relations, and bodies of knowledge. (See the definition of *postmodernity* in this glossary.)

Frankfurt School: The *Frankfurt School,* a German institute of social research frequented by the likes of Marcuse, Fromm, Horkheimer, Adorno, Habermas, Arendt, Brecht, Lukacs, and a great many others, had an enormous impact on the sociological, political, and cultural thought of this century. It was from this institute that the term "critical theory," and its ideas evolved. For a more in-depth discussion, see the following books in the annotated bibliography: Martin Jay, *The Dialectical Imagination: A History of the Frankfurt School and the Institute of Social Research, 1923–1950;* Susan Buck-Morss, *The Origin of Negative Dialectics: Theodor W. Adorno, Walter Benjamin, and the Frankfurt Institute;* Herbert Marcuse, *One Dimensional Man.*

grand, totalizing, and master narratives: These *narratives* represent any macro-theories that attempt to explain social reality in its entirety. However, such explanations, by subsuming every aspect into one narrowly defined lens, are overly simplistic in that they suppress differences into homogenizing schemes. For example, the modernist claim to universality, or the Marxist notion that class struggle is the unifying principle of human history, are totalizing narratives. In the case where there is a monopoly on the power structure in a particular social order, some of these theories, (*master narratives*) have a large impact on the structure of society.

hegemony: *Hegemony,* as derived from the work of Italian theorist Antonio Gramsci, is used to express how certain groups manage to dominate others. An analysis of hegemony is especially concerned with how the imposition of particular ideologies and forms of authority results in the reproduction of social and institutional practices through which dominant groups maintain not only their positions of privilege and control, but also the consensual support of other members of society. For a more in-depth discussion, see work by Gramsci. See also the following book in the annotated bibliography: Robert Babcock, *Hegemony*.

hermeneutics: *Hermeneutics* refers to the ongoing process of interpreting text for understanding the significance of lived experience, as opposed to believing that meaning is evident or understandable without need of interpretation.

hidden curriculum: This refers to the unspoken agenda in schools that socializes students into the dominant ideology and discourse in which they become uncritical tools of the work force. The *hidden curriculum* functions to erase or distort the experiences and perceptions of individuals and groups from specific backgrounds, such as class, race, gender, and sexual orientation. For a more in-depth discussion, see the following books in the annotated bibliography: Michael W. Apple, *Official Knowledge: Democratic Education in a Conservative Age;* Henry Giroux and David Purpel, *The Hidden Curriculum and Moral Education*.

historical amnesia: This term implies that people develop a limited and limiting sense of history through the socialization process in which selective historical memories are imposed. *Historical amnesia* is used to explain how negative and or dangerous memories that threaten or question the status quo are excluded from public consciousness and classroom inquiry. How, for example, do the histories of women, Blacks, Native Americans, working-class groups, and others whose past experiences contradict the "moral foundation" of the existing dominant structures of society get eliminated or simply rewritten. Critical pedagogy calls for the resurrection of such memories and buried knowledge for the purpose of creating more critically democratic societies. For a more in-depth discussion, see the following books in the annotated bibliography: Howard Zinn, *A People's History of the United States;* Donaldo Macedo, *Literacies of Power: What Americans Are Not Allowed to Know;* Noam Chomsky, *Year 501: The Conquest Continues;* Shoshana Felman and Dori Laub, *Testimony: Crises of Witnessing in Literature, Psychoanalysis, and History*.

internalized oppression: *Internalized oppression* occurs when a member(s) of an oppressed group, after a period of abuse and criticism, comes to believe in the dominant group's description of them as "inferior." As a result of such oppression, people often attempt to assimilate into the dominant culture. Critical pedagogy, while calling for an understanding of this psychological phenomenon, nevertheless insists that it not simply be reduced to the level of the individual. Psychology in the critical sense is shaped by one's sociocultural reality, and thus any understanding of the individual would require an examination of the root cause of that psychological state, which pertains to the realm of ideology. For a more in-depth discussion, see the following books in the annotated bibliography: Franz Fanon, *Black Skin, White Masks;* Paulo Freire, *The Pedagogy of the Oppressed;* Edward Said, *Culture and Imperialism;* Albert Memmi, *The Colonizer and The Colonized;* Edmund Sullivan, *Critical Psychology and Pedagogy: Interpretation of the Personal World;* Shoshana Felman and Dori Laub, *Testimony: Crises of Witnessing in Literature, Psychoanalysis, and History*.

logocentrism/Cartesian logic: Associated with the work of Descartes, who proposed a form of linear causality and a foundation for knowledge, modernist epistemologies center on the idea that there are universal truths, absolute logic, and thus "common sense" in the world. These absolutes (*logocentrics* or *Cartesian logic*) are thought to be the building blocks of society.

manufacture consent: *Manufacturing consent* refers to the process through which an individual or group internalizes certain values (or is indoctrinated), and thus conforms with particular practices, which are usually oppressive in nature. Other similar terms: domesticate, anesthetize, colonize the mind, dysconsciousness, and the social construction of not seeing. For a more in-depth discussion, see the essay by Donaldo Macedo in this book. See also the following book in the annotated bibliography: Edward S. Herman and Noam Chomsky, *Manufacturing Consent: The Political Economy and Mass Media.*

marginalize: To *marginalize* is to force an individual or group out of mainstream society, limiting their access to political and economic power, or to push ideas and concepts that conflict with dominant ideologies to the fringes of academic debate, labeling them as important only to special interest groups. William Tierney describes this process of marginalizing as it readily occurs around gay and lesbian issues. While critical pedagogy is certainly concerned with understanding the lives of those on the margins (and creating self-empowering conditions to escape such oppression), one of its central purposes is to deconstruct the ideologies and practices of the existing dominant center that in fact creates such segregation. For a more in-depth analysis, see the following book in the annotated bibliography: Russell Ferguson, Martha Gever, Trinh T. Minh-ha, Cornel West, *Out There: Marginalization and Contemporary Cultures.*

meritocracy: Under the assumption that institutions in this society are equally responsive to all groups, regardless of race, class, and sex, *meritocracy* refers to a system of education where the so-called "talented" are advanced by virtue of their achievements. Arguing that meritocracy is simply a mechanism of maintaining the status quo, David Spener contends, "Because the excellence movement seeks through its meritocracy to reward the 'excellent' student who 'excels' in the language and behaviors of the dominant elite, and to punish (through low grades and tracking) the 'inferior' student who does not master the language and behaviors of the elite, the outcome of the movement will be to maintain a job ceiling for minorities" (p. 145). For a more in-depth discussion, see the following books in the annotated bibliography: Antonia Darder, *Culture and Power in the Classroom: A Critical Foundation for Bicultural Education;* Samuel Bowles and Herbert Gintis, *Schooling in a Capitalist America: Educational Reform and the Contradictions of Economic Life.*

meta-narrative: A *meta-narrative* analyzes the body of ideas and insights of social theories that attempt to understand a complex diversity of phenomena and their interrelations.

modernity: See postmodernism/modernism.

object/subject of history: Critical pedagogy calls for a person to be an active participant and not simply an entity to be acted upon, manipulated, and controlled as an object of history. It is believed that only as active, critical subjects are we able to make substantive change. In the literature the term *objectification* is used to refer to people being seen/acted upon as objects. This is the process through which one becomes the object of learning strategies (for example, "this is designed for African Americans, you're Black, therefore..."), rather than a knowledgeable participant in the construction of deep and meaningful learning experiences. For a more in-depth discussion, see the following book in the annotated bibliography: Paulo Freire, *Pedagogy of the Oppressed.*

political awareness/clarity: Not to be confused with political correctness, *political awareness/clarity* (which Paulo Freire, throughout his work, refers to as "conscientization") is the awareness of the historical, sociopolitical, economic, cultural, and subjective reality that shapes our lives, and our ability to transform that reality. Lilia Bartolomé further explains that political awareness/clarity is "the process through which individuals come to better understand possible linkages between macro-level political, economic, and social variables and subordinated groups' academic performance at the micro-level classroom" (p. 235). For a discussion about the differences between "political education" and "politicizing education," see the essay by Henry Giroux, in this collection.

positionality (location, subject position, situated): Coming out of feminist scholarship, *position* or *location* refers to the place that a person occupies within a set of social relationships. This position is often determined by such categories as gender, class, race, language, ethnicity, sexual orientation, age, and physical ability. For a more in-depth discussion, see the following books in the annotated bibliography: Gloria Anzaldua, *Haciendo Caras: Creative and Critical Perspectives by Feminists of Color;* Chandra Talpade Mohanty, Ann Russo, Lourdes Torres, *Third World Women and the Politics of Feminism;* Judith Butler and Joan Scott, *Feminists Theorize the Political;* bell hooks, *Talking Back: Thinking Feminist, Thinking Black;* Michael Eric Dyson, *Reflecting Black: African-American Cultural Criticism;* Stanley Aronowitz, *The Politics of Identity: Class, Culture, Social Movements;* Henry Abelove, Michèle Aina Barale, and David M. Halperin, *Lesbian and Gay Studies Reader.*

positivism: Associated with the Enlightenment and modernism, *positivism* refers to a belief system or paradigm that makes claims to objectivity, truth, and certainty in defense of a scientific basis for the study of culture. As such, knowledge and reason are seen as neutral and universal, rather than as social constructions that reflect particular interests and ideologies. Refuting this prevailing notion, critical pedagogy focuses on the idea that any examination of culture is inherently subjective, that is, determined by one's own experiences, beliefs, values, and interests. See the definition of "technocratic" in this glossary. For a discussion of the ways in which "positivism" is embedded in public school curricula, see Henry Giroux, "Schooling and the Culture of Positivism," in *Ideology, Culture and the Process of Schooling* (Philadelphia: Temple University Press, 1981). For a more in-depth discussion, see the following books in the annotated bibliography: Herbert Marcuse, *One Dimensional Man;* C. Wright Mills, *The Sociological Imagination;* Renato Rosaldo, *Culture and Truth: The Remaking of Social analysis.*

postcolonialism: *Postcolonial* theoretical frameworks and practices confront the ideologies, authority, discourses, and social relations that have driven the oppressive legacy of colonialism and imperialism that structure Western institutions, practices, knowledge, and texts. For a more in-depth discussion, see the following books in the annotated bibliography: Albert Memmi, *The Colonizer and the Colonized;* Franz Fanon, *Black Skin, White Masks;* Chandra Talpade Mohanty, Ann Russo, and Lourdes Torres, *Third World Women and the Politics of Feminism;* Rodolfo Acuna, *Occupied America: A History of Chicanos;* Edward Said, *Culture and Imperialism;* Noam Chomsky, *Year 501: The Conquest Continues;* Wa Thiong'o Ngugi; *Decolonizing the Mind: The Politics of Language in African Literature;* Haunani-Kay Trask, *From A Native Daughter: Colonialism and Sovereignty in Hawai'i;* Trinh T. Minh-ha, *Women Native Other;* Bill Ashcroft, Gareth Griffiths, and Helen Tiffin, *The Postcolonial Studies Reader.*

postmodernism/modernity: There is no generic definition of either *modernity* or *postmodernity.* In fact, positions within these frameworks are often contradicting. This particular explanation will simply compare and contrast some specific points of modernism and postmodernism that are central to critical pedagogy (the individual, knowledge, schools).

the individual: The individual in the modernist (or liberal humanist) sense is considered to be an independent and rational being who is predisposed to be motivated toward social agency and emancipation — what Descartes believed to be the existence of a unified self. Postmodernists, on the other hand, don't believe that the mind has an innate universal structure or essence. They contend that consciousness and the self are socially and historically constructed, and are constantly changing within shifting contexts. Emancipation is also seen as uncertain and incomplete.

knowledge: Modernist epistemologies center around the idea that universal truths, absolute logic or common sense (referred to as *logocentrism* or *Cartesian logic* — associated with the work of Descartes, who proposed a form of linear causality) are a foundation for knowledge, morals, and social standards (referred to as *foundationalism*), and that a society can and should be built upon these values and truths. "Positivism" is the philosophy associated with modernity, which makes claims to objectivity, truth, and certainty, in defense of a scientific basis for the study of culture. Universal reason and objectivity are seen as the source for knowledge and emancipation. Postmodernists are radically opposed to any homogenizing and constricting social paradigm, and reject a scientific basis for the study of culture and of the possibilities of truth, certainty, and objectivity. They reject positivism, instrumental reason, and any theory that subsumes every aspect of social reality into one totalizing theory that goes unquestioned (these all-encompassing theories are referred to as *grand, master,* or *totalizing* narratives). Postmodernists don't believe that the mind has an innate, universal structure; rather, they see consciousness, identities, and meaning as socially and historically produced. Universals are thus rejected in the name of difference and diversity, and the uncertainty of knowing the world in a fixed and assured way. As postmodernists confront the relationships among power, ideology, and knowledge, critical pedagogy concerns itself with having students examine the values, assumptions, ideologies, and interests reflected in bodies of knowledge so that they are able to recognize whose interests have been advanced at the expense of others. Students within this process become knowledge producers rather than reproducers.

schools: Modernists believe that schools can contribute to the development of a democratic and egalitarian social order. Postmodernists argue that the modernist foundations of positivism, instrumental reason, universal knowledge, and bureaucratic control have historically been injected into public schools — that, in fact, they are at the center of curriculum, educational theory, and practice — and frequently operate in oppressive ways to shape the manner in which people interact and relate to each other with an agenda of constructing forms of cultural, gender, sexual, linguistic, racial, and socioeconomic domination. Critical pedagogues thus contend that schools do not provide the opportunity for self-empowerment and democratic struggle, in that multiple voices cannot be heard because of the modernist belief in objective truth, which means that only one voice is given legitimacy, and only one truth, one reality, will be heard. For a more in-depth discussion, see the following books: Jean-Francois Lyotard, *The Postmodern Condition* (Minneapolis: University of Minnesota Press, 1984); Jurgen Habermas, *The Philosophical Discourse of Modernity* (Cambridge: MIT Press, 1987); Henry Giroux, *Border Crossings: Cultural Workers and the Politics of Education* (New York: Routledge, 1992). See also the following books in the annotated bibliography: Steven Best and Douglas Kellner,

Postmodern Theory: Critical Interrogations; Colin Gordon, *Michel Foucault: Power/Knowledge: Selected Interviews and Other Writings 1972–1977;* Homi K. Bhabha, *The Location of Culture;* Herbert Marcuse, *One Dimensional Man.*

poststructuralism: While *poststructuralism* holds certain assumptions about language, discourse, and identity, it is important to note that it does not constitute a unified field. A major influence on postmodern thought, poststructuralists reject the notion of universal truth, and that the mind has an innate, universal structure. They also reject the possibility of conducting an objective study of culture. Consciousness, identities, meaning, and cognitive development are seen as socially and historically produced within the politics of everyday life. Poststructuralism works from the premise that language/discourse constitutes rather than merely reflects reality. Discourse in this sense refers to the way reality is perceived through and shaped by historically and socially constructed ways of making sense — that is, languages, complex signs, and practices that order and sustain particular forms of social existence. As such, systems of communication, which are all social and historical constructions informed by particular ideologies, play a significant role in shaping human subjectivities and reality, and can work to either confirm or deny the life histories and experiences of the people who use them. For a more in-depth discussion, see the following books in the annotated bibliography: Cleo H. Cherryholmes, *Power and Criticism: Poststructural Investigations in Education;* Maria-Regina Kecht, *Pedagogy is Politics: Literary Theory and Critical Teaching;* M. M. Bakhtin, *The Dialogic Imagination: Four Essays by M. M. Bakhtin;* Judith Butler and Joan Scott, *Feminists Theorize the Political;* James Paul Gee, *The Social Mind: Language, Ideology, and Social Practice;* Henry Giroux, *Disturbing Pleasures: Learning Popular Culture.*

praxis: *Praxis* is the relationship between theoretical understanding and critique of society (that is, its historical, ideological, sociopolitical, and economic influences and structures) and action that seeks to transform individuals and their environment. Arguing that people cannot transform a given situation through awareness or the best of intentions, nor through unguided action, Paulo Freire defines "praxis" throughout his work as a dialectical movement that goes from action to reflection and from reflection upon action to a new action. For a more in-depth discussion, see the following book in the annotated bibliography: Paulo Freire, *The Politics of Education: Culture Power, and Liberation.*

problematize: Associated with critical thinking/inquiry (that is, being able to understand, analyze, and effect the sociohistorical, economic, cultural, and political realities that shape our lives), *problematizing* is the process of posing questions in order to deconstruct a particular phenomenon so as to understand its construct. The term "deconstruction" is often used to describe this same process.

public sphere: *Public spheres* in the critical sense are public arenas for citizens in which political participation, outside of direct government and economic influence and intervention, is enacted through dialogue and debate. Schools are envisioned by critical pedagogues as "public spheres," wherein classrooms are active sites of public intervention and social struggle, rather than mere adjuncts of corporate and partisan interests. Because mainstream society is constituted by particular oppressive ideologies, these critical spheres are also referred to as "counterpublics." For a more in-depth understanding and critique of the multiple definitions and historical roles of "public spheres," from Jurgen Habermas' coining of the phrase on, see Nancy Fraser, "Rethinking the Public Sphere: A Contribution to the Critique of Actually Existing Democracy," in *Between Borders: Learning Popular Culture,* ed. Henry Giroux and Peter McLaren (New York: Routledge, 1994) and Hannah Arendt, *The Human Condition* (Chicago: University of Chicago Press, 1958).

reductionistic: To be *reductionistic* is to simplify a particular phenomenon so as to mask its complexity. For example, arguing that social reality is shaped solely by socioeconomic status and class conflict obscures the multiple and interconnecting relationships of other significant human experiences (such as race, gender, and sexual orientation) and their effects on perception and struggle.

representational politics: Public media, such as film, television, and magazines, work to actively control the ways in which identities are depicted in the mainstream. These images/representations can stereotype, silence, marginalize, or distort. Curricula also function in this way by depicting and/or shaping the identities of students. This struggle over identity and representation — that is, over who has the power to fashion images and identities, and with what agenda in mind — is referred to as *representational politics*. For a more in-depth discussion, see Henry Giroux's essay in this collection. See also the following books in the annotated bibliography: Edward S. Herman and Noam Chomsky, *Manufacturing Consent: The Political Economy and Mass Media;* Gina Dent, *Black Popular Culture;* Richard Dyer, *The Matter of Images: Essays on Representations;* Edward Said, *Culture and Imperialism;* Gayatri C. Spivak, *Outside in the Teaching Machine;* Toni Morrison, *Playing in the Dark: Whiteness and the Literary Imagination;* Michael Eric Dyson, *Reflecting Black: African-American Cultural Criticism;* Diana Fuss, *Inside/Out;* Coco Fusco, *English Is Broken Here: Notes on Cultural Fusion in the Americas;* Lucy Lippard, *Mixed Blessings: New Art in a Multicultural America;* Cameron McCarthy and Warren Crinchlow, *Race, Identity, and Representation in Education*.

resistance/oppositional identity: *Resistance (oppositional identity)* has traditionally been attributed to deviant behavior, individual pathology, learned helplessness, cultural deprivation, and genetic flaws. Critical pedagogy, on the other hand, sees resistance as a legitimate response to domination, used to help individuals or groups deal with oppression. From this perspective, resistance in any form should be part of a larger political project that is working towards change. For a more in-depth discussion, see: Henry Giroux, *Theory and Resistance in Education: A Pedagogy for the Opposition* (South Hadley, MA: Bergin & Garvey, 1983); Paul Willis, *Learning to Labour: How Working Class Kids Get Working Class Jobs* (Westmead: Saxon House, 1977); Lois Weis and Michelle Fine, *Beyond Silenced Voices: Class, Race, and Gender in United States Schools* (Albany: State University of New York Press, 1993). See the following books in the annotated bibliography: bell hooks, *Talking Back: Thinking Feminist, Thinking Black;* Michele Wallace, *Invisibility Blues*.

sociohistorical: A *sociohistorical* lens works from the assumption that we are never independent of the social and historical forces that surround us. That is, we all inherit beliefs, values, and ideologies that need to be critically understood and transformed where necessary. Arguing that history is not predetermined, critical pedagogy contends that we should be active subjects of history (shapers of history), rather than objects that are acted upon, manipulated, and controlled. For a more in depth discussion, see the following books in the annotated bibliography: Paulo Freire, *The Politics of Education;* Howard Zinn, *A People's History of the United States;* James W. Loewen, *Lies my Teacher Told Me: Everything Your American History Textbook Got Wrong*.

subjectivity: *Subjectivity* in the liberal humanist sense is described as being constructed by the independent choices and intentions of the individual. Rejecting the notion of an autonomous being, subjectivity, in the critical sense, is more of a product of historical, cultural, social, linguistic, and institutional structures and constraints. As such, subjectivity is always forged within particular relations of power.

subordinated cultures: *Subordinated* refers to cultural groups that have been historically, politically, socially, and economically disempowered in the greater society. As Lilia Bartolomé states, "While individual members of these groups may not consider themselves subordinate in any manner to the White 'mainstream,' they nevertheless are members of a greater collective that historically have been perceived and treated as subordinate and inferior by the dominant society. Thus it is not entirely accurate to describe these students as 'minority' students, since the term connotes numerical minority rather than the general low status (economic, political, and social) these groups have held" (p. 230).

technocratic (technicians/technicists): Emanating from the positivist tradition, *technocratic* models, which conceptualize teaching as a discrete and scientific undertaking, embrace depersonalized solutions for education that often translate into the regulation and standardization of teacher practices and curricula, and rote memorization of selected "facts" that can easily be measured through standardized testing. As such, the role of the teacher is reduced to that of an uncritical, "objective," and "efficient" distributor of information.

telecratic: A *telecratic* society is one, such as U.S. society, in which the electronic media have an enormous influence on the construction of meaning, identity, and social relations (that is, a media-oriented society). For a more in-depth discussion, see David Sholle and Stan Denski, *Media Education and the (RE)Production of Culture* (Westport, CT: Bergin & Garvey, 1994). See also the following books in the annotated bibliography: Gretchen Bender and Timothy Druckrey, *Cultures on the Brink: Ideologies of Technology;* Henry Giroux, *Disturbing Pleasures: Learning Popular Culture;* Dominic Stranati, *An Introduction to Theories of Popular Culture;* Edward S. Herman and Noam Chomsky, *Manufacturing Consent: The Political Economy & Mass Media.*

text: A *text* implies any aspect of reality that transfers meaning. This may include, but is not limited to, aural, visual, and printed materials. Examples of text include written passages, oral communication, music, body language, and visual representations such as movies, advertisements, photographs, and paintings. Magda Lewis and Roger Simon define text as "a particular concrete manifestation of practices organized within a particular discourse" (p. 254).

voice: *Voice* simply refers to people's authentic self-expression, with an understanding that people are situated in personal histories of engagement with their surroundings/communities through which voice is shaped by class, cultural, racial, and gender identities. Finding one's/using one's voice refers to a quality of authenticity, that one is speaking with integrity and from a position of self-empowerment, or even liberation. See the definition of "dialogue" in the glossary. For a more in-depth discussion, see Magda Lewis and Roger Simon's essay in this collection. See also: Lois Weis and Michelle Fine, *Beyond Silenced Voices: Class, Race, and Gender in the United States Schools* (Albany: State University of New York Press, 1993); Daniel McLaughlin and William Tierney, *Naming Silenced Lives: Personal Narratives and the Process of Educational Change* (New York: Routledge, 1993). See also the following books in the annotated bibliography: bell hooks, *Talking Back: Thinking Feminist, Thinking Black;* Catherine E. Walsh, *Pedagogy and the Struggle For Voice: Issues of Language, Power, and Schooling for Puerto Ricans.*

Recommended Reading

The following list is not meant to be exhaustive, nor is it meant to be a prescription. Its purpose is to introduce and challenge the reader to engage in an interdisciplinary exploration of the multiple issues, theories, and practices of some insightful critical thinkers. As the readings will show, there is a great deal of artwork, music, and videos that are not only useful in developing our own understanding of cultural politics and critical pedagogy. The books are listed in alphabetical order by title.

Academic Discourse and Critical Consciousness
by Patricia Bizzell. *Pittsburgh: University of Pittsburgh Press, 1992.*
This collection of essays explores the dilemmas that students from diverse backgrounds face when dealing with academic discourse. Bizzell develops theoretical and practical directions for composition studies that are both inclusive as well as critically engaging for both students and teachers.

The Asian American Educational Experience
edited by Don T. Nakanishi and Tina Yamano Nishida. *New York: Routledge, 1995.*
This collection of essays provides a comprehensive and interdisciplinary reader on Asian American education. The contributors offer historical, theoretical, and practical insights about a number of issues, including admission quotas, model minority stereotypes, bilingual education, and education for refugee and immigrant populations.

Black Atlantic: Modernity and Double Consciousness
by Paul Gilroy. *Cambridge, MA: Harvard University Press, 1993.*
Bringing together theoretical insights from cultural and African American studies, Gilroy's analysis of the Black Diaspora and Black popular culture sets a new agenda for understanding the debates over modernity.

Black Popular Culture
edited by Gina Dent. *Seattle: Bay Press, 1992.*
This collection of Black insurgent intellectuals, which includes the voices of Stuart Hall, Houston Baker, Hazel Carby, Tricia Rose, Manning Marable, and Kofi Natambu, provides a comprehensive look at the diversity and complexity of Black popular culture, as well as the intellectual debates that such diversity evokes.

Black Skin, White Masks
by Frantz Fanon. *New York: Grove Press, 1967.*
This widely circulated book has been a major influence in civil rights, anti-colonial, and Black consciousness movements around the world. Fanon's understanding of the Black

psyche in relation to White domination provides an abundance of postcolonial theoretical insights that are invaluable to any project for human liberation.

Bolivian Diary
by Ernesto Che Guevara. *New York: Path Finder, 1994.*
This book is a day-by-day account of the ever-evolving political consciousness and revolutionary movements of workers and peasants, as organized and led by Guevara, in their struggle for land and national sovereignty.

Borderlands/La Frontera: The New Mestiza
by Gloria Anzaldua. *San Francisco: Spinsters/Aunt Lute, 1987.*
Through a series of prose and poetry, Gloria Anzaldua describes her life of being trapped between two cultures on the Texas-Mexico border, and provides an important analysis of the coming together of many cultures.

Breaking Bread: Insurgent Black Intellectual Life
by bell hooks and Cornel West. *Boston: South End Press, 1991.*
This book consists of an insightful dialogue between two of today's central Black intellectuals. The conversation engages a wide range of issues pertaining to Black intellectual life, and calls for the necessary social, cultural, and political transformations that will ensure justice and equality for all peoples.

Breaking the Silence: Redress and Japanese American Ethnicity
by Yasuko I. Takezawa. *Ithaca, NY: Cornell University Press, 1995.*
This book depicts how wartime internment and the movement for redress affected Japanese Americans. Covering the period before, during, and after World War II, Takezawa captures the internal struggles of the Japanese American community.

Bury My Heart at Wounded Knee: An Indian History of the American West
by Dee Brown. *New York: Henry Holt, 1970.*
Rupturing the myth of how the west was won, this study documents the systematic destruction and colonization of Native Americans during the second half of the nineteenth century, and includes the voices of the many of the forgotten victims.

The Chicano/Hispanic Image in American Film
by Frank Javier Berumen Garcia. *New York: Vantage, 1995.*
This book examines the roots of media stereotypes, in their historical and political context, demonstrating how history itself is often revised to create a "screen world" of cultural inaccuracies and stereotypes.

Chilean Voices: Activists Describe Their Experiences of the Popular Unity Period
recorded and edited by Colin Henfrey and Bernardo Sorj. *Atlantic Highlands, NJ: Humanities Press, 1977.*
Salvador Allende's struggle to achieve "the peaceful way toward socialism" in Chile is depicted through the voices of seven activists who were involved at a grassroots level. This book addresses such questions as What difference did the "Popular Unity Movement" make in the lives of women? and What did "popular power" mean to workers? These seven activists describe what their ideas meant in practice, and how the general population contributed and reacted to them.

The Chomsky Trilogy: The Real Story Series
by Noam Chomsky. *Berkeley, CA: Odonian Press, 1993.*
In these three books — *Secrets, Lies, and Democracy* (1993), *The Prosperous Few and the Restless Many* (1993), and *What Uncle Sam Really Wants* (1992) — Noam Chomsky provides a powerful critique of U.S. domestic and foreign policy, revealing a disturbing agenda of domination, exploitation, and destruction. Chomsky clearly shows how we as a nation in fact work against the basic tenets of democracy.

The Colonizer and the Colonized
by Albert Memmi. *Boston: Beacon Press, 1991.*
Concerned with the anti-colonial struggle of the past two centuries, and the implications for contemporary postcolonial theory and practice, Albert Memmi's personal recollections of life in occupied Algeria and his theorizing about the relationship between the oppressed and those in power offers a portrait for understanding the ideological, psychological, cultural, and political ramifications of imperialism.

Critical Discourse Analysis: The Critical Study of Language
by Norman Fairclough. *New York: Longman, 1995.*
This book clearly illustrates how language and discourse are inextricably related to power, ideology, and contemporary social and cultural change. In addition, Fairclough provides educational applications for critical discourse analysis.

Critical Pedagogy and Cultural Power
edited by David Livingstone. *New York: Bergin & Garvey, 1987.*
This collection of essays depicts ways in which pedagogy in advanced capitalist societies is implicated in forms of domination and subordination. The various authors examine the ideologies of the media, the family, and the schools that drive contemporary class and gender relations in society.

Critical Pedagogy and Predatory Culture: Oppositional Politics in a Postmodern Era
by Peter McLaren. *New York: Routledge, 1995.*
Covering issues of identity, representation, resistance, culture, and schooling, McLaren shares a number of insights for developing a critical pedagogy capable of challenging and transforming standard academic boundaries and practices that are part of the deep structures of domination within schools and society.

Critical Psychology and Pedagogy: Interpretation of the Personal World
by Edmund Sullivan. *New York: Bergin & Garvey, 1990.*
Refuting the traditional notion of psychology, which often abstracts identity development from sociohistorical and ideological influences, this book provides some important insights, not only about understanding the process through which identities are constructed, but also about how to ground such critical psychology in critical pedagogical practices that are liberatory.

Critical Theory and Educational Research
edited by Peter L. McLaren and James M. Giarelli. *New York: State University of New York Press, 1995.*
With contributions by Nicholas Burbules, Joe Kincheloe, Kathleen Weiler, Carlos Alberto Torres, and Paulo Freire, among others, this book elaborates and refines the possibilities of research informed by critical theories.

Critical Theory, Public Policy, and Planning Practice: Toward a Critical Pragmatism
by John Forester. *New York: State University of New York Press, 1993.*
Providing an introduction to critical social theory, John Forester examines and illuminates how such theories are crucial in not only understanding, but more importantly transforming, public policy, planning, and organizational structures.

Cultural Pedagogy: Art/Education/Politics
by David Trend. *New York: Bergin & Garvey, 1992.*
This book illustrates how there should be a symbiotic relationship between education and the arts, and presents new critical theoretical insights and that link creative work to critical pedagogical practices.

Cultural Studies
edited by Lawrence Grossberg, Cary Nelson, and Paula Treichler. *New York: Routledge, 1992.*
Bringing together over forty scholars, including Stuart Hall, Paul Gilroy, Kobena Mercer, Marcos Sanchez-Tranquilino, and Lata Mani, this collection of essays captures the complexity of issues taken up in cultural studies, and provides important signposts for navigating a path through the cultural turmoil of the 1990s.

The Cultural Studies Reader
edited by Simon During. *New York: Routledge, 1993.*
This is an excellent source for representative examples and in-depth critiques of the diverse issues explored in the field of cultural studies. Unlike most other volumes, this particular book offers the reader access to a legacy of critical social thought by including the work of less recent, but highly influential, critical social theorists such as Theodor Adorno, Max Horkheimer, and Michel Foucault.

Culture and Imperialism
by Edward Said. *New York: Knopf, 1993.*
Exploring the great works of Western tradition — including Conrad's *Heart of Darkness*, Austen's *Mansfield Park*, Verdi's *Aida*, and Camus's *L'Etranger* — Edward Said exposes how Western imperialism, with its mechanisms for controlling the language and culture of dominated groups, shaped the ways in which the colonizer and the colonized saw themselves and each other. He describes this legacy of imperialism in the nineteenth and twentieth centuries as nothing less than devastating.

Culture and Power in the Classroom: A Critical Foundation for Bicultural Education
by Antonia Darder. *New York: Bergin & Garvey, 1991.*
Describing her own critical theoretical framework and liberatory practices, Antonia Darder examines the possibilities of critical pedagogy in the education of bicultural and bilingual students in the United States.

Culture and Truth: The Remaking of Social Analysis
by Renato Rosaldo. *Boston: Beacon Press, 1993.*
As part of a growing body of work in critical anthropology, this book provides a new way of thinking, researching, and writing about culture and social analysis. Discarding the positivist paradigm that makes claims to objectivity, truth, and certainty in defense of a

scientific basis for the study of culture, Ronato Rosaldo recognizes the inherently subjective nature of research and embraces difference, narrative, and emotion.

The Culture of Nature: North American Landscape from Disney to the Exxon Valdez
by Alexander Wilson. *Cambridge, MA: Blackwell, 1992.*
Wilson argues that the current environmental crisis has reached far beyond the land; it is a crisis of culture as well. The book thus examines North Americans', including Native cultures', relation to the natural world.

Cultures on the Brink: Ideologies of Technology
edited by Gretchen Bender and Timothy Druckrey. *Seattle: Bay Press, 1994.*
This collection of essays critically examines the influences that technologies, such as the electronic media, computerization, information processing, and cybernetic control systems have on everyday life — organizationally, socially, psychologically, etc. The book's authors challenge the notion of technological advancements and stress the need for critical public intervention in order to control the manipulation and exploitation embedded in the notion of "progress."

Decolonizing the Mind: The Politics of Language in African Literature
by Wa Thiong'o Ngugi. *London: James Curry, 1986.*
Shedding light on the complex relationship among language, experience, ideology, and power, Ngugi, through an examination of the language of African literature and theater, contends that throughout the twentieth century, Europeans have exploited the African mind to enrich their own language and culture. This book represents an effort to resist neo-colonial imperialism, and embodies the desire to take ownership of one's identity and heritage.

The Dialectical Imagination: A History of the Frankfurt School and the Institute of Social Research, 1923–1950
by Martin Jay. *Boston: Little Brown, 1973.*
The Frankfurt Institute of Social Research, frequented by the likes of Marcuse, Fromm, Horkheimer, Neuman, Adorno, Habermas, Mann, Arendt, Brecht, Lukacs, Mannheim, Lowenthal, Pollock, and a great many others, had an enormous impact on the sociological, political, and cultural thought of this century. Jay provides an introductory and comprehensive historical look into the Frankfurt Institute and the groundbreaking ideas generated by its members, both in Germany and the United States.

The Dialogic Imagination: Four Essays by M. M. Bakhtin
edited by Michael Holquist. *Austin: University of Texas Press, 1981.*
In this English translation of the Russian social and cultural theorist M. M. Bakhtin, Bakhtin analyzes how language and literature (the novel) are shaped by sociohistorical and ideological influences, and reveals the ways in which diverse languages, dialects, and subgenres compete with one another. He points out the ways in which we actually experience language as we use it, as well as how we are used by it.

Disability and Democracy: Reconstructing (Special) Education for Postmodernity
edited by Thomas M. Skrtic. *New York: Teachers College Press, 1995.*
The book's contributors situate special education reform within a broader discourse on the reconstruction of education through democratic renewal. The chapters in this book

examine the theoretical implications and influences of functionalism, interpretivism, radical structuralism, and radical humanism, in order to show how modern approaches and practices in special education are simply inadequate. The authors provide alternative ways of thinking about and doing special education.

Disturbing Pleasures: Learning Popular Culture
by Henry Giroux. *New York: Routledge, 1994.*
This book argues that pedagogy as the production of knowledge, values, and social identities takes place in a variety of sites, especially the sphere of popular culture. Giroux addresses how meaning and representation work through the advertising of Benetton, the cultural texts of Disney, in Whittle Communications, and elsewhere. He examines the strategies employed by these companies and at the same time suggests ways in which their deconstruction and transformation can be taken up as part of a broader pedagogical practice.

Don't Be Afraid Gringo: A Honduran Woman Speaks From the Heart: The Story of Elvia Alvarado
edited by Medea Benjamin. *New York: Harper Perennial, 1987.*
Trained by the Catholic Church to organize women's groups to combat malnutrition, Alvarado began to make the connections between malnutrition and systemic domination in Honduras. This book invites the reader to walk with her as she traveled her country by foot talking to the people. Discovering the internal and oppressive workings of her society, Alvarado worked as a *campesino* organizer, for which she was jailed and tortured at the hands of the Honduran military. This book is not only a testament to the struggle and political conflict of Honduras, but also provides a picture of the possibilities of growing political awareness and making alliances.

Ecological Economics: A Practical Program for Global Reform
by The Group of Green Economists. *London: Zed Books, 1992.*
These authors draw on the thinking of various environmental, women's, and human rights movements, arguing that there are practical alternatives to the vast inequalities and social and environmental dislocation caused by two centuries of market-led industrialization and European colonial rule. They propose basic principles for global ecological economics, and provide suggestions for restructuring international trade, reorganizing the global financial system, and controlling transnational corporations. Their alternatives are based on ecological balance, democracy, social equality, feminism, nonviolence, and respect for cultural identity and diversity.

Empowering Education: Critical Teaching for Social Change
by Ira Shor. *Chicago: University of Chicago Press, 1992.*
Making the links between education and democracy, Ira Shor examines the possibilities and obstacles for creating a self-empowering classroom (whether it be elementary school or college) in which both the students and the teachers engage and work, through critical dialogue, to transform traditional epistemological restraints and oppressive pedagogical practices.

English Is Broken Here: Notes on Cultural Fusion in the Americas
by Coco Fusco. *New York: New Press, 1995.*
This collection of essays, which discuss issues of biculturalism, bilingualism, nationalism, and cross-cultural arts and media criticism, provides an important and insightful examination of contemporary cultural politics.

The Essential Difference
edited by Naomi Schor and Elizabeth Weed. *Bloomington: Indiana University Press, 1994.*
Representing a wide range of fields— philosophy, deconstruction, theology, history, literary studies, etc. — as well as of perspectives, including Teresa De Lauretis, Diana Fuss, and Gayatri Chakravorty Spivak, this collection of essays examines and extends the heated feminist debates over nature (biological predispositions) versus nurture (the social construction of identity).

Faces at the Bottom of the Well: The Permanence of Racism
by Derrick D. Bell. *New York: Basic Books, 1992.*
Derrick Bell illustrates how racism is an integral part of the American cultural landscape, and how the status quo is a serious threat to all democratic possibilities in this country. This book moves beyond the liberal efforts of the Civil Rights Movement and advocates a more radical approach to eradicating racism.

Feminists Theorize the Political
edited by Judith Butler and Joan Scott. *New York: Routledge, 1992.*
This collection of feminist scholars takes a look at the role of poststructuralism within the feminist debates. The book addresses what happens to the feminist critique when traditional foundations of the movement are critically examined (for example, how have the role of race, class, and sexual orientation been included or excluded), and in doing so, it reformulates questions over social agency, power, and sites of political resistance.

Framing Dropouts: Notes on the Politics of an Urban High School
by Michelle Fine. *New York: State University of New York Press, 1991.*
Through the use of critical ethnography, Michelle Fine reflects on the ideological and material forces that create the social conditions within which young people drop out of school. Arguing that public schools have never been designed for the benefit of low-income students of color, Fine illustrates how the institution of education, by focusing on one school in particular, routinely and traditionally has reproduced social injustice and "failure." By unpacking the prevailing discourse about "dropouts," Fine creates the possibility for change.

From a Native Daughter: Colonialism and Sovereignty in Hawai'i
by Haunani-Kay Trask. *Monroe, ME: Common Courage Press, 1993.*
Trask offers an inside view of the racism, injustice, and domination that has driven the history of U.S. imperialism in Hawaii, and depicts the struggle of Native Hawaiians to regain their human rights and land.

Gender Trouble: Feminism and the Subversion of Identity
by Judith Butler. *New York: Routledge, 1990.*
Critically appropriating insights from philosophy, anthropology, literary theory, and psychoanalysis, Butler provides a critique of the essentialist notion of fixed gender identities rooted in biology. Engaging the work of Lacan, Freud, Beauvoir, Kristeva, Foucault, and others, she shapes and refines her own theory of gender.

The Green Peace Guide to Anti-Environmental Organizations
by Carl Deal. *Berkeley, CA: Odonian Press, 1993.*
Arguing that industries have set up elaborate front groups, that masquerade as environmental organizations — legal foundations, think tanks, charitable endowments, and pub-

lic relations firms — in order to exploit and destroy the environment, Deal puts critical pedagogy into practice by doing the necessary critical research to expose fifty of these fraudulent organizations.

Haciendo Caras: Creative and Critical Perspectives by Feminists of Color
edited by Gloria Anzaldua. *San Francisco: Aunt Lute Books, 1990.*
This collection of essays by women of color explores a wide range of issues that are crucial in understanding the complexity of the politics of identity and difference. Examining and challenging neo-colonial models, mechanisms of internalized oppression and silencing, and the rocky road of inter/intragroup alliance building, this book creates the critical theoretical space in which coming to voice is a practice of freedom.

Hegemony
by Robert Babcock. *New York: Tavistock Publications, 1986.*
Robert Babcock introduces the reader to Italian theorist Antonio Gramsci's concept of "hegemony," and expands Gramsci's notion by moving beyond his focus on class analysis and into the struggles for power in religious, nationalist, women's rights, and environmental movements.

The Hidden Curriculum and Moral Education
edited by Henry Giroux and David Purpel. *New York: McCutchan, 1983.*
This book is important for understanding the meaning and practices of the hidden curriculum — that is, the unspoken agenda in schools in which students are socialized by and into the dominant ideology. The various authors explore how such an agenda functions to erase or distort the experiences and perceptions of individuals and groups from specific backgrounds, such as class, racial, gender, and sexual orientation.

Hold Your Tongue: Bilingualism and the Politics of "English Only"
by James Crawford. *New York: Addison-Wesley, 1992.*
This book explores the contentious debates over bilingual education, and examines the politics of the "English Only Movement." Crawford takes a critical look at legislation and classroom practices across the country and attempts to portray all sides of the argument over language and national identity. He embraces cultural diversity by calling for the improvement of English-as-a-Second-Language and bilingual maintenance programs.

I . . . Rigoberta Menchú: An Indian Woman in Guatemala
edited by Elisabeth Burgos-Debray. *New York: Verso, 1984.*
This book depicts the social and political struggle, as well as the evolving feminist and socialist theoretical framework, of a Guatemalan peasant woman in her efforts as a national leader to achieve social justice for her Indian community and country.

Ideology: An Introduction
by Terry Eagleton. *New York: Verso, 1991.*
Written with the intention of introducing the unfamiliar reader to the current conflictual debates over the complex issue of ideology, this book explores the conceptual development of the notion of ideology, from the Enlightenment to poststructuralism and postmodernism. Eagleton travels through the multiplicity of definitions of "ideology," engaging the reader in the critical and enormously influential work of Marx, Freud, Nietzsche, Lukacs, Gramsci, Adorno, Bourdieu, Schopenhauer, and Sorel, among others.

In the Spirit of Crazy Horse
by Peter Matthiessen. *London: Penguin, 1991.*
This book tells the story of Leonard Peltier and the F.B.I.'s war on the American Indian Movement. In fact, Matthiessen exposes the Lakota tribe's long struggle with the U.S. government.

Inside/Out: Lesbian Theories, Gay Theories
edited by Diana Fuss. *New York: Routledge, 1991.*
Featuring the theoretical work of gay and lesbian scholars, this collection of essays investigates representations of sex and sexual difference in literature, film, video, music, and photography. They also address issues of AIDS, pornography, authorship, pedagogy, and activism.

Intifada
by Zachary Lockman and Joel Beinin. *Boston: South End Press, 1989.*
Exploring the Palestinian uprising in Jerusalem, this book not only attempts to deal with the historical and political complexity of the Palestinian situation, but also unpacks the Western medias' portrayal of such a struggle.

An Introduction to Theories of Popular Culture
by Dominic Strinati. *New York: Routledge, 1995.*
This book is a clear and comprehensive map through the major themes and theories of popular culture. Introducing the reader to the debates over mass culture, the Frankfurt School and the culture industry, semiology and structuralism, Marxism, feminism, and postmodernism, Strinati provides a critical assessment of the ways in which these theories have tried to understand and evaluate popular culture in modern societies.

Invisibility Blues: From Pop to Theory
by Michele Wallace. *New York: Verso, 1990.*
Drawing from cultural studies, Black feminism, critical theory, and personal history, Michele Wallace takes a look at popular culture, examining the collective legacy that Black artists must contend with in carving out a distinctive cultural practice that is critical, more theoretically profound, inclusive, and liberatory.

Iron Cages: Race and Culture in 19th-Century America
by Ronald Takaki. *New York: Oxford University Press, 1990.*
Takaki's work encompasses the broad political, social, and economic influences on the formations of foundations of racial and cultural domination in the United States. The author analyzes White attitudes toward Blacks, Asians, Native Americans, and Mexicans, as well as ways in which the experiences of different groups related to one another in the nineteenth century.

Jews and Blacks: Let the Healing Begin
by Michael Learner and Cornel West. *New York: Grosset & Putnam, 1995.*
Exploring the possibility of whether or not Jews and Blacks can be allies again, Learner and West look at the problems facing contemporary America through the lens of the relationship between these two communities. This dialogue examines issues such as economic inequalities between the two communities, crime, and affirmative action, and takes a critical look at both Louis Farrakhan and Zionism. Modeling what dialogue, in the Freirian sense, is all about, they conclude with a plan for bridging the gaps and healing the rifts between Blacks and Jews.

Language and Control
by Roger Fowler, Bob Hodge, Gunther Kress, and Tony Trew
Boston: Routledge & Kegan Paul, 1979.
These authors argue that the language used in social institutions and mainstream practices is deeply implicated in the oppressive ideology of the dominant elite. They provide a conceptual framework for critical linguistic practices that works to lay bare and challenge such subtle discursive mechanisms of social control.

Latina Politics, Latino Politics: Gender, Culture, and Political Participation in Boston
by Carol Hardy-Fanta. *Philadelphia: Temple University Press, 1993.*
This book provides an in-depth study of the evolving political consciousness of the Latino community in Boston, Massachusetts. Through a series of interviews with Puerto Rican, Dominican, and Central and South American women and men, Hardy-Fanta examines the ways in which culture and gender interact in the political mobilization and empowerment of ethnic communities.

Lesbian and Gay Studies Reader
edited by Henry Abelove, Michèle Aina Barale, and David M. Halperin. *New York: Routledge, 1993.*
This collection of essays provides a deep and thorough understanding of the diversity of issues, concerns, concepts, theories, and practices of Lesbian and Gay studies.

Lies My Teacher Told Me: Everything Your American History Textbook Got Wrong
by James W. Loewen. *New York: New Press, 1995.*
Having examined twelve contemporary high school American History textbooks, Loewen deconstructs some of the myths and distortions that are readily taught in history classes across the country. Contesting the misinformation, lack of information, and blind patriotism that are so characteristic of such schoolbooks, Loewen challenges such limited and limiting notions of history, and fills in the missing information in order for students to have a better understanding of who they are and how they are shaped by and shapers of history.

Literacies of Power: What Americans Are Not Allowed to Know
by Donaldo Macedo. *Boulder, CO: Westview Press, 1994.*
Dealing with the politics of race, class, gender, language, literacy practices, and educational reform, this book clearly illustrates how schools, the media, and other social institutions perpetuate ignorance, apathy, and social injustice. Macedo argues that without the ability to think critically and make linkages between what we learn, the work that we do, and the broader social implications, Americans are easy prey for manipulation and exploitation. *Literacies of Power* offers some important insights for preparing students in the kind of broad, critical thinking necessary for responsible democratic citizenship.

Literacy and Empowerment: The Meaning Makers
by Patrick L. Courts. *New York: Bergin & Garvey, 1991.*
Courts contests traditional literacy approaches, arguing that they are designed to produce readers, who, through the development of prepackaged reading and writing programs, are unable to create meaning. Courts reveals how the exclusion of social and political dimensions from the practice of reading results in a lack of critical participation in society.

Literacy: Reading the Word & the World
by Paulo Freire and Donaldo Macedo. *South Hadley, MA: Bergin & Garvey, 1987.*
Examining literacy as a form of cultural politics, this book explores the possibilities of literacy and pedagogy as a form of empowerment. Looking at adult literacy, various literacy campaigns during the era of decolonization, the illiteracy in the United States, and literacy as a form of critical pedagogy, Freire and Macedo promote critical, democratic change.

Living in Truth
by Vaclav Havel. *London: Farber and Farber, 1989.*
Havel reveals the core philosophy of his efforts towards social and political transformation of former Czechoslovakia. *Living in Truth* explores Havel's notion of culture, oppression, political consciousness, human resistance to domination, citizenry, and democratic struggle.

The Location of Culture
by Homi K. Bhabha. *New York: Routledge, 1994.*
Working from an interdisciplinary theoretical framework — using postcolonial, postmodern, literary, and cultural criticism — Bhabha rethinks questions of identity, social agency, and nationalism in this series of essays. Taking a critical look at the cultural phenomenon of Western modernity, Bhabha carves out some challenging possibilities for global survival.

Loose Canons: Notes on the Culture Wars
by Henry Louis Gates Jr. *New York: Oxford University Press, 1992.*
This book takes a critical and illuminating look at the controversial issue of multiculturalism. Gates calls for integrating the American mind through the development of educational practices and a civic culture that respects both difference and commonality.

Malcolm X: The Final Speeches, February 1965
edited by Steve Clark. *York: Pathfinder, 1992.*
During the three weeks before his assassination, Malcolm X spoke in a number of countries about racism, anti-immigrant sentiments, U.S. global military exploits, and women's issues. This collection puts a face and a voice to a revolutionary who is widely misunderstood and misrepresented.

Manufacturing Consent: The Political Economy of the Mass Media
by Edward S. Herman and Noam Chomsky. *New York: Pantheon Books, 1988.*
Herman and Chomsky examine how the ideological underpinnings of the dominant elite in the United States shape the information of the news media. Using the media's portrayal of the struggles in Nicaragua, El Salvador, Russia, Vietnam, and Cambodia, as well as the Iran-contra affair as examples, this book vividly illustrates how the general population in this country is manipulated by various forms of propaganda. The authors also provide insight as to how to develop and put to transformative use the ability to critically engage the media's functions and outcomes.

The Matter of Images: Essays on Representations
by Richard Dyer. *New York: Routledge, 1993.*
This book provides an insightful analysis of the complexity of images of gays and lesbians in popular culture. Dyer reveals the importance of understanding and challenging the social and political function of representations that can stereotype, distort, or silence.

Mixed Blessings: New Art in a Multicultural America
by Lucy Lippard. *New York: Pantheon Books, 1990.*
Exploring the creative art by women and men from many different ethnic backgrounds, this book discusses the cross-cultural process and social critique taking place in such work, and consequently situates the artists in relation to their culture.

Multicultural Education, Critical Pedagogy and the Politics of Difference
edited by Christine Sleeter and Peter McLaren. *New York: State University of New York Press, 1995.*
Bringing together the fields of critical pedagogy and multicultural education, this collection of essays, which includes contributions from Donaldo Macedo, Stephen Haymes, and Antonia Darder, not only contests mainstream educational practices that are systematically exclusive and inherently unjust, but also provides clear pedagogical and curricular insights for creating a more critical, multicultural, and democratic learning environment.

Multiculturalism: A Critical Reader
edited by David Theo Goldberg. *Oxford: Blackwell, 1994.*
This collection of critical essays, which includes work by Charles Taylor, Michele Wallace, Michael Dyson, Henry Louis Gates Jr, and Ramon A. Gutierrez, addresses cutting-edge theories, issues, concerns, concepts, and practices that are part of the pedagogical struggle towards more inclusive and liberatory forms of education and social practice.

Nation and Narration
edited by Homi K. Bhabha. *New York: Routledge, 1990.*
Asking such questions as "What forms of narrative express the ideology of the modern nation?" and "How do questions of race and gender, class, and colonialism change the boundaries of national identity?" this collection of essays and authors examines the complex constructs of nation and nationalism.

Notes of a Native Son
by James Baldwin. *Boston: Beacon Press, 1955.*
Baldwin's first piece of nonfiction, *Notes of a Native Son* is a collection of essays that takes a hard look at life in Harlem, posing some serious questions about resistance and identity.

Occupied America: A History of Chicanos
by Rodolfo Acuna. *New York: Harper & Row, 1988.*
Exploring the history of the Southwestern United States, Acuna vividly depicts the legacy of hate and destruction perpetrated by the United States against Mexico, in which Mexicans became, and in fact remain, victims of a colonial process through which violence, exploitation, racism, and occupation were/are the norm.

Official Knowledge: Democratic Education in a Conservative Age
by Michael W. Apple. *New York: Routledge, 1993.*
Apple provides an analysis of the ways in which the political right is tightening its grip on education. Taking a close look at the politics of knowledge construction and dissemination, textbook content and distribution, pedagogy, curricula, and the increased pressure to privatize public education (as motivated by such private interests as Whittle Communications), this book charts a new course for more critical and democratic education.

Old Nazis, the New Right, and the Republican Party: Domestic Fascist Networks and Their Effect on U.S. Cold War Politics
by Russ Bellant. *Boston: South End Press, 1988.*
This book exposes the roots and growth of domestic fascist networks, which include Nazi collaborators, within the Republican Party. Bellant reveals how such members, during the Reagan era, held positions of power on the Republican Ethnic Heritage Groups Council, an ethnic outreach division of the GOP. He also scrutinizes the American Security Council for its participation in anti-Semitic and racist practices under the guise of anticommunism.

One Dimensional Man
by Herbert Marcuse. *Boston: Beacon Press, 1966.*
Rupturing the traditional notion of the "neutrality" of technology, Herbert Marcuse, a major player in the development of critical theory and the Frankfurt Institute for Social Research, argues that technology and capitalism are totalitarian in nature in that their social and political effects shape the work force, cultural identities, and social relations. Scrutinizing this inherent logic of domination, he contends that advanced industrial societies are nevertheless capable of giving rise to transformative practices.

The Origin of Negative Dialectics: Theodor W. Adorno, Walter Benjamin, and the Frankfurt Institute
by Susan Buck-Morss. *New York: Free Press, 1977.*
Buck-Morss's introduction to the historical origins, traditions, evolution, and influences that shaped Adorno's work in critical theory provides an important scaffold for approaching Adorno's original text, *Negative Dialectics.*

Out There: Marginalization and Contemporary Cultures
edited by Russell Ferguson, Martha Gever, Trinh T. Minh-ha, and Cornel West. *Cambridge, MA: MIT Press, 1990.*
This diverse collection of authors, including Audre Lorde, John Yau, Kobena Mercer, Toni Morrison, and bell hooks, confronts the exclusionary practices that readily occur in dominant cultural processes and institutions. The book addresses various points of view on issues of race, class, sexual orientation, gender, ethnicity, the politics of identity, postmodernism, postcolonialism, AIDS, art, representation and popular culture, and resistance.

Outside in the Teaching Machine
by Gayatri Chakravorty Spivak. *New York: Routledge, 1993.*
Spivak explores how the debates over the canon, ethnicity, "Third World" feminism, and cultural studies are shaping our understanding of culture.

Pedagogies of the Non-Poor
by Alice Frazer Evans, Robert A. Evans, and William Bean Kennedy. *New York: Orbis Books, 1990.*
This collection, which includes a dialogue with Paulo Freire, makes use of case studies that are designed to have readers confront a number of conflictual situations, and analyses that explore ways to help privileged students reach a level of political awareness capable of rupturing their complicity in perpetuating oppression.

Pedagogy and the Struggle for Voice: Issues of Language, and Schooling for Puerto Ricans
by Catherine E. Walsh. *New York: Bergin & Garvey, 1991.*
This book explores how Puerto Rican students struggle to make sense out of and fashion a voice from the multiple and often contradictory realities that comprise their daily existence. Walsh challenges generally accepted perspectives among teachers and calls for new pedagogies that respond to the complex needs of these students.

Pedagogy Is Politics: Literary Theory and Critical Teaching
edited by Maria-Regina Kecht. *Chicago: University of Illinois Press, 1992.*
Examining the relationship among ideology, power, and knowledge, the twelve essays in this book not only explore some of the central concerns of poststructuralism, but also offer concrete ideas and strategies for an educational process that embraces political consciousness, resistance to oppressive practices, and transformative action.

Pedagogy of the Oppressed
by Paulo Freire. *New York: Continuum, 1970.*
This seminal revolutionary work examines the dialectical relationship between the oppressor and the oppressed. His first book, this is the perfect place to begin to explore Freire's prolific work and ground oneself in an understanding of some of the central concepts, theories, and practices that recur throughout his lifework: "generative themes," "dialogue," "praxis," "political consciousness," the "banking notion of education," etc.

A People's History of the United States
by Howard Zinn. *New York: Harper Perennial, 1980.*
This history of the United States includes the voices of those people who have been systematically excluded from telling their side of the American story: the working class, Blacks, immigrants, Native Americans, women, and many others. Zinn's research reveals how the history of this country has not been motivated by the struggle for democracy, but, rather has been driven by greed, domination, violence, and exclusion.

Playing in the Dark: Whiteness and the Literary Imagination
by Toni Morrison. *Cambridge: Harvard University Press, 1992.*
This piece of literary criticism takes an engaging look at the ways in which American literature has been shaped by the presence of Africans in the United States — discussing the Black identity as portrayed in the work of Poe, Cather, Hemingway, and Melville. Morrison also reveals ways in which writers can and do transform parts of their social reality and struggles into aspects of language as a form of resistance and self-affirmation.

The Politics of Education: Culture, Power, and Liberation
by Paulo Freire. *New York: Bergin & Garvey, 1985.*
Exploring his ideas on adult literacy, political consciousness, liberation theology, and the process of social and cultural change, Freire extends his earlier works, still providing a view of pedagogy and praxis that is not only just, but also liberatory.

The Politics of Identity: Class, Culture, Social Movements
by Stanley Aronowitz. *New York: Routledge, 1992.*
Exploring the notion of working-class identity, Aronowitz presents an in-depth examination of the ways in which class, politics, and culture are interconnected.

Postcolonial Studies Reader
edited by Bill Ashcroft, Gareth Griffiths, and Helen Tiffin. *New York: Routledge, 1995.*
This is perhaps the most comprehensive, diverse collection of key works in postcolonial theory and criticism. It covers a wide range of topics and issues from some of the most influential and innovative scholars in the field.

Postmodern Theory: Critical Interrogations
by Steven Best and Douglas Kellner. *New York: Guilford Press, 1991.*
For those interested in understanding the complexity of postmodern theories, in all of their historical, sociological, cultural, and philosophical origins, variations, contradictions, contributions, limitations, and ongoing evolutions, Best and Kellner walk the reader through, and critique, the likes of Foucault, Deleuze and Guattari, Baudrillard, Habermas, Lyotard, Jameson, Mouffe, Laclau, among others.

Power and Criticism: Poststructural Investigations in Education
by Cleo H. Cherryholmes. *New York: Teachers College Press, 1988.*
This book provides an important bridge between pedagogy and poststructuralism. Cherryholmes's work is crucial because he is one of the only theorists who has used this connection not only as part of a project of critique, but more importantly as a possibility for changing education for the better.

Power/Knowledge: Selected Interviews & Other Writings 1972–1977
by Michel Foucault, edited by Colin Gordon. *New York: Pantheon Books, 1980.*
This collection of essays and interviews offers the reader an accessible guide to the wide range of topics and concerns, social visions, and political aims of one of this century's seminal critical social theorists. The purpose of the book is to act as a primer and thus facilitate access to other of Foucault's works by using the author himself to informally explain the underpinnings of his own work.

Race, Identity, and Representation in Education
edited by Cameron McCarthy and Warren Crinchlow. *New York: Routledge, 1993.*
This collection of essays, which includes contributions by Ali Behdad, Roxana Ng, William Pinar, Fazal Rizvi, Hazel Carby, Manthia Diawara, and Gladys Jiménez-Munoz, provides important perspectives on the relationship between race, class, gender, ethnicity, nation, and education. These authors address issues ranging from postcolonialism, anti-racist pedagogy, White teachers' construction of race, Black Studies, Chicana/os, postmodernism, multiculturalism, and the politics of representation.

Race Matters
by Cornel West. *Boston: Beacon Press, 1993.*
Drawing from religious and critical traditions, West addresses some of today's most urgent issues concerning Black Americans: the crisis in Black leadership, nihilism in the Black community, affirmative action, Black-Jewish relations, Black rage, the problems with traditional progressive theorizing about race, and the new Black conservatism.

Reflecting Black: African-American Cultural Criticism
by Michael Eric Dyson. *Minneapolis: University of Minnesota Press, 1993.*
Reflecting Black explores issues ranging from the culture of hip-hop, rap, and soul, to a critique of the work and representational politics around Spike Lee, Michael Jackson, Michael Jordan, Bill Cosby, John Singleton, to issues of Black leadership, religion, and

nationalism. Dyson, with an understanding of the complex interaction of race, class, and gender, provides a compelling perspective on Black cultural criticism.

Reproduction in Education, Society and Culture
by Pierre Bourdieu & Jean-Claude Passeron. *London: Sage, 1992*.

These two critical social theorists argue that dominant ideologies and knowledge are built into social institutions that both privilege and exclude particular perspectives, voices, authorities, and representations. Bourdieu and Passeron provide an examination of the mechanisms of ideological control that work to reproduce and maintain dominant beliefs, values, norms, and oppressive practices.

Rethinking the Borderlands: Between Chicano Culture and Legal Discourse
by Carl Gutierrez-Jones. *Berkeley: University of California Press, 1995*.

Drawing from gender studies, psychoanalysis, critical legal and critical race studies, this book explores the ways that Chicana and Chicano writers, musicians, artists, and film directors engage their history in ways that resist and challenge the racist and oppressive nature of the legal institutions that Gutierrez-Jones contends have significantly shaped Chicano history. The author explores how the Mexican-American image has become associated with criminality, and presents a new way of understanding this subordinated population's social experience.

The Return of the Political
by Chantal Mouffe. *New York: Verso, 1993*.

French political philosopher Chantal Mouffe presents the case that the confining vision of modernity inhibits us from realizing a democratic theory that embraces and engages the multiplicity of political positions and antagonisms in society, as well as the diverse and competing conceptions of our role as citizens. This is an important read for anyone interested in the debates over the realities and possibilities of cultural democracies, liberalism, and citizenship.

Rewriting Literacy: Culture and the Discourse of the Other
edited by Candace Mitchell and Kathleen Weiler. *New York: Bergin & Garvey, 1991*.

This collection of essays, which includes contributions by Jim Gee, Adrian Bennett, Linda Brodkey, and Jonathan Kozol, places literacy in its historical, cultural, and ideological context. Mitchell and Weiler provide profound insights in helping teachers to develop with their students the necessary practical solutions for eradicating oppressive educational practices.

Savage Inequalities: Children in America's Schools
by Jonathan Kozol. *New York: Crown, 1991*.

This is a shocking testimony from a teacher about the "savage inequalities" that exist in public schools, especially in the inner-city, in which poor children are systematically abused and neglected by policies, practices, and a system that claims to be democratic.

Schooling in Capitalist America: Educational Reform and the Contradictions of Economic Life
by Samuel Bowles and Herbert Gintis. *New York: Basic Books, 1976*.

Bowles and Gintis examine the history of public education, educational reform, and class conflict in the United States, and dissect the notions of the "American Dream" and "meritocracy," detailing how the system, with all of its built-in injustices, reproduces itself to the benefit of very few.

The Social Mind: Language, Ideology, and Social Practice
by James Paul Gee. *New York: Bergin & Garvey, 1992.*
Gee illustrates how memories, beliefs, values, and meanings are not formed in a psychological vacuum that is void of the influences of ideology and political struggle, but, rather, they are the products of a particular sociohistorical context. Providing an analysis of how we are shaped through discourse, this book sets the tone for what a new socioculturally situated linguistics needs to look like.

The Sociological Imagination
by C. Wright Mills. *London: Oxford University Press, 1959.*
Critiquing what he refers to as "this age of fact," in which we are overwhelmed with information with little opportunity for analysis, Mills calls for the quality of mind in which critically engaging the historical and ideological nature of social reality — the world around and within us — is essential. His views on the role of the sociologist, and methods of conducting research, are of extreme importance across the social sciences.

The Souls of Black Folk
by W.E.B. DuBois. *New York: Gramercy Books, 1903.*
From one of the most influential thinkers in the history of the United States, these essays depict the plight of generations of Blacks at the turn of the century, laying bare the injustices they faced: the failures of federal policy, the lack of opportunities that were available in public schools, and the racist nature of the job market. At the heart of this biographical and sociopolitical work, which stands as a testament to the African American struggle in this country, DuBois sees the legacy of slavery as the problem of the twentieth century.

Studying Culture: An Introductory Reader
edited by Ann Gray and Jim McGuigan. *London: Edward Arnold, 1993.*
This book, which includes contributions by Stuart Hall, Raymond Williams, Fredric Jameson, Paul Willis, Bhiku Parekh, Jan Nederveen Pieterse, and Roland Barthes, provides a broad spectrum of the work that has been done in cultural studies. As an introductory reader, it is an invaluable resource that moves the newcomer through the history, the shifting perspectives, and various theoretical frameworks and practices. The three main sections: "Foundations," "Difference and Identity," and "Meaning and Power" are provocative and inspire questions about educational practice, social research, and public policy.

Talking Back: Thinking Feminist, Thinking Black
by bell hooks. *Boston: South End Press, 1989.*
Black insurgent intellectual bell hooks writes about the meaning of feminist consciousness in everyday life, surviving and rupturing White supremacy and sexism, self-recovery, a pedagogy and political commitment, and about theories and transformative practices that strive for liberation.

Teachers and Crisis: Urban School Reform and Teachers' Work Culture
by Dennis Carlson. *New York: Routledge, 1992.*
Carlson, through empirical studies of two urban high school districts, illustrates how the conservative back-to-basics reform efforts, which devalue students' need to think critically, result in extremely limited possibilities for democratic struggle and socioeconomic empowerment.

Teaching Against the Grain: A Pedagogy of Possibility
by Roger I. Simon. *New York: Bergin & Garvey, 1992.*
This book provides an important look into the obstacles, avoidable pitfalls, and democratic practices of critical pedagy in the classroom. Simon presents a number of ways in which educators can work against the epistemological and relational limitations of traditional pedagogy.

Testimony: Crises of Witnessing in Literature, Psychoanalysis, and History
by Shoshana Felman and Dori Laub. *New York: Routledge, 1992.*
These authors explore, from both clinical and literary perspectives, how the process of testimony — bearing witness to a crisis or a trauma — can be used to teach. Using art, literature, videos, and autobiographical accounts of Holocaust and war survivors, *Testimony* offers both pedagogical and clinical lessons on listening to human suffering and traumatic narratives, and the possibilities for liberation from such experience, as well as the need to keep such memories alive so that we as a society can learn from them.

Texts for Change: Theory/Pedagogy/Politics
edited by Donald Morton and Mas'ud Zavarzadeh. *Urbana: University of Illinois Press, 1991.*
Through a series of poststructural analyses, the authors in this collection provide insights as to the possibility of political and cultural intervention in the oppressive dominant social organization through pedagogy.

Third World Women and the Politics of Feminism
edited by Chandra Talpade Mohanty, Ann Russo, and Lourdes Torres. *Bloomington: Indiana University Press, 1991.*
This volume of essays, which includes work by Rey Chow, Barbara Smith, Nayereh Tohida, Nellie Wong, Carmen Barroso, and Cristina Bruschini, takes a critical look at the construction of the self, the intersection of race, class, gender, and sexual orientation, the process of decolonization, and the oppressive nature of multinational capitalism. This book brings the issues, concerns, voices, and perspectives of "Third World" women to the center of feminist debates of the 1990s.

Thirteen Questions: Reframing Education's Conversation
edited by Joe L. Kincheloe and Shirley R. Steinberg. *New York: Peter Lang, 1994.*
This collection of critical educators, which includes Maxine Greene, Magda Lewis, William Pinar, Deborah Britzman, and Madeleine Grumet, takes up such questions as "What are the basics and why are we teaching them?" "Who decides the forms schools have taken?" "What is good teaching?" "Should the fact that we live in a democratic society make a difference in what our schools are like?" "In what ways do gender, race, and class affect the educational process?" and "What are schools for and what should we be doing in the name of education?" The contributors' insights are crucial for both educational theory and practice.

Tribes and Tribulations: Misconceptions about American Indians and their Histories
by Laurence M. Hauptman. *Albuquerque: University of New Mexico Press, 1995.*
These essays debunk the plethora of myths circulating about Native American–White relations. Hauptman looks at a wide spectrum of issues, ranging from campaigns to pacify and Christianize Native Americans, policies of their removal from the land, and stereo-

types of Native Americans that emanate from the images of mascots for sports teams or Hollywood film sidekicks.

An Unquiet Pedagogy: Transforming Practice in the English Classroom
by Eleanor Kutz and Hephzibah Roskelly. *Portsmouth, NH: Boynton/Cook, 1991.*
Rather than viewing multiple identities and perspectives in the English classroom as a problem, this book explores the kinds of teaching that respect and engage — without romanticizing — the realities, histories, and views of diverse students and educators.

The Vanishing Race and Other Illusions: Photographs of Indians by Edward S. Curtis
by Christopher M. Lyman. *New York: Pantheon, 1982.*
This book examines the role of photography in misrepresenting Native Americans.

Welcome to the Jungle: New Positions in Black Cultural Studies
by Kobena Mercer. *New York: Routledge, 1994.*
Drawing from psychoanalysis, postcolonial theory, and Black and Queer cultural art practices, Kobena Mercer discusses the politics of ethnicity, sexuality, and race during the 1980s, and examines Black cultural forms such as hairstyles, dress, music, film, and other forms of visual art therein.

When Heaven and Earth Changed Places
by Le Ly Hayslip. *New York: Plume, 1990.*
This is a personal account of a Vietnamese woman who talks about the price villagers paid for the Vietnam War: her experience of being forcefully removed from her village and relocated in Saigon, her marriage to a U.S. GI, and her subsequent move to, and culture shock in, the United States.

Woman Native Other: Writing Postcoloniality and Feminism
by Trinh T. Minh-ha. *Bloomington: Indiana University Press, 1989.*
Critically appropriating the theoretical insights of anthropology, cultural studies, literary criticism, postcolonialism, and feminist theory, Minh-ha addresses questions of identity and difference, language and writing in relation to the notions of ethnicity and femininity, and authenticity. She provides important insights about building historical and political consciousness and coming to voice.

Year 501: The Conquest Continues
by Noam Chomsky. *Boston: South End Press, 1993.*
Chomsky, beginning with the coming of Columbus, finds a great deal of commonality between the genocidal era of colonialism and the barbarism associated with modern-day imperialism. Analyzing the role of the United States in Latin America, Indonesia, Haiti, and Cuba, he challenges all of us to work against the forces that will surely lead to global destruction.

About the Contributors

Lilia I. Bartolomé is Assistant Professor and Director of the masters program in Language and Literacy at the Harvard Graduate School of Education. Her research interests center on home/school cross-cultural language and literacy practices, and on oral and written classroom discourse acquisition patterns of language minority children in U.S. schools. She is author of "Effective Teaching Strategies: Their Possibilities and Limitations" in *Cultural Diversity and Second Language Learning* (edited by B. McLeod, 1994), and *The Misteaching of Academic Discourse* (forthcoming).

Dennis Carlson is Associate Professor in the Department of Educational Leadership and Director of the Center for Education and Cultural Studies at Miami University (Ohio). Interested in urban school reform and cultural studies, he has published in the area of critical analysis of power relations within educational contexts. He is the author of *Teachers and Crisis: Urban School Reform and Teachers' Work Culture* (1992).

Noam Chomsky, Institute Professor at the Massachusetts Institute of Technology, is a linguistics professor and social theorist. A prolific writer, his most recent works include *The Prosperous Few and the Restless Many* (1993), *Language and Thought* (1993), and *World Orders, Old and New* (1994). He was the 1994 recipient of the Homer Smith Award from the New York University School of Medicine.

Paulo Freire is a world-renowned educator who has conducted literacy campaigns throughout the world, particularly in developing countries. Among the many books he has written, he is best known for his classic work, *The Pedagogy of the Oppressed* (1970). Freire was exiled from Brazil for over sixteen years for teaching peasants to read. Upon his return, he became Secretary of Education in São Paulo. He is presently a professor of literacy, educational theory, and political writings at Pontifícia Universidade Católica São Paulo in Brazil.

Henry A. Giroux is Waterbury Chair Professor at Pennsylvania State University in State College. His professional interests center on the links between critical pedagogy and cultural studies. His recent publications include *Border Crossings: Cultural Workers and the Politics of Education* (1992), *Living Dangerously: Multiculturalism and the Politics of Difference* (1993), *Disturbing Pleasures: Learning Popular Culture* (1994), and *Fugitive Cultures: Race, Violence, and Youth* (1996).

Maxine Greene is Professor of Philosophy and Education (Emeritus) at Teachers College, Columbia University; Philosopher-in-Residence at the Lincoln Center Institute for the Arts in Education; and founder of the Center for Social Imagination at Teachers College. Her books include *Landscapes of Learning* (1979), *The Dialectic of Freedom* (1988), and *Releasing Imagination* (1995).

Joe L. Kincheloe is Professor of Cultural Studies and Pedagogy at Pennsylvania State University. He is interested in postformal thinking, urban education, and critical thinking. His latest books include *Teachers as Researchers: Qualitative Paths to Empowerment* (1991) and *Toward a Critical Politics of Teacher Thinking: Mapping the Postmodern* (1993). He is also coauthor of *The Stigma of Genius: Einstein and Beyond Modern Education* (with S. Steinberg and D. Tippins, 1992).

Magda Lewis is Associate Professor and Queen's National Scholar in the Faculty of Education at Queen's University in Kingston, Ontario. She is interested in feminist/critical theory and practice, feminist pedagogy as a method and a politics, and the politics of radical critique as this applies to education, schooling, and culture. Her published works include *Without a Word: Teaching Beyond Women's Silence* (1993) and *Rewriting the Gender Curriculum* (forthcoming).

Donaldo P. Macedo is Professor of English and Director of the Graduate Program in Bilingual and English as a Second Language Studies at the University of Massachusetts-Boston. His research interests are critical literacy, linguistics, and bilingual education. His publications include *Issues in Portuguese Bilingual Education* (1980), *Literacy: Reading the Word and the World* (with Paulo Freire, 1987), and *Literacies of Power: What Americans Are Not Allowed to Know* (1994).

Cameron McCarthy teaches curriculum theory and cultural studies at the University of Illinois at Urbana-Champaign, where he is also a Research Associate in the Institute for Communication Research. His professional interests include institutional support for teaching, and school ritual and adolescent identities. Widely published, his recent works include *Race and Curriculum* (1990), *Race, Identity, and Representation in Education* (coedited with W. Crichlow, 1994), and *Sound Identities* (with C. Richards and G. Hudak, forthcoming).

Peter McLaren is an Associate Professor at the Graduate School of Education and Information Studies at the University of California, Los Angeles. His research interests include critical literacy and a Marxist materialist critique of the sign. His books include *Schooling as a Ritual Performance: Towards a Political Economy of Educational Symbols and Gestures* (1986), *Life in Schools: An Introduction to Critical Pedagogy in the Social Foundations of Education* (1989), and *Critical Pedagogy and Predatory Culture: Oppositional Politics in a Postmodern Era* (1995).

Roger I. Simon is a Professor in the Department of Curriculum at the Ontario Institute for Studies in Education, Toronto. His current work focuses on commemoration as a pedagogical practice and the intersection between memory and history. Widely published, his books include *Popular Culture, Schooling, and Everyday Life* (with H. Giroux, 1989), *Learning Work: A Critical Pedagogy of Work Education* (with D. Dippo and A. Schenke, 1991), and *Teaching Against the Grain: A Pedagogy of Possibility* (1992).

David Spener is Research Director of the Program in Border and Migration Studies at the Population Research Center, University of Texas at Austin. His research interests include comparative international development, economic sociology, international migration, and race and ethnicity. He is editor of *Adult Biliteracy in the United States* (1994), and author of "Small Firms, Social Capital, and Global Commodity Chains: Some Lessons from the Tex-Mex Border in the Era of Free Trade" in *Latin America in the World Economy* (edited by R. P. Korzeniewicz and W. C. Smith, in press).

About the Contributors

Shirley R. Steinberg, an Educational Consultant and Lecturer, teaches pre-service teachers; she is also Senior Editor of *Taboo: The Journal of Culture and Education.* She is coeditor of *Thirteen Questions: Reclaiming Education's Conversation* (with J. Kincheloe, 1995), and coauthor of *The Stigma of Genius: Einstein and Beyond Modern Education* (with J. Kincheloe and D. Tippins, 1992), and *Kinderculture: Corporate Production of Childhood* (with J. Kincheloe, forthcoming).

William G. Tierney is a Professor and Director of the Center for Higher Education Policy Analysis in the School of Education at the University of Southern California. He is author of *Curricular Landscapes, Democratic Vistas: Transformative Leadership in Higher Education* (1989), *Building Communities of Difference: Higher Education in the 21st Century* (1993), and coeditor of *Naming Silenced Lives: Personal Narratives and the Process of Educational Change* (with D. McLaughlin, 1993). He is presently working on a book that looks at the intersections of cultural studies and queer theory.

About the Editors

Pepi Leistyna is a doctoral student in Learning and Teaching at the Harvard Graduate School of Education. His research centers around issues of language and experience, democracy and education, and the implementation of critical multicultural curricula. For the past eight years, he has been teaching community-based adult education, as well as at the college level in the areas of English as a Second Language, bilingualism and literacy, anti-racist multicultural education, and education for social and political change.

Stephen A. Sherblom is a doctoral candidate in Human Development at the Harvard Graduate School of Education, with a special focus on moral development and violence. His doctoral work involves talking with young children about their moral sensibilities in conflicts and pain in their close relationships, especially with friends. His dissertation study integrates moral philosophy with relational psychology, with a goal of gaining greater understanding of how and why people hurt others.

Arlie Woodrum is a doctoral candidate in Administration, Planning, and Social Policy at the Harvard Graduate School of Education. His research explores the ways the values and expectations of culturally distinct groups influence their interaction with leadership (and one another) in diverse, urban social institutions, with a particular interest in the ways schools, their communities, and social serivce organizations work together. He was formerly headmaster of an international school in Spain.